Nan'yō

Mori Koben, 1869–1945. (Linda Mori)

Pacific Islands Monograph Series, No. 4

Nan'yō

The Rise and Fall of the Japanese in Micronesia, 1885–1945

MARK R. PEATTIE

Center for Pacific Islands Studies
School of Hawaiian, Asian, and
Pacific Studies
University of Hawaii
UNIVERSITY OF HAWAII PRESS • Honolulu

05 06 07 08 09 10   9 8 7 6 5 4

Library of Congress Cataloging-in-Publication Data

Peattie, Mark R., 1930–
  Nan'yō : the rise and fall of the Japanese in
Micronesia, 1885–1945.

  (Pacific islands monograph series; no.4)
  Bibliography: p.
  Includes index.
  1. Micronesia—History. 2. Micronesia—Relations—
Japan. 3. Japan—Relations—Micronesia. I. Title.
II. Series.
DU500.P43   1988   996'.5   87-19437
ISBN 0-8248-1087-2

ISBN 0-8248-1480-0 (pbk)

University of Hawai'i Press books are printed on acid-free
paper and meet the guidelines for permancence and
durability of the Council on Library Resources.

Printed by The Maple-Vail Book Manufacturing Group

www.uhpress.hawaii.edu

*Dedicated to
the memory of Mori Koben
(1869–1945),
pioneer and patriot*

Editor's Note

TODAY AND AFTER more than four decades of American rule, four new political entities are emerging from the U.S. Trust Territory of the Pacific Islands (USTTPI). The Northern Marianas will become a Commonwealth of the United States. The Marshall Islands and the Federated States of Micronesia (composed of the former USTTPI districts of Pohnpei, Kosrae, Truk, and Yap) will enjoy a measure of self-government as states freely associated with the United States, a status first suggested by the Cook Islands' arrangement with New Zealand in 1965. Although there are some unresolved problems, Belau may follow suit.

Japan was ejected from these portions of Micronesia at the end of World War II, yet a strong Japanese presence has continued. Older Islanders have memories of the Japanese period, and some still speak textbook Japanese. Many Micronesians are of part-Japanese descent, including two of the first presidents of the newly emerging states. Today, Japan is exhibiting a renewed influence in the area through commercial activities and tourism.

Professor Peattie's monograph explains much of this history, and it is an atypical volume in this series. As Peattie makes clear in his preface, his concern is not with the Islanders but with the Japanese in the islands. To the surprise of some old Pacific hands, Japanese activities in Micronesia began long before Japan acquired the area with the onset of World War I in 1914. Representatives of Japan had penetrated Micronesia three decades earlier; they helped lay the foundation for Japan's eventual rule of the islands as a mandated territory under the auspices of the League of Nations.

Japan's influence was pervasive and well orchestrated; the Japanese had clear objectives in mind. Micronesians were to be absorbed into the Japanese empire, and eventually Japanese and other Asians would come to outnumber Islanders in their own homeland by a ratio of two to one.

While his focus is upon the Japanese, Peattie helps us to understand much of Micronesia's history and why things are the way they are today.

The publication of the Pacific Islands Monograph Series is subsidized by private funds raised by the University of Hawaii Foundation. From the outset, the Foundation's staff members have shown great interest and support for the series, and their assistance and that of the Foundation is greatly appreciated.

ROBERT C. KISTE

Contents

Figures

Photographs

Preface

THE PREFACE to any book is the first statement that an author makes to a reader, but it is usually the last part of the book to be written. Besides providing space to acknowledge authorial debts, it thus serves a retrospective, as well as a prefatory function, for it allows the author, after a long backward glance over the text, to offer a clear statement of purpose, in order to warn the unsuspecting, make explanations to the skeptical, and encourage the interested.

The writing of this particular book—a history of the appearance, activities, and ultimate expulsion of the Japanese in Micronesia—is linked to my research, past and present, in broader areas of modern Japanese history. It arose, essentially, from my interest in the evolution of Japanese expansionism and, more specifically, is an extension of my recent work in the history of the Japanese colonial empire, of which most of Micronesia once formed a part. It has also served as an introduction to my current interest in the development of the modern Japanese drive toward the Asian and Pacific tropics from late Meiji times until the beginning of the Pacific War.

It must be clear at the outset that what I have dealt with in these pages is a portion of Japanese history, specifically a small segment of the history of Japan's imperial expansion, which took place in a setting that was both exotic and geographically vast. It is equally important to make clear at the outset what I have *not* done. I have not attempted to write a history of Micronesia during the Japanese period, nor have I attempted to write a history of Micronesia or Micronesians under Japanese rule. As a specialist in modern Japanese history by training and interest, I hope that it is understandable that it is the Japanese, not the Micronesians, who come into sharpest focus under my lens. Yet there are undoubtedly those who will, with some reason, object that more space should have been devoted to the meaning of the Japanese presence and occupation in terms of the development of the Micronesian peoples. To this I can only respond that it is my distinct impression that, while still somewhat fragmented, the study of the Micronesian response to Japanese rule and culture contact has been pursued by a good number of qualified social scientists, whereas the response of Japanese colonials to their Micronesian environment has been virtually ignored. Over the past forty years relevant studies concerning Micronesians under the Japanese have been undertaken by both established and younger scholars equipped with the necessary area and language skills. Nor has this effort run its course. An example of the continuing interest in the Micronesian response to the Japanese period is the extensive oral history on the Japanese administration of Palau now being compiled by the Micronesian Area Research Center at the University of Guam and based entirely on interviews with older Micronesians who remember the period. While I myself have none of the qualifications necessary to undertake such studies, I have gratefully used and acknowledged them at points in my account where it was important to discuss the impact of the Japanese presence on Micronesian communities.

The prism of indigenous response to an alien administrative elite is, in any event, hardly a satisfactory approach to the study of any people. It should be obvious by now that Micronesian history is itself fully worthy of serious academic study. In the long run, the best persons to write it are undoubtedly Micronesians themselves. Indeed, as more young Micronesians are able to combine the rich insights of traditional Micronesian oral history with the refined research techniques of modern social science, such histories will inevitably appear, studies that will accord with the highest standards of scholarship while being true to the Micronesian character. Given my own background and interests, I leave that important task to them. As a historian of modern Japan, my concerns have been with the restless, opportunistic, and materially dominating people who lived for a while among them. If they engendered slight Micronesian affection, they appear, in balance, to have earned Micronesian respect.

I have embarked on a relatively new venture. Not only has the subject of the Japanese in the tropical Pacific been bypassed in the evolution of Pacific Islands historiography, but those more interested in East Asian history are generally unfamiliar with the chronology, actors, and setting of the Japanese presence in Micronesia. These facts not only caused me to include a considerable number of maps in the volume, but also led me to shape it in an overall narrative, rather than analytical, form. I have attempted neither to establish nor to reevaluate any theoretical approach to either imperial history or the history of the Pacific Islands. I have, in certain chapters, dealt with specific historical problems that inevitably arise in providing an account of the Japanese in Micronesia:

the question of Japan's fidelity to its mandate charter in the treatment of its Micronesian charges (chapter 4); the relative merits and demerits of the Japanese economic development and exploitation of Micronesia (chapter 5); and the relative guilt or innocence of Japan in the alleged militarization of Micronesia between the world wars (chapter 8). But, for the most part, I have simply tried to tell the story of the rise and fall of a vigorous, aggressive, and enterprising people on distant and far-scattered fragments of land during the course of a half century or more.

If there is one continuing theme that runs through this work it is that of Japan's drive to the tropics. Of themselves, the island territories that Japan possessed in the Pacific counted for little in the Japanese imperial ledger, but as stepping stones toward a greater maritime and southward destiny, their value glittered in the imagination of a growing number of Japanese between the world wars. The *nanshin*—the 'southward advance' toward tropic lands and seas—existed for many Japanese as a kind of national holy grail, one that was pursued in late Meiji times with romanticism, in the 1920s and 1930s with methodical attention, and in the early 1940s with fatal consequence for the nation.

Given the focus and setting of this study, a few explanations are necessary concerning my use of names and terminology. I have employed the accepted arrangement of Japanese names, that is family name first. Matters of Micronesian place names have been far more difficult to deal with, mainly because there appears to be so little agreement on correct usage. Wherever possible I have used the most commonly accepted prewar spelling of Micronesian places instead of their Japanese variants (for example Palau, not Parao), while recognizing that many of these have been altered in recent years (for example, Belau for Palau; Kosrae for Kusaie; Pohnpei for Ponape). I have also referred throughout this work to the "Pacific War," because it is a far more useful term for discussing Japan's conflict with the United States from 1941 to 1945 than "World War II," which designates a conflict that began in 1939, a date of much lesser significance in terms of Japan–United States hostilities.

Most difficult of all, for any American writing a history of the Japanese in Micronesia from the ending of the nineteenth century to almost the middle of the twentieth, is the tangle of terms, both English and Japanese, used to describe the historical as well as the geographic setting of the subject. To begin with, the Japanese word *Nan'yō*, literally, the 'South Seas,' is an extremely vague term. At various times, it has included Micronesia, Melanesia, the South China Sea, and Southeast Asia from the Andaman Islands to Papua. The English term "South Seas," as Americans generally understand it, vaguely embraces all the tropical waters of the Pacific, but, thanks to fiction and motion pictures, is perhaps most closely identified with Polynesia. The difficulties surrounding the English term "South Pacific" are just as great, as I have discovered since I first began writing about Japanese expansion into Micronesia. For Americans, the term encompasses Polynesia (including Hawaii), Micronesia, and Melanesia, sometimes with particular emphasis on island groups where American military and naval forces were stationed or involved in combat from 1942 to 1944, which would include islands from Samoa to Saipan. The Japanese are far more literal in their use of the term. For them the South Pacific can only include territories in the Pacific that lie south of the equator. As Micronesia is north of that line, the Japanese recognize it as being in the "north Pacific," a notion that would strike most Americans as bizarre, since to them the term conjures up images of Eskimo, icebergs, and the fur trade. Other terms are equally inappropriate when used cross-culturally: the Japanese place the Mariana Islands in the "central Pacific" (chūbu Taiheiyō); seen from the United States the same islands are obviously in the "western Pacific."

There are, of course, other terms in English and Japanese that are much more restricted in scope, but each creates problems for someone writing about the historical evolution of the Japanese in Micronesia. "Southwest Pacific" excludes Polynesia, but has the disadvantage of including Melanesia as well as Micronesia. Micronesia is clearly an area-specific term, but was not in common use by Japanese or Americans when my story begins. The Japanese appellations, *Nan'yō guntō* 'South Sea islands' and *Nan'yō shōtō* specifically refer to Micronesia, but encounter the same difficulties as the English term—as do *uchi Nan'yō* 'inner South Seas' and *ura Nan'yō* 'back South Seas', designations for Micronesia that came into use only during the late 1920s.

In the earlier chapters of this book, working toward a term that would be reasonably flexible, stylistically attractive, and relatively acceptable, I have occasionally used a narrower definition of the Japanese word *Nan'yō*, in general use in the late nineteenth century and the early decades of the twentieth. In that period, the *Nan'yō* still centered on Micronesia (as witness the title Nan'yō-chō, the designation of the Japanese governmental bureau that administered Japan's mandate territories from 1922 to 1945). The English translation, of course, is still "South Seas," but my use of this English term in its narrower Japanese context in the first part of this study (when I am not using "tropical Pacific" or Micronesia) is done consciously, as a convenience, with full awareness that it has been used in both English and Japanese in other, broader contexts.

Acknowledgments

In RESEARCHING and writing this work, I hold no one higher in my gratitude than Dr. Dirk Anthony Ballendorf on the faculty of the University of Guam. From the time he first appeared in the doorway of my office at UCLA to propose that I undertake this project, Dirk has been an expert and invaluable counselor, jovial companion and correspondent, and trusted friend. As director of the Micronesian Area Research Center (MARC), it was Dirk, moreover, who arranged for the funding which made it possible to do the basic research for this book, beginning with a two-month-long tour of Micronesia and Japan in the summer of 1983. Everywhere along my route through the Marshalls, Carolines, and Marianas, Dirk's introductions to a procession of interesting and knowledgeable friends and acquaintances made that passage as informative as it was delightful. Since my return to the Boston area, Dirk's expertise concerning Micronesia, his ever tactful suggestions and corrections, and his unfailing enthusiasm have been vital to the writing of this book.

Probably no one in the Pacific or on either side of it knows more about the history of the Japanese in Micronesia than Nakajima Hiroshi, executive director of the Pacific Society (Taiheiyō Gakkai), whose counsel and assistance is constantly sought by Japanese and non-Japanese alike. Over the past several years, Mr. Nakajima has not only generously provided me with a steady flow of hard-to-obtain Japanese-language materials, but has taken time from his busy schedule to devote careful and helpful attention to the draft chapters I have regularly sent to him. His extensive suggestions and comments have continually saved me from countless small errors of fact and interpretation. I can only hope that the volume in its final form will measure up to his rigorous standards of accuracy.

From the beginning of this project I was convinced that well-drawn maps would be essential to the reader's understanding of places and

events. Of the maps included in this work, some have been reproduced
from the relevant volumes of Samuel Eliot Morison's *The United States
Navy in World War II*, with the permission of Little, Brown & Company; some have been adapted from the fourth volume of the *Pacific
Islands* series issued by the British Royal Navy in World War II; but
most have had to be drawn from the beginning. Fortunately, in com-
missioning someone for this task, I have been able to call upon Noël
Diaz, one of the ablest craftsmen in his profession, under arrangements
that were most generous on his part.

During my research travels in the summer of 1983, a host of people
offered kind and helpful assistance to me in my efforts to gather materials and to acquaint myself with the Micronesian environment. At the
University of Hawaii, Masato Matsui, curator of the East Asian Collection at Hamilton Library, opened the valuable collection of Japanese-
language materials on the *Nan'yō;* similarly, Karen Peacock of the
library's Pacific Islands Collection brought my attention to a number of
rare English-language materials; Dr. Robert Kiste, director of the university's Center for Pacific Islands Studies, and Dr. Leonard Mason,
Professor Emeritus, offered useful counsel; and Sophia Lee provided
meticulous and conscientious research assistance, as well as unstinting
logistical help before, during, and after my visits to the Manoa campus.

On Majuro in the Marshalls, where I first became acquainted with
the wonders of a Pacific atoll, Enid McKay, long-time resident of
Majuro, was a hospitable, knowledgeable, and patient guide, and Jerry
Knight, director of the local library and museum, was kind enough to
arrange an afternoon of interviews with older Marshallese who remembered the wartime years on the islands. On Ponape, Iris Falcam, on the
library staff of the College of Micronesia, was of great help in reproducing valuable materials from the library's Pacific Islands Room. Dakio
Syne, head librarian, and Madison Nena, historic preservation specialist at the same institution, also offered help.

In the Truk group I could not have had a more congenial companion
than Brother Henry Schwalbenberg, S.J., then on the faculty of Xavier
High School, Moen Island, and one of the most informed and level-
headed young men I have known. On Dublon and Eten islands Antolin
Sotan proved an expert guide through the jungle-covered ruins of
Japan's military and naval facilities and recalled for me his childhood
memories of Dublon as a flourishing town. I also recall with pleasure a
delightful luncheon hosted by Father Amando Samo at his church on
Dublon after a morning of poking about the ruins. On Moen Island it
was my great good fortune to be invited to the home of Masataka Mori,
grandson of Mori Koben, just at the time when the members of the large
Mori family were hosting a delegation of Japanese relatives and
interested visitors from Kochi, Mori Koben's home prefecture, to commemorate the transfer of his remains from their original gravesite on Tol

to the family estate on Moen. At those ceremonies I also had the pleasure of meeting Mr. Nakaya Yujirō, principal of the Tosa Preparatory
School, who kindly presented me with a set of articles on Mori printed
in the *Kochi Shimbun,* which I have mined extensively for the details of
Mori's early life in the islands.

On Koror, in the Palau Islands, the late David Ramarui, then minister of Social Services and Dr. Minoru Ueki, then director of Koror Hospital, gave generously of their time in sharing with me their recollections of their childhood education during the Japanese period in Palau.
I came away from these interviews not only with a sheaf of notes, but
also with a profound respect for both these men and confidence that
their newly independent country has been well served by public servants of such character and caliber. At the Micronesian Occupational
College on Koror I was able to consult with a knowledgeable specialist
on Micronesia, Dr. Donald Shuster, whose work on the social and educational effect of Japanese colonial policies on Micronesian communities has greatly influenced my discussion of that subject in chapter 4, as
well as with Higuchi Wakako, a free-lance journalist who has a sensitive
understanding of the Japanese-Palauan relationship and who, over the
past several years, has offered a number of helpful comments on my
work.

On Saipan, Dirk Ballendorf himself joined me on a tour of the island,
which he has known for twenty years or more. My visit was made memorable by a tour of the battlegrounds, shattered redoubts, and sites of
the mass wartime suicides, expertly guided by D. "Colt" Denfeld whose
knowledge of the military archaeology of World War II in the Pacific is
unsurpassed. On Saipan, too, Scott Russell, director of the Office of
Historic Preservation for the Trust Territory of the Pacific, who has
actively presided over the publication of the valuable Micronesian
archaeological surveys cited frequently in this work, offered useful comments and materials for this study. On Rota, I spent a delightful morning walking along the island's southwestern coast with Dr. William
Peck—poet, former administrator for the Trust Territory, and sensitive
interpreter of the island's past—and was absorbed by his dark tales of
Rota's wartime travails, gleaned from island friends over the years.

In Tokyo, in addition to the invaluable counsel provided to me by
Nakajima Hiroshi, I was materially assisted by Mr. Kuribayashi Toku-
goro and Mr. Kosuge Teruo of the South Sea Islands Association (Nan'yō
Guntō Kyōkai), Mr. Kobayashi Izumi of the Japan-Micronesia Association (Nihon-Mikuroneshia Kyōkai), and by Mr. Yoshihisa Akira of the
Asian-African Section of the Diet Library, who has also been most helpful since then in locating various materials at that library.

I am indebted to various persons for photographs of some of the principal Japanese who appear here and there in my narrative. Mr. Yamaguchi Yoji, who probably owns the world's finest private collection of

photographs of the Japanese in Micronesia, was kind enough to let me browse through his numerous books and albums and to make a selection of photographs for reproduction in this volume. Linda Mori supplied me with a superb portrait of her great grandfather, Mori Koben, in his last years; Mr. Morizawa Takamichi of the *Kochi Shimbun* staff provided the earlier photo of Mori, his wife, and two of his children; Hijikata Keiko made available the photograph of her late husband, Hijikata Hisakatsu; and to Matsue Hiroji I am grateful for the photograph of his father, Matsue Haruji, the "Sugar King."

In addition to Dirk Ballendorf, Nakajima Hiroshi, and Professor David Evans of the University of Richmond, who read the manuscript in its entirety, I should also like to thank a number of specialists who have read various sections of the manuscript and offered expert criticism and suggestions, including, Father Francis Hezel, S.J., of the Xavier High School, Truk, the late Professor J. L. Fischer, Department of Anthropology, Tulane, and Professor Shimizu Hajime of the Institute for Developing Economies in Tokyo. Naturally, I alone am responsible for whatever errors of fact and interpretation may have eluded their kind and helpful scrutiny of these pages. In matters of style I received invaluable advice from my brother, Noel Peattie—gifted poet, small press editor, and incredible polymath—whose mastery of the English language continues to astound and delight me and all who know him. Most important of all, I could not have had a more informed, exacting, and conscientious copy editor than Linley Chapman of the Center for Pacific Islands Studies, University of Hawaii. Without her meticulous scrutiny and her gentle but persistent questioning and correction in details of style, consistency, and sometimes fact, this would have been a far poorer manuscript.

In addition to the funding provided to me by the Micronesian Area Research Center, without which it would have been difficult to begin this book, let alone complete it, I should like to gratefully acknowledge a grant made to me by the American Philosophical Society of Philadelphia as supplemental support for my research trip to Micronesia in the summer of 1983. I am also indebted to the Center for Pacific Islands Studies of the University of Hawaii, as well as to my own institution, the University of Massachusetts at Boston, for financial support which helped defray the costs of producing the maps for the volume.

In this extensive list of acknowledgements I have left until the last that one which affords me the greatest pleasure to set down. To Alice, dear wife and true friend for over thirty years, who typed nearly the entire manuscript (aided at the end by my son David), offering careful and tactful editorial suggestions, while at the same time holding down a highly demanding position at the Massachusetts Institute of Technology, go thanks of a very special kind.

CHAPTER 1

Distant Shores
The First Japanese in Micronesia,
1885–1914

FEW COUNTRIES have occupied a more geographically distinctive position throughout history than Japan. An island nation situated off a continental land mass, Japan has always been close enough to fall within
the gravity of China, the center of East Asian civilization, yet sufficiently distant to stand apart from its authority. Only the circumstance
of Britain, off the coast of Europe, has been similar. Like Britain, Japan
has been subject to two opposing cultural tensions: the landward pull of
the neighboring continent and the maritime impulse to move out upon
the open seas. Like Britain, the basic orientation of Japan in ancient
and feudal times was continental. Culture and politics peacefully
inclined Japan toward China in the seventh and eighth centuries;
aggressive designs pulled Japan onto the continent in the sixteenth century. Yet the maritime orientation was compelling. In the same century
that Toyotomi Hideyoshi's armies fought their way up the Korean peninsula, Japanese traders, pirates, and even colonists made their way
south into tropic lands and seas—to the Philippines, along the coast of
southern China to Siam, and even as far as the Malay Peninsula. About
the time that Elizabethan seamen had established a commanding maritime presence off the coast of northern Europe, Japanese ships ranged
from the East China Sea to the Strait of Malacca.

After the first few decades of the seventeenth century, the seclusion
policies of the Tokugawa government slowed the maritime expansionism of nearly a century and turned Japan away from affairs on the
continent as well. For two hundred fifty years these twin drives were
suppressed, as Japan, immobile in self-imposed isolation, turned in
upon itself. When the country was reopened in the mid-nineteenth century, the expansive energies of Japan were once again released, but were
now given greater dynamism by the prevailing environment of world
imperialism. For the remainder of the century the major thrust of Japa-

1

nese expansionism was to be continent-directed, as Japan sought a
foothold on Asian soil against the eastward advance of Russian power.
Yet, at this dawn of the nation's new age, there were Japanese of various
stations and professions who sought to revive the notion that Japan also
had a maritime destiny.

The Meiji Interest in the South Seas

Thus was born, by the end of the nineteenth century, the concept of a
"southward advance," *nanshin*, whereby the nation would find glory,
prosperity, and new territory by moving into the "South Seas," the
Nan'yō, a geographical concept as nebulous as the ambitions directed
toward it, but which, in the first years of the Meiji era, was generally
defined as the tropical Pacific, particularly Micronesia.[1] Few Japanese
knew much about distant waters in those days, but by the mid-1880s a
number of impulses had stirred a sudden interest in the tropical Pacific.

To begin with, there was the decision by the early Meiji government
to move outward to clarify Japanese authority over nearby island territories—the Kuriles, Sakhalin, the Ryūkyū Islands, and the Bonins—
which had at one time or another been associated, however loosely,
with Japan. Inevitably, this activity, essentially completed by the 1870s,
turned Japanese attention overseas. In particular, the effort to recover
the Bonins, farthest out in the Pacific, stirred the imagination of the
curious and adventurous about lands farther south.

This impulse to expand was more than just a matter of clarifying the
national unit. It was impelled even more by the early Meiji recognition
of the vulnerability of the nation and of the correlation between expansion and national power, a point made ominously clear by the advance
of Western warships into Asian waters. Parallel with these new convictions there had arisen in early Meiji a waxing interest in maritime
power. The scramble by European nations for the remaining island territories of the Pacific had brought about a sudden recognition of the
nation's inability to play a role upon that ocean, compounded by disturbing evidence that Japan's few vessels were faulty in design or
manned by inexperienced crews, and that the nation's maritime commerce was pitifully dependent on foreign merchant ships.[2]

Subsequent efforts to magnify the Japanese maritime presence in the
western Pacific inspired a modernization program for Japan's fledgling
navy and the construction of a modern merchant marine, heralded by
the slogan *kaikoku Nippon* 'maritime Japan'. By the end of the 1880s,
Japan had indeed begun to act like a maritime nation, sending its vessels
of war and commerce abroad upon the high seas. Inevitably, Japanese
ships began to enter tropical waters in the first two decades of the
Meiji era.

Meiji interest in tropical lands and seas was also invigorated by a general admiration for Western overseas expansion and by the introduction into Japan of Malthusian fears of population growth. By the 1880s these ideas had moved Japanese views on colonization beyond a concern for the domestic settlement of Hokkaido to a consideration of colonizing distant territories. Along with America, Mexico, Hawaii, and Southeast Asia, the islands of the Pacific, as yet little known or even identified by contemporary Japanese, were imagined to be places where an overcrowded and overburdened people might settle.

Finally, the tropical Pacific beckoned a number of former samurai. In many members of the warrior class the twin impulses of political idealism and personal ambition, repressed by the Meiji government's concern for order, stability, and rationality, could find outlet on distant shores, where the quest for personal fulfillment could be justified by a sense of national mission. To an extent, the Japanese continental adventurers—the famed *tairiku rōnin* of Meiji times—have their counterparts in those Japanese who set out singly or in groups for the distant reaches of the Pacific in search of profit, adventure, and glory.

By the mid-1880s all these elements—the recovery of the Bonin Islands, the surge of maritime concerns, the interest in overseas settlement, and the ambitions of individual adventurers and expansionists— had prepared the way for the first tentative Japanese entry into the tropics. But by that decade the Pacific was not unknown, nor were its islands uncounted. To understand the innocence, the acquisitiveness, and the anxiety with which Japanese of the time looked out upon that ocean, we must undertake a general survey of the tropical Pacific in 1885.

By that year, the Pacific was for all practical purposes explored; the final phase of Pacific discovery had ended with the voyages of Charles Wilkes more than forty years before. Westerners were increasingly in residence throughout the Pacific: missionaries with their pride, bibles, and convictions had come to both high and low islands; planters and settlers were to be found in all the larger island groups; castaways and beachcombers had even reached some of the remoter atolls. Western trading companies were already thriving in the equatorial Pacific: Burns Philp, the Australian firm, had spread its activities throughout the Gilberts; the German firm of J. C. Godeffroy & Son, operating in the Marshalls and Carolines, had launched a brisk trade in copra, tortoiseshell, and sundries; and the American David Dean O'Keefe had been managing his private trading kingdom on Yap for over a decade. Western writers and artists had already taken up pen and brush to depict an idealized South Seas: Herman Melville had written his *Typee* and *Omoo* some four decades before; Pierre Loti had already begun to beguile a generation of French with the beauty of Tahiti in his *Mariage*

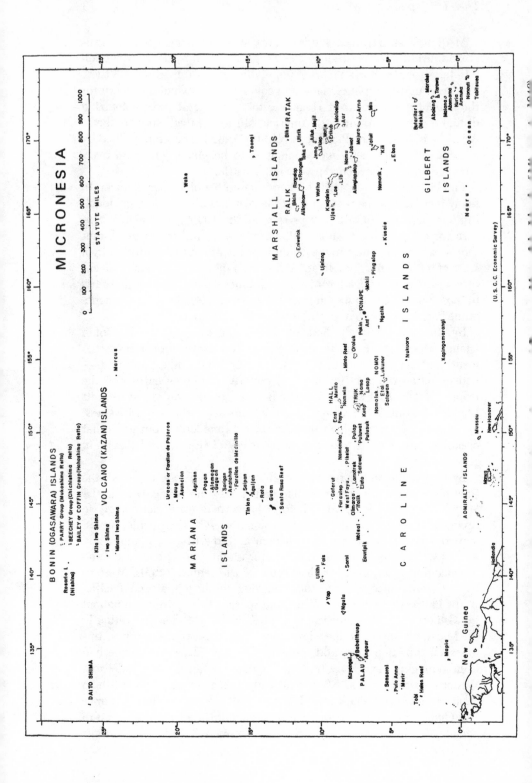

MICRONESIA

(U.S.C.C. Economic Survey)

de Loti; Stevenson would take up his South Sea idyll at Vailima in three years; and Gauguin would arrive in Papeete several years after that.

The Western presence in the Pacific was now official and permanent. European nations had planted their flags all across the ocean: France had acquired Tahiti and the Tuamotus; Britain, after some reluctance, had made a colony of Fiji; Spain had long held the Marianas, had recently acquired the Carolines, and had just ceded the Marshalls to Germany, which had shouldered its way into the Pacific with surprising vigor (Figure 1). This burst of territorial acquisitiveness was part of the larger scramble for the remaining unclaimed portions of the globe in the last quarter of the nineteenth century that historians have labeled the "new imperialism." In the Pacific, it meant that almost all island territories of any size or value were already spoken for.

To Japanese at the time, the tropical Pacific—what little they knew of it—presented an image that was at once alluring and troubling: alluring, in that it was relatively unknown and therefore still apparently pristine and open to the play of ambition, profit, and adventure; troubling in that it seemed to be rapidly filling with Western ships, guns, and traders, at a cost to Japan that was uncounted, but possibly dangerous. To some of the Japanese entry into the Pacific was a matter of personal fulfillment, to others a question of national interest.

Enomoto Takeaki and the Tropical Pacific

At a time when most of the leadership of Meiji Japan was concerned with the perils and opportunities of a Japanese presence on the Asian continent, one of its leading members saw the problem of the Pacific as a matter of his nation's power and prestige. Enomoto Takeaki (1836–1908, Photo 1) had seen naval service under the Tokugawa Shogunate and had been a crew member aboard a Dutch-built naval vessel that sailed on its maiden voyage through the Strait of Malacca and the East Indies in 1867, a voyage that inspired in him a vision of a Japanese expansion into the tropics. Dogged in his loyalty to the tottering feudal regime of the Shogun, Enomoto had led the Tokugawa navy in the last futile resistance to the new imperial government in 1868. After his defeat he was imprisoned briefly by the victors; he was pardoned in 1872, and his leadership and experience were rewarded by his appointment as vice admiral in the fledgling Meiji navy. Like other early Meiji leaders, Enomoto had administrative talents that were versatile; in the years that followed he occupied a series of positions that gave him a range of experience, influence, and contacts: minister to St. Petersburg in 1874, deputy foreign minister in 1879, navy minister in 1880–1881, minister to Peking in 1882, minister of communications, 1885–1889, of

Photo 1. Enomoto Takeaki, 1836–1908.

education, 1889–1890, and of foreign affairs, 1891–1892, and minister of agriculture and commerce, 1894–1897.

During those years, Enomoto appears to have done more than any other leader to promote the idea of Japan as a maritime power, moving out into the Pacific, vigorously engaged in trade settlement on new shores, and acquiring new territories to add to the nation's prestige and strategic position. But if he was a central figure in the "South Seas boom" of the decade 1885–1895, his role was shadowy, for he acted as an instigator and facilitator in ministry offices and in boardrooms, rather than as a navigator, explorer, or entrepreneur.

Enomoto's interest in the Pacific was unflagging, his schemes for a major Japanese role there were grandiose, and his initiatives concerning them were sometimes impetuous. On a number of occasions he advocated the purchase or occupation of territories in the Pacific: in 1876, he initiated inquiries, apparently unauthorized by his government, as to the willingness of the Spanish government to sell the Mariana and Palau islands; in later years he proposed that his government should occupy and colonize New Guinea and that it should purchase the whole of Borneo.[3] While nothing came of these expansionist schemes, Enomoto did play a major part in the creation of institutions that would enlighten his compatriots about the Pacific and the countries around its rim. Chief among these was the Tokyo Geographic Society (modeled on the Royal Geographic Society of London), whose bulletin in the years that followed frequently carried articles advocating overseas expansion and settlement, and whose membership included both the titular and actual leaders of early Meiji Japan, including Inoue Kaoru, Ōkuma Shigenobu, and Fukuzawa Yukichi. Not content with an armchair interest in the Pacific, Enomoto, while navy minister, began meeting with kindred enthusiasts, as well as interested colleagues, to consider some kind of enterprise involving settlement and commerce in the South Seas. The problem was that little was known either in or out of government about specific conditions in the Pacific tropics. In 1885, to fill this gap Enomoto had encouraged the founding of the South Seas Assembly—Nan'yō Kyōkai—an organization established to collect information, consult with knowledgeable persons, translate foreign language books on the Pacific, and act as a lobby within the upper levels of the Meiji government.[4]

Beyond these initiatives, Enomoto also actively encouraged discovery. In 1887, while he was minister of communications, Enomoto placed one of the survey ships of the ministry's lighthouse service at the disposal of a group of amateur explorers, including the governor of Tokyo Prefecture, who hoped to locate any uninhabited island territories in the western Pacific on which Japan could place its claim. Their area of search was the ocean southeast of the Bonins and their reward was the discovery of the barren, lonely Volcano Islands, including Io (Iwo) Jima, which Japan formally annexed two years later.[5]

Enomoto was first and last a sailor, and nothing that he did to stimulate Japanese interest in the Pacific was more important than his promotion of high seas voyages by Japanese naval vessels. Beginning with the cruise of the screw sloop *Tsukuba* in 1875, the early Meiji navy, spreading its sails and pressing on steam, began a series of training missions to the far shores of the Pacific. During a cruise from late 1882 to the early autumn of 1883, the corvette *Ryūjo*, with the entire tenth class of the Naval Academy aboard, stopped at Kusaie and Ponape in the eastern Carolines; it was the first Japanese warship to enter Micronesian waters. Later, the navy sent other warships to show the Japanese flag in Australia and in ports along the western coast of South America.[6]

Circumstantial evidence suggests that the navy brass in Tokyo regarded these voyages as more than training cruises for selected naval cadets. They may well have been regarded as reconnaissance missions, searching for unclaimed island territories in the Pacific. We know that the Meiji government was already seeking new homes for Japanese emigrants and that tropical islands were considered along with continental sites. Besides, there was the intriguing practice of allowing certain extracomplement civilians aboard these ships, a practice that began over two decades earlier when, as a young samurai, Fukuzawa Yukichi, the famed publicist and educator of Meiji times, had boarded the *Kanrin Maru* to accompany Japan's first diplomatic mission to the United States. It appears that Enomoto Takeaki was instrumental in arranging passage on these naval cruises for journalists and writers who were known to be enthusiastic supporters of the navy and of Japanese expansion in the Pacific. A number of these civilian volunteers, men like Shiga Shigetaka and Miyake Setsurei, rose to literary prominence, or, like Suzuki Tsunenori and Hattori Tōru, became explorers themselves. Their books, essays, and travelogues were the first to evoke a compelling vision of the tropical Pacific for the Japanese reading public.

Shiga Shigetaka (1863–1927) became the most influential of the civilian writers who took passage courtesy of the Japanese navy. Inspired by the account of the round-the-world voyage of Charles Darwin aboard HMS *Beagle*, and aided by his navy connections, particularly his close acquaintance with Enomoto, Shiga sought and obtained passage aboard the *Tsukuba* in 1886 for its ten-month cruise to the Caroline Islands, Australia, New Zealand, Samoa, Fiji, and Hawaii. His account of that passage, *Nan'yō Jiji* (Conditions in the South Seas), published in 1887, established him in the contemporary world of Japanese letters and marked the first appearance of an authoritative work on the Pacific Islands for Japanese readers. Beginning his account as a travelogue, Shiga transformed it into an appeal for the establishment of a Japanese presence in the Pacific while there was still time. Though he did not invent the word, Shiga made the public aware of *Nan'yō* as a regional concept, distinct from what was Western *(Seiyō)* or Eastern *(Tōyō)* and warned his compatriots that through their ignorance and passivity the Pacific would soon be controlled by Westerners.[7]

Other enthusiastic young expansionists followed Shiga aboard Japanese warships. The Tosa journalist Hattori Tōru, who had traveled through Micronesia in 1887, told Japanese readers in his *Nihon no Nan'yō* (Japan in the South Seas) that the nation's destiny lay not on the Asian continent, but "in the vast reaches of the hazy ocean"; there were undoubtedly still unclaimed islands where Japanese might settle and bestow the blessings of their civilization and commerce.[8] The thought that not all the islands of that ocean were entirely spoken for appealed to Shiga and to other Japanese pioneers in the Pacific, though the German annexation of the Marshall Islands in 1885 made it obvious that the number of island groups as yet unclaimed was rapidly shrinking. Among these civilian expansionists and their counterparts in the navy the hope existed that Japanese ships might yet find some small unclaimed land mass in that equatorial world where the Japanese flag might be planted and trade and settlement follow. Miyake Setsurei, who sailed aboard the *Hiei* on its training voyage into the Pacific in 1891, recalled years later that the hunger for territory in the Pacific had been so strong that the ship's officers had searched their charts in vain for unclaimed islands.[9] For his part, Shiga Shigetaka urged that exploration for island territory be made a national priority:

> Every year [he wrote in 1890] on the anniversary of the Emperor Jimmu's accession, February 11, and on the anniversary of his passing, April 3 . . . we should ceremonially increase the territory of the Japanese empire, even if it only be in small measure. Our naval vessels on each of these days should sail to a still unclaimed island, occupy it, and hoist the Rising Sun. If there is not an island, rocks and stones will do. Some will say this is child's play. It is not. Not only would such a program have direct value as practical experience for our navy, but it would excite an expeditionary spirit in the demoralized Japanese race.[10]

The Suzuki-Gotō Expedition to the Marshalls

Such considerations may have caused the Japanese government to dispatch two official representatives on a mission to the Marshall Islands that seems as curious as it was ultimately fruitless. In the mid-1880s, the Marshalls, a double chain of atolls scattered at the eastern end of Micronesia (Figure 1), were already well known to Westerners: American missionaries had spread their works and their pulpits throughout the southernmost atolls, Godeffroy & Son had founded commercial stations on Ebon, Mili, Namorik, Maloelap, and Jaluit atolls by the 1870s, and by the end of that decade the senior chief in the islands, Labon Kabua, had concluded a treaty with Germany granting that nation the right to build a naval base at Jaluit should the need arise.

Early in 1884, a party of Japanese pearl divers returning from Australian waters were blown off course and cast ashore on the atoll of Lae in the Ralik chain of the Marshalls, where they were set upon and murdered by the inhabitants. Their remains—skeletons, clothing, and some bottles with Japanese labels—were discovered some months later by the crew of the British schooner *Ada*, which brought news of the massacre to Yokohama.[11]

Gunboat imperialists of the nineteenth century were probably delighted with such a pretext for a little territorial plundering. The loss of a couple of missionaries to a savage mob, an imagined insult to the flag by an upstart local potentate, the murder of some fishermen by "primitive islanders" were viewed as a small price to pay for the excuse to take over a harbor, an island, or even some atolls. Such considerations may well have been discussed around the conference tables of the Japanese foreign ministry, but in the end the government decided merely to dispatch two very young ministry employees—Gōto Taketarō and Suzuki Tsunenori (Keikun)—who were to proceed to the Marshalls aboard the *Ada* (chartered for the purpose), ostensibly to investigate the incident and to secure an apology from the chiefs responsible.

At twenty, Gotō Taketarō seems to have had little to recommend him as the principal investigator of the mission, other than that he was the profligate son of the Meiji politician Gotō Shojirō and that he was burning to go. Suzuki Tsunenori, on the other hand, had already crammed a good deal of adventure into his thirty years. The son of a shogunal official from Tosa, Suzuki had studied Western languages and had knocked about the northern Pacific as a fur hunter in the 1870s, before being hired as an interpreter at the Foreign Ministry, in part through the good offices of the elder Gotō, who had been a friend of Suzuki's father. His experience in the wild seas off the Kuriles and the coast of Alaska had given him a taste for exploration and adventure and a hearty fund of self-reliance. Together with his language skills and his considerable facility as a quick-sketch artist, these qualities must have seemed valuable to the Foreign Ministry; the two young tyros were entrusted with this particular mission because no seasoned specialists in the South Seas were at hand.

The corroborated facts of the Suzuki-Gotō expedition to the Marshalls are simple enough[12] and, in a sense, anticlimactic. After receiving their instructions from the Foreign Ministry to proceed to the Marshalls, "some two thousand leagues south of the Bonins, in the direction of Australia," Suzuki and Gotō left Yokohama on 1 September 1884 aboard the *Ada*. The Japanese government had chartered the vessel for four months, a period long enough, it was judged, to complete the investigation into the circumstances of the massacre at Lae Atoll. On 23 September the *Ada* hove in view of Ujae Atoll in the Ralik chain of the Marshalls. Using Ujae as a base, Suzuki and Gotō explored a number of other atolls in the chain—Ailinglapalap, Lae, Kwajalein, and Namu— while Suzuki made copious notes and sketches of Marshallese village life, and of the fauna and flora of the islands.

At Ailinglapalap the Japanese first met Labon Kabua, the principal chief of the Marshalls, who, though cordial, was extremely reluctant to have outsiders prowling about his islands. Kabua appears to have put forward every possible excuse to avoid providing any help in the search for information relevant to the massacre and told the envoys that the Marshalls, with the exception of Jaluit Atoll, were not only dangerous, but closed to foreigners. Eventually, he did agree to assist in the investigation and promised that upon the apprehension of the offending islanders they would be brought to Ujae to be executed before the two Japanese.[13]

By November, Suzuki and Gotō were back on Ujae. There they

waited while the time remaining on their charter of the *Ada* dwindled away. At last, in late December, the *Ada*'s captain brought word from Kabua on Ailinglapalap. Yes, he had apprehended the culprits, but unfortunately he himself had become ill and could not possibly come to Ujae. He would instead await instructions from the Japanese. But by this time the charter on the *Ada* had run out, and its captain insisted on returning to Japan. Gotō and Suzuki boarded and, after a typhoon-wracked passage back, anchored at Yokohama on 18 January 1885. Several weeks later, Suzuki (in Gotō's name since Gotō was the ostensible leader of the expedition) submitted his report to Foreign Minister Inoue Kaoru, along with a sheaf of maps and illustrations made from the sketches he had done in the Marshalls. Inoue thanked the two men, filed the report in the confidential archives of the Foreign Ministry, and let the matter drop.[14]

Much about the Suzuki-Gotō expedition is both odd and intriguing, partly because its circumstances and apparent outcome raise so many questions, and partly because the public accounts of it in later years, largely by Suzuki himself, are contradictory. The problem is not only that Suzuki often changed the details of this and other explorations in his extensive writings, but also that he was, in his old age, a great raconteur who, often aided by the friendly ministrations of sake, never let the truth get in the way of a good story.

To begin with, Suzuki's first public account of the Marshall Islands expedition, *Maasharu guntō tanken shimatsu*, published eight years after the event, does not elucidate the purpose of the mission.[15] In it, the Foreign Ministry's reference to the Marshalls as being in the "direction of Australia" seems incredibly, perhaps even suspiciously, vague given that the Foreign Ministry had available to it expert foreign advisers who could easily have located the Marshalls with greater accuracy. There is also the fact that in Suzuki's fairly meticulous diary of the expedition there is an unexplained gap—the whole month of October 1884—which has led at least one researcher to speculate that Suzuki and Gotō may have secretly reconnoitered the Solomons and the north coast of New Guinea, territories of supreme interest to Enomoto Takeaki and other maritime expansionists.[16]

Whether or not Suzuki and Gotō were given oral instructions to explore so far from the Marshalls, we do know that their complete and confidential instructions from the Foreign Ministry committed them to investigate far more than the specifics of the atrocity at Lae Atoll. They were commanded to determine the number and arrangement of the Marshall Islands, the density and customs of the indigenous populations, the exact locations and conditions of all harbors and anchorages in the group, and the nature of the Western presence there. The possibility arises, therefore, that the investigation of the incident at Lae was merely a cover for a reconnaissance of the Marshalls prior to their annexation by Japan. In support of this supposition is the statement in Suzuki's published account that on the eve of the voyage, pondering the dangers and obstacles that lay ahead, he hoped that he would not only be able to provide a satisfactory report on the incident, but also "to place the islands under our Emperor's flag, to the glory of our country." There is also the assertion, which Suzuki made in his memoirs, published a year before his death, that before leaving the Marshalls, he induced Chief Kabua to run up the Japanese flag over his house on Ailinglapalap, an impetuous initiative that so unnerved his government that upon his return to Japan he was ordered to return to the Marshalls to have it hauled down.[17]

Some consider that Suzuki's claim to have been the first to have unfurled his nation's banner in the Pacific—an assertion often repeated by later chroniclers of the expedition—was just another of his tall tales.[18] We cannot be sure, but one thing seems clear: both young men seem to have been naive and misinformed about the Marshalls and their peoples. Suzuki and Gotō arrived in the islands believing that all Marshallese were poor and primitive savages. But Labon Kabua had for some years owned a schooner, and his trading activities, which extended as far as Ponape, had made him a far richer man than Suzuki. The Japanese were also both taken in by Kabua's spurious assertion that no foreigners were allowed in the Marshalls (when in fact Western missionaries and traders had been in the islands for a decade). This evasive tactic was taken at face value by the Japanese explorers and reinforced by the coincidence that they touched only at atolls where there was no Western presence. Suzuki and Gotō were left with the impression that the Marshalls were not yet within the orbit of any Western power when in reality Germany was rapidly moving toward claiming the group. It may be that Suzuki thought of himself as a scout for his nation, but during his months of exploration in the Marshalls he seems to have demonstrated no very great skill in discovering the political realities surrounding the islands.

Puzzles and contradictions abound concerning the end of the expedition and its return to Japan. Why were Suzuki and Gotō so easily turned aside by Kabua's "illness" and by the termination of the charter of their vessel? Was it because identification and punishment of the guilty were no longer important, and the envoys were anxious to hurry home with word that the islands were ready for the taking? We are left in doubt. There is also the scandalous secret of the home passage. For its return the *Ada* embarked two Marshallese, the chief of Namu Atoll and a lesser chief of Ailinglapalap, under circumstances that are not entirely clear. In his memoirs, Suzuki was to claim that the two chiefs were sent back to the Marshalls after a brief visit to Japan. In fact, it is both a shocking commentary on conditions on board the *Ada* and sad proof of the physical vulnerability of Pacific Island peoples in the nineteenth century that the Micronesian passengers had died of cold by the time the ship docked at Yokohama.[19]

Finally, there is the matter of Suzuki's report to Foreign Minister Inoue. The formal written report makes no mention of the flag-raising incident, whereas Suzuki's later published account indicates that he briefed the foreign minister on the substance of that initiative. Whatever intentions Inoue may have conveyed to Suzuki and Gotō before the expedition about acquiring the Marshalls, he now chose to disavow them. Whether his mind had been changed by foreign advisers at the ministry with a better understanding of the imminence of the German takeover in the Marshalls, or whether the government was now too involved with other foreign matters to be concerned with a few distant patches of coral, Inoue, with feigned or real exasperation, exclaimed to Suzuki that occupation of the islands would be prohibitively expensive and diplomatically hazardous. There, in the spring of 1885, the matter rested. The government quietly closed the books on the affair and some months later Germany formally annexed the islands, much to Suzuki's disgust.[20]

Perhaps because those in high places felt guilty about having given Suzuki misleading orders in the first place, or perhaps because they concluded that he should have a more fitting reward for completing an arduous and thankless enterprise, the government presented him with the schooner, the *Chūshin Maru*, in which he could indulge his passion for Pacific exploration. In the spring of 1887, he set off to continue the search for pristine island territories in the central Pacific. His itinerary evokes a sense of the obscurity of his landfalls: Ocean (Kure Atoll), Midway, Lisianski and Laysan islands, Maro Reef, Gardner Pinnacles and French Frigate Shoals (all to the northwest of Hawaii). But his account of the voyage, *Nan'yō fūbutsushi* (Customs and landscapes in the South Seas, 1893), would be one of the first to provide the Japanese reading public not only with interesting descriptions of the fauna and flora of the Pacific Islands, but with a sense of what it was like to sail tropical seas. He told his readers of the glories of a sunrise at sea, the way the horizon shifted under different weather conditions, the sea birds—boobies, seagulls, and stormy petrels—that could herald the approach of land, the look of a ship under sail as it crested a wave, the unpredictability of squalls, the fearful beauties of a waterspout, how to catch sharks, and what to do when suddenly caught in foul weather.[21]

But Suzuki had a more immediate task than spellbinding the reading public. In 1887, sunburned and weatherbeaten, he returned home, overjoyed that he had found land—mere specks on a map perhaps—but land, unclaimed and uninhabited, which awaited the Japanese flag, if only the government, specifically the navy, would act. But at the Navy Ministry his excited recommendations met only with amusement and were set aside. The next year his hopes for further exploration were dashed when the *Chūshin Maru*, in other hands, foundered off the northwest coast of Honshu. Yet 1889 found him aboard the warship *Kongō* on a training cruise to Hawaii, Samoa, and Fiji. That voyage gave him ample time to visit islands of some importance, yet filled him with despair at the rapid advance of other industrial powers in the Pacific and exasperation at the failure of his own government to enter the scramble for possessions. His account of the voyage, *Nan'yō junkō nisshi* (1892), was both a travelogue and a polemic, introducing Japanese to Hawaiian customs, music, cooking, and such now familiar tourist attractions as the Nuʻuanu Pali and the Koʻolau Mountains. At the same time, it urged the public to stake a claim to the islands, whose inhabitants Suzuki thought "were lacking in patriotism and vigor." But a government unwilling to confront the United States over the islands nearly ten years later, when Japan at last had a battle-tested navy, was unlikely to be prodded to such an adventure by a single Japanese traveler. Indeed, his call for territory, trade, and colonization in the Pacific was honored as prophecy only decades later, when Japanese ships were everywhere in tropic waters.[22]

The Floating Castle: Romantic Fiction of the South Seas

Not everyone who wrote about the South Seas for an avid Meiji public had been there, of course. Indeed, all that was needed to get the attention of an enthusiastic readership was pen, paper, and a strong imagination. But the romantic fiction concerning the Pacific did more than anything else to create a fevered excitement about that ocean among Japanese youth in the mid-Meiji period. Nearly all of these works were political novels whose inspiration stemmed from the largely abortive political activism in Japan of the 1880s and 1890s, and whose themes were those of adventure, exploration, resurgent navalism, and colonization of tropical utopias. Their authors, many linked to the Kaishintō, one of the early political parties in Japan, were usually frustrated liberal reformers who sought an outlet for their disappointed ideals in both literary romances and political chauvinism. As works of literature, these political novels, a preposterous mixture of outlandish plot, exotic settings, and political posturing, seem laughable today. Yet to a whole generation of Meiji youth seeking wider horizons outside Japan, they had massive appeal.[23]

Not surprisingly, the central figures of these ocean melodramas were young officers in the Japanese navy who stumbled upon some pristine island in the Pacific. *Bōken kigyō: rentō daiō* (A hazardous enterprise, or The great king of the Pacific), written by Komiyama Tenko in 1887, is a novel of exploration in which a Japanese naval officer, on his way to Australia to become a trader, makes his fortune as a sort of freebooter in a war between France and China, then discovers an uncharted island in the Pacific, over which he is eventually proclaimed monarch. In *Hinomihata* (Rising sun flag, 1887) by the journalist Sudō Nansui, a young Japanese naval lieutenant is shipwrecked on a lonely island in the South Pacific and claims it for his country. Hisamatsu Yoshinori's *Nanmei iseki* (Great exploits in the South Seas), published the same year, employed similar contrivances to sound the call for a greatly expanded navy. A young Japanese navy officer, returning from study in Britain on a newly constructed warship, is shipwrecked on a "savage island" in the Pacific, drifts ashore, and, finding a home among the inhabitants, instructs them on the dangers of the outside world and the need to look to their own defense—a somewhat heavy-handed message for the novel's Meiji readers.[24]

The work that gained the greatest fame and circulation and left the greatest mark on a generation of young Japanese, was the wildly imaginative adventure-romance, *Ukishiro monogatari* (The story of the floating castle), written in 1890 by the newspaper editor and naval enthusiast Yano Ryūkei (Fumio) and originally serialized in Yano's newspaper, the *Yubin Hōchi Shimbun*. The story is centered, appropriately, on three young adventurers who band together to seek their fortune aboard a ship bound for the East Indies. They capture a modern pirate warship, rename it the *Floating Castle* and sail through southern seas, visiting strange and exotic lands and looking for an island paradise to use as a base for the exploration and conquest of the Indian Ocean. The novel remained unfinished, but its descriptions of places like Hong Kong, Borneo, and Sumatra and of events such as a naval battle between modern fleets were devices sure to catch the wonder and enthusiasm of youthful Japanese readers in mid-Meiji.[25]

Taguchi Ukichi and the Vision of Profit and Adventure in the South Seas

By the beginning of the 1890s Enomoto Takeaki's vision of trade, settlement, and maritime expansion in the tropical Pacific had captured the popular imagination through the writings of like-minded novelists and armchair strategists, as well as seasoned travelers and explorers. It was inevitable that a few Japanese, lured by rumors of profit and adventure, should make the first attempts to act upon that vision. In small groups, Japanese traders began sailing out into the Pacific, first to the Bonins, then south into Micronesian waters, largely Spanish in those times, to trade and barter for copra and coconut oil with the inhabitants of the Marshalls and the eastern Carolines.

In 1887, a Japanese cattle farmer in the Bonins, one Mizutani Shinroku, with some ability as a sailor and a good deal of pluck, set sail in a small schooner heavily loaded with various goods to trade with the Micronesians. Touching at several small ports in Ponape in the Carolines, he was soon apprehended by Spanish officials for trading illegally, fined, and ordered to leave immediately. Having come several thousand miles to trade, Mizutani was not ready to head back to Japan with his ship still loaded and set a course for the nearest atolls, Mokil and Pingelap, where he quietly traded his goods before starting the long voyage home. Two years later Mizutani took his ship to Guam, Truk, and once more to Ponape. Over the next several years, others followed this general route.[26]

We do not know a great deal about these first Japanese trading voyages to Micronesia. They do not seem to have brought any great riches to those who undertook them, at what must have been considerable hardship and no little risk. But the prospects of greater profit they offered, combined with the growing public myth of a new Japanese frontier in the equatorial Pacific, meant that eventually other Japanese, who were better known and had more money and better organization, would try their hand at such long-range commercial ventures. The entry of such a man into the commercial opening of Micronesia marked a new level of Japanese interest in the Pacific.

At thirty, Taguchi Ukichi (Teiken, 1855–1905) already possessed an enviable reputation and valuable connections (Photo 2).[27] He was not only deputy chairman of the Tokyo city assembly, but had made a reputation as a politician, journalist, businessman, magazine editor, and most prominently, as an articulate and vigorous advocate of free trade. In his widely read journal, *Tokyo Keizai Zasshi* (Tokyo Economic Review), his criticism of economic protectionism had earned him fame in Japanese political and economic circles as "the Japanese Adam Smith." Yet, like many Japanese of his generation, Taguchi believed that his government should promote colonization and mercantile expansion. A decade earlier, he had been content to urge that these activities be directed toward the settlement of Hokkaido; but by the end of the 1880s, perhaps through his acquaintance with Enomoto Takeaki, perhaps because of the enthusiasm of his associate, Takazaki Goroku, governor of Tokyo Prefecture, who had participated in the Enomoto-backed voyage that discovered the Volcano Islands (Figure 1), Taguchi had become increasingly caught up in the vision of Japanese commerce in southern oceans.

Taguchi's brief but important involvement with Meiji southward expansionism began in the winter of 1890. Word of Mizutani's trading

Photo 2. Taguchi Ukichi. (Teiken, 1855–1905)

voyages in the South Seas began to circulate among the Japanese business community and political circles, along with the idea of setting up a trading company that would be a commercial pioneer in Micronesia. Among those most eager to pursue the idea was Takazaki Goroku, who approached a number of business and political figures, including Taguchi, seeking their support. But reading about ocean adventures was one thing and risking capital halfway across the Pacific was another; Takazaki could find no one prepared to put up the funds.[28]

Then, in the early spring of that year, a number of developments brought life to the scheme. First, Enomoto Takeaki (then minister of education) became interested and encouraged Taguchi and several individuals who had already been active in South Seas trading ventures to join. The commercial scale and geographic scope of the enterprise were reduced, perhaps to make it seem less hazardous. It was now to concentrate on gathering marine products in the waters around the Bonin Islands (Figure 1). Moreover, in his discussions with the charter members, Takazaki himself suggested a source of support: a grant from the fund provided by the national government to the Tokyo prefectural office for the retraining of former samurai. He justified his use of the money by the argument that those who would be employed by the firm would indeed be former samurai. These arrangements agreed upon, Taguchi Ukichi accepted the directorship of the newly formed Nantō Shōkai (South Sea Islands Company), and used some of the funds to buy a trading vessel, the 90-ton schooner *Tenyū Maru* (Heaven's Help). He started loading it with various liquors, canned goods, small arms, and sundries—an odd cargo for a marine products company—and lined up a crew and a list of passengers, headed by himself as company director. Among those enrolled was Suzuki Tsunenori, just back from his voyage through the central Pacific in the warship *Kongō*.[29]

Taguchi now became chief propagandist for the venture and for Pacific expansion in general. The *Tokyo Economic Review* began printing a stream of commentary and informational articles on the South Seas that would continue for six months. The lead essay, published two months before Taguchi's departure for Micronesia, restated all the contemporary themes of maritime expansion: the importance of overseas colonization and trade, the necessity for an expanded merchant marine, and the possibility of acquiring as yet unclaimed Pacific Island territories, all of which would contribute to the security and prosperity of the nation.[30]

Despite the glorious perspectives set forth in Taguchi's journal, the circumstances and purposes of the South Sea Islands Company were highly irregular and somewhat underhanded. There was first the question of the propriety of dipping into public funds to finance a private business enterprise; and there was also the wide discrepancy between the understood purpose of the company—an essentially commercial fishing enterprise off the Bonin Islands—and Taguchi's grand vision of trade and colonization in the South Seas. Within a short time the nature of the financial arrangements became public knowledge, raising a storm of criticism against Takazaki and Taguchi. The chairman of the prefectural assembly tried to beach the whole venture by taking steps to impound the *Tenyū Maru* before it could leave Yokohama Harbor. A number of charter members, unhappy with other arrangements for the enterprise, dropped out. At this point, even Taguchi began to waver, but Enomoto Takeaki urged him to pay no attention to the critics and to push ahead. "People today," Enomoto scoffed, "are just like snails shut up in their shells. They can't understand the advantage of looking around them at the world outside."[31] Suitably braced, Taguchi decided to stick with the endeavor and on 15 May 1890, while his enemies in the assembly were attending a local festival, the *Tenyū Maru*, with a crew of sixteen aboard, slipped its moorings and headed out to sea. Two days later, as the ship pointed south toward the Bonins, Taguchi's *Review* published a long exhortatory poem:

Three thousand years have passed and our land remains inviolate,
And yet we live our unreal dream,
While other nations break new soil and redeem their peoples
What of Japan? Now is the time to wake and rise!

After only a week in the Bonins the *Tenyū Maru* sailed on to Guam and then Yap. Problems of clearances and competition from other traders forced Taguchi to push on to the Palau Islands, where the ship anchored off Koror for nearly a month while Taguchi and the others explored the hilly, wooded interior of the main island of Babelthuap (Figure 1). Early in August the *Tenyū Maru* headed eastward, battling foul weather and heavy seas. Two weeks later the ship fetched Ponape, the largest and most rugged of the Carolines, where the jungle-covered mountains are forever in mist and the heat and humidity are as enervating to the first-time visitor as they are life-giving to the brilliant profusion of tropical growth. They entered a pass through the great fringing reef encircling the island and put into Ronkiti on the southern coast, but heavy weather caused them to sail around to the north side of the island to seek a more sheltered harbor. There, the *Tenyū Maru* anchored off the ugly little Spanish town of Santiago del Asuncion (now Kolonia). To their surprise, the Japanese found that they shared the harbor with a Spanish cruiser. Ponape, which had an evil reputation in the late nineteenth century for the intransigence of its inhabitants, was in the throes of one of its frequent rebellions. The Spanish colonial authorities had called in naval reinforcements and now set a watch against any smuggling trade that might lend support to the rebels. The Spanish officials refused to allow the Japanese to land, but after prolonged negotiations the company was allowed to build a small trading store close to the shore. The Japanese were permitted to trade only with the Spanish settlers and a few carefully selected villages, a restriction that slowed their business and lengthened their stay. It was November before two-thirds of the ship's cargo had been sold. Funds would not permit Taguchi to stay longer, and by mid-month the *Tenyū Maru* weighed anchor and headed home, leaving one of their number to manage the store until the ship's next call at Ponape.[32]

A month later the *Tenyū Maru* entered Yokohama Harbor. The voyage built on grandiose visions of trade and profit, had accomplished very little, for, as Suzuki was later to write, "the cruising trade is not really suitable to the South Sea islands. The only real advance must come through emigration there."[33] Worse than the disappointment he must have felt, Taguchi now had the charge that he had misappropriated the funds added to the indignant discord concerning their source, since he had made no effort to start the marine products enterprise in the Bonins, as stipulated in the arrangements setting up the company. Within a few months Taguchi was obliged to pay back most of the monies issued to him and to surrender control of the company and the *Tenyū Maru*, both of which the government put up for sale. At this point, Taguchi leaves our story. Restless and ambitious, and undoubtedly only too glad to turn the page on this damaging chapter in his career, he soon turned to writing history, to national politics (and election to the Diet), and eventually to the Asian continent, where he observed Japanese operations in the Boxer Rebellion and the Russo-Japanese War.

What is important about Taguchi's brief and almost accidental role in the evolution of Japanese interest in the South Seas is not his ill-starred trading voyage to Micronesia in 1890, but the writings that stemmed from that voyage. The *Tokyo Economic Review* printed more than sixty articles relaying information from the expedition and commenting expansively on the prospects for the dawn of a new age in Micronesia. No publication in Japan had given more extended publicity to the idea of a "southward advance" for the Japanese nation.

A more permanent account of the expedition, *Nantō junkōki* (A record of a voyage to the South Sea Islands), was published in 1893. Though purportedly written by Taguchi, it was in fact the work of Suzuki Tsunenori (and, to a lesser extent, of Inoue Hikosaburō, treasurer and manager of the South Sea Islands Company). Experienced sailor that he was, Suzuki kept detailed notes on all that he saw; the book, besides being an account of the passage among the Micronesian islands, is filled with details about weather, anchorages, indigenous peoples and their customs, local products, and all manner of information about the islands—a classic of its kind.[34]

After returning from this first voyage of the *Tenyū Maru*, Suzuki decided to try his own hand at trading in the equatorial Pacific, but bad luck dogged him once more. His trading vessel was wrecked off the coast of Honshu (the second time this had happened to him). To replace it, Suzuki raised money by selling his family property in Shizuoka. Then his commercial venture foundered. With no more funds, Suzuki was forced to turn his back on the ocean that had become his passion and to try his hand at other pursuits. He was never to return to the South Seas.[35]

Hardship and Heartbreak: The First Japanese Traders in Micronesia

If the first voyage of the *Tenyū Maru* brought no great riches to its backers, the publicity that surrounded it nevertheless inspired others to try similar ventures. It is perhaps a mark of the cumulative effect of the various writings on the tropical Pacific—the travel accounts, the essays, the flood of romantic fiction—that despite the brief and troubled history of the South Sea Islands Company, other Japanese were eager to undertake demanding, distant, and financially hazardous enterprises in southern waters. Over the next quarter century, by dogged and determined effort, by skill and initiative, and by occasional chicanery, a few score entrepreneurs, impelled by a dream that fused personal gain and national advantage, were able to create a small, tenacious, and often-imperiled Japanese presence in Micronesia. Their mini-trading companies, as one scholar has called them, usually operated on the margin of financial disaster; their small schooners crossed vast ocean distances to reach remote islands where lone representatives remained to manage small trading stores. These were established from the Marianas to the Marshalls, in order to distribute their Japanese wares—cloth, axes, cooking utensils, lamp oil, and sometimes weapons and liquor—as well as to collect the natural products of Oceania—copra, turtle shell, mother-of-pearl, and bêche-de-mer—for shipment to Japan. Sometimes the entrepreneurs sacrificed their modest personal fortunes in a futile effort to make their companies a success. Frequently their vessels— overloaded, one suspects—were lost with all their cargoes as they approached the rocky coasts of Japan on the return voyage. Often they operated under the most discouraging restrictions and harassment from suspicious Spanish and then German colonial regimes. But, limpet-like, they established a commercial foothold in the South Seas and by the second decade of the twentieth century had driven their commercial competition to the wall.[36]

After the South Sea Islands Company had been disbanded, and its assets, including the *Tenyū Maru*, put up to the highest bidder, they were purchased by one Komida Kigi who renamed the firm Ichiya Shōten (Ichiya Company). Under new management, the *Tenyū Maru* returned to Micronesia on two separate voyages, once to Ponape in June 1891 and a year later to Truk, where the company set up another store. But despite the high hopes of its new managers, the Ichiya Company, without either sufficient funds or profit, began to founder, and eventually, its assets, too, passed to other hands.

The fleeting history of the Kaitsu Company illustrates the perils and heartbreak that frequently awaited Japan's early commercial pioneers in Micronesia. The company was founded in 1891 by Mizutani Shinroku, whose 1887 voyage had first suggested the possibilities of South Seas trade. The company vessel, the *Kaitsu Maru*, reached Truk in 1892. There, Mizutani set up a small trading store—most probably on Moen Island—and after its cargo had been sold, loaded his ship with copra and other island products. On the return voyage the *Kaitsu Maru* was wrecked off the coast of Hokkaido with all its cargo. Undaunted, Mizutani chartered a leaky old tub belonging to the American missionary community on Truk. Some members of the company remained in the islands while others chose to return to Japan aboard the vessel. Somewhere between Truk and Japan the ship sank without a trace and with it the last fortunes of the Kaitsu Company, which seems to have disappeared almost as completely.

Similar tribulation haunted Yokō Tōsaku, one of the members of Enomoto Takeaki's circle of "southward advance" enthusiasts who had founded the South Seas Assembly. His ideas were sometimes as bizarre as they were grandiose (one was a scheme to settle the Pacific with the entire propertyless and criminal populations of Japan), but his commitment to furthering trade and immigration in the South Seas was total.[37] In 1891, with the backing of his mentor, he set up a joint-stock trading firm, Kōshin Sha (Kōshin Company) and purchased a schooner which plied the sea-lanes between Japan and the western Carolines. Within five years, however, the company ran into heavy financial seas. The disaffection of his original backers caused Yokō to reorganize the firm, and his business losses forced him to sell the schooner. In its place he chartered another, which foundered off Izu on its return from Palau. He leased still another, and that too was lost, this time in a storm off Kyushu. He sold his home in order to buy a fourth vessel, the *Matsuzaka Maru*, a purchase that left him with crushing debts, a six-mat room in a dingy tenement house in Tokyo, and an empty ship. In 1899, he somehow raised enough money for a crew and cargo for one last trading voyage to the Carolines. Miraculously, this last gamble seemed to have turned his fortunes. The Kōshin Company began showing a profit again and in 1903 Yokō at last stood on the threshold of success. But at sixty-five, perhaps worn out by his years of struggle and poverty, Yokō suddenly died. His now thriving company was inherited by his son, who emigrated to Palau where the firm owned an extensive coconut plantation. It continued in business until the advent of the Japanese administration, when it was bought out by the South Seas Trading Company.[38]

Japanese firms with larger capital resources were usually more fortunate. In 1893, two members of the Ichiya Company, recognizing its frailty and yet determined to stay in the South Seas trade, decided to form their own firm. Somewhere along the line they persuaded a wealthy landowner from Wakayama Prefecture, one Mitsumoto Rokuemon, to bankroll the venture. In deference to Mitsumoto (and his money) the organizers named the company after his birthplace, Hiki Village, in Wakayama. Thus was born the Nan'yō Bōeki Hiki Gōshigaisha (Hiki South Seas Trading Company Limited), which became a joint-stock company in 1899. Through aggressive tactics the Hiki Company established a number of commercial stores and agricultural enterprises in the Carolines and the Marianas. It operated four sailing vessels that plied between the islands with cargoes of sundries and then made the long haul back to Japan, their holds filled with the exotic and often odoriferous products of the tropical Pacific. In 1901, a rival firm, the Nan'yō Bōeki Murayama Gōmeigaisha (Murayama South Seas Trading Company, Unlimited), got started and, through aggressive trading, established a number of commercial outlets on Palau and Yap, as well as on a number of the smaller atolls in the western Carolines. Eventually, it was able to extend its activities eastward to Truk and Ponape.[39]

These were not easy years for these Japanese commercial pioneers. The great distances, the cramped quarters, the monotony of weeks at sea, the sudden squalls, the constant hazards of reef and rock, must have made life aboard their small ships arduous, wretched, and not a little dangerous. For those who remained on the islands and lonely atolls to mind the small stores and warehouses that were the distribution points for Japanese wares and the collection places for island cargoes to be sent back to Japan, the months of solitude without news from their homeland, the enervating heat and humidity, and the sense of extreme isolation, must have often mattered far more than the breathtaking beauty of their surroundings.

Added to these physical and psychological hardships was the constant struggle for economic survival, not just in the face of commercial competition from rival German, American, British, and Japanese firms, but also, after 1899, from the harassment by a new and actively hostile colonial regime. That year, Spain, driven from the Philippines, had withdrawn from the Pacific entirely, selling her remaining Pacific territories to Germany. Where the Spanish had rarely been able to command unquestioned authority over their Micronesian territories, the new colonial rulers took active steps to patrol the islands and to secure obedience to German law. Not only were they concerned about the growing Japanese competition to German firms like the Jaluit-Gesellschaft (Jaluit Trading Company), but they were also annoyed to discover that the Japanese had bought significant amounts of land on some of the larger high islands. The Germans were suspicious—with some reason—that the Japanese were dealing in two contraband items: liquor and firearms. Within months after they assumed authority in Micronesia, German colonial officials began to take steps to discourage this commercial poaching in the Kaiser's newest colonial territory, though they stopped short of closing the islands to foreign trade.[40]

The Japanese activities to expand their commercial presence in the South Seas and the German efforts to limit it became an episodic struggle of prohibitions and confiscations by local German colonial authorities and evasions by Japanese traders (who were occasionally aided by the intercession of their government). On Palau, the German governor called into question the ownership of land purchased by the Kōshin

Trading Company, but the firm produced legal deeds to the land dating from the last years of the Spanish administration. The governor replied with an order reducing the size of the holdings, the company appealed to the Japanese Foreign Ministry to intercede, and the subsequent wrangling continued up to the eve of the Japanese annexation of the islands in World War I.[41]

The Hiki Trading Company was the next firm to be harassed by German colonial authorities, who suspected the company of running guns and liquor to the Truk Islanders. In January 1901, while the entire Japanese community of Truk—some fourteen traders and planters—were celebrating the New Year at the company's branch headquarters on Moen Island, a German warship appeared offshore and disembarked the German colonial governor and a company of Melanesian soldiery who marched up to the building and surrounded it. Finding liquor and weapons on the premises, the governor ordered all the Japanese placed under arrest. A few days later all but one of the Japanese were expelled from the island and the company forbidden to do business in the Carolines. To circumvent the ban, the Hiki Company then set up a dummy firm and a few months later dispatched a schooner under its registry to Ponape and Truk. The Germans were not fooled and the Japanese were not allowed to land at either place. Undaunted, the schooner's captain doubled back to a number of isolated atolls in the western Carolines, where he set up several trading posts. The Murayama Company also ran into stern German prohibitions when it tried to start trading on Ponape, but subsequently, through persistent protest and negotiation, along with Hiki, it was able to establish stores on Saipan in the Marianas, on Yap and Palau, and on a number of atolls in the western Carolines.[42]

From Mini-trade to Monopoly: Japanese Success in Micronesian Trade

Within a few years, both Hiki and Murayama had been able to maneuver their way back into Micronesia. Their success over the next few years opened the way for an emerging Japanese commercial dominance in the Marianas and the Carolines. By 1906, of the total trade of German Micronesia, more than 80 percent was shipped between Japan and the islands. In the Palaus, nearly all trade, import and export, was in the hands of Japanese traders, who were as resourceful as they were determined. When the price of copra dropped on the open market the Japanese turned with skill and rapidity to commercial fishing. They pioneered freight routes among the islands and their ships began to carry interisland passengers. Often, to hear their critics tell it, they were unscrupulous, keeping prices artificially high in those places (like Guam) where they came to have a near monopoly, and selling goods that were cheaply made and overpriced.[43]

Whether by skill or by shoddy practices, they began to drive most of their foreign rivals out of Micronesian waters. By 1908, in the Marianas and the Carolines, the stiffest competition faced by the Hiki and Murayama trading companies was from each other. Concluding that continued commercial rivalry was neither healthy nor necessary, the two firms merged that year to form a new and larger enterprise, the Nan'yō Bōeki Kabushikigaisha (South Seas Trading Company, NBK), with Mitsumoto, the wealthy backer of Hiki, as its first president.

Over the next five years, "Nambō" (as it became familiarly known), with five ships and a growing commercial network throughout Micronesia, came to occupy a leading economic position in the islands. From copra and bêche-de-mer it moved into commercial fishing, interisland mail, freight transportation, and passenger service, which together provided the basis of a commercial network that by World War I had gained a near monopoly of trade in central and western Micronesia.

While German imperial ensigns floated from Micronesian customhouses and landing jetties, and an occasional German warship, resplendent in white paint and gleaming brass appeared in Micronesian waters to proclaim that these were indeed the Kaiser's islands, the trade and much of the economic life of Micronesia passed to Japanese hands. Only in the Marshalls, where the Jaluit Company monopolized trade, and in the Palaus, where the Deutsche Sudseephosphat A.G. (German South Seas Phosphate Company) dug out the rich mineral from Angaur Island, did the Germans hold the reins of economic activity.

What is surprising about the aggressive Japanese commercial drive is that those who undertook it were so few in number. On the eve of World War I there were scarcely more than one hundred Japanese living in Micronesia, divided almost evenly between the western Carolines (principally the Palaus) and the Marianas. In small groups they sailed the Pacific, leaving behind a Japan too cheerless in prospect and too inhibiting to their ambitions. In threes and fours—seldom more than a score in any spot—they had built their small wood and thatch trading stores, started their small coconut plantations (when they were able to buy land), and dickered with German colonial authorities for permission to fish the waters and ply the interisland trade routes. Exclusive in their tiny communities, as Japanese living abroad often are, they kept apart from the German centers, forming their inevitable *nihonjinkai* 'Japanese associations', which preserved their sense of identity and provided psychological support. Since there were no Japanese women in the islands and since it helped to cement their relations with the communities in which they lived, they often took Micronesian wives, who assumed Japanese names, cooked them Japanese food, and raised their children.

Mori Koben: The Man Who Would Be King

None of these early settler traders in Micronesia more embodied the themes discussed here—the romanticism, the exaggerated political idealism, the sense of national mission, the skill and tenacity, the willingness to tolerate the most trying conditions—than the remarkable Mori Koben (1869–1945). Distilling the facts of his life,[44] one feels that he had the character and capacities to have succeeded at any of a number of orthodox careers in his homeland. Yet he chose a life of hardship and danger in the South Seas. Born in Kochi City on the island of Shikoku, the son of a Tosa samurai who later became a judge, Mori showed an early aptitude for both Western learning and East Asian classical studies. His knowledge of the mathematical and physical sciences was extensive; he was able to discuss differential calculus with ease; and he was thoroughly grounded in the Chinese classics. He had numerous interests (including in later life an avid interest in photography) and a questing, restless mind. Like many young men in mid-Meiji he was a political romantic, but in Mori this trait was tempered by an iron will and exceptional fortitude, qualities he sorely needed in his youth.

It is said that as a young man Mori was a fervent admirer of his fellow Tosa countryman, Itagaki Taisuke, the melodramatic champion of the People's Rights Movement of early Meiji and a foremost advocate of an aggressive Japanese influence on the Asian continent, particularly in Korea. If true, this may explain how Mori in his youth became criminally involved in the so-called Osaka Incident of 1885. In brief, this dramatic political scandal centered on the plans of Japanese political dissidents, frustrated by their government's abandonment of the reformist cause in neighboring Korea, to cooperate with the members of a Korean reform party for the overthrow of the Korean government and its replacement by a "progressive" regime. The leader in the conspiracy was Oi Kentarō, a former samurai, in whose person was combined an explosive mixture of political liberalism and unrestrained chauvinism. In 1884, fifteen-year-old Mori left Tosa to become a houseboy to Oi, who was involved at the time in plotting with his fellow conspirators to gather weapons and raise an armed force for the assault on Korea. In order to obtain the money for the filibuster the conspirators resorted to robbery and extortion. Police investigations eventually led to the arrest of Oi and one hundred thirty suspects in Osaka and Nagasaki, of whom thirty were eventually sentenced to prison. Young Mori was caught up in the police dragnet, but, as a minor, was quickly released. Indignant at such leniency as an affront to his youthful pride as a true *kokushi* 'patriot expansionist', and unwilling to sit quietly while his fellow activists were in prison, Mori managed to get himself hired as an office boy in the courthouse where Oi and the others were being tried in order to steal some of the evidence that was to be used in their trial. This rashness earned him his proper place in prison for a year.

Several years after his release, Mori moved to Tokyo where he fell in with an old Tosa acquaintance, Oe Taku, whose father-in-law was Gotō Shojirō. Through Oe's introduction, in 1890 Mori came to stay at the Gotō mansion in Takanawa (now the location of the Prince and Pacific hotels) as a doorman. Apparently, during this Tokyo period Mori, now twenty-one and filled with a restless idealism and romanticism, somehow succumbed to a wanderlust for the South Seas. Perhaps it was because the great house was filled with the artifacts—spears, fishhooks, coconut shells, headdresses—brought back from Micronesia by Gotō's son Taketarō after his voyage there with Suzuki Tsunenori some years before. Possibly it was because he came across the spate of articles in Taguchi's journal publicizing Taguchi's impending voyage to the South Seas. Almost certainly, it had something to do with his reading Yano Ryūkei's *The Floating Castle,* a work that seems to have swept him up in its vision of the tropics as the stage for personal as well as national heroics. Like the heroes of that romantic melodrama, Mori began to nourish the fantasy of ruling over some tropic isle, of living out a life of exotic adventure that would fuse his personal destiny with that of his nation.

In any event, Mori quit the Gotō household in May 1891 to join the Ichiya Company, which had taken over from Taguchi's firm after its collapse. Six months later, with eight others, he boarded the *Tenyū Maru* at Yokohama to sail to Micronesia to become a resident representative of the company. Only twice, and then for only very brief periods, was he ever to see Japan again.

An incident on the outward voyage, perhaps apocryphal, illuminates the almost mystical spirit of adventure with which Mori set out for the South Seas. When the *Tenyū Maru* stopped at Chichijima in the Bonins, Mori disembarked with his fellow passengers to tour the island. While strolling about he came across a monument erected by the Japanese government in 1875 to commemorate the annexation of the Bonins by Japan. Engraved on the monument was a poetic allusion to the Bonins in relation to an expanding Japanese nation:

> The mountain chain of Izu stretches far and distant
> Ending here at our nation's gateway to the south

In the intervening years some unknown Japanese visitor had tried to chisel out the two characters which indicated that the mountain range

and, by implication, Japan's southward expansion, "ended" at the
Bonins. Struck with the nationalistic ardor of this small act of vandal-
ism, Mori supposedly made a vow on the spot to dedicate his life to the
South Seas and to Japan's southward advance.[45]

From the Bonins the *Tenyū Maru* plodded southward until, north of
the Marianas, it was struck full force by one of the hurricanes that periodically sweep the western Pacific. Battered and leaking, the ship
fetched Ponape in February 1892 and dropped off one of its passengers
to manage the company's store. Some weeks later, the schooner entered
the great lagoon at Truk and anchored off Moen Island where Mori
Koben, twenty-two years old, without friends or allies, and armed only
with a sword and two daggers, disembarked to start his life in the South
Seas.[46]

Deserved or not, the Truk group, comprising Moen, Tol, Dublon,
Fefan, Udot, and a scattering of smaller islands within an enormous
lagoon (Figure 2), had long had an evil reputation for violence to foreign visitors. In 1892, the Trukese were certainly warlike and Spanish
colonial authority almost negligible, conditions that might have intimidated any newcomer. Mori quickly turned them to his advantage. Per-
ceiving that the islands, particularly Moen, were in a continual state of
internecine warfare, Mori soon offered his services as a military adviser
to Manuppis, the most important chief on the island. Armed only with a
spear, Mori led the complete rout of an opposing Trukese clan, a victory
that earned him the lifelong friendship of Chief Manuppis and, eventually, the chief's daughter in marriage.

After he settled on Moen, Mori formed, in effect, a private army,
equipped with the latest Murata repeating rifles brought on the company schooner from Japan. By this time a few other Japanese had
arrived on Truk, much like Mori in outlook and ambition. Shirai Mago-
hira, for example, had fought alongside Enomoto Takeaki in the wars of
the Meiji Restoration and, after the defeat of the shogun's forces, had
fled to the Bonins and from there made his way to Truk. Along the way
he had been joined by Akayama Shirosaburō, a former customs inspector from Yokohama who had forsaken his ledgers for the perilous beauty
of the tropical Pacific. Their tiny *nihonjinkai* was a gathering of kindred spirits. Mori captured their adventurous audacity in a poem he
dashed off after a night of drinking and talking with Akayama:

> If you join me to lead an army in these southern ocean lands
> I'll take Tol, and you can have Dublon

If this was a bit of swagger, the members of the tiny Japanese community more than once had occasion to risk their lives in confrontation
with the Islanders. Their most stunning success followed an attack upon
two of their number by the Islanders on Udot. Mori gathered his forces,

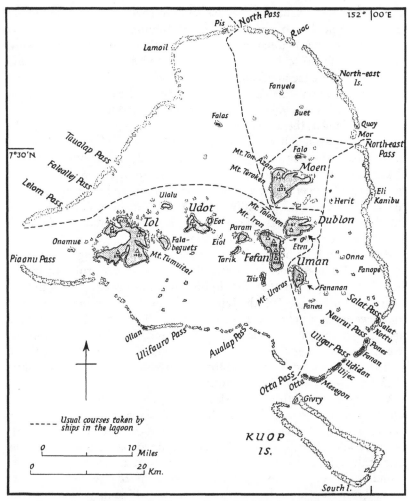

Figure 2. Truk Atoll: The Barrier Reef and Islands within the Lagoon.
(UK Naval Intelligence Division 1945, 391; British Crown copyright,
reproduced with the permission of the Controller of Her Britannic Majesty's
Stationery Office)

led them over to Udot, and in three days of fighting smashed the offending Trukese completely. But life on Truk continued to be as dangerous as
on any wild frontier. In 1896 Akayama was ambushed and murdered on
Tol by the inhabitants and that same year Mori nearly lost his life in a
frightful accident. As he was preparing gunpowder for ammunition,
the mixture suddenly exploded, blowing the fingers off his right hand.
There was no doctor on Moen in those days and, knowing that the
injured flesh might soon become gangrenous, he sliced off the affected
parts with his own knife. Somehow he managed to stanch the blood and

bind up his wound, so that he was able to survive until, some weeks later, he could board one of the small trading schooners bound for Japan. Arriving in Yokohama after a voyage that must have been agony, he went to Tokyo to have his wound dressed and then spent several months convalescing at his hometown in Kochi.

At twenty-seven Mori Koben had already sailed a course of adventure that most of his generation had only dreamed about. Given the hardships, the danger, the isolation, and the physical pain that had been the cost of that passage, it would have been natural had he now chosen to anchor his life in the relative comfort and security of his homeland.

Yet, after nearly five years of separation from Japan, his country seemed to offer even fewer and duller prospects than before as a place to live and to work out his destiny. More than that, his vision of personal fulfillment and national mission in the South Seas had not dimmed. Inevitably, he chose to return to Micronesia.

Back on Truk he built a house on Moen at Irais Village (where the sleek Air Micronesia jets now streak down the runway), ruled by his old friend, Manuppis. In 1898 Manuppis gave him his daughter—not yet twelve—in marriage. Isa (the Japanese name Mori gave her) was gentle and devoted and bore him twelve children, the first at this precocious age; she was also to provide him with an understanding and appreciation of the Micronesian environment. Through her, Mori became fluent in Trukese, adopted Trukese customs, and wove a skein of friendships with Trukese throughout the islands.

Yet, despite everything—his decision to return to the South Seas to stake his happiness and fortune there, his increasing sense of comfort and ease in his Micronesian surroundings, and the affection of his Trukese wife and children—Mori Koben remained passionately and unequivocally a Japanese, for whom separation from his country was a profound sacrifice. In true expatriate fashion, he took care to preserve around him the cultural symbols of his national identity. He taught his children Japanese, built up a small library of Japanese books, and on the most important national holidays proudly flew the Japanese flag on the flagstaff before his house.

In his efforts to maintain the tiniest Japanese presence on Truk, Mori was aided by a small number of compatriots. He had come to the islands as a representative of the Ichiya Company, and when it folded had gone into business for himself, but in 1897 the Hiki Company opened a branch on Moen, and Mori became its resident agent. Then, in 1899, he became an independent trader once more, though he picked up a contract to act as agent for the Jaluit Trading Company—no mean feat, considering the suspicion and antipathy with which the Germans soon viewed their Japanese competitors.[47] With the establishment of Hiki's branch store in Truk, other Japanese had drifted into the islands and the Japanese association had come to number fourteen. Unhindered (and protected) by the few Spanish officials on the island, Mori and his companions traded as they pleased, cultivated their coconut plantations, and met frequently at the company store to talk, drink, and exchange news.

All at once, the transfer of Micronesia from Spanish to German authority interrupted this idyllic existence. The extinction of the Hiki Company's activities in Truk came about during a New Year's party at the company store early in 1900. The scene is not hard to recreate: The Japanese are sitting on the veranda of the company store, expansive perhaps, with sake and beer, and watching the sun sink into the sea. The cruiser *Kondor,* thick black smoke streaming imperiously from its funnels, comes steaming around the point and drops anchor off Irais Village. The Papuan constabulary march up the beach, the store is surrounded, and the imperious colonial governor enters the building and orders it ransacked for contraband. The astounded Japanese are arrested and marched down to the launch. Mori, amazingly, was not among them. Whether because he was the local agent for a German firm or whether by quick-witted explanation he was able to disassociate himself from suspicion,[48] he was left on Moen while his compatriots were bundled aboard the *Kondor* for a trip to Ponape and eventual expulsion from Micronesia. But the price he paid was high.

Without assurance that Japanese trade or traders would ever again be permitted to enter the islands, Mori now faced an agonizing choice: to return to Japan, perhaps having to forsake his Trukese wife and children for the companionship of his countrymen, or to remain in the South Seas as a virtual exile. For undoubtedly the same reasons that he had chosen to return to Truk in 1897, strengthened now by the bonds of family, Mori decided to stay, though it was a decision that was to subject him over the next eight years to prolonged periods of overwhelming loneliness and despair. Because of German suspicions, any overt displays of Japanese nationality increasingly risked the possibility of deportation. To escape the attention of the colonial authorities, he moved with his family to Tol, the largest, most lofty, and most fertile island in the Truk group. There, even more isolated, the Mori family lived in peace and grew in size (Photo 3). But Koben's patriotism remained as resolute as ever and he took heart in each scrap of news about his country, even though it reached him long after the event. Hearing of Japanese victories in the Russo-Japanese War literally years after the war's end, Mori wrote to a friend in Japan: "Living as I do on this far-off island, news of our nation's triumph has made me as proud as if I wore a golden crown."[49]

Mori's isolation ended in 1907 when a Japanese merchant ship entered the lagoon. Paddling out in a canoe to meet it, Mori was over-

Photo 3. Mori Koben, wife Isa, and children. *(Kochi Shimbun)*

joyed to discover that the vessel belonged to the Murayama Company, which had been given permission by the German authorities to restart Japanese trade in Truk. Eventually, other Japanese, some in trade, some in fishing, others in farming, began to enter Truk again, but, as always, in small numbers. They kept to themselves, careful not to create any occasion for German retribution. To Mori, who prospered as a trader and plantation owner during these years, this almost furtive existence of the Japanese community must have seemed a discouragingly pale image of the glittering vision he had once held of the southward sweep of Japanese trade and power.

Then, one day in October 1914, almost without warning, the capricious drift of international events, far from Mori Koben's sheltered world, brought that vision to Truk Lagoon in dramatic and majestic form. Japanese warships, or so Mori heard, had come to anchor inside the great lagoon. That could only mean Germany had been expelled from the South Seas and Japan had come to stay. Decades later, as an old man, Mori recalled running down to the beach on Tol to see if it were true. There, out in deeper water, floating in gray majesty, was a Japanese warship, her sunburst naval ensign hanging limply from her taffrail. Mori sat down on the beach and wept for joy. Japan had come south at last.

CHAPTER 2

South into the Pacific
The Japanese Acquisition of Micronesia, 1914–1922

THE APPEARANCE of Japanese warships in Truk Lagoon in October 1914 was the immediate result of a sudden and dramatic shift in global events. But it was also due to the emergence, over the previous two decades, of Japan as a maritime power of the first magnitude. With skill, determination, and the friendly assistance of Britain, the world's greatest seapower, Japan had built a modern navy, trained it, and sent it into battle in two wars, thereby achieving a dominant position in East Asia. The Sino-Japanese War of 1894–1895 had demonstrated both the vigor of modern Japan and its alacrity in assimilating Western naval technologies and strategies, to the great cost of China. With the acquisition of Taiwan as part of the victor's spoils, Japan secured the cornerstone for a colonial empire and a stepping-stone to the lands and seas to the south. The victory in the Russo-Japanese War a decade later was an even more impressive accomplishment. The defeat of the world's greatest land power and the shattering of one of its fleets were due in equal measure to Japanese daring, tenacity, and luck. By 1905, Japan, which had embarked upon the oceans just two decades before, was the predominant naval power in East Asia.

The Emerging Strategic Importance of Micronesia

Just as Japanese fleets had begun to exercise a commanding role in East Asian waters, American naval power had begun to ply the western Pacific with similar energy and ambition. The Spanish-American War of 1898 not only demonstrated American military and naval prowess, but also brought the United States the territorial spoils of empire—the Philippines and Guam—to which Hawaii and Samoa were soon added. Though this fresh intrusion of American power into the Pacific came at a time when Japan's maritime and territorial horizons were similarly expanding, it did little to alter the essentially friendly relations between the two countries. The United States had little reason to suppose that Japan possessed the means, let alone the desire, to compete for a dominant role in the Pacific or to alter the essentially unbalanced relations between a greater and a lesser power. This American complacency about Japan's naval capacity was destroyed when the Japanese Combined Fleet crushed the Russian Baltic Fleet at the Battle of Tsushima in 1905. In the ensuing clear-headed reassessment of Japanese strength, Japan's military and naval potential became as important as its intentions. To those in command of the United States Navy, Japanese energy, ambition, and valor now reinforced a potential threat to America's new Philippine territories, which lay less than a day from Taiwan by steam. Much more ominous to ordinary Americans was the challenge to white American institutions and society posed by the growing stream of Japanese "aliens" into Hawaii, the Pacific Northwest, and California. The American response—alarmist, racist, and vehement—reached a climax in the discrimination episodes of 1906–1907 in California. These profoundly shocked Japanese optimism about the relationship with America and called into question the seemingly unlimited possibilities of Japanese expansionism. For the first time, public discussion of an open and violent rupture appeared on both sides of the Pacific, though it was largely limited to the war scare literature exemplified by Homer Lea's *The Valor of Ignorance*, a scenario of a possible Japanese invasion of the Philippines and the Pacific Northwest, and Mizuno Hironori's *Tsugi no issen* (The next battle) which included a description of an annihilating battle between Japanese and American fleets in the Pacific.

For their part, the Japanese and American governments attempted to damp down the rhetorical fires, recognizing that a Pacific war was neither inevitable nor in the interests of either country. Yet, as the naval establishments in each nation brought into sharper focus their strategic priorities for the immediate future, the adversary navy clearly emerged as the salient hypothetical enemy in a naval war. Each began to ponder the strategic problems of a Japan–United States conflict. In the staff colleges on both sides of the ocean the study of a Pacific war centered on two common assumptions: that the Japanese would conduct offensive operations against the Philippines at the outset of the war, and that the United States Battle Fleet would move westward across the Pacific to come to the aid of the American garrison and naval units there. To struggle with the problem, the American Army-Navy Board, as part of its contingency "color plans" dealing with interservice cooperation in wartime, drafted Plan Orange, which provided the strategic concept and mission in the event of war against Japan.[1] Over the next thirty years Plan Orange was kept under constant review and was frequently revised in keeping with changes in the strategic situation in the Pacific.

But the central dilemma of how to bring distance and time into a closer ratio in order to effect the rescue of the vulnerable American position in the Philippines remained nearly insoluble.

For the Japanese, the problem was how to confound and defeat an American battle line superior in numbers and firepower. The first Japanese fleet maneuvers, with the United States Battle Fleet as the hypothetical enemy, were held in the waters off Kyushu in 1908, and the first concrete study of operations against the Philippines and against a westward-moving American battle fleet were begun in 1910. From these exercises Japan's naval high command concluded that Japan's best hope of victory lay in a strategy of attrition whereby the size of the American fleet would be reduced by continuing flank attacks by light Japanese forces until at some point, probably in the western Pacific, an eventually superior Japanese fleet could challenge it in a final encounter.[2]

Initially in the study of the strategic considerations of a Pacific war, Micronesia was not seen as an area of critical importance by either Japan or the United States, largely because in German hands the islands had posed slight threat to either side. Certainly, few strategists in either Japan or the United States had given much thought to the importance of Micronesia before 1905. America had evinced so little interest in the islands prior to that time that Germany's annexation of the Marshalls in 1886 had passed almost unnoticed in America. At the conclusion of the Spanish-American War, however, the Naval War Board had recommended that one coaling station be retained in the Marianas.[3] Accordingly, Guam, already occupied by American naval forces, became the sole American possession in Micronesia. Yet when Germany purchased the remaining Marianas and the Carolines from a beleaguered and sullen Spain, the United States government raised no objection. In the fourteen years prior to World War I the German naval presence in the Pacific was symbolic rather than strategic, as the largest German naval force was based far to the north at Tsingtao on the Shantung peninsula. After the Russo-Japanese War, however, the officers in the naval staff colleges in both Japan and America gradually became aware of the potential importance of Micronesia.

To the Japanese at the end of the nineteenth century, Micronesia was viewed, along with the rest of the tropical Pacific, as an area where they could realize that vaguely formed and romantic concept, "the southward advance." Yet in the 1880s and 1890s, with the exception of a few enthusiasts in high places like Enomoto Takeaki, the South Seas and the "southward advance" were the stuff of dreamers, novelists, and isolated explorers, not the concerns of the Japanese navy. Once the "South Seas fever" among the reading public subsided, the Nan'yō no longer caught the public imagination.

Yet, even as this romantic public interest in the South Seas subsided, an increasing number of influential professionals in politics, business, and the navy began to give more sober thought to the southward expansion of Japanese influence and power. Their views, expounded in lecture platforms, in the national press, and in a steady flow of professional articles, began collectively to demarcate a gradually emerging debate as to the proper orientation for Japan's expansionist energies, a choice between an advance onto the content in north Asia, *hokushin*, or expansion southward, *nanshin*. Influential proponents, like Navy Commander Satō Tetsutarō and the journalist and Diet member, Takekoshi Yosaburō, grounded the concept of an advance of Japanese interest and power into equatorial lands on the serious concerns of economic advantage, national security, and geopolitics. Japan's future lay not in the north, but in the south, not on the continent, but on the ocean, insisted Takekoshi. Admonishing his compatriots to realize that it was Japan's great task as a people to turn the Pacific into a Japanese lake, he urged them to support an increase in the Japanese navy, an expansion of the merchant marine, an extension of trade routes, and unfettered emigration to the tropic lands south of Japan. To Takekoshi the importance of equatorial regions to Japanese national ambitions was critical. "Whoever controls the tropics controls the world," he declared.[4]

Because the concept of a southward advance was essentially a maritime strategy, it is not surprising that in the decade that followed the Russo-Japanese War the Imperial Japanese Navy came to support these somewhat nebulous aspirations with enthusiasm. In doing so, the navy's priorities ran counter to the demands for continental expansion urged by the army. The *hokushin-nanshin* debate went on within the context of competition between the two services for funds and national attention to support their large expansion or construction programs, claims which each service made by identifying a hypothetical enemy (the United States for the navy, Russia for the army) and assigning a geographical priority. In developing the concept of a "southward advance," the Japanese navy linked it with the need to protect Japanese commerce in the western Pacific and the consequent necessity to establish naval hegemony in those waters against the advance of American naval power.

Yet by the beginning of the new century's second decade, Japan had no foothold in either the South Seas or Southeast Asia, only economic aspirations in both areas. Japanese business and commerce had begun to make important inroads into Malaya, the Philippines, and the Netherlands East Indies, but operated at the indulgence of the colonial governments in those areas. In German Micronesia a few hundred Japanese traders and fishermen in the Carolines and Marianas constituted the only Japanese presence in the South Seas. To some expansionists like the journalist Tokutomi Sohō the idea of marking time on the continent while pursuing illusory riches in tropic lands far to the south was a very roundabout way to advance Japanese interests. "How many rubber groves, pearl fisheries, and sugar plantations can we really expect?" he asked, urging that instead Japan put its energies and resources into expanding its power near at hand, in Manchuria and north China. But in 1913, the popular monthly *Taiyō* devoted most of its November issue to an exploration of the economic, strategic, and political choices posed by the *hokushin-nanshin* controversy.[5]

Opportunity Beckons: Japan's Decision for War, August 1914

All at once, by a stroke of amazing luck, it seemed possible with but slight effort to advance both strategies simultaneously, by exploiting the suddenly vulnerable situation of Germany in East Asia and the Pacific. No other consideration seems adequate to explain the rush with which Japan chose to enter the outer edges of the maelstrom of international conflict that swept over Europe in the summer of 1914. In a sense, Japan's decision to join Britain in a war against Germany underscored the priorities of the Imperial Japanese Navy, which had been seeking to recoup prestige lost in a shabby contract scandal the previous year, as well as to drum up public support for a much larger battle fleet. Furthermore, the navy had for many years cherished its British connection. The Royal Navy had helped train the fledgling Japanese navy in the early Meiji years, infusing it with an admiration for everything British, from Players cigarettes to the British heroes of the Great Age of Sail. (As Tōgō Heihachirō, victor at Tsushima, had put it, "My god is Nelson.") The Anglo-Japanese Alliance of 1902 was the most important tie, having aimed largely at isolating Russia, a purpose it had admirably served during the Russo-Japanese War. But the claim—or at least that of some Japanese statesmen at the time—that Japan joined in the fight against Germany because of obligations under that alliance was specious, since its terms could not be so interpreted within the conditions that prevailed in the crisis of August 1914. It is clear that Japan went to war that month because it was to its very obvious advantage to do so.[6]

Separated from Berlin by half the globe, the prize German colony and naval base at Tsingtao on the Shantung Peninsula lay just across the China Sea. Its main protection, the German East Asiatic Squadron, was out of port when the war began. The German territories in Micronesia, New Guinea, and Samoa had no permanent naval units or military garrisons whatsoever. To move swiftly against these territories and wrench them from Germany's feeble grasp would be a simple strategic effort that could be made with minimum military risk, particularly since, as everyone in the government expected, the Allies would be victorious, or, at the very worst, stalemated. The real problem was the diplomatic and political task of maneuvering the nation into war on the Allied side and finding a suitable pretext for the dispatch of naval and military forces to occupy the German territories in China and the Pacific without antagonizing the Allied powers, particularly Britain. Undoubtedly, everyone at the top level of the government recalled the painful national humiliation of two decades before, when the intervention of Germany, France, and Russia had forced Japan to retrocede Port Arthur, wrested from China at the end of Japan's stunning victory in 1895. This time the support, or at least the acquiescence, of Britain was essential. With it, Japanese forces could move swiftly against the German colonial territories, occupy them, and be in a position to argue at the peace table for the right to retain them permanently as a reward for contributing to the Allied victory. But how to arrange it?

As it turned out, the key was provided by Germany itself. The German East Asiatic Squadron, under Admiral Maximilian von Spee, was the most powerful single group of warships of their class at the time, but was divided and far from Tsingtao when the war broke out. The squadron's two principal warships, the battle cruisers *Scharnhorst* and *Gneisenau*, had sailed south in June on a cruise to show the flag in Germany's Pacific territories. Should they choose to return to join with the other units of the squadron they could, for a time at least, ravage Allied shipping in East Asia and the western Pacific, though soon, without a home base and faced with superior numbers, von Spee's fleet would be destroyed. Unknown to Britain or Japan, von Spee, at Ponape when the war began, chose instead to rendezvous quickly with his supply vessels in the Marianas, then turn back eastward across the Pacific, around the Horn, and through the Atlantic, to try to reach Germany. In this attempt, he was fated to smash up a weak British blocking force off Chile and then, in December, to meet annihilation under the guns of a powerful British squadron off the Falklands.

All this lay ahead. In the first week of August 1914 the uncertainty as to von Spee's whereabouts and the possibility of attacks on Allied shipping by German raiders provided Japan with the pretext to exploit the international crisis. Britain, for its part, was ambivalent about having Japan as an active ally. The British government was concerned about von Spee's isolated force in the Pacific, though it was in no panic. Moreover, from the first tremors of the world crisis, Britain was suspicious of Japan's intentions and apprehensive of its appetites. Because of the proximity of Tsingtao to Japan, the British government was resigned to giving Japan a free hand on the Shantung Peninsula, but was extremely reluctant to countenance a Japanese thrust into the tropical Pacific.

In the first few days of the war, Sir Edward Grey, British foreign secretary, had fended off eager Japanese offers of assistance. Then, on 7
August, the British government, as yet possessed of no adequate naval
force in the East and momentarily unnerved by reports of German
raiders attacking British shipping in the East China Sea, provided Japan
with the wanted pretext: a request to the Japanese government for
naval assistance in seeking out and destroying these enemy vessels. Has-
tening to exploit the opening thus presented, the Japanese cabinet met
to "consider" the request. The nation's elder statesmen were consulted
the following evening, and the emperor briefed. On 9 August, the Japanese government informed Britain of Japan's intention to go to war with
Germany in order to honor its commitments under the Anglo-Japanese
Alliance and in order to preserve the safety of the sea-lanes in the
Pacific. Japan also assured the British government that in going to war
it had no thought of territorial aggrandizement.[7]

Too late, Britain sought to put the cork back in the bottle. On 9
August, Sir Edward Grey informed the Japanese ambassador in London
that recent intelligence indicated the naval alarms to be unfounded and
that Britain, withdrawing its request, desired Japan to postpone military and naval operations until further notice. But the Japanese government brushed past this awkward diplomatic maneuver. Foreign Minister Katō Takaaki told the British ambassador in Tokyo that the Japanese
government had made its decision, that the emperor had been informed, and that preparations for war had been set in motion. To
reverse these would cause the downfall of the cabinet. Reluctantly, Britain conceded the point and agreed to recognize that Japan was entering
into war on the basis of the Anglo-Japanese Alliance. The British aim
now was to persuade Japan to limit its military and naval operations to
East Asia.[8]

But in Tokyo, the leadership was impatient with such efforts to narrow Japanese options or to lessen the nation's new strategic opening.
Moreover, to the diplomatic offensive was brought the logic that Japan
was entering the war to destroy the threat to the sea-lanes posed by German warships, as Katō pointed out. Von Spee's most powerful ships
were known to have sailed into Micronesia, and the most recent intelligence was that German warships were operating near Jaluit Atoll in the
Marshalls. The Japanese navy had to be able to pursue them there for
the same reasons that Australian naval units had begun to move toward
German territories south of the equator. The British effort to keep its
unwonted ally in check now crumbled. On 12 August, in London, Grey
summoned the Japanese ambassador to explain that Britain hoped
Japan would not occupy any of the German island territories in the
Pacific, except for direct operational necessity; but in Tokyo, the government merely repeated its denial of any territorial ambitions.[9]

Moderates versus Fire-eaters: The Japanese Navy Occupies Micronesia

On 23 August, Japan declared war on Germany and a few days later began to assemble a military expedition that would land on the Shantung Peninsula and a special naval force that would enter Micronesian waters. On 14 September, the South Seas Squadron—a battleship, two cruisers, two destroyers, and three transports—steamed out of Yokosuka under Vice Admiral Yamaya Tanin, flying his flag on the battlecruiser *Kurama*, ostensibly in pursuit of the German East Asiatic Squadron. Yet by this time von Spee had left the Marshall Islands far behind, heading for Tahiti and the chance to sideswipe the French port facilities there as he made for Cape Horn.

If there is much seeming ambiguity about the Japanese naval expeditions to the South Seas in the early autumn of 1914 it is because there apparently was vehement disagreement in Tokyo as to how rapidly and aggressively Japan should move in exploiting the opportunity the war had provided. There were some, particularly in the top echelons of the Foreign Ministry and the Navy Ministry, who urged caution and counseled against flouting Britain's opposition to the outright occupation of German territory. Foreign Minister Katō was noted within the Foreign Ministry for his keen admiration and respect for the British. So too were Navy Minister Yashiro Rokurō and Vice Minister Suzuki Kantarō (destined, as an old man, twenty-one years later, to preside over the cabinet deliberations to end the Pacific War). For these men, establishing a foothold in the South Seas, desirable as that might be, was less important than retaining the trust and support of Japan's allies, especially Great Britain. Through the first six weeks of Japan's participation in World War I, their influence seems to have kept the mission and activities of the naval expeditions to the South Seas limited to their original ostensible purpose: the location and destruction of an enemy fleet.[10]

Arrayed against this policy of caution and moderation were a number of groups and individuals who sought, by lobbying, by stimulation of public enthusiasm, or by powerful bureaucratic pressure, to bring about an aggressive exploitation of the new opportunity. There were various nationalist groups ready to support any effort at territorial expansion, as well as commercial firms that obviously welcomed the possibility of Japanese sovereignty in Micronesia and a friendlier environment for their enterprises. In the first few weeks of the war one such firm bombarded the press, members of the Diet, and numerous government officials with arguments concerning the economic value and strategic importance of the islands. The more nationalist newspapers saw the Japanese movement into Micronesia as breaking the stranglehold on Japan's natural expansion into the Pacific that they believed America had attempted through its occupation of Guam, Hawaii, and the Philippines.[11]

But the most telling pressure for a swift and permanent occupation of Micronesia came from within the navy itself, where powerful bureaucrats within the Naval General Staff and the Naval Affairs Division of the Navy Ministry saw the opportunity to acquire advance bases that would give Japan a vital strategic advantage in any future conflict with the United States. These individuals provided the impetus behind the change in the character and purpose of Japan's naval expedition into Micronesia.

Several incidents illuminate this change, though they do not explain exactly how it came about. The first of these concerns the battle group sent south under Admiral Yamaya. After touching at the Bonins, the squadron stopped at the Marianas, but, finding no sign of the enemy, pushed on as rapidly as possible toward the Marshalls, arriving at Eniwetok Atoll on 29 September. Yamaya's ultimate objective, however, was Jaluit Atoll, the German commercial headquarters in the central Pacific. He anchored off Jaluit on 30 September and, finding the vast lagoon empty, put a landing party ashore. The handful of German authorities on the island wisely made no attempt to resist or to stir up the indigenous population, who willingly accepted the atoll's new occupiers. After gaining control, Yamaya radioed his report to naval headquarters in Tokyo. Back almost immediately came instructions that he was to withdraw the landing party at once and retire to Eniwetok. Yamaya complied and steamed westward once more, only to receive further orders a few days later that he was to return to Jaluit and land a permanent occupying force. This he did, putting ashore a permanent landing party of three officers and one hundred enlisted men on 3 October.[12]

In the meantime, a second naval task force had been formed, supposedly at the request of the British government, which wished to have a battle group sent to Australia to protect troop transports carrying ANZAC contingents on the first leg of their journey to Europe. This Second South Seas Squadron (Yamaya's group being renamed the First South Seas Squadron), consisting of the battleship *Satsuma* and two light cruisers, was commanded by Rear Admiral Matsumura Tatsuo. The day after assuming his new command and before his departure from Sasebo, Matsumura called to pay his respects at the principal offices in naval headquarters in Tokyo. His first stop was the Navy Ministry to consult with Navy Minister Yashiro who cautioned him that, considering the importance of maintaining good relations with Japan's Anglo-allies, it would be most unwise to occupy any of Germany's Pacific island territories. If the military situation compelled him temporarily to do so, he was to withdraw the landing force as quickly as necessity permitted, and on no account was he to raise the Japanese flag. He received similar warnings from Vice Minister Suzuki, who added that he was to be particularly circumspect in any operations near Yap and Saipan, since Britain had announced its intention to send landing parties to both these islands.[13]

After his calls on the minister and vice minister, Matsumura visited the Naval General Staff offices. When he relayed the instructions given him at the Navy Ministry he met a sulfurous response. The vice chief of staff and Admiral Inoue Yoshika stormed that these were ridiculous orders. Why on earth shouldn't enemy territory be occupied, and why withdraw a naval landing party for no operational reason? Akiyama Saneyuki at the Naval Affairs Division of the Navy Ministry was equally derisive of the ministry's policy of caution. The whole thing was rot, he insisted. Yamaya had been sent on a fool's errand, chasing von Spee around the vastness of the Pacific with only three ships. In any event, Japan ought to have something to show for its efforts and if Matsumura wanted to be of real service to his country, Akiyama argued, he ought to pick up a few of the islands in Micronesia, particularly those like Angaur, which were rich in phosphates. Matsumura himself seems to have warmed to Akiyama's arguments that the South Seas were an undeveloped, underpopulated treasure house of natural riches, waiting to be developed by Japanese enterprise and resourceful immigrants.[14]

These two separate developments—the altered instructions sent to Admiral Yamaya and the demonstration of an open rift at navy headquarters noted by Admiral Matsumura—form the background to the new instructions sent to these two commanders, now both at sea, by the navy minister. Both squadrons were instructed to carry out "temporary occupations" of the principal German territories in Micronesia.[15] It is clear that at some point in the four days between Matsumura's conversations in Tokyo and Yamaya's occupation of Jaluit, the expansionists in the navy had triumphed. Though the cabinet still equivocated, the navy, in effect, had decided to run up the flag in the South Seas. On 5 October the First South Seas Squadron anchored off Kusaie; on the seventh it sailed past the great rock at Sokehs (Jokaj) and entered Ponape Harbor; and on the twelfth the battleship *Kurama*, followed by a cruiser escort, entered the enormous lagoon at Truk where Mori Koben saw it at anchor. To the west, Matsumura in the battleship *Satsuma*, escorted by two cruisers, sailed into the harbor at Yap (to the consternation of the Australian navy, which had been on its way north to do so); on 7 October, his squadron put a landing party ashore at Koror in the Palaus; on the ninth Angaur and its German phosphate mines were in its hands; and on the fourteenth, when the battleship *Katori* dropped anchor in the roadstead off Garapan Town on Saipan, the Japanese occupation of Micronesia (except for the American colony of Guam and the British Gilberts) was complete.[16] The effort had been swift, bloodless, and easy.

It had also been furtive. Except for the initial landings on Jaluit Atoll in the Marshalls, Japan gave little publicity to its occupation of the other island groups in Micronesia. And, after taking control of the islands, the Japanese navy made it plain that it did not welcome the entry of any other ships into Micronesian waters, even those of its allies.[17] Admittedly, this was a policy little different from that pursued by the United States in the decade following its conquest of Micronesia in World War II. Yet the element of secrecy that pervaded the Japanese occupation of Micronesia from its earliest beginnings was to create unnecessary suspicion and ill will for Japan.

A Clever Hand: Japan's Secret Diplomacy, 1915–1917

In point of equity, Japan can hardly be chided for the alacrity with which it snapped up the German Pacific islands north of the equator, since Australian and New Zealand naval units had been no less tardy in occupying the German territories to the south: Kaiser Wilhelmsland in New Guinea, the Bismarcks, Nauru, and Samoa. Indeed, to prevent an accidental clash between Japanese and Australian warships, the British and Japanese governments had reached agreement in October, making the equator the operational dividing line between Japanese and British naval forces.[18]

Yet the outright Japanese seizure of German Micronesia provoked the sort of alarmed reaction from Britain and the dominions that moderates in the Japanese government had feared. What aroused the ire of the Anglo-Saxon nations was what they considered to be the rank opportunism and the furtive and devious manner by which Japan had acquired its spoils of war, followed by Japan's obstinate refusal to expend men, ships, or material in other theaters of war where the Allies could have used real help. Although the historical record offers extenuating circumstances to explain Japanese conduct during World War I, to their embattled Allies at the time, it was cause for suspicion.

Alarmed by the speed with which Japan had moved into the South Seas, Britain now attempted to prevent Japan from establishing a permanent claim to its Micronesian spoils. Sir Edward Grey cabled Katō Takaaki that, in Britain's view, the respective British and Japanese occupations of Germany's Pacific territories should be considered a temporary wartime measure and that the final disposition of the islands should be left to discussion between the Allies at the end of the war. Katō's rather evasive answer came back on 1 December. He agreed that the matter should be left "without prejudice to the final arrangements" at the conclusion of the war. But he pointed out that, in view of the very extensive operations in which the Japanese Navy has been engaged and is still engaged in cooperation [with the British navy], the Japanese nation would naturally insist on the permanent retention of all German Islands north of the equator and the Imperial Government will have to rely on the support of the British government for the accomplishment of that objective when the proper moment arrives.[19]

This amazing bit of artifice—partly accommodating, partly insistent—must have strained the patience of Sir Edward. Noting dryly that Japanese operations since entering the war "have been greater in extent than was contemplated," he commented that Katō's statement was inconsistent, to say the least. To insist on Japan's permanent possession of the Pacific islands and to expect advance British support for Japanese claims to them at the peace table hardly squared with Katō's acceptance of the principle that all such matters should be decided at the end of the war, let alone Japan's professions in August that it harbored no territorial ambitions whatsoever. Katō was at once conciliatory and obstinate, replying that his statement had simply been an expression of friendship for Britain, but noting also that Japan had gone to a rather great effort as an allied belligerent and would find it impossible to quit the islands after the war.[20]

There the matter rested for several years, while the Japanese navy set about establishing a firm administrative presence in Micronesia, untroubled by war's alarms or by the critical observation of other powers. Early in January 1915 the First South Seas Squadron returned to Yokosuka. Two weeks before, the Second South Seas Squadron had been transformed into the Provisional South Sea Islands Defense Force (Rinji Nan'yō Guntō Bōbitai), which, for the next eight years, was to administer the "newly occupied territories," *shinsenryōchi,* the wartime term for the ambiguous legal status of Micronesia. In this first rapid stage of the Japanization of Micronesia, Japan's naval government undertook a vigorous effort throughout the islands to place a permanent Japanese imprint on them. The administrative structures, the education and indoctrination of the indigenous population, the encouragement of Japanese enterprises, and the discouragement of involvement by other foreign powers, all reflected the official assumption that Japan was in the islands to stay.

Displaying the Japanese talent and obsession for information gathering, the government in Tokyo also sought to buttress its future claims to Micronesia by studying its new territorial acquisitions in meticulous detail. In the spring of 1915 a government-sponsored investigating team, composed largely of specialists in medicine, agriculture, and natural science from Tokyo University, arrived at Truk aboard a navy steamship to begin a two-month tour of all the island groups, investigating all manner of questions concerning them. Their massive report, published several years later by the Ministry of Education, was obviously intended, among other things, to demonstrate to other powers that Japanese claims to Micronesia were based on a solid understanding of the territories they wished to administer.[21]

For over two years, European armies ground each other into the blood and muck of the trenches and opposing fleets collided in titanic and fruitless battle in the North Sea. Japan, with great common sense and uncommon parsimony, looked on from distant and tranquil shores, resistant to all entreaties from Europe for a commitment of lives and treasure to European battlefields, yet determined not to lift its hand from the territories it had so easily seized at the outset of the war. Occasionally, amid the world's chaos, Japanese statesmen would attempt to catch the attention of one or another of the embattled Allies regarding Japan's claims. In the summer of 1915 the ambassador to France, Viscount Ishii Kikujirō, passing through London on his way back to Japan for reassignment, revealed to Sir Edward Grey his view that, while he himself did not consider the former German islands in the Pacific as being of vital importance, "they appear to the Japanese people as the only memento of their sacrifices of the war." If they did not become a Japanese possession, public opinion in his homeland, Ishii noted pointedly, would reach fever pitch. Sir Edward replied laconically that he would keep that in mind.[22]

Unable through such sly hints to obtain firm advance commitments from its allies for support for its territorial aspirations, Japan tried a different tack. In the spring of 1916, the Foreign Ministry leaked word of roundabout offers made to Tokyo by Germany for cession of the Pacific territories to Japan in return for a termination of hostilities between the two nations. Quickly, Britain squelched this initiative by reminding Japan of its pledge upon entering the war that it would not enter into a separate peace.[23]

Not until January 1917 did the Japanese government see an opening by which it could make effective overtures to the Allies for the sort of commitment it sought. In that month, Britain had sent one of several appeals for help in the European theater, this time a request for Japanese naval units to assist in antisubmarine patrol work in the Mediterranean. Early in February, Motono Ichirō, the new foreign minister, let it be known that the Japanese cabinet could be moved to provide such assistance if firm British assurances regarding disposition of Shantung and the Pacific islands were forthcoming. Two weeks later Motono had his guarantees.[24]

Several reasons, beyond the need for Japanese naval assistance, were behind this sudden change of heart by Britain. Undoubtedly, Britain recognized that Japan's retention of the islands in some form was inevitable. It was undeniable that Japanese naval garrisons were scattered throughout Micronesia, and none of the Allied powers seemed tempted to try to dislodge them. Undeniable, too, were the ambitions of Britain's own dominions in the South Pacific, ambitions that equalled those of Japan north of the equator. Australian naval garrisons were posted in New Guinea and the Bismarck Archipelago, and New Zealand had occupied German Samoa. Australia was determined to retain these territories upon the conclusion of the war, if for no other reason than to prevent further Japanese southward expansion in the Pacific. As a major force within the empire, Australia was able to press its views upon Britain. Thus, the Foreign Office note of February not only conveyed Britain's guarantee of support for Japan's claims to the German islands north of the equator, but contained a demand for similar Japanese support for British claims to those to the south.

Once Japan had Britain's support, commitments from the other Allies, none of whom had competing interests in the Pacific, were easy enough to acquire. France sent in its agreement on 1 March, Russia agreed four days later, and on 28 March, Italy approved.[25] By the spring of 1917 Japan had quietly collected all the IOUs necessary to feel confident about the disposition of the Micronesian islands at the peace table.

The United States Navy Looks at Micronesia, 1914–1918

Of these arrangements, Japan's chief rival in the Pacific knew nothing. It is entirely understandable that during the first few years of the war Japan felt no obligation to convey to the United States any information about the secret agreements entered into with its European allies. Yet even after America's entry into the war in April 1917, Japan kept its own counsel on the matter. Viscount Ishii, now ambassador to Washington, in his call on Secretary Lansing in the summer of 1917, mentioned Micronesia, remarking that "no government in Japan could survive if it did not retain some of the South Sea islands as souvenirs of the war," and adding that Sir Edward Grey had practically assented to Japan's insistence on this point. Like Grey, Lansing let Ishii's remark pass without comment.[26] Perhaps he did not grasp its full meaning, or perhaps he felt that, even if true, it was of small consequence. There is some evidence that he subsequently learned of the Anglo-Japanese accords in greater detail, but if so, he failed to pass the word along, either to his president or to his subordinates at State. At war's end, therefore, the United States had no coordinated or effective policy toward Japan's Pacific advance.

Nevertheless, Japan's occupation of the German Pacific islands north of the equator in the early autumn of 1914 had been alarming to American strategists, particularly in view of the cluster of antagonisms between the two countries that had emerged over the past five years.

American phobias about Japan—the racial stereotypes, the issue of Japanese immigration, the continuing babble about the Yellow Peril—had deepened antagonisms on both sides of the Pacific. By 1913, the tide of mutual resentment had reached ominous levels and was held in check only by the common sense of both governments and the redirection of the attention of both publics to the cloudburst that had broken over Europe in the summer of 1914.

For military and naval planners in Tokyo and Washington, developments in the first years of the war hardly lessened the critical strategic problems of the Pacific. Japanese naval strategists had reason to be concerned in 1914 by the opening of the Panama Canal, which greatly enlarged the American capacity to exert a formidable naval presence in the Pacific, and in 1916 by the obvious American effort to establish naval supremacy by constructing a navy "second to none." For American naval planners, the global crisis seemed to increase the basic strategic dilemma of protecting American territories in the western Pacific. On the eve of the war, the navy's General Board had revised Plan Orange to take into account the possibility of a coalition between Japan and Germany. Then, in the autumn of 1914, American strategists became alarmed by the alacrity of Japan's move into the western and central Pacific and grew disturbed about Japanese intentions, particularly in view of the veil of secrecy the Japanese navy had dropped around its new conquests. In the strategists' view, a permanent armed Japanese occupation of Micronesia would make an already difficult American strategic mission in the Pacific almost impossible, since, in enemy hands, all the Micronesian groups bristled with potential danger: the Marianas curved menacingly down toward the lone American naval station at Guam; the Carolines and Marshalls lay strewn like caltrops across the path of any American force moving toward the Philippines.

From its unheralded beginning in the autumn of 1914 to its violent end thirty years later, the importance of the Japanese occupation of Micronesia as an international issue, and as a point of tension in Japan–United States relations, was strategic. In matters of general naval strategy these tiny, remote flecks of land assumed global significance. In that context, the problem of their disposition at the end of World War I provoked an intense diplomatic tug-of-war between the United States and Japan in the immediate postwar years, and, once settled, left a legacy of suspicion and resentment between the two great naval powers of the Pacific.

Lacking adequate information about Japan's intentions regarding the islands and about the web of diplomatic support that Japan had stretched around them, the United States was unable during World War I to develop either a realistic policy or a unity of views concerning them.

Some American naval leaders and diplomats indulged in quite optimistic speculation about the ultimate disposition of the islands. One battleship admiral surmised that since the Japanese already held Shantung, they would see the need for equity and would willingly part with their Micronesian territories. The assistant secretary of state believed that the islands should be returned to Germany after the war and then claimed by the United States as a down payment on war reparations. The navy's General Board wanted America to acquire the Marianas, while the Committee for Planning Operations thought the Carolines and Marshalls should be internationalized.[27]

Gradually, by war's end there emerged a widely held view in the top echelons of the navy that the critical point about the German Pacific islands was not who held title to them, but what their strategic value would be. As undefended territories, effectively neutralized by international agreement, they were exotic, beautiful slivers of tropical real estate and no more; fortified with dry docks, barracks, coast-defense guns, and storage facilities, they were seen to have vital strategic importance. It was insistence on the military neutralization of Micronesia, therefore, that the naval advisers to the American delegation at Paris urged upon President Wilson and his staff.[28]

Noble Visions and Hard Realities: Micronesia and the End of World War I

Lastly, there was the outlook of the American president himself, though it cannot be said that Wilson *had* a specific viewpoint on Germany's Pacific territories prior to December 1918. The profile of those distant tropical islands hardly appeared on the horizons of a man absorbed in a grand vision for the remaking of the world. Yet Wilson, committed to the radical reform of international affairs, was to make the most determined stand against the Japanese acquisition of Micronesia. Vexed to learn in the last months of the war of the various clandestine arrangements that the Allied powers had made between themselves for the redistribution of conquered territories, he was determined to block such claims by creating new standards of international conduct and new institutions for internationalizing the spoils of war. In place of the established, cynical, and collusive arrangements of the old imperialist diplomacy—the gentlemen's agreements that slid around formal treaties, the spheres of interest mutually arranged behind closed doors, the territories traded and bargained for over brandy and cigars, the countless betrayals of the aspirations of subordinated peoples—Wilson proposed a new set of principles to govern the rearrangement of territories: "open covenants, openly arrived at," "territorial integrity," "self-determination of peoples," and the "impartial adjustment of colonial claims." Territories wrenched from the hands of the defeated nations were not to be annexed by the victors, but were to be placed under some sort of international guardianship supervised by the new League of Nations.

If this program of world reconstruction could be realized at the forthcoming peace conference it would surely sweep away all claims to conquered territory based on prior agreement, Japan's included. But ranged against such an idealistic program were formidable realities, chief among them being the reluctance of imperialist powers to renounce the diplomatic practices of more than a century for the untried idealism of this schoolmasterish American president. Specifically, in the case of the Pacific islands, Britain was understandably reluctant to go back on its 1917 pledge to Japan, no matter what new moral light it might be placed in by the United States. Moreover, there was the problem of similar arrangements for the annexation of German Pacific territories south of the equator by Australia and New Zealand. As early as 1917, the British government had made it clear to the State Department that loyalty within the British Empire made it essential that those nations retain the territories captured by British imperial forces during the war. For their part, Australia and New Zealand, as deeply suspicious as the United States about the new advance of Japanese power into the Pacific, seemed determined to annex certain of those same territories on the grounds of national security. Inevitably, the logic of honoring any such claims would lead to a similar concession to Japanese demands for title to its Pacific conquests.

It was undeniable, too, that Japan was already established in the islands and that each passing year had served to consolidate its presence there. By the time the Allies gathered at Paris to discuss the postwar settlement, Micronesia had virtually been a Japanese colony for five years. If the islands were not to be returned to Germany, what nation could present a better claim to them than Japan? And what nation or group of nations would be willing to try to force Japan out of them?

Finally, although Micronesia did not burn as an issue in the Japanese public consciousness, there was a widespread assumption, across a range of interest groups and in the government, that Japan deserved the islands for its security and for its contribution to the war effort. This view was strongest in the navy, of course. Navy Minister Katō Tomosaburō and Admiral Takeshita Isamu, the senior naval adviser to the Japanese delegation at Paris, were convinced that the islands were necessary as a strategic screen that would block America's access to its Philippine bases.[29] But beyond questions of security there glittered new possibilities for the expansion of Japanese trade and influence south of the equator. Despite the navy's initial efforts to limit public information on the affair, the sudden thrust of Japanese power into the tropical Pacific in the autumn of 1914 had seized the imagination of the Japanese press

and had reignited public discussion of a "southward advance."[30] From
this perspective, the newly occupied territories of Micronesia, valuable
as they might be in a defensive strategy, were of greater importance as
steps on the road to far richer territories further south, lands that
appeared open to the play of Japanese investment and economic influence. The navy also saw Micronesia in these terms. "The newly occupied territories in the South Seas fill a most important position as a link
between Japan and the East Indies, the Philippines, New Guinea, and
Borneo," declared an internal navy memorandum. "Even if our occupation brings no immediate advantage the islands must be carefully kept
in our possession as stepping-stones to the treasure houses of the southern regions [Southeast Asia and Melanesia]."[31] Civilian commentators
had begun to sound similar arguments in the years immediately following the naval occupation of Micronesia. Yamamoto Miono, a young professor of economics who was to go on to a distinguished career at Kyoto
University as a specialist in colonial economies, had been a member of
the research team dispatched to Micronesia in 1915. Obviously influenced by the briefings provided to the team by the naval garrison in
Micronesia, he wrote in the popular monthly journal *Taiyō* that while
the islands were but tiny specks of territory with small resources,

> it is appropriate that we add them to our colonial empire. They are impor-
> tant to us for several reasons. First, they can serve as a stepping-stone in
> the event of the southward advance of the Japanese people. Second, in the
> event of a future crisis in the Pacific, possession of the islands, situated as
> they are between Hawaii and the Philippines, may be of critical impor-
> tance to our nation.[32]

Other voices within and without the government spoke quietly or
loudly for retention of the islands. The Foreign Ministry had committed
its prestige to confirmation of the 1917 agreements, and some members
of the Diet urged no retreat on the issue as a matter of national honor. In
the last few days of the war, a federation of various nationalist and
expansionist organizations issued a manifesto that included a demand
for retention of the conquered territories.[33] Statements by various prominent Japanese collected and cabled to Washington by the American
naval attaché in Tokyo, overwhelmingly asserted Japan's right to the
territories. Among them was a pronouncement by Prime Minister
Ōkuma Shigenobu, who in the summer of 1914 had flatly asserted that
Japan had no territorial ambitions, but now insisted that Japan had
earned the right to possess Micronesia. Moreover, more than a few Japanese shared the suspicions of Japan's navy men about the motives
behind the international moralizing of the American president as well
as the navy's concern that it threatened Japan's permanent title to its
wartime acquisitions.

Some in Japan believed that neither Japan nor any other nation had a moral right to annex the former German territories in the Pacific. The distinguished liberal journalist and scholar Yoshino Sakuzō agreed with Wilson that the islands ought to be internationalized under a League of Nations mandate. If Japan were to assume guardianship of the islands under such an arrangement it should not expect unilateral annexation. The only justification for annexation, Yoshino argued, would be a situation in which Japan, by the nobility of its intentions and the worth of its good works, so captured the loyalties of the island peoples that they would ask to become citizens of the empire.[34]

To most commentators, such lofty motives were irrelevant and the Japanese claim was one of necessity. For some the need was economic and material. As the publicist K. K. Kawakami, writing in English, explained to an American readership: "The masses of Japan do not base their clamor for the South Pacific islands upon such pretentious abstract arguments. Their claim is more spontaneous, more direct, more straight from the shoulder . . . . They . . . plainly assert that they want to keep those islands because they need them more badly than any other nation." For others, like old South Seas hand Shiga Shigetaka, the economic argument for such a tiny land mass was spurious; the matter was rather one of national destiny. Shiga had noted that, though they had few people and little water, the thirteen hundred islands strung across Micronesia would serve as a base for Japan's advance into the South Pacific and thus for its development as a great maritime power.[35]

By January 1919, when the Allied representatives met at Versailles to establish the League of Nations and to settle the issues of the war, including Japan's claim to Micronesia, they were confronted with a tangle of selfish interests and noble visions, no nation having a monopoly on either. The inevitable compromises, including the settlement of the mandates question, were roundly condemned by many at the time and have been criticized by historians through the subsequent decades. But they were the product of an imperfect world and, to a degree, they represented at least an incremental step on the path toward a more equitable international order as well as toward the formal recognition by imperial powers of their responsibilities to their dependent peoples. Such was the decision made at Paris to award Japan a mandate under the League of Nations for the administration of the former German Pacific islands north of the equator.

Woodrow Wilson, the doomed star of the Paris peace conference, went to Europe in the winter of 1919 fiercely opposed to the annexation of any of Germany's former colonial territories by any nation. He conceived, instead, that the German colonies should be governed under a system of mandates from the League of Nations. In Wilson's view such a system should be bound by a number of qualifications: that the mandatories should be drawn from the smaller, disinterested nations of the globe; that the mandatories should, in any event, refrain from fortifying the islands; that freedom of trade and commerce should be preserved in all the mandates; and that mandatory powers should protect the welfare of the inhabitants of their mandate territories.

By general principle, then, Wilson was adamantly opposed to the permanent acquisition of Micronesia by Japan and unprepared to recognize the secret treaties of 1917 by which Japan had sought to bring that about. Alerted at last to the strategic importance of Micronesia, he was not even prepared to grant Japan a mandatory role there. But from the outset of the conference Wilson was handicapped in his effort to deal with questions that affected Japan, since both Georges Clemenceau and David Lloyd George, the other two members of the inner power group at Versailles, were bound by the 1917 agreements with Japan. Undoubtedly, Japan's representatives to the conference counted on this hard reality.

Annexation versus Guardianship: The Mandate Compromise, 1919–1920

On 27 January 1919, in the enormous and drafty audience hall of the old Palais Bourbon, decorated with heavy tapestries and frescoes in the classical style, Japan's chief delegate, Baron Makino Nobuaki, stood up to make his country's case before the meeting of the so-called Council of Ten. After describing Japan's contribution to the elimination of Germany's "piratical activities" during the recent war, Makino declared that Japan should be confirmed in its possession of Micronesia because of its record of humanitarian accomplishment there:

> As Japan has been endeavoring to secure a stable livelihood for the inhabitants of these islands by giving them work and providing them with schools for the education of their children, they are quite satisfied with their present arrangement . . . . [Moreover, they] still remain in a primitive state and have no ability to establish political, economic, and social organizations, in a modern sense, by themselves. For Japan, which has actually occupied these islands, it is necessary, in view of her contribution in bringing about the current situation and of the agreed popular opinion in Japan, to continue to protect these islanders and to improve their living conditions by making her possession of these islands definite.[36]

While much about this statement can be faulted, it is worth quoting at length because its chief appeal is much closer to the argument advanced by Yoshino Sakuzō than it is to any of the justifications of necessity or compensation hitherto advanced by Japanese spokesmen. It took into account the new tone of moral rectitude, set for the conference by Woodrow Wilson, which all the other delegates might ridicule behind closed doors, but few dared openly challenge.

After Makino was finished, Woodrow Wilson, speaking for those who opposed all annexations of territory, proposed his alternative of mandates issued by the League of Nations. Wilson's proposal quickly opened up acrimonious debate, the most vehement criticism coming from the British dominions, particularly Australia. Prime Minister William Hughes, angry and insistent, made the case for full sovereignty over the former German colonies and argued that Australia's annexation of certain of those territories south of the equator was vital to "insure her national safety and to guarantee her industrial, social, and racial policies."[37] Perhaps the irony implicit in this argument is clearer today than it was to those assembled in the Palais Bourbon on that dreary afternoon in 1919. Japan was the power that Hughes undoubtedly regarded as the greatest industrial, social, and racial threat to Australia, a threat increased by its southward advance into the Pacific in 1914. Yet, by waging the battle for Australia's right to annex German territories south of the equator, Hughes unwittingly acted as a proxy for the international confirmation of a permanent Japanese presence to the north.

Recognition of that fact undoubtedly influenced the conduct of the Japanese delegation during the debate. Makino, at least, understood that Japan, distrusted and resented by the Anglo-American maritime powers, had the most to lose by leading a bruising argument on the issue. For most of the three days of protracted wrangling in that grand and musty chamber, Makino, except for some brief expressions of doubt concerning the practicality of Wilson's mandate scheme, kept his own counsel, letting the irate Australian carry the weight of Japan's contention.

It became clear over the course of the debate that neither the new idealism of Wilson, nor the spoils-of-war stance of Hughes could completely carry the day. Indeed, Hughes contributed to the search for a compromise on the mandates question, declaring that, while he was in general opposed to the mandate principle, he was prepared to accept the idea if, in the Pacific territories it now occupied, his nation could make the same laws and exercise the same powers as existed in Australia.

This concession led to a proposal being advanced by the South African delegate, General Jan Christian Smuts, and formally introduced by Lloyd George, under which the mandated territories were to be divided into three categories, ranked according to the development and autonomy of the indigenous populations and the degree of authority of the mandatory powers. The Class C mandated territories were defined as those which, "owing to the sparseness of their population, or their small size, or their remoteness from the centers of civilization . . . can best be administered under the laws of the Mandatory as integral portions thereof . . . ."[38] Further, the powers that held mandate over such territories would be obliged to report to the League of Nations on the progress of their mandate administrations, to forswear the construction of any fortifications there, and to guarantee that the territories would be open to the trade and commerce of all nations—all points on which Wilson had insisted.

This formula, which applied to the former German territories in the Pacific, was, of course, a fig leaf for the annexation of the territories coveted by Australia, New Zealand, and Japan, while it preserved the fiction of guardianship by the League of Nations.

In Tokyo, the Japanese government warmed quickly to the compromise, sensing that it would be both futile and hazardous to press the case for outright annexation. Navy Minister Katō Tomosaburō reversed himself on the need to occupy the islands in full sovereignty and professed that the navy was not concerned about Wilson's principle of non-fortification in mandated territories. In the event of hostilities, Katō argued, Japan could quickly develop whatever bases it needed. Although history would prove him only partly right on that score, his support for the mandate compromise proposed by Smuts enabled Prime Minister Hara Kei, who backed the compromise, to press the rest of the government to go along and in consequence to cable Makino to accept the proposal.[39]

A few die-hard annexationists outside the government grumbled at the idea of anything less than total integration of the new territories into the Japanese empire. Shiga Shigetaka, who had been a foremost advocate of planting the flag in the tropics thirty years before, expressed alarm that Wilsonian principles might be extended to the Marianas, the Carolines, and the Marshalls. Writing in a popular journal, he scoffed at the hypocrisy of the Anglo-American backing of the Smuts plan and urged the government to accelerate its efforts to create a permanent physical presence in Micronesia—imposing administrative buildings, docks and warehouses, schools, and such—that would stamp the islands as indelibly Japanese.[40] But advocates like Shiga were out of touch with diplomatic realities and with what the government had already accomplished to establish a Japanese presence in Micronesia.

In Paris, Wilson remained cool to any arrangement that left the islands to be administered in any capacity by Japan, whose pledges and intentions he did not trust. Now sensitive to the strategic value of Micronesia and still resentful about the secret treaties of 1917, he threw up a flurry of objections: Britain and Japan had had no right to hand round the islands in the first place; the language of the Smuts proposal was too vague in its terms and too inconsistent in its principles; and he wished, in any event, to set aside the disposition of the island of Yap, because of its international importance as a cable station. By late April, however, resigned to the prospect of a Japanese mandate and absorbed by other, weightier issues facing the conference, Wilson reluctantly agreed, reserving (he believed) only the matter of Yap, on which he wished further consideration.

Wilson was right about the vagueness and inconsistency of the Smuts compromise. While it spoke of the territories in the "South Pacific," it made no mention of the islands north of the equator and omitted reference to the principles of nonfortification and equal opportunity of trade, which applied to Class B mandates. These problems were taken up over the next few months in a succession of meetings, deliberations, and the drafting and revising of agreements, each infused with the national ideals, prejudices, fears—both justified and groundless—of bureaucrats, diplomats, and military men. By and large, they had never seen the distant mountain ranges, the rain forests, or the lagoons over which they bargained and debated so doggedly. For the naval advisers to the American delegation the principal issue was the demilitarization of the mandates, since in their view unfortified Japanese islands in the Pacific would be vulnerable to superior American naval power. For the Japanese, it was important to guarantee in the Pacific the principle of the Open Door, which would allow Japanese trade and commerce to move southward into Melanesia. For Australia and New Zealand, and thus for Britain, it was vital to keep Japan—its ships, its goods, and its settlers—out of the South Pacific in order to preserve the racially isolated position of which William Hughes had spoken so emotionally.

Early in May, the Supreme Council of the Allied Powers agreed that the former German islands north of the equator should be awarded to Japan as a Class C mandate, pending final approval by the Council of the League of Nations. Three months later a special mandates commission meeting in London set forth the precise terms that were to govern all Class C mandates. Initially, it seemed, these terms worked to the strategic disadvantage of Japan. Wilson and his advisers obtained the proviso on which they had been so determined: the demilitarization of the mandates. While Japan was now bound to keep its new Pacific territories defenseless, the United States, whose own colonial possessions in the Pacific were not mandates and thus not under such restrictions, was free to strengthen Hawaii, Guam, and the Philippines. Moreover, Japan was not free to extend its influence any further into the Pacific. Britain and the dominions rejected all Japanese entreaties that the mandated territories, specifically including those held by Australia and New Zealand, be open to the trade and immigration of all nations, including Japan. Together, these two limitations, the one military and the other economic, turned back, at least temporarily, whatever aspirations

Japan may have had for a "southward advance" across the equator. Because of the suspicions aroused by the force, speed, and secrecy with which Japan had seized Micronesia in 1914, its wartime allies were determined that it would not be allowed to use the islands as either naval or economic bases for the penetration of Melanesia or Southeast Asia.[41]

Yet a closer look confirmed that in significant ways America had failed to limit Japanese control over Micronesia—and that control had now been tightened. For all practical purposes, the islands were now to be administered as Japanese possessions, not as territories under quite temporary guardianship by the international community. Moreover, the failure to obtain agreement on the principle of the Open Door in the Pacific would provide Japan with a pretext to keep its Micronesian waters off limits to the ships and commerce of other nations.

The Yap Controversy, 1920–1922

It is incongruous that such a tiny scrap of land as Yap should have become over the next several years the focus of jealousies and suspicions, the subject of great stacks of cables and memoranda, and the wedge by which the United States sought to challenge the legality of Japan's advance into the Pacific. Indeed, Yap itself was not even the immediate object of this attention, which, rather, was focused on the transoceanic cables that met there, connecting such distant terminals as Shanghai, Guam, and Manado in the Netherlands East Indies. American spokesmen were to make much of the fact that the struggle over the Yap cables was in reality a question over whether transoceanic communications would be monopolized by other countries and, in the event of war, imperil America's link with its Pacific territories. But, in truth, the United States already had other cables that connected the American mainland with Hawaii, Guam, and the Philippines. The Yap cables were an important supplement to those links, but only that. In wartime, moreover, the Yap cables would have been either denied to the United States or severed by its naval forces.[42]

Indeed, the sheer volume of the diplomatic correspondence surrounding the Yap controversy induces the suspicion that it was a bogus issue and that American representatives, at least, were seeking something else. Was it prescience or petulance that caused Wilson to ask in April 1919 that Yap be set aside in considering the general award of the other Micronesian islands as a mandate? Whatever it was, Wilson's inattention let the May 1919 decision of the Supreme Council slip by without a protest that it failed to exclude Yap. Within three months, as his grand pattern of international government began to unravel in the United States Senate, Wilson had reason to rue his negligence. As Henry Cabot

Lodge and his "little group of willful men" in the Foreign Relations Committee began sifting through the negotiations that had led to the Versailles settlements, seeking reasons to deny Senate ratification of the peace treaty, certain revelations about the secret treaties of 1916–1917 and Wilson's reluctant acquiescence to them emerged—and did not help the cause of the treaty in the Senate. Then, in Wilson's testimony to the committee on the negotiations involved in the treaty, the problem of Yap bobbed to the surface. Confidently, Wilson asserted that he had reserved the question of the island from discussion at Paris. When his senatorial critics uncharitably pointed out that the Supreme Council of Allied Powers had made no explicit exception of Yap in awarding the Micronesian mandate to Japan, and that the United States had made no objection at the time, neither Wilson nor anyone else in his administration could provide contrary evidence. Wilson could only argue that he had *assumed* that Yap had been included in the mandate provisions of May 1919 to which he had given his consent. Wilson's flawed testimony on Yap made it seem that either he had been duped at Paris or he had attempted to deceive the Senate. Both appearances contributed to the gathering congressional opposition to the Paris accords and to American membership in the League of Nations. Moreover, Wilson received no help from any of the powers in his efforts to reopen the issue. In December 1920, a year and a half after the Allied powers had decided to award Micronesia to Japan, the Council of the League of Nations confirmed the Japanese mandate, again without reference to Yap.[43]

By this time America had dropped out of the League, shattering Wilson's grand vision for humanity. Whether for the sake of his personal honor and pride or in order to salvage some tattered remnant of his Fourteen Points, Wilson continued to pursue the impossible object of an international rehearing on the disposition of Yap. From his sullen and obstinate refusal to give ground on the issue, one might suppose that this sliver of hills and jungle at the western edge of the Carolines (did he ever imagine it this way in his mind's eye?) became for Wilson a repository for his frustrations and shattered hopes. At his direction, the United States announced in November 1920 that it would not recognize the disposition of Micronesia made in May 1919. Two months after the League of Nations had confirmed the 1919 agreement, the secretary of state sent in the American protest, arguing that no such award could be made without the consent of the United States, which, as an Allied power, had an equal concern in the disposition of German territory. To this the Council of the League merely responded that, as the original agreement on the mandates was drafted by the victorious Allied powers, America's complaint should rest with those nations. Wilson himself, bitter and obstinate, refused to let go. In one of his last official acts, he denied that the United States had ever given its consent to the disposition of Yap and thus, by extension, considered invalid the award of the Japanese mandate as a whole.[44]

The succeeding Republican administration was no less determined to defend American interests in the Pacific, including the matter of Yap. But as the new administration had no ties to the League and was compelled by no ideological imperative to campaign for the internationalization of the island, something else may have impelled the continuing American concern with this dot in the Pacific. Almost certainly, the motives behind the diplomatic maneuvering by the United States in 1921 were a fear of Japanese perfidy, on the one hand, and a search to gain strategic advantage in the Pacific, on the other. The first related to American suspicions that arose from the continuing Japanese restrictions on the entry of foreign trade and vessels into Japanese waters. For the United States Navy, bedeviled by the possibility that, behind a veil of secrecy, Japan might be violating its pledge and be constructing a network of formidable naval bases, access to Micronesia by American vessels and commerce became a vital objective. For its part, the War Department saw the possibility of using the issue of the Yap cables to seek access to any and all cables in Micronesia. Both services thus pressed the Harding administration to secure a modification in the arrangements by which Japan controlled Micronesia. To bring this about Harding's secretary of state, Charles Evans Hughes, took a strikingly different approach to the problem. Instead of arguing over what had or had not been agreed upon at Paris, Hughes informed all the Allied powers, including Japan, that as the United States had not signed the Versailles treaty, it was not bound by its provisions and therefore refused to recognize the Japanese mandate over any part of Micronesia.[45]

Yet there were pressures at work leading to a resolution of the issue. In 1921, Yap was but one of an array of bristling controversies that had emerged after World War I to reinflame relations between the United States and Japan: the massive Japanese intervention in Siberia, the collapse of ambassadorial talks over immigration problems, American indignation over Japan's continued occupation of Shantung, and, most ominous of all, the quickening naval arms race between the two powers. To deal with these problems in an international context, the United States issued an invitation to the maritime powers to attend a grand conference in Washington on naval arms limitation and the settlement of outstanding problems in East Asia and the Pacific.

Along with the major European powers, Japan accepted the American invitation, though it feared that such a gathering might be used by the West, particularly the United States, to force Japan to relinquish its wartime gains. But Japan's political elite, beginning with Prime Minister Hara, were sensitive to the need to lessen their nation's isolation from the West and to adjust Japan's course to the changing currents of international cooperation set in motion by Woodrow Wilson. To minimize the chance of being isolated at the Washington conference and thus becoming the object of American antagonism, the Hara cabinet decided, in the summer of 1921, that it would be well to settle as many outstanding problems as possible on a bilateral basis with the United States before the conference began.

Only this background can explain why Japan, having occupied Micronesia for seven years and been confirmed in that occupation by the agreement of a majority of the international community on terms that were very nearly Japan's own, nevertheless agreed in the summer of 1921 to treat directly with the United States over the issue of Yap. In these negotiations, Japan gave way, by stages, to American demands. In September, the Japanese government essentially accepted American insistence on access to Yap and on use of the cables there, as well as on American rights of residence and property. In December, Tokyo agreed to the right of free entrance into Micronesian territorial waters by American commercial vessels and agreed to extend to the mandated islands the provisions of the existing Treaty of Commerce and Navigation between the United States and Japan. These concessions were formalized in a convention signed in Washington on 11 February 1922, by which the United States finally recognized Japan's mandate over Micronesia and Japan reiterated the pledges it had given to the League not to fortify its mandate.[46]

A Temporary Calm: The Washington Naval Treaty, 1922

In the meantime, the Washington conference on naval armament and the outstanding issues of East Asia and the Pacific had been convened. It culminated in agreements between the powers that guaranteed the territorial and administrative integrity of China, an Open Door in East Asia (though not necessarily in the Pacific) for the commerce of all nations, and limitations on the naval tonnage to be maintained by the principal naval powers. This last problem had been the subject of heated controversy. After prolonged and difficult bargaining, the Japanese delegation had agreed to accept a ratio of naval tonnage less than that of the Anglo-American naval powers. But Admiral Katō Tomosaburō and his colleagues in the Japanese delegation had extracted a high price: a freeze on all insular fortification in the Pacific west of Hawaii. Such a concession, embodied in Article 19 of the subsequent Washington Naval Limitations Treaty (the Five Power Treaty), left the Japanese navy dominant in the western Pacific and, in the event of war, made the Philippines and Guam as vulnerable and open to attack as Japanese Micronesia.

But, for the decade after 1922 at least, hostilities between the two Pacific powers seemed less likely than they had for the past fifteen years or more. After the clearing away of a number of old disputes at Washington in 1921 and 1922, the animosities of the immediate past seemed substantially ameliorated on both sides of the Pacific. In Japan, not only party politicians and professional bureaucrats, but significant elements within the military and naval leadership, accepted the fact that the imperialist policies of the past were outdated and that Japan would have to adjust to the new principles of international openness and cooperation espoused by the United States. American images of Japan also quickly changed for the better, so much so that in mid-1923, Franklin Roosevelt, who had sided with the hardliners in the Navy Department five years earlier, could write that Japan and the United States "have not a single valid reason, and won't have as far as we can look ahead, for fighting each other."[47]

Perhaps this calm that settled over the Pacific goes far to explain the irony that lies at the end of the three-year American effort to challenge the advance of Japan into Micronesia. Having secured the rights and privileges, not only on Yap, but throughout Micronesia, for which it had maneuvered so intensely and argued so vehemently, the United States failed to exercise them in the years that followed. It never sought to use the communication facilities on Yap, nor to exercise treaty rights elsewhere in Micronesia. Few American ships sought entry into Micronesian waters, nor did Americans seek to settle or trade in Micronesia. Almost unnoticed, on the other hand, was a gathering thicket of bureaucratic hindrances by which Japan complicated free access to its island territories. By the 1930s, when Japanese-American relations once again worsened and Micronesia again became the subject of international dispute, this sequestering of Japan's Pacific territories would lead to reawakened American fears of Japanese perfidy and reemerging phantoms of secret Pacific bastions and "impenetrable Japans."

In the meantime, Japan, for better or for worse, had a mandate to work its will among the islands and peoples of Micronesia, subject to only the most feeble and tenuous restrictions imposed by the international community. The structure, style, and substance of Japan's mandatory rule were, inevitably, those of a colonial power.

CHAPTER 3

The Iron Cherry Blossom
The Structure of Japanese Authority in Micronesia

FROM ITS BEGINNINGS, the Japanese administration in Micronesia was marked by cool efficiency and strict discipline. The tone was set at the outset by the naval landing parties that swept ashore in a series of swift and bloodless occupations of Jaluit, Kusaie, Ponape, Truk, Yap, Palau, and Saipan in October 1914. Provided with civil as well as military powers under special regulations, the naval landing parties collectively constituted the first Japanese government in the islands. The commanding officers of these units were under instructions to deal swiftly with any resistance, German or Micronesian, and also to see that their men observed the strictest military discipline, "since by their words and actions the landing parties will have great influence on the future development of our rights and interests in the South Seas." In particular, the occupation forces were to respect property, religion, and local customs and traditions, as well as to enforce, for the time being, those German laws not prejudicial to Japanese order and sovereignty.[1]

The scrupulousness with which the naval landing parties by and large carried out these instructions is exemplified by an account of the Japanese occupation of Ponape left by a German observer at the time, Salvator Walleser, Catholic bishop of Micronesia. Standing below the walls of his newly built church, which overlooked Kolonia Town, on the morning of 7 October, the bishop witnessed the entry of Admiral Yamaya's First South Seas Squadron into the harbor, the setting out of launches packed with sailors, and the precision operations with which the landing party came ashore. Once they had landed, the sailors dog-trotted along the main street of the town, entering all the houses, and even the church, mission, and convent, searching for weapons. Finding none they moved beyond the town to scour the coast and hinterland for German soldiers and officials.

Bishop Walleser recounted:

A few days after the seizure, the chief of the occupying forces appeared
and explained with polite excuses that Japan had conquered the island and
would administer it from now on. For the present, everything was to
remain as it was. Private property was [to be] respected and religious and
intellectual freedoms guaranteed . . . . We were left in peace to perform
our usual work . . . . By and large, the conquerors—officers and troops—
acted with decorum during and after the takeover of the island. Although
the troops had gone through everything and had ample opportunity to
steal whatever they wanted, not the least little thing was missing after they
left.[2]

The commander of this exemplary landing party was a most unusual
naval officer, whose exposure to the tropical Pacific during this assignment was to change his life. At thirty-six, Lieutenant Commander Matsuoka Shizuo (1878–1936), younger brother of the famed ethnologist
Yanagida Kunio, had already attained a distinguished professional
career, including four years in Vienna as naval attaché and an assignment as second in command of the battle cruiser *Tsukuba*, from which
he had just disembarked. Frail and uncommonly given to intellectual
pursuits for a navy man, Matsuoka had been on the verge of resigning
his commission because of ill health. But the outbreak of the World War
and the formation of the South Seas battle group of which the *Tsukuba*
was a part kindled his excitement at the prospect of a voyage to the
remote tropics and induced him to stay on.[3]

Now he had come ashore to take possession of this lush and mountainous island for his emperor, thankful, no doubt that he and his men did
not have to fight for it. The small armory in the town was empty, the
hundred or so Papuan policemen offered no resistance, and the few
German officials supposedly on the island were nowhere to be found.
After most of the landing party had reembarked, and the battle group
had sailed out of the harbor to complete the campaign of occupation
elsewhere in Micronesia, Matsuoka stayed on for several weeks to head
a small naval garrison charged with the administration of Ponape.
Though the Japanese naval personnel appropriated certain buildings
for this purpose, they generally left the small German community to
itself. As part of his effort to insure that Ponape was completely paci-
fied, Matsuoka traveled with a small naval party for two weeks, going
around the coast by boat and into the interior, staying in thatched
houses, tasting for the first time the delights of fresh coconut juice, and
listening with increasing interest to the flow of the Ponapean language.
For Matsuoka it was a magical time, the beginning of a lifelong passion
for the languages and cultures of the South Seas. Four years after his
return from Ponape he resigned his commission in order to pursue the
life of a scholar, eventually becoming one of Japan's most distinguished

cultural anthropologists, the author of numerous books on Micronesia and its languages.[4]

But at least one of the commanders who led his men ashore in Micronesia in October 1914 had little of Matsuoka's cultural sensitivity and tact. In Palau, the Japanese occupation began in a more threatening fashion. Incensed at learning that German authorities had incarcerated Japanese nationals on the island at the outset of the war, the landing party commander threatened to execute all Germans in Koror, including the Capuchin missionaries, but was dissuaded from doing so by the Japanese released from jail. A short time later, the Japanese commander ordered all the Germans to be tried by a Japanese naval court on a charge of having attempted to incite the Palauans against the Japanese occupation, but the charge was dropped for lack of evidence. By the end of the month, however, all Germans had been banished from Palau.[5]

The Navy in Charge, 1914–1922

By the end of 1914, confident that its occupation of the islands was militarily secure, the Japanese navy withdrew its major warships from Micronesian waters, disbanded its two South Seas squadrons, and settled down to the business of occupying Japan's new territories. In late December of that year, the work of its naval landing parties was coordinated under a unified command, the Provisional South Seas Defense Force (Rinji Nan'yō Guntō Bōbitai), led by a rear admiral with headquarters in Truk and comprising five naval districts—Saipan, Palau, Truk, Ponape, and Jaluit—each headed by a commander or lieutenant commander (Photo 4). In addition, the Palau garrison dispatched detachments to Yap and Angaur, and the Ponape garrison established a detachment on Kusaie. In 1915, Yap was added as a sixth naval district, with its own naval garrison and civil affairs responsibilities.

The zeal and energy with which these naval officers undertook to transform the districts under their charge gave evidence that from the beginning of its presence in Micronesia the Japanese navy intended to stay. In addition to issuing laws and regulations necessary to insure peace and order, on the larger islands the officers saw to a host of public works—roads, navigation buoys, docks, and wharves; undertook the detailed charting of coasts and reefs; directed surveys and censuses; supervised justice, education, hygiene, and sanitation; subsidized steamship services between the islands; encouraged agriculture and trade; promoted Japanese language instruction; controlled village life through a cautious restructuring of traditional political hierarchies; and drafted extensive reports and recommendations to Tokyo for the future administration and development of the islands.[6]

Photo 4. Naval District Headquarters, Jaluit Atoll, Marshall Islands, c. 1918.
(Yamaguchi Yoji)

Consistent with the general pattern of compliments by foreign observers of the "civilizing" efforts of Japanese colonial administrations in Asia and the Pacific during these years, the occasional Western visitors who passed through the islands usually gave the naval administrators high marks and saw the coming of Japan as good fortune for Micronesia. Their lavish praise, preserved for us in the yellowing pages of professional journals and travel magazines, may have been based on an understandable gratitude for Japanese naval hospitality and cooperation, particularly in primitive surroundings that lacked Western amenities, and on an uncritical acceptance of their hosts' assertions about the advance of civilization and enlightenment under Japanese rule. At Japanese naval headquarters on Saipan, for example, the American zoologist H. E. Crampton worked out the pleasant details of his visit to the Marianas with the naval district staff. William Hobbs, the geologist, shared similar hospitalities on the veranda of the headquarters building on Truk and wrote, not surprisingly, of the "Conspicuous Courtesies of Commanders." Thomas McMahon, visiting the Marshalls, seemed struck with wonder at the transformative efforts of Japanese officials, teachers, doctors, scientists, and traders in creating "a New Japan" in the South Seas.[7]

But one or two foreign observers noted that if the Japanese administration during the war years had a major fault it was simply that there was too much of it. To begin with, it was a bureaucracy far larger than anything put in place by the previous German administration. Moreover, the Micronesian peoples, unaccustomed to directives, instructions, or restraints other than those imposed by their own cultural traditions, were now subject to an array of instructions and prohibitions that compelled conformity to Japanese values and customs and rooted out practices judged to be uncivilized, all in the name of a modernizing emperor. George Blakeslee, who visited the Marshalls toward the end of the naval regime, remarked that "there has been over-administration, a too careful supervision of details, too many officials, occasional injustice due to petty naval officials, and an attempt to hustle the simple natives too fast."[8]

Nevertheless, considering that these naval men had no civil affairs training, unlike their American counterparts who came to administer the islands during and immediately after World War II, it is remarkable that their administration was as informed and intelligent as it was. In carrying out their tasks they were fortunate to be able to call on long-term residents of the Japanese communities in the islands who now served invaluably as island guides, interpreters, and advisers on Micronesian life and culture (and who in the process attained for themselves positions of influence and profit). On Ponape, Sekine Sentarō, Nan'yō Bōeki manager since 1901, guided Matsuoka Shizuo around the island on his inspection by launch and by foot during the first few weeks of the Japanese occupation. On Truk, Mori Koben, appointed adviser to the naval administration, quickly gained the stature and authority that had eluded him for so many years, since his understanding of Trukese life and culture, which probably surpassed that of any Japanese scholar of the day, was eagerly sought by the new naval administrators. Mori's "Outline of the Customs and Culture of the Truk Islands," drafted at the request of the Defense Force commander, not only became a useful guide for local administration on Truk, but also gained recognition as an important ethnographic study when it appeared in Japan.[9]

But if old South Seas hands like Mori were a help in the navy's effort to establish a permanent presence in Micronesia, there were Japanese interlopers—speculators, dishonest traders, and assorted riffraff—who proved to be a blight. Their appearance in Micronesia in these early months was another example of an unsavory feature of all of Japan's colonies. In the initial military phase of Japan's administration, in Taiwan and Korea particularly, unscrupulous individuals—some with money and some without—had followed closely behind Japanese ships and troops, sniffing the air for quick profit and easy pickings. With the establishment of firm Japanese control, their often-shady activities came to the attention of colonial authorities and they were usually bundled unceremoniously back to Japan.

That such economic adventurers almost immediately turned up in Micronesia, however, was of particular embarrassment to the navy, since they had been unwittingly encouraged by bureaucrats within the naval high command. Admiral Akiyama Saneyuki, for example, had not only pressed for a major naval role for Japan in the South Seas at the outset of World War I, but had argued for substantial Japanese immigration and aggressive economic investment in order to consolidate the occupation of Micronesia. For this reason, Akiyama had used his influence to have the exclusive rights to work the German phosphate mines on Angaur awarded to a private firm, the South Seas Construction Syndicate (Nan'yō Keiei Kumiai) headed by one Nishizawa Yoshitsugu. Scarcely a month after the occupation of the Palaus, a freighter chartered by the company, with Nishizawa and a hundred Japanese passengers aboard, put into Angaur to begin operation of the mines and to start up a copra trade. Nishizawa recruited indigenous labor to work the mines and had shipped nearly fifty thousand tons of phosphate ore to Japan before it was discovered that he had done so at the cost of physical abuse of his labor force, whom he "paid" in certificates printed by himself. Red-faced, the navy revoked Nishizawa's privileges in October 1915 and took over the mining operations on Angaur, until 1922, when they were turned over to the South Seas Government.[10]

The abuses by the South Seas Construction Syndicate were only the first example of the callousness of certain Japanese entrepreneurs in this early period and soon naval commanders from Palau to the Marshalls were complaining to the naval high command in Tokyo about the reckless and disreputable activities of some Japanese commercial firms in Micronesia. By the end of the navy's rule in the South Seas, strict supervision had curbed the problem, but not before a major business scandal in the Marianas was to shock the government.

Getting the navy out of the business of running Micronesia was established by slow stages. Though the navy had intended to remain on station in the islands, it had for some years planned to replace a large portion of its administrative staff of naval officers with civil bureaucrats responsible to the commander of the Provisional South Seas Defense Force. As civilians were filtered into the civil affairs branches in Micronesia, the purely naval character of Japanese rule began to lessen. On 1 July 1918—later celebrated as Foundation Day—a civil affairs bureau was created within the Defense Force, provided with branches in all its naval districts, and composed entirely of civilians who began to perform all administrative functions other than police duties. But the Civil Affairs Bureau functioned as part of a wartime naval garrison, and by 1919, with the award of Micronesia as a mandated territory, the Navy Ministry was obliged to consider various plans to shift to peacetime administrative mechanisms, though all of them called for the navy to maintain its warships and garrisons in the islands. In July 1920, the

Defense Force commander relinquished all his authority over the Civil Affairs Bureau (now responsible to the Navy Ministry) and the next year the Civil Affairs Bureau was transferred from Truk to Palau, a move that brought the capital of Japan's future colony within several days' sailing of the Philippines and within just a few more days of New Guinea. Fixed on the strategic importance of Micronesia, the navy maintained its garrison there until late 1921, but it was clear from the terms for Japan's mandate set down by the League of Nations that the navy was inevitably obliged to quit the islands altogether.[11] On Truk the naval flag that flew from the headquarters building on Dublon Island was hauled down, and one by one the naval garrisons packed up and sailed away. The only official link the navy maintained with Micronesia was a naval liaison office, *kaigun bukan-fu*, attached to the civilian government at Koror, headed by a single officer below flag rank and throughout the 1920s seeming to have no functions of any consequence.[12] In March 1922 a purely civilian administration, the Nan'yō-chō—South Seas Government[13]—was established under a governor charged with administering the new island territories and with fulfilling Japan's obligations under its mandate authority.

The South Seas Government (Nan'yō-chō)

Given the tiny land mass and modest population of Micronesia, Japanese rule was intensive and dominating. Where the Spanish had neglected, and occasionally tyrannized, the islands, and the Germans had seen them as little more than remote trading stations where Pacific breezes might lift the Kaiser's flag, the new rulers, after some initial miscues, set about administering their mandate with an intensity of attention, purpose, and industry unrivaled elsewhere in the Pacific. As in all Japanese overseas territories, the administration was far larger than those of other colonial powers in East Asia and the Pacific. Whereas the Germans had posted some twenty-five officials to administer some two thousand islands scattered over some three million square miles, by the mid-1930s the Nan'yō-chō employed nearly nine hundred fifty. Moreover, the style of administration was, like the rest of the empire, heavily bureaucratic. The government played the leading role in providing the modernizing institutions—the schools, the hospitals, the wharves, the research institutes. A small army of administrators, unhindered by any local assemblies, indigenous dissidents, or insistent immigrants, zealously executed the laws and regulations of the realm, preserving the Japanese concern for order throughout the mandate.

The agency of Japanese rule in Micronesia, the Nan'yō-chō, was the last of Japan's colonial governments to be set in place. In status and authority it ranked in the lesser tier of Japan's overseas bureaucracies, considerably below the prestigious and powerful governments general, *sōtoku-fu*, of Korea and Taiwan, but on a par with the colonial governments, *chō*, of Karafuto (the Japanese southern half of Sakhalin) and the Kwantung Leased Territory (on the Liaotung Peninsula, Manchuria). Like each of Japan's colonial administrations, the functions and organization of the Nan'yō-chō were set out by *kansei*, an imperial ordinance, the ponderous translation of which, 'organic regulation', provides the proper tone for the heavy bureaucratism of all Japanese colonial government.

This bureaucratic cast, shaped by the intent of the government in Tokyo and free from the legislative interference of the Japanese Diet, led to intricate and occasionally contradictory distinctions of legal status among the several colonies. In turn, these influenced the way administrative authority was exercised in each. The Nan'yō was a case in point. In accepting the mandate to govern Micronesia, Japan had insisted to the world that it would rule these nearly two thousand island territories as if they were an integral part of the Japanese empire, a condition that permitted the nearly untrammeled exercise of Japanese authority. Yet, following its own internal administrative reasoning, the Japanese government declared that the Nan'yō, like the Kwantung Leased Territory, was not a "sovereign colony," in that Japanese authority was limited by having to be exercised in accord with international agreement. This legal fiction made it possible to declare that the Meiji constitution, the supreme law of the metropolitan homeland, was not applicable in these two colonies, which could therefore be ruled through imperial ordinances, *chokurei*, without interference from Diet-enacted laws.[14]

Yet, in his subordination to the central government in Tokyo, the governor of the Nan'yō-chō *(Nan'yō chōkan)* was distinctly the administrator of a lesser colony. Unlike those great proconsuls, the governors general of Korea, who were officials of *shinnin* rank, the highest in the Japanese bureaucracy and in theory responsible only to the emperor, the governors of the Nan'yō-chō occupied subordinate *chokunin* rank and were directly responsible to the prime minister.[15] When, in 1929, Japan belatedly established a colonial ministry, *takumushō*, the governors of the three lesser colonies were appointed by the colonial minister. Even then, their lines of responsibility were indicative of their lesser status in the colonial hierarchy. For the most part—that is, for the general administration of the colony—a governor was responsible to the colonial minister, but was also responsible to other cabinet ministers for specialized activities: in matters of posts and telegraph to the minister of communication; in currency, banking, and customs duties to the minister of finance; in weights and measures to the minister of commerce and industry. Indeed, the degree of administrative control of the home government over the governor of the Nan'yō-chō was such that his power was reduced to being comparable to that of a prefectural governor.[16]

Within the mandated territory itself, however, the governor exercised complete executive authority, subject only to the veto of the colonial minister. His word flowed down along the cool passages of the Nan'yō-chō headquarters in Koror to the various bureaus and divisions it housed —the Secretariat, General Affairs, Finance, Police, Colonization, and Communications, as well as the branch government of the Palau Islands (Photo 5). And the governor's word flowed outward across the seas to the other branch governments, *shichō*—the Mariana Islands (on Saipan), the Yap District (on Yap), the central Carolines (on Truk), the eastern Carolines (on Ponape), and the Marshalls (on Jaluit)—whose branch governors, *shichōkan*, were appointed by and responsible to him for the execution of all laws and for the conduct of all administrative matters within their districts. In addition, as the Japanese presence and commitment in Micronesia expanded over the next two decades, the governor came to preside over schools, courts, and hospitals spread throughout Micronesia, as well as a cluster of research stations and institutes providing a range of information—on marine products, meteorology, engineering, mining, tropical agriculture, and industry.[17]

The colonial governor also wielded complete authority in legislative and judicial matters in the Nan'yō. Whereas in Taiwan and Korea there existed the merest fictions of legislative representation, none existed even on paper in the lesser colonies, including the Nan'yō. All legislative power was held by the governor at Koror, who was empowered to issue executive ordinances, *chōrei*, and to punish violations of such laws. Since the Meiji constitution was not applicable in the Nan'yō, the judicature was simply considered part of the executive function of the gov-

Photo 5. Headquarters, South Seas Government, Koror, Palau Islands.

ernor. While there existed a complete court system, with a court of appeal at Koror and three district courts, the judges were appointed and could be dismissed at will by the colonial governors.[18]

Japan's Colonial Administrators in the South Seas

Whatever else may be said about Japan's administration of Micronesia, its colonial bureaucrats there—as in Japan's other overseas territories— were top-drawer professionals. Indeed, the competence and quality of the average Japanese colonial bureaucrat is remarkable, considering that they had few of the professional advantages of their counterparts in the British or French colonial systems. Not only did Japan lack a colonial tradition, but there was no specialized colonial service or colonial school, like those in Britain or France, to provide particular training in colonial administration. Neither was administration in the colonies a time-honored profession, as it was in Britain, where a distinguished colonial career could be an important ladder to social promotion, and where a far-flung "old-boy" network kept alive the traditions of the Colonial Service and a steady supply of talent flowing into it.

This general degree of competence in all of Japan's colonial administrations, including the South Seas Government, was largely due to the caliber of the senior and middle-level officials who, for the most part, were drawn from the graduates of Japan's imperial universities, particularly the Law Faculty of Tokyo University (Japan's most prestigious) and had passed the demanding civil service examinations. They were not selected from the public at large, nor from the growing pool of private individuals—entrepreneurs, scientists, or academics—who had long experience or specialized knowledge of colonial territories. Instead, they were chosen from the various ministries, bureaus, and offices of civil government in metropolitan Japan, though as the years passed it was natural that an increasing number of those assigned to the South Seas Government were officials who had prior experience in either the Colonial Ministry or one or more of Japan's other colonies.

The thinking behind this general arrangement for the selection, training, and posting of Japan's colonial officials seems to have been that it was best to have individuals to administer the emperor's overseas territories who met the exacting and uniform standards of the Japanese bureaucracy as a whole. They could therefore be moved from colony to colony like interchangeable parts, and their ambitions would be held in check by national traditions of loyalty and conformity. The brilliant innovator and the unconventional expert, who, over decades of service in some remote outpost, dominated it by sheer force of personality, were not to be found in the South Seas Government, because neither the culture nor the official policy of Japan encouraged their emergence. One looks in vain on the roster of Japanese administrators in the South Seas for dramatic personalities like J. B. Thurston, British governor of Fiji, who, it has been written, "acquired the sway and persona of the Viceroy of the Pacific," for elegant, urbane administrators like Sir Basil Thomson of Tonga, or for eccentric specialists like the naturalist Charles Morris Woodford, who virtually ruled the Solomon Islands for twenty years. Rather, the governors of the Nan'yō-chō were all competent and colorless bureaucrats. Of the longest serving of Japan's governors in the South Seas, Yokota Gōsuke, who occupied the post for an unprecedented eight years (1923–1931), apparently nothing is remembered. Only Hayashi Hisao (1933–1936), a tough police bureaucrat in Mukden before he came to Micronesia, is at all remarkable in terms of career interest, largely because of his active, energetic efforts in both subversion and counterespionage during the turbulent years of Japan's takeover of Manchuria, 1931–1932 (Photo 6).[19]

Moreover, the transfer of most of Japan's administrators from colony to colony, or in the case of the South Seas Government, from district to district, tended to make them aloof from the indigenous peoples they administered, though it also contributed to a growing pool of administrators familiar with a wide range of administrative problems in different regions. Yet, because they were imbued with a vigorous sense of public duty typical of Japanese civil government, and because they were openly given preferential treatment and reward, the administrators were almost never touched by corruption or tainted by malfeas-

Photo 6. Trukese *seinendan* (Young Men's Association) and Japanese officials. (Truk District Branch Governor in center)

Photo 7. Departure of the governor and naval officials from the South Seas Government Building, Koror, c. early 1930s.

ance. Their sense of status as functionaries was as starchy as the white linen uniforms on which brass buttons and epaulettes gleamed, each embossed with a circlet of palm fronds enclosing a cherry blossom to symbolize their South Seas service. Their efficiency seemed incapable of lapse, even under the most trying conditions. Despite the remoteness of their station and the vast distances that separated the islands under their charge, despite the hot, damp, enervating climate, and despite their responsibilities toward indigenous populations with whom they shared little in the way of culture, ethos, or attitude to work, they labored ceaselessly with zeal, pride, and purpose. From the broad verandas of the Nan'yō-chō headquarters in Koror (Photo 7) to the tidy little district office standing behind its proud stone gateposts at Jaluit in the Marshalls, these men earnestly and diligently collected statistics, drew up laws and regulations, and drafted reports to the ministries in far-off Tokyo. Pith-helmeted, they presided over a host of public works and programs involving health and sanitation, fisheries, agriculture, harbor improvement, road construction, and land surveys; regularly making the rounds by schooner and launch, they maintained their emperor's writ on the remoter atolls of his tropic domain.

At the lowest rung of Japan's colonial bureaucracy was the policeman. Yet, in many ways, his position was the most important, because, as in Japan's other colonial territories, the police became the backbone of local administration. Carefully selected, rigorously trained, and assigned a wide range of functions beyond general police duties—tax collection, enforcement of sanitary regulations, dissemination of public information, supervision of road building—the Japanese policeman became a colonial functionary whose responsibilities and quality of performance bore strong resemblance to those of the district officer in the British colonial territories or the gendarme in the French.

The Japanese police structure in Micronesia was a three-tiered hierarchy: at the top, in the South Seas Government in Koror, was a police section, *keimuka*, headed by a superintendent, *keishi*, under whom served police inspectors, *keibu*, and assistant inspectors, *keibujō*, and still farther down, policemen, *junsa*. Each branch government in the islands duplicated this structure on a smaller, truncated scale, starting with a police station located in the branch capital and headed by an inspector who supervised the work of the two- or three-man substations situated in some of the more important villages and on some of the larger islands. The Japanese police posted in these remoter locations were the only regular point of contact between the Japanese government and the island populations. For example, the police substation on Wotje Atoll *was* the Japanese government for the sixteen atolls of the Ratak chain in the Marshalls.[20]

In his tasks the Japanese policeman was assisted, though never supplanted, by *junkei* 'native constables', recruited from island males who were under forty, were in good health, and had completed the optimum five years of primary school. Given three months of Japanese language training and police methods, the *junkei* were assigned to investigate misdemeanors and to supervise public health, farming, and road construction, though not until 1929 were they allowed to handle cases involving Japanese citizens. While they were always sharply subordinate in authority and pay to Japanese police, in deportment, dress, language ability, and general knowledge of their communities, they seemed to have earned the respect of Japanese visitors (Photo 8).[21]

Though operating as he did on the farthest fringes of the empire, often acting alone as the supreme law within the small confines of his authority, the average Japanese policeman, like the middle and senior officials above him, seems to have been untouched by corruption or scandal. However, there is little doubt that police treatment of Micronesian offenders was often severe and, occasionally, brutal (as it was of their own compatriots in metropolitan Japan). On a number of islands, the reputation of the Japanese police in their administration of corporal punishment was such as to inspire fear and dislike among the local populations. Yet such cases must be balanced against evidence that other police officials were a good deal more moderate and took an intelligent interest in the Micronesians in their charge.[22]

Photo 8. Trukese patrolmen, c. 1932.

Local Administration: Turning Chiefs into Bureaucrats

Below the lowest Japanese functionary in the branch government of the Nan'yō-chō, below the stern eye of the resident Japanese policeman, was the traditional Micronesian leadership.[23] In their dealings with these individuals the Japanese were aided, at least to a degree, by Spanish and German precedents that had somewhat lessened the authority of the traditional leaders of the islands. Wisely, the Japanese made no sudden or dramatic change in the scope or prestige of that leadership during the initial years of the naval administration, and were content to leave in place the system of essentially indirect rule through chiefs and paramount chiefs. However, in 1922 the newly established South Seas Government promulgated its "Rules for Native Village Officials," *sonri kitei*, which embodied the "village," *mura*, system of rural administration in Japan, thus beginning a slow dissolution of traditional chiefly authority in most of the islands.[24]

The new regulations created two types of Micronesian leaders, the village chief, *sosonchō*—or in Chamorro villages in the Marianas, *kuchō* 'district head'—and a village headman, *sonchō*—or *jōyaku* 'assistant official' in the Marianas. In theory, the village chiefs, subject to the supervision of the General Affairs section of the branch government, directed the activities of the headmen in several villages. In fact, there was seldom a real distinction between the functions of the two types of leaders. Both were appointed by the branch governor and were responsible to the nearest Japanese authority, most often the resident Japanese policeman.[25]

From the Micronesian perspective, more important was the distinction that soon arose between village chiefs, who came from traditional royal lineages or were chosen by their communities, and "government office chiefs," who might have no legitimacy in a traditional sense, but were appointed by the branch government because they were believed to be more amenable to direction by the Japanese. The branch governors prudently maintained a flexible policy in making these appointments, sometimes bypassing the traditional indigenous leadership in order to lift up someone in whom they had greater confidence, as in Palau, sometimes confirming traditional chiefs in their office, as in Truk.[26]

Whether drawn from established lineages or not, the village chiefs and headmen under the Japanese system exercised but a fraction of their traditional authority. Gone was their power to manage village affairs under the old customs and traditions, to settle land disputes, to chastise or reward subjects at will. No longer autocratic leaders, chiefs and headmen now became minor functionaries in a bureaucratic structure and were directed to act as agents of Japanese government, notifying their communities of the laws and regulations that came to them from the branch government. They collected the taxes, gathered the statistics, and made the reports it demanded, citing members of their communities who violated the long list of offenses punishable under the *Nan'yō guntō keisatsu shōbatsu rei* (Police and Penal Regulations of the South Sea Islands).[27] One chief on Ponape, recalling his subordination to Japanese authority, put it succinctly at the end of Japanese rule: "The Japanese policeman gave the orders; I was forced to see that they were carried out."[28]

To preserve the illusion of status for these figurehead leaders, the Japanese paid them a small salary and provided them with a white duck coat, matching trousers, and a cap with distinctive insignia denoting their rank—a uniform for ceremonial occasions when they were in the company of Japanese officials. The government also made available a small allowance for them to hire a local scribe, *shiki*, to help them keep records and a village constable, *shinkei*, to aid them in the fulfillment of their tasks and in dealing with the Japanese. In practice, these arrangements served only to weaken the traditional prestige of chiefs and headmen still further and to confirm them as holders of sinecures. Lacking adequate understanding of either the Japanese language or administrative matters, usually dependent on the two assistants, who held no official position at all, but whose limited training at least gave them greater confidence in dealing with the colonial rulers, and resigned to having their decisions appealed or amended at any time, the village chiefs saw their power weakened year by year.[29]

This redirection of the channels of ancient authority, this interference by alien rules and regulations, punishments and exhortations, with the time-honored custom and usage of Micronesian communities, was greatly moderated on the remoter atolls of the Carolines and Marshalls, where there was no official Japanese presence. There, the slow rhythms of island life, shaped by the sun, the sea, the wind, and the narrow land, continued undisturbed, month after month. All at once, the occasional visitation of some functionary from the branch government would intrude upon the quiet splendor of those lonely landfalls. Borne by launch from the government ship standing off the reef, the visitor would come strutting up the beach, sparkling in his whites, sword at his side, trailed by an aide or interpreter or two, and bringing efficiency and determination to his tasks—collecting census figures, checking on a rumored outbreak of dysentery, handing out a reward here, a warning there, or perhaps presiding stiffly over a village celebration. Then the chiefs and headmen of Bikini or Woleai, Ulithi or Satawal, who waited for him in a nearby grove of palms, would be reminded of the power of the alien race he represented and comprehend something of the authority invested in those distant centers—Kolonia, Jabor Town, Dublon— that most of them had never seen.

The Iron Cherry Blossom

Despite the distance of the South Seas from Japan, the vastness of the administrative boundaries of the mandate, and the more than occasional discomforts of the tropics, those who governed Micronesia in the emperor's name were untroubled in the daily exercise of their authority by indigenous resistance, domestic complaint, or foreign criticism.

To begin with, the island peoples, whose destinies these men now controlled, had accepted the imposition of Japanese rule with scarcely a whisper of resistance and, in the years that followed, had offered no violence against either officials or settlers. Unlike the interiors of the Australian mandate in New Guinea, the remotest atolls and the deepest back country of the larger islands were safe to traverse and to inhabit. Given the warlike reputation of the Trukese when young Mori Koben stepped ashore on Moen Island, the record of attacks on foreign ships and crews in the Marshalls in the half century before Suzuki Tsunenori's arrival in those waters, and the ferocity of the Sokehs (Jokaj) Rebellion on Ponape in 1910—which required a German cruiser and a landing party equipped with artillery to put down—this peaceful acquiescence to Japanese rule by the Micronesians is remarkable. It may have been due to the gradually ameliorating effects of foreign trade and evangelism in the islands. More likely, it had to do with the fact that the Japanese were quickly spread throughout Micronesia in considerable numbers and were, at least initially, backed up by such a show of overwhelming military force that resistance was inconceivable.

Indeed, there emerged but one shadowy center of opposition to Japanese rule, a nonviolent cult, *Modekngei,* which appeared in Palau around 1918. The aims of the movement were directed toward a revitalization of Palauan culture and, by implication, toward a rejection of the efforts of the South Seas Government to compel them to adopt the trappings of Japanese civilization. But the founder was imprisoned soon after the movement began, and though *Modekngei* continued to gain adherents during the remainder of the Japanese period, it never seriously threatened the colonial order on Palau until the last year of the Pacific War, when aerial bombardment and isolation enfeebled the colonial administration. More important, in more than two decades of existence, it never spread beyond Palauan shores to the other island groups.[30]

Essentially, there was no spark of Micronesian nationalism to kindle defiance of Japanese authority. Collectively, the Micronesians constituted a small population scattered through hundreds of widely separated islands, on some of which they were rapidly outnumbered by swelling masses of Japanese. Without any common language, without any collective pan-Micronesian sense of national or cultural identity, without any educated elite or representative assemblies to express the inevitable resentments of a subordinated people, lacking any means to petition the League of Nations or the court of world opinion—even had they thought of doing so—and socially conditioned by the Japanese language and other assimilative devices, the Micronesians were neither able nor disposed to offer articulate or open opposition to the rule of their islands by Japan.

Nor were the diligent bureaucrats of the Nan'yō-chō greatly bothered by inquisitive or critical inspectors from the home islands. Like most colonial matters, questions concerning Japan's Pacific mandate rarely came to the floor of the Diet in Tokyo and when they did, even more rarely did they reflect popular interest provoked by an aroused press. Few members of the press or the Diet ever showed up in Micronesia. The only visitors who ever caused a flurry of official preparations were the occasional imperial prince, shown around the islands like a flag, or an admiral or two passing through on a training cruise.

For their part, the Japanese communities on the larger islands contributed to the authoritarian colonial rule. Unlike the rambunctious community of individualistic French expatriates in Tahiti, who took to the pages of their virulently antiadministration newspaper to shrill their objections against any attempt by the French colonial government to curb their interests, the swelling numbers of Japanese settlers in the Marianas and the western Carolines were conditioned by their cultural traditions to work harmoniously and obediently with authority. Usually grateful for the subsidies and assistance provided to them by the colonial government in their initial endeavors, they came to constitute a rootwork of loyal and unquestioning support for the administration.

Finally, the South Seas Government, by delay, evasion, or outright refusal, was increasingly successful in screening the islands from foreign visitors, official or unofficial, whose presence in Micronesia could be considered potentially detrimental. Few foreigners attempted to tour the islands and only the United States made even halfhearted attempts to gain access to Micronesian waters for its vessels or citizens (see chapter 8).

In its administration of Micronesia, the Japanese government was limited only by one restraint, a distant and passive one at that: the annual scrutiny of the Permanent Mandates Commission of the League of Nations. The commission was charged with the supervision, not only of the terms of the charter for Japan's specific mandate, but of all mandatory powers in the fulfillment of the principles of Article 22 of the Covenant of the League, which established the mandate system.[31]

Yet "supervision" is too active, too vigorous a term to describe the deliberate, circumspect, and almost courtly discussions that took place each year behind closed doors in the stately chambers of the League in Geneva, half a world away from the sprawling Nan'yō-chō headquarters in Koror. Composed of nine members, the majority of whom represented nonmandatory powers, the commission met twice a year, in June and November, the Japanese mandate coming up for review at the June session. The commission distributed to each mandatory a questionnaire designed to elicit information relevant to the specific terms of its mandate. The responses formed the general framework (but not necessarily the boundaries) for the annual report submitted to the commission by each mandatory's accredited representative, sometimes a colonial specialist, more often not.

In turn, these reports—bland in tone, self-serving in content, festooned with statistical tables—often formed the sum of the commission's understanding of a particular mandated territory and the bounds for the cautious and gentlemanly interlocutory sessions between the commission and the accredited representative who presented the report. In the case of the Class C mandates, including that of Japan, the members of the commission had no direct knowledge of the mandated territories under discussion, nor did they ever seek to acquire any by first-hand observation. The commission considered that inspection of the territories might hamper the work of the mandatory and, even worse, imply suspicion concerning the word and good faith of the mandatory. For themselves, the Japanese accredited representatives to the commission were scarcely better informed, since none of them ever appears to have visited the islands on which they reported each year.

With their understanding of the mandate thus limited to the official explanations placed each year before them, the commission members largely restricted themselves to questioning the accredited representative on the basis of a careful reading of the current report. Rarely did they criticize or recommend changes in the policy of the mandatory power, though it says much about Japanese policy in its mandated territory that they did so on several occasions when Japan's representative sat before them. Those rare occasions when Japanese policy in Micronesia—regarding labor conditions, education, population ratios, immigration, public health, and adherence to the nonfortification provisions of the mandate—became the object of critical questioning and sharp comment produced no effect upon the Japanese government. In reality, the Permanent Mandates Commission was as impotent as its parent body in the monitoring of international order. Limited in their understanding of the subject at hand, lacking any inclination to undertake on-site inspections, fearful of any stance that might put them in direct opposition to a mandatory power when they encountered dark corners of mandatory misconduct, powerless to punish violators of the terms or principles of a mandate covenant, unable to compel adherence to a recommendation, or indeed to undertake any action whatsoever—the members of the Permanent Mandates Commission possessed "supervisory" authority over the mandates that was so attenuated as to be almost invisible. Confronted on a number of occasions by delay, evasion, and even obduracy when the Japanese government did not wish certain subjects concerning its mandate to be explored, the commission was not only powerless to force the issue, but became incapable of judging whether or not Japanese rule over fifty thousand Micronesians continued to justify the "sacred trust of civilization."

It is left to the historian, drawing on a greater range of information and more sophisticated analysis, to attempt a judgment on the question.

CHAPTER 4

A Trust Betrayed?

Japanese Policy toward the Micronesians

IT HAS BEEN SAID that when Japan took possession of Micronesia under its League of Nations mandate, it was presented with a set of minimal obligations and a far greater range of opportunities.[1] Undoubtedly, this was true of most, if not all, of the mandatory powers after World War I. The question the historian must ask in the Japanese case is whether, in the pursuit of its opportunities for national self-interest, Japan betrayed its obligations to the international community and, more important, to the indigenous peoples placed in its trust.[2] To attempt to answer the question is to review Japanese policies toward the Micronesians across a range of issues.

Two basic documents, mentioned in chapter 3, together constitute a starting point for sorting out judgments on Japan's treatment of its Micronesian populations. Article 22 of the Covenant of the League of Nations etched the broad principles and purposes of the mandate system; and the charter of Japan's specific mandate over the former German possessions north of the equator set forth specific requirements that Japan was to follow in its administration of Micronesia.

Within Article 22 of the Covenant, several concepts that illuminate the intent of its framers are prominent. The first paragraph of the article refers to "peoples [of the mandated territories] not yet able to stand by themselves under the strenuous conditions of the modern world," and declares that "the well-being and development of such peoples form a sacred trust of civilization." The second paragraph states that this principle is to be realized by "entrusting the tutelage of such peoples to advanced nations who by reason of their resources, their experience, or their geographical location can best undertake this responsibility, and who are willing to accept it, and that this tutelage be exercised by them as mandatories on behalf of the League."

If these words had any meaning at all, they were based on certain fundamental assumptions.[3] To begin with, the phrase referring to peoples "not yet able to stand by themselves" implied that, ultimately, no matter how long it might take, these same peoples should *learn* to stand by themselves. In short, they should be instructed as to how to be eventually free and self-governing. Secondly, the tutelage of such peoples by advanced nations, such as Japan, as a "sacred trust of civilization" implied the principle of "trusteeship," the idea expressed by Edmund Burke that "all power which is set over men . . . ought in some way to be exercised in their benefit." The trust held by the mandatory power implied not only a humanitarian concern for the material well-being of the peoples of the mandated territory, but also tutelage toward their ultimate emergence as a free, self-governing people. It is difficult to read Article 22 of the Covenant in any other light. Even the sixth paragraph of Article 22, which, in certain cases, such as that of Micronesia, permitted a mandatory to govern its mandate as integral portions of its territory, subjected such governance to safeguards protecting the indigenous peoples.

The text of the mandate charter, which specifically assigned to Japan the German islands in the Pacific north of the equator, was essentially similar to that of other Class C mandates in the Pacific and imposed upon Japan responsibilities of both an active and a negative sort. From today's standpoint, some of those obligations and prohibitions seem remarkably thin and others are distressingly vague. I shall look at each of them, not in the order they were set forth, but in order of their increasing importance, the better to view how Japanese policy related to each. (I have set aside the charter's prohibition on militarization or fortification of the islands as a separate issue, to be discussed in chapter 7.)

Among the least consequential and most easily summarized of the prohibitions imposed upon Japan were those in Article 3 outlawing the slave trade and arms traffic within the mandate. There is not the slightest reason to believe that the Japanese tolerated either of these activities during their administration of the mandate. Article 3 also banned any forced labor, "except for essential public works and services, and then only for adequate remuneration." Here, the Japanese record is a good deal more dubious and deserves some comment. Compulsory labor existed in Micronesia in three forms: communal duties of a traditional sort (organized by the village and undertaken without pay); public works projects—roads, schools, and so on—organized by Japanese branch governments (sometimes with pay and sometimes without); and paid work in the Japanese-owned mines in the Carolines, particularly the phosphate mines at Angaur, in southern Palau. This last category of labor earned the ongoing mistrust of the Permanent Mandates Commission. The Japanese government, which owned the mines until

1936, relied primarily on Micronesian labor to work the open pits; Chamorros from the Marianas and Carolinians from Yap, Palau, and Truk, were recruited by village chiefs and headmen, who were paid a small bonus for each "volunteer," supposedly to compensate them for the loss of tribal labor. There appears to have been circumstantial evidence that many Micronesians, particularly Carolinians, transported far from home for a year of exhausting work totally unsuited to their temperament, were recruited for mine work against their will.[4]

Nor was this all. Far from representing "essential public works," the phosphate mines were instead an enterprise worked for the exclusive benefit of Japan—a classic case of exploitation by foreign capital. Despite the ease and low cost with which the government had purchased the mines and existing machinery at Angaur, and notwithstanding the rapidity with which they had begun to show a profit, for most of those employed there, wages actually decreased after 1930. Moreover, none of these conditions were ever rectified through pressure from the League. The evasions and delays of the Japanese government in answering the questions of the Permanent Mandates Commission about recruitment, pay, and conditions in the mines deepened the suspicions of the commission that Japan was in violation of this article of its mandate charter. But, as the commission never sent a member to Micronesia to investigate the matter, no formal charges against Japan were ever prepared.[5]

The third article of the charter also prohibited the sale or supply of intoxicating spirits to the indigenous population. The Japanese government complied by making it illegal for Micronesians to imbibe any liquor more than three percent alcohol by volume, unless for strictly controlled medicinal or religious purposes. The South Seas Government included in this ban the various native beverages, from *sakau* (kava), a mild narcotic made on Ponape from a root of the same name, to the potent coconut toddies concocted throughout Micronesia. Yet drunkenness continued to be the single greatest reason for arrests by police and constables during the Japanese period (though it was a far smaller problem during Japanese rule than in the decades since). About 1938, the government relaxed these injunctions slightly to allow village chiefs, when in the company of Japanese officials, to down a small glass or two of sake on ceremonial holidays, such as the emperor's birthday, on the obvious assumption that it would not do to drink that monarch's health in water.[6]

I noted in chapter 3 that the text of the mandate charter called for Japan to make annual reports to the League of Nations in answer to questions put by the Permanent Mandates Commission and thus to demonstrate what progress had been made in fulfilling the terms of the mandate. For the Japanese, who traditionally have been indefatigable compilers of information, this was a familiar and natural task. The collection of oversized volumes that Japan sent to the commission every year, each filled with masses of statistics on population, education, industry, navigation, and trade, attests to the scrupulousness with which Japan met this bureaucratic responsibility during its membership in the League and even for the five years following its withdrawal from that body. The reports provided the essential data, not only for consideration of Japan's mandate administration behind the closed-door sessions of the commission in Geneva, but also for investigations by foreign scholars and commentators seeking to write about Micronesia, few of whom ever visited the islands and almost none of whom knew Japanese, which would have opened a far greater range of sources to them. Although the statistics in the reports were and still are of value, they cast only a half-light on conditions in the mandate and it is hard to see how the bland, palliative prose of the reports could have satisfied the curious or skeptical observer or commentator outside Japan.

Of considerable concern to the Western powers when the mandate was drafted, was a provision for freedom of conscience, the free exercise of all forms of worship, and the unrestricted activity and movement of foreign missionaries located in the islands. For the first decade of the Japanese mandate, there is little to criticize in the efforts of the Nan'yō-chō to meet this obligation. During those years, Micronesia under the Japanese displayed remarkable religious diversity. Although German missionaries, both Catholic and Protestant, had been expelled as enemy nationals by the Japanese navy within a year of the Japanese takeover, Christian evangelism was quickly reestablished in Micronesia after the war. In 1920, a Japanese Congregationalist group, the Nan'yō Dendō Dan (South Seas Mission) received permission to send four missionaries co Micronesia: two each to Truk and Ponape. Negotiations with the Vatican reinvigorated the Catholic presence in Micronesia and led to the assignment of a number of Spanish Jesuit fathers throughout the region. In 1927 the Liebenzell Mission, a Protestant order, was given permission to work in the islands, as well as a number of American mission groups that had been in Micronesia for years.[7]

Not only were these activities tolerated, but a number of groups, including the Catholic Church and the Nan'yō Dendō Dan, actually received small subsidies during the 1920s. In the official Japanese view, their attempts to "civilize" the Micronesians complemented the efforts of the South Seas Government to do so.[8]

At the same time, Buddhist, Shintō, and Tenrikyō missions had begun to enter the South Seas with encouragement from the Japanese government. The East Honganji Temple of the True Pure Land Buddhist sect established a branch in Saipan in 1919, and a second Buddhist temple was founded in Palau in 1926. But Shintō, with its unique links to

Japan's cultural traditions, was specially favored by the South Seas Government. In particular, State Shintō, the spiritual edge of Japanese nationalism by the 1930s, was seen as a means to bring about the acculturation—the Japanization—of the Micronesians. For this reason it flourished under government encouragement and support, its shrines dotting the Pacific from Angaur to Arno. The most imposing of them was the great shrine at Koror, established in 1940 amid ceremonies that symbolized the high tide of Japanese dominion in the South Seas.[9]

In the 1930s, as the Japanese empire, including Micronesia, began to undergo the forced assimilation of its colonial populations, and all creeds and beliefs that did not support this national effort began to fall under official disapproval, the relative religious tolerance of the South Seas Government began to shrivel. The foreign mission schools had already felt the pressure of state interference, when the Nan'yō-chō made it compulsory for Micronesian children to attend government schools. Then, in the late 1930s, as hardening Japanese nationalism displayed growing hostility toward the West, foreign missions came under increasing suspicion from the colonial government. The movement of foreign missionaries was increasingly restricted, Japanese teachers in the government schools spoke with mounting contempt of Christian institutions, and the replacement of mission personnel was increasingly discouraged. In the few years preceding the Pacific War, foreign churches and missionaries were subjected to outright harassment and interference, until by 1941 little remained of Japan's original commitment to fulfill this particular obligation of the mandate charter.[10]

One provision in the mandate charter lies at the heart of the question covering Japan's fidelity to "the sacred trust of civilization" it had accepted: "The Mandatory," the charter stated, "shall promote to the utmost the material and moral well-being and the social progress of the inhabitants of the territory subject to the present mandate." With hindsight, the language of that provision is exasperatingly vague. Because of that vagueness, one can understand how Western scholars and commentators in the interwar period, having access only to Japan's annual English-language reports to the League, could believe that Japan's accomplishments in Micronesia—harbors improved, docks and roads built, schools established, medical services provided—were collective proof that Japan was improving the conditions of the colonial population in its charge and was attempting to fulfill this clause of the mandate charter.

But this provision in particular, unlike some of the simpler and more mechanical injunctions of the charter, derived its meaning from the League of Nations Covenant, specifically Article 22, which implied both humanitarian concern and the principle of trusteeship for self-government. If the "material well-being" of the Micronesians meant their health, their stability, and their prosperity, their "moral well-being" could only have meant their happiness, their sense of human worth, their virtue, in the profoundest sense of the word. Their "social progress" most reasonably meant progress through encouragement, through education, and through a gradually increasing transfer of responsibility, toward freedom and independence. Finally, the use of the phrase "to the utmost" in the provision would seem to mean that it was Japan's duty to exert every resource and every effort it could muster in attempting to fulfill the terms of this portion of the charter; half-hearted measures or the diversion of Japanese resources and energies to other objectives would mean that Japan had failed to meet its obligations.

In seeking to gauge Japan's relative success or failure in meeting this critical provision, one must therefore try to evaluate the commitment, purpose, and results of those policies that directly or indirectly affected the well-being and the social progress of the Micronesians. The indicators I have chosen—public health, education, land ownership, and economic opportunity—seem critical to the problem. Toward the end of chapter 3, I commented on a fifth standard, freedom, or more precisely, the absence of it under Japanese rule. What freedom remained to Micronesians—the freedom simply to be left alone to be themselves—was undermined, at first through subtle inducements and then, by the late 1930s, through efforts at forced assimilation.

Population and Public Health

With the exception of the question whether Japan had kept its pledge not to use the islands for military purposes, no issue of the Japanese mandate administration subjected Japanese rule in Micronesia to as much outside query, including that of the Permanent Mandates Commission, as the stagnant condition of Micronesian population growth, particularly when juxtaposed with the rocketing upward curve of the Japanese immigrant communities in the islands. The issue put the Japanese government on the defensive, for behind the questions lay the implication that Japanese policies were contributing to the problem. Indeed, one member of the commission asserted that "if the native races were dying out, it was clear that their moral and material welfare were being sacrificed."[11]

Of course, the demographic stagnation of Micronesia was not so simple that its root causes could be found in Japanese policy. Most of the Micronesian populations, like those of other Pacific islands, having already reached a stasis, had suffered a decline in numbers ever since contact with the industrial nations of the West had intensified in the first half of the nineteenth century. The scourge of the innocent populations of the Pacific had been the bacteria, the rickettsias, and the viruses borne onto their island shores by the whaling crews, the traders, the settlers, and perhaps even by the missionaries. Their effects had been devastating to the island communities, whose social customs, living practices, and ideas concerning sickness often made the spread of disease inevitable. Addiction to European liquor, the depredations of the notorious blackbirders, and the general disruption of native society by aggressive and ruthless interlopers had added to the ruin. Of all the Micronesian groups, the Marianas, by the end of the Spanish period, had suffered the greatest decline; as a pure race, the Chamorros were sharply reduced in number by the end of the nineteenth century.

In fairness, it must be said that Japan inherited the population problem in Micronesia. Yet it is clear that the demographic decline had leveled off by the time the Japanese navy moved into the islands in 1914. On all the larger islands, except Yap, island populations had become static or were actually showing a slight increase. Had they not then been crowded to the wall by an inundation of aggressive, determined, immigrant Japanese, their recovery might have been robust.

The immediate response of the Japanese government to the discouraging health conditions it encountered appears admirable. In February 1915, the Japanese navy's *Nan'yō guntō shōbyōsha kyūryō kitei* (Regulations concerning the medical treatment of sick and injured persons in the South Seas) authorized navy doctors of the various garrisons to provide free medical treatment to indigenous populations as well as Japanese civilians in the islands.[12] At each naval district headquarters a small hospital was established as an affiliate of the civil affairs branch, and vigorous, pioneering efforts were made to improve the sanitation and personal hygiene of the island populations. These programs were continued and expanded by the succeeding civilian administration, in keeping with the high priority on the pacifying effects of modern medicine begun by Gotō Shimpei on Taiwan two decades before. In the Japanese colonial mind, at least, the doctor's smock and stethoscope and the dentist's drill were as much symbols of civilization and order as were the census table, the accountant's ledger, the telegraph form, or the policeman's badge. In 1922, government hospitals were established on Saipan, Yap, Palau, Angaur, Truk, Ponape, Jaluit, and later Kusaie, and were staffed with fully trained doctors, nurses, and pharmacists. Compulsory vaccination programs were implemented throughout the islands, and medical teams traveled by motorboat to treat both Micronesians and Japanese on the smaller, remoter islands. Some Micronesian women were given paramedical training and sent back to their villages to spread their understanding of basic hygiene and sanitation.[13]

In its effort to improve public health and reverse the demographic decline, the South Seas Government concluded that changes in Micronesian lifestyles were necessary. The thatch house, so picturesque to armchair travelers and visiting anthropologists alike, was often damp, poorly lighted, ill ventilated, and vulnerable to tropical rains. To provide a better alternative, the Nan'yō-chō designed a model, one-room house, to be raised one meter from the ground, solid, of wooden construction, roofed with corrugated metal, and provided with adequate window space; for this the government would pay half the cost of construction. Exemplary efforts were also made on some of the larger islands to improve drinking water facilities and to build public baths and public latrines along sanitary lines.[14]

Given that Japanese health care for Micronesians was a great improvement over anything they had known before, one might expect that by the eve of the Pacific War the health of the islanders would have been blooming and their numbers markedly increased. Yet neither condition came to pass. To understand why, one must look at the priorities of Japanese policy.

A fundamental reason for the discouraging results of Japan's public health programs was that, by the high noon of Japan's rule in Micronesia, its priorities in terms of budget and attention were placed on industrial development—the exploitation of the islands' natural resources—not on social services. The statistical evidence for this is striking. In 1935, for example, the subsidy for Japanese shipping in Micronesia alone was almost ¥665,000, while the sum total expended for social purposes—medicine, public health, sanitation, education, and so on—was less than ¥170,000.[15] Even more critical was the fact that, as wave upon wave of Japanese immigrants washed into the islands, they came to absorb an increasingly greater share of government expenditures for social services in general and health care in particular. With major Japanese resources being taken up with the prevention, quarantine, and eradication of contagious diseases—typhus, smallpox, cholera—among the Japanese, fewer were available to treat the continuing afflictions of the Micronesians. A fee structure that, ironically, had been erected to counteract their suspicions that free medical treatment was inferior, soon worked against the Micronesian communities, since not all Micronesians could afford even a small charge. The best hospitals as well as the best medical services were to be found on the larger islands—Saipan, Palau, and Ponape—where there were larger concentrations of Japanese. What medical treatment was left for the Micronesians may have been better than anything they had known before, but that says little. Public health and public works that affected the Islanders' health were severely limited. Model houses are a splendid idea, but of little use if few of them get built, as indeed, few did. (How many Micronesians could afford even half the cost?) Public health education is admirable, but the nine Micronesians trained in sanitation work in 1932 could hardly be expected to have much impact on public health in Micronesia as a whole.[16]

Despite the image of brisk professionalism in public health and medicine purveyed in the government's annual report to the League of Nations, the old maladies—yaws, amoebic dysentery, dengue fever, and others—remained to afflict the island populations. Their numbers continued to increase at a negligible rate throughout Micronesia as a whole, yet the mortality of Micronesians was higher than that of Japanese for every year between 1922 and 1937.[17]

Of all the demographic profiles, that of Yap was the most discouraging. Despite doing all it could, or thought it could do, to reverse the downward trend, the South Seas Government watched the Yapese population decrease yearly, a situation that caused ever more insistent mutterings in Geneva and such mounting embarrassment in Tokyo and Koror that in the late 1920s the Yap Branch Government was instructed to look into the problem. To take charge of the investigation the government called upon Dr. Fujii Tamotsu, director of the Yap hospital and distinguished parasitologist from Hokkaido University, who had undertaken similar studies among the Ainu.

The immediate causes were obvious enough: high death rates due to tuberculosis and infant diarrhea; low birth rates due in large part to a shocking incidence of gonorrhea.[18] From the outset of his investigations Dr. Fujii was convinced that the population decline was a result of these afflictions and that they, in turn, were particularly acute because the Yapese were the most stubbornly resistant of all the Micronesian peoples to any change in their traditional ways, including those the Japanese considered to be unsanitary living practices, religious customs, and misguided ideas concerning disease, illness, and sexual relations. The solution, Dr. Fujii and his government believed, was to break down tribal practices and customs that were obviously retarding the health and vigor of the island population, while redoubling whatever efforts were necessary to improve medical care for the islanders. The colonial authorities seem to have undertaken both approaches with genuine determination and concern.[19]

To the Yapese, however, the Japanese modernizing policies themselves had stunted the growth of the island's population, since they had served to dislocate Yapese society as a whole. The authority of their traditional leaders had been destroyed and the weakening of traditional social controls had led to the disorganization of family life, the undermining of traditional morals among Yapese youth, and the consequent spread of venereal disease. Similarly, they considered the shortage of food and poor nutrition to result from the Japanese requirement of compulsory labor for certain public works, which took men away from their villages. Convinced that Japanese medical efforts to reverse the depopulation of the island were simply intended to abolish Yapese customs, the Yapese regarded all attempts to improve their welfare with uncooperative suspicion.[20]

Undoubtedly, this resistance was, in part, that of a fearful, obdurate, and bewildered preindustrial community. Yet, looking at Micronesian societies as a whole, there was perhaps some small truth in the view that the particular processes of Japan's disruption of traditional Micronesian social patterns and functions did help to enfeeble the collective powers of generation among the island populations, particularly when those processes were borne on a rising tide of alien immigration.

To Yanaihara Tadao, the distinguished colonial scholar and Christian thinker who visited the islands in the 1930s, it was not Japanese modernization per se that led to this situation, but rather the social and economic halfway state of Micronesian societies that had been created by the Japanese presence. The islands' natural economy had been invaded by foreign capitalism, yet its benefits had been incompletely diffused among island communities; their traditional authority structure had been broken up with no system to replace it that might have reinforced Micronesian pride and dignity; age-old amusements and pastimes had been prohibited or restricted without being adequately replaced by communal incentives that could engage Micronesian enthusiasm. All of these situations had contributed, Yanaihara argued, to a lassitude, a depression, and in a few cases, to an impoverishment among Micronesian peoples. In Yanaihara's view, these conditions could not be improved by a return to the old order. What was needed, he believed, was the complete and systematic assimilation of the Micronesian into modernity, which in this case meant Japanese modernity.[21] But by implication this meant access to education, wages, position, land, and economic opportunity on a scale which, if it did not immediately equal that available to the Japanese immigrants who were filling up the islands, would at least so improve over the years that it would demonstrate Japan's urgent concern for the material well-being of the island peoples, as demanded in the League Covenant and the mandate charter.

Japanese Schools for Micronesians: Education for Dependence

No Japanese policy more clearly illustrated the contradiction between Japanese self-interest and Japan's obligations under its mandate than the education programs which the South Seas Government made available to Micronesians. Intended to be a showpiece to demonstrate Japan's commitment to its mandate obligations, they also served as a means to perpetuate Japanese rule and to keep the indigenous population in a state of perpetual dependence.

Before the arrival of the Japanese navy in 1914, education for Micronesians—what there was of it—came from the mission schools in the islands. A few months after the navy came ashore that autumn, the mission schools were shut down and on the larger islands the various naval garrisons began setting up makeshift classrooms. Hundreds of youngsters during the early years of Japanese rule in the South Seas had their first introduction to Japanese civilization provided by the intimidating figure of a Japanese naval officer, or sometimes by a sailor or two. At the naval garrison headquarters on Truk, Saipan, Ponape, and the other large islands, Japanese navy men, occasionally assisted by a staff member of the South Seas Trading Company, gathered their small charges every morning beneath the sunburst ensign and initiated them into the wonders of arithmetic, geography, the Japanese language, and the benevolence of Emperor Taishō, all served up with naval rigor and discipline.[22]

But since fighting, not teaching, was its trade, the navy was soon willing to turn over its classrooms to civilian teachers and to bring in officials from the Ministry of Education to frame policies and guidelines for the instruction of island children. These initial regulations set the tone for the indoctrination as well as the education of Micronesian youth through language training and heavy doses of moral education of the sort that weighted contemporary curricula in Japan—with stress on filial piety, obedience to authority, and the rest. In 1923, the new South Seas Government issued a *chorei*, *Nan'yō-chō kōgakkō kisoku* (South Seas Government regulations for public schools), which reorganized the existing school system and, in words that hewed to both Japanese interests and the mandate charter, declared that the fundamental objectives of education in Micronesia should be the moral guidance of the students, provision of knowledge indispensable to the advancement and improvement of their lives, and training directed toward their physical development.[23]

Under the regulations, the basic program of education in the "public schools," *kōgakkō*, was to be three years of primary education, with a supplementary two-year course for youngsters who showed promise. Because the colonial authorities considered facility in the Japanese language essential to the rest of their education, language instruction consumed almost half the class time of the children. The remainder was taken up with the inevitable Japan-oriented moral education classes, arithmetic, geography, agriculture, gymnastics, and handicrafts.

After World War I, the Nan'yō-chō had allowed the mission schools to start up again in the islands, but gradually they began to give way to the government schools as public education began to make rapid strides in the 1920s. In 1935 they were driven into a supplementary role, when they were no longer permitted to serve as an alternative to the government *kōgakkō*.[24]

Because Japan's mandate obligations compelled a central place for Japanese education in the administration of Micronesia, and since Japan, as in its other colonies, saw education as a means to insure the obedient and loyal acquiescence of Micronesian peoples, school was made compulsory for all children on the larger islands. On the distant, isolated atolls, a predetermined number of children were selected by the village chief or headman for study at one of the larger centers, where they were expected to board with relatives or friends. By the 1930s, the Nan'yō-chō had established twenty-four public schools and more than half the school age children of Micronesia were enrolled (though on Palau the figure reached nearly one hundred percent).[25]

Considered by the South Seas Government an important element of Japan's mandate rule, the public school occupied a highly visible place on the Micronesian scene. Looking at old photographs in the massive history of Japanese education in Micronesia published before the war, one sees that Japanese school buildings came in all sizes and styles, though they were most commonly patterned after the elementary school in Japan. A long, rectangular wooden building contained classrooms and storerooms with a central portico in front, before which was an open area large enough for an athletic field. Here the photographs invariably show rows of children lined up for drill, moral exhortation, or calisthenics directed by a white-uniformed teacher standing on the school steps. Occasionally, off to the side is a smaller building to house the Japanese teaching staff, which, in some of the remoter locations, might consist of a solitary Japanese teacher whose influence and prestige, since he was the only Japanese functionary about, carried far beyond the school yard. Acting as doctor, counselor, and quasi-policeman, as well as teacher, such a school principal assumed the perquisites of a village chief, receiving gifts of food and the services of the schoolchildren who helped him about the house.[26]

In the early years of Japanese navy rule in the South Seas, the focus of educational efforts was the Micronesian population, but by 1918, with increasing Japanese immigration to the islands, the authorities felt obliged to make a distinction in student assignments, on the basis of facility in Japanese. Those who spoke and read the language—Japanese children—went into the eight-year primary schools, *shogakkō*, structured according to the basic educational pattern in Japan. Those who didn't—island children—went into the two- to three-year public schools. The Japanese made little effort to deny that the separation was for cultural as well as linguistic reasons. In the Japanese view, the "special circumstances" of a preindustrial people meant that Micronesians had no place in the competitive environment of a Japanese schoolroom. "Education for the natives," asserted an early policy statement, "cannot be carried out the same way as that for the Japanese. One must consider the special circumstances affecting the length of study, course work, level of instruction, and so on, in the case of the islanders and deal with these problems separately."[27]

Thus began, in purpose, curriculum, and facilities, two decades of segregated and largely discriminatory education in Micronesia. Japanese primary schools there indoctrinated Japanese children in the traditional values of their homeland—diligence, obedience, frugality, filial piety, and devotion to the emperor. Yet in the breadth and depth of the instruction they offered, they also honored the idea of study for itself and set goals designed to raise the aspirations of Japanese youngsters. In public schools for Micronesians, the teachers placed emphasis on honesty, hard work, and obedience to authority, but did so without raising the students' expectations about individual advancement or self-fulfillment.[28] The whole thrust of the limited education offered to Micronesian youngsters was to be practical education, *jissai kyōiku,* by which was meant teaching the manual skills necessary to perform well at the lower social and economic level that was to be their lot. "The system was geared," as one American scholar has written, "to produce a supply of general laborers and domestic servants who understood Japanese, plus a small elite of skilled laborers and petty officials."[29]

The late David Ramarui, distinguished civil servant of the Republic of Belau (as the Palau Islands are now known), who was a product of Japanese public school training in Koror as a youngster, years later recalled two symbols that demonstrated the disparity in purpose between the public and primary schools in Palau. At the gate of the public school he attended was a concrete pillar that bore four Japanese ideographs in gold-plated brass, admonishing all who entered to be diligent, honest, obedient, and mindful of their obligations. Lest any schoolchildren forget, the school day opened with a recitation in unison of those four instructions. Across town, at the Japanese *shogakkō,* the symbol was subtly different. Standing at the main gate was a statue of Ninomiya Sontoku, the peasant sage of late feudal times, as a schoolboy, carrying firewood on his back, but reading from an open book as he strode forward. Diligence and hard work were symbolized here, but also the joy of reading and independent study, which promised advancement.[30]

Few Micronesians could expect the same. The study of the Japanese language took up the largest single block of classroom time in the public schools, indeed so much that there was insufficient time for other subjects. This imbalance was defended by Japanese colonial authorities on the grounds that Japanese language facility was critical to everything else they were trying to teach Micronesian children and because the government believed Japanese would provide a common language for all Micronesians. Yet after leaving school, few Micronesians could read anything of any difficulty in Japanese; the written language was too complex and their time in school too brief. Moreover, most Micronesians who left public school after three years seldom again had much opportunity to hear or use Japanese, unless they lived or worked near one of the Japanese towns that sprang up in the islands. Even those who remained in school to take the supplementary two-year course never learned to read much more than *kana,* the simple phonetic syllabary, and thus, unfamiliar with any *kanji,* the Japanese ideographs, were unable to read either a newspaper or the regulations promulgated by the South Seas Government. This would have been tolerable had the Japanese colonial educators encouraged written facility in any of the Micronesian languages, but the vernacular tongues were ignored and even denigrated, students being punished for using them in class. In consequence, Micronesians couldn't really read Japanese, but weren't trained to read their own languages either.[31]

Indeed, little was provided to Micronesians, either in their textbooks or by their Japanese teachers, that gave them pride in their own history, their culture, or themselves. In large classes, often of eighty or more students, with one teacher for all subjects, Micronesian children were drilled, pushed, pummeled through a few years of schooling that stressed their subordinate role in a Japanese system. Learning generally consisted of rote memorization and group recitation (standard Japanese classroom procedure), with heavy doses of corporal punishment—slapping and hitting—for apparent laziness or for giving incorrect answers.[32]

Yet the Japanese sincerely considered this educational castor oil, forcefully dispensed to Micronesian youth for a few short years, to be education appropriate to their cultural level. Konishi Tatehiko, retired naval officer and old South Seas hand, recalled with hearty approval the opening day of the first school on Truk, in late October 1915, when the principal, a naval lieutenant, accompanied by an interpreter and three or four sailors, addressed the awed group of children assembled before him. "You and these sailors are all human beings," the lieutenant declared, "but who do you think is better?" "The sailors," the children meekly replied. "Good. Remember that and become just like these sailors here. And if you don't study hard you'll get this," he barked, waving his fist in the air.[33] With such rough and ready methods the modern education of Micronesians began under the Japanese.

Perhaps the most crippling limitation on Japanese education for Micronesians was the fact that the overwhelming number of Islanders could expect no more than a few years of elementary school. There were no middle schools open to Micronesians and only the smallest possibility of further schooling in Japan, where the few Islanders who managed to enter middle school almost invariably dropped out, unable to keep up with the work or to adjust to the competitive environment of a closed educational system.[34] Aside from a few agricultural training programs on some of the larger islands, the one exception to this limited educational horizon was the *Mokkō totei yōseijō* (Carpentry Apprentice Training School) established in Koror in 1926 to train young Micronesian men in carpentry and woodworking. For a handful of Micronesians (mostly Palauans) selected on a highly competitive basis, the school opened doors of great economic opportunity, for it provided skills that came to be greatly in demand as Japanese immigrants began to pour into the Marianas and the Carolines. Expanded in 1940 to include blacksmithing, automotive mechanics, and electronics, the school gained fame throughout the Pacific, a "must" on the itinerary of every distinguished visitor touring the mandate.[35]

Yet it is significant that this most prestigious educational institution for Micronesians was a school that taught manual arts. Nowhere in the mandate was there an institution that trained Micronesians to assume any of the administrative, economic, or educational positions occupied by Japanese. Since there were no middle schools there were obviously no colleges, not even teacher training centers. Though Micronesian assistants were used as interpreters by Japanese teachers, few received special training or ever became full teachers themselves.[36]

In sum, formal Japanese education for many Micronesians was at worst a cultural humiliation; for most it was of limited permanent value; and at best—for the minority who gained some facility in the Japanese language—it was good training for certain useful but subordinate roles as clerks, interpreters, assistant teachers, personal servants, labor supervisors, and village scribes. Indeed, the highest position to which a Micronesian with five years of primary education and some specialized training could generally aspire, was that of village constable. There was no institution to train Islanders to assume leadership responsibilities or to direct Micronesian destinies, even for some distant day.[37]

Referring to Article 22 of the Covenant of the League, in 1948 the distinguished Australian scholar Duncan Hall wrote: "The positive conception of the article is surely education for self-government . . . the self-government of a free people standing on its own feet as the result of a process of education . . ."[38] Judged by such a standard, the education dispensed to most Micronesians was surely a betrayal of Japan's "sacred trust."

Yet this severe judgment needs qualification. To begin with, there were a few Micronesian students who, by good luck, family circumstances, or family connections with Japanese, were able to obtain schooling considerably beyond the usual *kōgakkō* education. Some were able to enter the small, private Japanese academies that were established in the larger island centers in the late 1930s and early 1940s, and a handful successfully completed secondary school in Japan. For these individuals, a number of whom came, upon maturity, to fill leadership positions in postwar Micronesia, the values—loyalty, hard work, discipline, and ambition—as well as the skills imparted by their Japanese schooling have stood in sharp contrast to what they regard as the indifferent education provided to Micronesian youngsters after the passing of the Japanese era.[39]

It is necessary to recognize, moreover, that to view the Japanese education provided to the great majority of Micronesians as having failed to live up to the ideals of the League of Nations Covenant is to assume the anticolonial perspectives of the postwar world. It is certain that few Japanese at the time were willing to consider Japan's limited efforts to educate Micronesians as a failure to meet its mandate commitments, though Yanaihara Tadao's veiled criticism came close to making that charge. For their part, Micronesians had as yet too little information about the outside world to feel a keen sense of deprivation about the educational fare provided to them. Moreover, the handful of Western observers passing through the islands reflected the patronizing prejudices of the era in their approving commentary on Japan's "education in the jungle," as the American scholar Paul Clyde called it. "The Japanese administration," Clyde declared, "has wisely modified the curriculum to meet native intelligence and needs." Willard Price, the peripatetic journalist of the thirties, agreed and, after several months in the islands, concluded that Japan's sacred trust was being exercised "exactly as so intended by the League."[40]

Land Policies: Japanese Order and Micronesian Custom

Considering that there was so little of it, land was the single most valuable commodity in Micronesia. It was natural that the South Seas Government should consider its control and allocation to be a major administrative function.

When the Japanese came to the islands they encountered a patchwork of native landowning systems, varying from island to island in three different modes: clan or communal property, feudal claims, and private ownership. At the outset, the Nan'yō-chō made several important decisions. First, it chose to consider that all communal land apparently unused or uncultivated should belong to the colonial government. In order that private Micronesian land should be protected against the incursions of Japanese land speculators, it also declared that no Japanese individuals or corporations could buy, sell, or mortgage land in Micronesia, though it placed no restrictions on the sale or transfer of land between Micronesians themselves. Lastly, the regulations permitted Micronesians to lease land to Japanese citizens for a period of no more than ten years.[41]

It soon became apparent, however, that land ownership was impossible to determine, since most Micronesian claims were based on oral testimony or tribal custom. Moreover, on most islands, the indigenous boundary markers—such as special plantings, notches on tree trunks, or coral rocks—between separate claims were not obvious to outsiders; on others, previous attempts to clarify land titles had come to naught. Land surveys made in German times on a few of the larger islands, like Saipan and Ponape, were largely incomplete, and the maps and documents on which land titles were based had somehow become lost.

For these reasons the South Seas Government began land survey and registration programs that identified ownership, measured boundaries, and confirmed or established land titles, thus simplifying the sale and purchase of land, promoting land obligation, and providing accurate assessment of land for tax purposes. The first phase of this activity, begun in 1923, was a survey of land declared to belong to the government, which started in the Marianas and, like every other Japanese activity in Micronesia, then moved through the western and the eastern Carolines, finally ending in the Marshalls nine years later. In 1933, the process was started all over again, this time concentrating on land in private ownership. By 1937 this task was at last completed.[42]

In view of the gathering dispossession of Micronesians of their land and its acquisition by Japanese individuals and corporations in the last decade of Japanese rule in Micronesia, it is easy to view these administrative assessments as merely preplanned administrative cover for the alienation of the land. Yanaihara Tadao, in his classic study of the Japanese mandated islands, stopped just short of making such an assertion when he speculated that the colonial government had decided to stake out the boundaries of government land before settling private claims in order to determine the extent of land available for immediate exploitation and settlement by Japanese immigrants.[43] In 1923, however, the central government in Tokyo was far from certain that the settlement and development of the South Sea Islands were practical matters. Moreover, such assertions overlook the fact that the clarification of land ownership had been a priority of all new Japanese administrations throughout Japanese history, ever since the great cadastral surveys of Toyotomi Hideyoshi in the sixteenth century. In the nineteenth century such a rationalization of land tenure in Japan had been one of the first priorities of the fledgling Meiji government. Its successful completion had launched the economic modernization of Japan and had been the model for land survey and registration programs in each of the Japanese colonial territories. To the Japanese, it was a task essential to good order, economic prosperity, and proper management, and it appears to have been undertaken with painstaking care and scrupulous honesty.

Yet, if there was no premeditated plan to alienate Micronesians from their land, there is no doubt that the long-run effect of Japanese policy led in that direction, and that those conducting the surveys and the registration programs were sometimes insensitive to the complexities and subtleties of Micronesian land tenure. For example, to begin with, on some islands, such as Ponape, clan or communal land that may have appeared to the eyes of a Japanese surveyor to have been unclaimed and unused, was in fact traditionally open to hunting, farming, fishing, and logging by the island populations. With the appropriation of this land by the colonial government, Ponapeans were obliged to buy licenses if they wished to continue these activities on what was now government land. On other islands, communal lands had been opened to private purchase with the consent of the local chiefs; the new regulations now made this impossible. It is also undeniable that in acquiring "unused" communal land, the colonial government expropriated some of the best of it. In the Mortlock Islands, for example, the government declared that land between the high and low tide marks was to be government property, resulting in the disruption of indigenous use of the lagoon and reefs and the outlawing of Micronesian fish traps.[44]

In other cases, the Islanders were either too afraid to contradict the terms of the survey or unclear as to Japanese intentions concerning the land. On Kusaie, large tracts in the interior were understood by the Japanese authorities to be unused communal land and were consequently counted as government territory. In fact, these lands had passed some years before into private Micronesian ownership, but Kusaieans were too intimidated to contradict the surveyors. In other cases, the Nan'yō-chō, in an effort to allow landless Micronesians to have the use of land, made it available to them on a temporary basis, but the terms of the agreement by which this was done were written in Japanese and the Islanders were not aware that they had no clear title to the land. Moreover, though the South Seas Government in its registration effort did not set out to defraud Micronesians, neither did it make it easy for them to obtain a favorable government decision on their claims. The land commission created for the 1933 land survey accepted petitions seeking confirmation of land titles, but these had to be presented in Japanese and the ultimate decision was conveyed in the same language, which placed considerable burden on Micronesian petitioners, few of whom could negotiate in Japanese.[45]

Perhaps most galling to Micronesians was the fact that the land policies obviously came to benefit the swelling numbers of Japanese immigrants who began to fill up the larger islands—Saipan, Palau, Ponape, and Truk—in the late 1920s. It is easy to understand how Micronesians could harbor suspicions about the motives behind Japanese surveys when again and again they saw the best communal land taken by the South Seas Government, which then leased it to Japanese farmers and settlers. On islands such as Ponape, when the government leased government land to Micronesian cultivators on the condition that they clear it, the suspicion arose that Micronesians were being asked to break the ground, after which they would be moved off and Japanese settlers moved in.[46]

On the other hand, the pressure on privately owned Micronesian land was ameliorated by the economic benefit to Micronesians themselves. The ultimate success of Matsue Haruji and the South Seas Development Company in establishing a sugar industry in the Marianas both pressured and induced Micronesian landholders to lease their land on the broad uplands of Saipan to the company for sugarcane cultivation, as well as to the hundreds of independent farmers who came to try their hand at planting cane and sharing in the sugar boom. Similarly, the towns that sprang up across Micronesia—Garapan, Koror, Kolonia, Dublon, and Jabor—became overwhelmingly Japanese, as much due to the economic inducement offered to Micronesian residents to lease their property and move to the countryside, as to Japanese pressure for them to leave.[47]

In 1931, the drift toward alienation of Micronesian land increased when the South Seas Government revised the law that forbade the legal transfer of land between Micronesians and private Japanese individuals or corporations. Such transactions still required the permission of the government, but it is easy to see how the government, acting increasingly in the interest of its own citizens, would be increasingly open to lobbying by Japanese immigrant, agricultural, and industrial interests to authorize such purchases.[48]

Until the mid-1930s, Micronesian landholders had their titles protected by the Japanese colonial administration and at the same time, as a rentier class, were brought into the modern economy by which Japan had begun to transform village life throughout Micronesia.

Although Japanese land policies and the increasing acquisition of Micronesian land by burgeoning Japanese communities throughout the larger islands may have caused growing unease and even resentment among Micronesians, the course of this process was orderly through the decade of the 1930s, and the laws by which it evolved were applied with a general concern for the Islanders' interests.

With the militarization of the islands in the years prior to and during the Pacific War, however, the place of the Micronesians on their land, like all other aspects of their life under Japanese rule, drastically worsened. Houses, beaches, agricultural plots, recreational areas, all lands and buildings deemed necessary for the Japanese defense of the islands were seized by the military, at first with monetary compensation, and then, as the islands were either attacked or besieged in the last few years of the war, without any payment whatsoever.[49]

The postwar legacy of Japanese land policies in Micronesia—the land survey and registration programs in particular—has been mixed. On some islands the policies served to legitimize the claims of individual Micronesians to specific land holdings. On others, the registration records were lost in the destruction and chaos of the war and could make little difference in the subsequent allocation of the land. On a few islands, such as Kusaie, they became the focus of disputes between American officials of the Trust Territory trying to make sense of local land tenure, and indigenous landowners who disputed every acre of territory appropriated by the Japanese in the days when the verdict of the Japanese land surveyor had been supreme.[50]

Working for the Yen: Exploitation and Opportunity

The coming of Japanese trade and industry to Micronesia in the 1920s was to transform the tropical landscape and to quicken the infusion of energetic, land-hungry immigrants from the Japanese islands. In the process, the indigenous Micronesians found themselves at once exploited for their labor and enriched by the new economic opportunities available to them.

There is little reason to doubt that, in their role as employers in Micronesia, both Japanese business and government deserve low marks, though perhaps no worse than those of other colonial powers. The sinister reputation of the recruiting practices at the phosphate mines at Angaur lingered year by year in the conference rooms of the Permanent Mandates Commission in Geneva like an unexpelled mephitis. Yet it did not arise solely from questions of compulsion and exploitation, but was due as well to the inequities in the wages and treatment of the mine workers. Salary scales at the mines were blatantly discriminatory, wages being paid in a sharply descending scale for Japanese, Chinese, Chamorros, and Carolinians. Whereas the Japanese acted almost entirely in a managerial capacity, the Carolinians, far from home and alone (they were the only group not allowed to bring their families) furnished the bulk of the labor for the pick-and-shovel work, yet received the lowest wages and the smallest food ration.[51]

The pattern of economic discrimination in salary as well as in position ran throughout the fabric of Japanese trade and industry as it developed in Micronesia. In general, the maximum wage for the small numbers of skilled Micronesian laborers was half that of their Japanese counterparts and only slightly above that of the unskilled miners on

Angaur. When Micronesians were employed by Japanese business it was usually as stevedores or day laborers, or at best as mechanics, almost never as managers or overseers; when the government employed them it was always as assistants, office workers, postal clerks, or interpreters. Almost never were they provided with advanced training or assigned positions of responsibility. In the burgeoning sugar industry in the Marianas during the 1920s, for example, Micronesians were not even hired as manual laborers, since in the Japanese view, no Micronesians could be found who could cope with the new techniques of cane cultivation or sugar manufacture. The never-failing official explanation was that the government had neither the time nor the resources to train Micronesians for more demanding economic positions and that, in any event, their inherent backwardness and laziness made them unsuitable for such work.[52]

Yet it would be a distortion of history to say that indigenous Micronesians were merely victims exploited in the path of the Japanese economic juggernaut. The coming of the Japanese did mean economic gain and a higher standard of living for most island communities. Even at the most debased wage scales Micronesians began to have what they had not had (and admittedly, had not wanted or needed) before—money to buy things. They were soon attracted by the small but growing array of cheaply made consumer goods from Japan—knives, pots, pans, lamps, clothes, rubber sandals, canned goods, and the like. Their small earnings inevitably drew them into a modern money economy and changed their lives in countless small ways, making their daily chores a little easier, their living arrangements more comfortable, their tastes and outlook somewhat wider. At the same time, their former economic self-sufficiency began to be eroded.

But the Micronesians benefited most from the Japanese economic presence in certain limited areas of entrepreneurship, of which the copra trade was one. As Japanese traders, particularly those employed by the South Seas Trading Company, began to expand the planting, cultivation, and harvesting of coconut trees, they sought to induce Micronesians to increase production of copra by giving them a small subsidy to clear the land, set out more trees, thin the groves, and put up drying sheds. Copra thus became the first cash crop for numerous village communities and the growing profitability of the trade in the 1930s was proof of the effectiveness of the inducements offered to the Micronesians. Though insect blight ruined the copra business in the Marianas in the 1920s, the trade flourished in the Marshalls and Carolines and transformed the pace of village life by markedly increasing the amount of individual and community work the inhabitants had to do. In the Marshalls and most of the Carolines, the Islanders sold their copra to Japanese brokers, who served as intermediaries between the indigenous producers and Nambō (South Seas Trading Company) as well as acting as retailers for consumer goods from Japan sold on the village level. Yet in Palau, at the height of the copra business, Palauan copra brokers were at the forefront of a small but growing Micronesian middle class whose livelihood was based on modern currency.[53]

Because they had neither the technical skills nor the capital, most Micronesians were unable to enter into commercial fishing or other areas of commercial agriculture—economic activities that were quickly dominated by Japanese and Okinawans. But here and there, resourceful Islanders broke the near monopoly of the Japanese. The Mortlockese harvested and smoked dried trepang for export to China and Japan, and some Trukese were able to fish commercially for bonito. Palauan vegetable and fruit markets flourished around Koror and, by the 1930s, so large had Palauan agricultural production become that indigenous farmers organized their own agricultural producers' cooperatives in association with the South Seas Government.[54]

A significant minority of Palauans in Koror also successfully entered retail trades, becoming petty shopkeepers—bakers, fishmongers, barbers, restaurant owners, and such—selling goods and services to the indigenous market. For a few Micronesians, particularly those living in the Marianas, the coming of the Japanese produced a windfall in rents. Larger landowners who were able to lease land to the South Seas Development Company at lucrative rates had the means to buy fine new houses, boats, and even cars.[55]

These economic trends quickened during the 1930s. The Japanese government had offered economic assistance and encouragement to help the island peoples, but in addition they came to enjoy a higher standard of living because of the goods and services available to them. In the late 1930s, Japan's war in China and the heightened demands for certain raw materials, and the labor to produce them, led to an unprecedented boom in the Micronesian economy. On Ponape, for example, Japanese needs led to new island industries in fibers, tannin, and certain drugs. Incomes to Ponapeans from exports to Japan tripled between 1936 and 1940. Then, in the next few years, the arrival of Japanese military and naval units further increased the needs for indigenous labor and local foodstuffs. On the remoter islands, where Japanese garrisons were placed, the indigenous populations were obliged to sell all their livestock, fruit, and vegetables, but, at least in these early wartime years, seem to have been fairly compensated.[56]

In sum, the economic prosperity enjoyed by a considerable number of Micronesians during the three decades of Japanese rule was the brightest aspect of Japan's treatment of the Islanders, an incomplete and unintended fulfillment of its mandatory obligations for their welfare. Had the Pacific War never occurred, it is probable that this modest affluence would have caused the Japanese era to be remembered with a good deal more enthusiasm by Micronesians. As it was, older Micronesians in the postwar decades recalled the bustling economic activity with a good deal of approbation, particularly since it was scarcely equaled immediately after the war. "Under the Japanese we had more money and there were more things to buy," was a constant complaint to American civil affairs staffs in the early postwar decades. Economic prosperity was the one positive recollection of the Japanese period, generally accepted and widely repeated amid the litany of woes stemming from the agonies of the war itself.[57]

Assimilation as the "Japanization" of Micronesia

Throughout the fifty-year history of Japan's overseas empire no issue was more important or more sensitive than that concerning the proper place of the nation's colonial peoples within a Japanese order. Imbedded in it were two questions that implied fundamentally opposite answers: Were those colonial peoples distinct races, deserving permanently separate, though sharply subordinate, destinies? Or, through the benevolent agency of Japanese civilization, could they become members of one undifferentiated cultural, spiritual, and geographic entity with Japan?

The issue was never really resolved by those who governed the empire or who wrote or thought about it, largely because the logic of all Japanese attitudes toward colonialism foundered on the fundamental contradictions among the four basic principles that underlay most of Japanese colonial doctrine. The first of these asserted the unique and hence, superior, qualities of the Japanese race, centering on its link to an unbroken imperial line, whose origins were held to be mystical and divine. The second was that, except for the Micronesians, all Japan's colonial peoples, since they inhabited East Asia, shared a common cultural heritage with Japan—the "Great Tradition" of Chinese civilization—centering on the classical written language. Third, Japan's colonial rulers stressed that all who came under the sway of the Japanese sovereign shared *equally* in his benevolence, though it was a matter of great controversy whether this meant that they were invested with the same rights, as well as being subject to the same obligations. Lastly, Japanese commentators delighted in interpreting Japan's premodern history in a way that "proved," sometimes in the face of adverse evidence, that Japan had shown itself to be uniquely qualified to assimilate foreign peoples and ideas.[58]

Out of these discordant themes Japanese colonial bureaucrats began to shape a policy of colonial "assimilation," an approach to the administration of overseas colonial territories not unlike the doctrine first articulated by French colonial thinkers in the nineteenth century. In theory, at least, assimilation was meant to erase all differences between colonial territories and the metropolitan homeland, working toward a point where the colonies would be an integral, if noncontinuous, part of the mother country, their peoples made over in the image of the ruling power. In the French theory, assimilation implied a distribution of both the rights and the obligations of citizens in the metropolitan country to their subjects overseas.[59]

Assimilation never really materialized in the French colonial empire since, in practice, the French government constantly compromised its principles. Yet, based as it was on the republican ideals of 1789, French assimilationist doctrine had an inner logic, whereas its Japanese counterpart amounted to squaring the circle. Although they endlessly asserted the obligations that bound Japanese, Koreans, Taiwanese, and Micronesians to a common emperor, Japanese colonial rulers excluded these subject peoples from the rights held by Japanese citizens in the homeland under the Meiji constitution. Far from regarding assimilation as a means by which the "lesser" peoples of the empire could gain eventual equality with the Japanese, Tokyo's colonial bureaucrats too often viewed assimilation as a useful administrative concept, a mechanical means by which to "Japanize" the thinking, appearance, and lifestyles of the colonial peoples, and thus remold them into loyal, law-abiding subjects who could become almost, but not quite, Japanese.[60]

Through the 1920s, when Japan was still open to the winds of liberalism, there was a good deal of debate among Japanese colonial bureaucrats and thinkers on the meaning of assimilation; in the colonies, assimilation, as a policy, proceeded gradually. Then, beginning in the early 1930s, as a growing sense of national crisis at home and international danger abroad seized the attention of the Japanese government and people, assimilation took on a rigid orthodoxy directed toward an increasing exploitation and regimentation of Japan's colonial peoples. No longer open to discussion, assimilation under force became the guideline for all Japanese colonial policy, an attempt to inculcate aggressive Japanese patriotism throughout the empire. Under the pressure of national and international crises, the tempering of colonial races to the institutions, values, and national objectives of Japan now proceeded at white heat as the nation drifted toward war.[61]

In brief, Japan's effort to "assimilate" the indigenous populations of its mandate toward Japanese values and institutions was pursued through four specific means: education of Micronesian children, the exaltation (if not propagation) of state Shintō, the organization of Micronesian youth, and the arrangement of observation tours to Japan for Micronesian community leaders.

Although the objectives of the public school system in the Japanese mandate were designed to provide Micronesian children with such skills as they would need to fulfill a limited role in the Japanese order, Japanese education for Micronesians was as much a program of indoctrination undertaken to shape a favorable Micronesian outlook toward Japan, to induce Micronesians to think well of their new Japanese neighbors, and to think of themselves as part of a beneficent Japanese order. This purpose lay at the heart of the moral education courses, *shūshin kyōiku*, that occupied a considerable part of each school day.

Such "moral guidance" was intended to help in the assimilation of future generations of Micronesians, but the segregated nature of Japanese education in the islands demonstrated the artificiality of the whole concept. Without the integration of Japanese and Micronesian students in the classroom and on the playground, which could have strengthened both Japanese language skills and some degree of loyalty to Japan among Micronesian children, the results of their "moral" indoctrination, though purveyed by the most earnest and determined teacher, would be as thin as their understanding of Japanese national traditions.[62]

In the late 1930s, as the sense of national crisis deepened, Japanese educators in Micronesia began to supplement this moral instruction with heaping portions of aggressive Japanese patriotism, which added to the already burdened class day. In Palau students were organized every month to march to the Kampei Taisha Nan'yō Jinja, the great Shintō shrine outside Koror, where they offered up prayers to Japanese deities for the success of a greater Japan in Asia and the Pacific, or paraded with lanterns and national flags to celebrate Japanese victories on the Chinese mainland. To a few dispassionate outside observers, this induced chauvinism seemed somewhat preposterous. The American journalist Willard Price, visiting a schoolroom on Truk in the mid-thirties, was shown stacks of childish drawings of flag-waving Islanders, demonstrating, their Japanese teacher proudly claimed, "the pleasure of the natives when the Japanese came to Truk." The sensitive writer Nakajima Atsushi, visiting a public school on Truk in 1941, observed with faint distaste island children marching around the school yard to a Japanese patriotic march, led by a fellow student who carried a Japanese flag and bawled out commands.[63]

Visiting Palau the same year, the journalist Ishikawa Tatsuzō recognized the hollowness of such efforts to promote youthful loyalties. In his small classic, *Akamushijima nisshi* (A diary of red insect island), Ishikawa set down a memorable vignette of his visit to a girls' school in Koror, where the principal spoke in the thick dialect of northeastern Japan and pounded out patriotic marches on an organ:

> Somehow he blundered through the organ pieces and when they were through the girls began to sing in chorus in their high little voices. Despite the fact that they sang in perfect Japanese, I felt the fraudulence of the whole thing. The children rendered "The Patriotic March," "Commander

Hirose," "The Great Hero," "Kagoshima Valiants," and others, but lacking
any understanding of Japanese tradition, and without the slightest reason
to comprehend phrases like *hakkō ichiu* [the eight corners of the world
under one roof] and *isshi hōkoku* [dying for one's country], their singing
was a beautiful, but parrot-like effort.[64]

Religion was also invoked to assimilate Micronesians into a Japanese
order. Although in the home islands, state Shintō had long claimed to
perpetuate the traditional beliefs of the Japanese people, its first shrines
in Micronesia were founded in the 1920s to minister to the spiritual
interests of the Japanese communities, rather than to serve as missions
for the propagation of the faith among the indigenous population. But
in the next decade, as state Shintō in Japan took on an increasingly mili-
tant and nationalistic character, its branches throughout the empire
were enlisted in the attempt to assimilate Japan's colonial people. By
the 1930s state Shintō had become more than just a religion by which
Micronesians were to be led from savagery to civilization; it was seen as
an activity that could strengthen the identification of island people with
the national ideals of Japan, now infused with a mystical and divine
character, linked as they were to a living god.[65]

Government offices and schools began to encourage active involvement with Shintoism. Micronesians were taught not only to pray at
Shintō shrines and to venerate their elements—torii, lanterns, guardian
statues, memorial tablets, and sanctuary buildings—but also to partici-
pate in the rituals, particularly the boisterous shrine festivals in which,
as in Japan, young men chanting and jostling in rhythm, carried aloft
the *mikoshi* 'sacred palanquin' along a predetermined route.

Photographs of the period show young Micronesians dutifully performing these increasingly obligatory rituals. Here on Saipan we see a
group of schoolchildren, their young backs burdened with the custom-
ary rucksacks of Japanese primary school, bowing to the small shrine
before them (Photo 9). There on Yap, a party of young stalwarts, naked
to the waist, dances along the palm-lined quay, the small peak-roofed
omikoshi bobbing along in their midst (Photo 10). Three more groups
jostle along the narrow road behind them, the whole procession
watched approvingly by the inevitable uniformed Japanese officials.

Looking at these scenes, now distant in time and place, one has the
sense that they are at once natural and fictitious. Certainly, the basic
animism and naturalism of Shintō could appeal to peoples whose own
religions were similarly animistic, with no complicated liturgy, no elaborate canon, no vast pantheon of deities. Yet Shintō had always been a
particularistic religion and, by the 1930s, had become aggressively so.
Without the transcendent appeal of personal succor or salvation, its
spiritual boundaries coterminous with the priorities of one nation,
Shintō could hardly have taken root in the sympathies of any of Japan's

Photo 9. Micronesian school children before Shintō shrine.

Photo 10. Japanese-organized shrine festival, Yap, Caroline Islands.

colonial peoples, including the Micronesians. Indeed, the assimilative objectives for which it came to be propagated were offset by its very aloofness, an aspect reinforced by official policy. Shintō's most magnificent edifice in the South Seas, the Kampei Taisha Nan'yō Jinja outside Koror, was never intended as a place of worship for the empire's humblest subjects, only as a focus for their awe and respect. "Though we were allowed to visit [it]," recalled one prominent Palauan after the war, "it was for Japanese only." It is small wonder that today one never hears of any practicing Shintoists among Micronesians, and that no Micronesian is able to explain Shintō or what it meant at the time.[66]

But Japanese attempts to promote Japanese loyalties among Micronesians were not without their successes. Chief among these was the formation of the *seinendan* 'youth groups' among young Micronesian men and women. These associations grew out of the Japanese language classes organized by the navy during World War I, as well as from the men's house traditions on islands such as Palau and Yap. Promoted to further "knowledge and virtue, physical training and public service," *seinendan* soon sprang up on all the main islands and were invariably advised and led by Japanese officials or schoolteachers. Yanaihara Tadao considered them highly beneficial, since they filled the vacuum left by the decline in modern times of traditional Micronesian amusements and entertainment. The associations sponsored athletic competitions, song fests, community construction projects, handicraft exhibitions, and the like.[67]

Yet the prewar photographs of various *seinendan* give a hint as to how they could be exploited for nationalistic purposes. Almost invariably the emphasis in these pictures is on uniforms, flags, and drill: members of the Palau young men's association are shown in uniforms and military-style caps, clustered around a fringed banner embroidered with the Nan'yō-chō seal; those on Dublon Island, Truk, are sailor-suited for calisthenics; on Udot Island, Truk, the *seinendan* are marching off, young pioneer fashion, shovels on shoulder, for road repair under the watchful eye of the white-uniformed police official who steps along beside them (Photo 11). Yet, parades, uniforms, and banners, fused with imperial rhetoric and appeals to local pride, seem to have won the loyalty and approval of hundreds of youngsters throughout Micronesia. From these community associations organized for sports, outdoor amusements, and local pride, it was an easy transition to the *teishintai* 'volunteer units' formed in the immediate prewar and early wartime years as labor battalions under the Japanese army and navy to aid in preparations for the defense of the islands. It is testimony to the effectiveness of Japanese indoctrination efforts directed toward Micronesian youth, that so many young men were willing to swell their ranks, and that even a few *kesshitai* 'do-or-die units' for noncombat service overseas, were formed of Micronesian volunteers early in the war.

Photo 11. *Seinendan* parade, Truk.

Perhaps the most effective programs to win over the hearts and minds of Micronesians were the government-sponsored observation trips to Japan organized for local Micronesian leaders (Photos 12 and 13). The concept behind these tours was a sound one, which has influenced the cultural exchange programs of most countries since World War II: the invitation of selected foreign leaders, current and potential, for a carefully orchestrated tour of the host country, with the safe expectation that they would favorably influence their compatriots upon their return. In Micronesia, such tours began within a year of the Japanese takeover. The first group was organized in 1915 by the navy and accompanied by five interpreter-escorts from the South Seas Trading Company; it consisted of twenty-one island leaders drawn from all the major island groups and ranging from great chiefs to deputy village headmen. In Japan, they visited all the great cities on Honshu, boarded trains, toured factories and naval arsenals, were wined and dined, lectured to, and given gifts. Their every move was captured on the flickery and primitive motion-picture film of the day. If this group accomplished nothing else upon its return, it contributed to the increasing acceptance of Japanese (Western) attire in Micronesia. Departing the islands in loincloths, without shoes, and with their hair bundled up with combs, the Micronesian chiefs returned in suits and shoes, and with close-cropped hair.[68]

Other tours followed and, with the establishment of the South Seas Government, became annual affairs, arranged on a cost-sharing basis,

Photo 12. Micronesian tour group members with Japanese army officers.

Photo 13. Micronesian tour group with Japanese civilian guides.

with the Japanese government paying half the expenses and local communities usually raising the remainder. The members were generally drawn from at least three of the major island groups and, as the steamer headed west and north, stopping to pick up tour members from different islands, Trukese, Palauans, Yapese, and Chamorros would meet for the first time. After the initial landing in Yokohama, the tour would usually last about three weeks. Typically, the group would be hosted in Tokyo at the offices of the South Seas Trading Company and other firms doing business in Micronesia. Perhaps they would be invited to call at the home of former Commander Matsuoka Shizuo, now a distinguished, white-maned scholar, who delighted in these renewed contacts with his beloved South Seas. Then, after a visit to the Meiji and Yasukuni shrines, they would be trotted along the Ginza, tour the wonders of the Mitsukoshi Department Store, and, after crossing Meganebashi and Nijūbashi, would arrive footsore (those shoes hurt terribly) before the Imperial Palace, to be led around its walls and to give three banzais to the living god who dwelt within and who extended his benevolence unto the smallest atoll of his realm.[69]

Micronesians as a "Third Class People"

In the economic boom years of the late 1930s Japanese efforts to win the hearts and minds of Micronesians seemed, on the surface at least, to have been successful. Money in their pockets, and goods and services to buy with it, undoubtedly ameliorated the attitude of Micronesians toward their shrinking place in the islands, and the more mechanical manifestations of Micronesian loyalty toward Japan allowed colonial bureaucrats to believe that their efforts produced results. In 1939, for example, one highly placed official in the Nan'yō-chō expressed the prevailing optimism concerning the attachment of Micronesians to the Japanese cause:

> Recently, the islanders realize the value of Japanese policies and they contribute money for the national defense. Some Chamorros enjoy a high style of living, some of them even have a piano at home. On the other hand, the *kanakas* are still poor, but even in their poverty, they still contribute money for the national defense effort, having raised a few yen from their income. They visit the shrines to pray for good luck and long life to the Japanese military. They hoist the Japanese flag on holidays and sing marching songs. They realize that they are governed in the name of the Emperor, and some request to join the Japanese military forces. This allows us to think that we have made good friends.[70]

But this was self-delusion, a frame of mind that all too often seized Japanese officials when thinking about their colonial peoples. In fact, the bonds that held Micronesians to Japan were made of straw, not steel, and were quickly sundered in the first gusts of adversity. The relationship was too inequitable, too unjust to have been made of stronger sinew. Despite the endless incantations about imperial benevolence equally apportioned throughout the empire, Micronesians were accorded the lowest place of all its subjugated peoples. In the case of Koreans and Taiwanese, Japanese colonialism paid lip service to the idea of a cultural affinity between ruler and ruled. But Micronesians, because they were outside the cultural as well as the geographic limits of East Asia, were always viewed by Japanese colonial administrators as lesser peoples in an empire that, ethnically, was sharply hierarchical. At the top were the Japanese, who enjoyed overseas most of the rights and privileges accorded their compatriots at home. Next came those Koreans and Okinawans who emigrated to the South Seas as farmers, fishers, and laborers. Last came the *tōmin,* 'Islanders' who were designated as a "third class people" *(santō kokumin)* and seen by the Japanese government as being different in status from imperial subjects *(Nihon teikoku shimmin).* No Micronesian could acquire the status of an imperial subject other than by naturalization or marriage. The difficulty of doing so by either means was demonstrated by the fact that by 1934, of all the Micronesian women who had married Japanese men (and there were more than a few), just three had managed to acquire Japanese citizenship.[71]

Within this category of "third class people," Japanese colonial policy made further ethnic distinctions. For example, the Japanese always tended to favor the Chamorro of the Marianas as the most advanced and adaptable of the Micronesian peoples. Below the Chamorros, on the lowest rung in the imperial order, were the so-called *kanaka,* a general, and today completely pejorative, term applied to all Carolinians and Marshallese. Within this lowest group the Yapese, stubbornly resistant to Japanese institutions, values, and ministrations, were singled out as "savages" who were "rather difficult to keep in order."[72]

In addition to the fundamental contradictions between the assimilationist rhetoric of Japanese colonial bureaucrats and the degraded status they assigned to Micronesians, the very idea of assimilation contravened the mandate concept. The League of Nations never intended that mandate peoples be integrated into the societies of the mandatory powers, but rather that they be given such protection, encouragement, and assistance as would prepare them to stand by themselves some day, however distant. Yet, even as a violation of the Covenant of the League, assimilation could have been justified in the light of history if it had awarded Micronesians political, economic, and social advancement as full participants in a Japanese order. Ironically, the Japanese representative to the League of Nations, Matsuda Michikazu, contributing to the League's early deliberations on the status of the mandated peoples, stated this proposition most clearly. "It is contrary to the spirit of Article 22 of the Covenant," he declared, "to assimilate the native inhabitants of a mandated territory to the subjects of a mandatory power. On the other hand, having in mind the interests of these peoples, they should be accorded every advantage granted the subjects of a mandatory power."[73] For three decades Japanese policy toward the Micronesians directly contravened both principles.

At the Margins of Empire

The abject status to which Micronesians were relegated by the Japanese colonial bureaucracy stems from two fundamental causes. The first is clear from the evidence: Japanese officials harbored prejudices toward

Micronesians that arose from the superior attitudes generally typical of a technologically advanced society toward a preindustrial one, as well as from the particular ethnocentrism of East Asia. The evidence for the second is more circumstantial, yet it may be argued that Micronesians were shunted aside because the growing scale of Japanese immigration in the islands made a proportionately shrinking Micronesian population seem increasingly irrelevant to Japan.

At the outset of its mandate responsibilities, distance made it relatively easy for Japan to assume the mantle of obligations toward Micronesia and its indigenous population. On the floor of the Japanese Diet, Foreign Minister Uchida Yasuya had grandly proclaimed: "It is the determination of the Japanese government to spare no efforts in the discharge of this noble mission in promoting the welfare and development of the people of this territory."[74] If the statement was admirable, it was also vacuous, a rhetorical flourish made by a statesman untroubled by the experience of administering foreign peoples and territories, and scarcely cognizant of the effort required to live up to the responsibilities imposed by the League.

Sadly, Japanese frustrations with the Micronesian temperament, as well as bureaucratic inexperience and exasperation with traditional island cultures, quickly dissolved official hopes for quick success in the advance of their Micronesian charges. By 1922, when Japan filed its second annual report, its colonial administrators had begun to express their view that Micronesians were as yet in the infancy of their development. Over the years, later reports came to refer to Micronesians as a lazy, uncivilized, inferior people, whose barbaric and objectionable habits would take a long time to overcome.[75]

Indeed, the image of the Micronesian as carefree, primitive, and indolent had already been fixed in the Japanese mind through the observations of Japanese navy officers during the early years of their occupation. A navy lieutenant who served in the garrison on Yap, for example, wrote contemptuously of the Islanders:

> Without any concept of progress, they have no sense of industry or diligence. Theirs is a life of dissipation: eating, dancing, and carnal pleasure absorb their waking hours. For these reasons they have not escaped the common traits of tropic peoples: lewd customs, barbarity, laziness, and debauchery.[76]

A semischolarly work voiced the same opinion almost twenty years later:

> Because their life is extremely simple and primitive, it is needless to say that their thought is also childish. They do not possess any desire or spirit of self-improvement. Their pleasures are eating, dancing, and satisfying their sexual desires . . ."[77]

As the American scholar Donald Shuster has pointed out, these pejorative views came to influence Japanese social policy toward the Micronesian population. They lay at the heart of the Japanese decision to limit the schooling of Micronesians to "practical education" in manual skills, rather than training for political or economic leadership; they were basic to the low positions and wages assigned to Micronesian labor; and they were the source of nearly every Japanese response to criticism at the League of Nations that Japan was moving too slowly in promoting the development of its Micronesian charges. "The slow pace of progress," Shuster has written, "was attributed to the inferiority of the human raw material rather than to the social processes instituted by the governing authority."[78]

When representatives of the Permanent Mandates Commission asked why, with eleven thousand of them having graduated from the public school system, the mandate population should still be so underdeveloped, the Japanese representative claimed that the aptitude of native children was inferior; when the commission members expressed puzzlement as to the absence of Micronesians in responsible governmental posts, the response was that Micronesian "society did not fit them for the special duties inherent in administrative work."[79]

It is easy to stigmatize Japanese colonial policy as particularly bigoted and reactionary in its attitude to Micronesian peoples. Undoubtedly, certain traditional customs and practices in Micronesian communities would be viewed as noxious by any reasonable Micronesian today and understandably they vexed the Japanese bureaucrat of the time.[80] More importantly, pejorative Japanese attitudes toward Micronesians were no worse than many Western colonial outlooks that degraded and derided indigenous peoples in order to make them accept subordinate places in Western colonial systems. Considering the ways in which European colonials often created images of Africans or Asians to suit European material needs, Japanese views of Micronesian society were far from being unique.[81]

Yet what made Japanese attitudes toward Micronesians different from those Western perceptions of most other colonial peoples, was that they were formed against the background of a growing movement of emigrants from the mandatory power into the mandated territory (see chapter 6). This migration, not unlike the mass influx of whites into Hawaii, Australia, New Zealand, and New Caledonia in the nineteenth century, was duplicated in no other territory mandated by the League of Nations. Through the dominance of Micronesia by weight of numbers, not merely by stern administrative authority, official Japanese policy came to view the original inhabitants of the islands not only with an attitude of superiority, but ultimately with indifference.

There is no reason to believe that at the outset of its occupation of

Micronesia the Japanese government anticipated the volume of Japanese immigration into the islands, let alone planned it. At the end of World War I, the Japanese population in the islands was no more than a few hundred—mostly merchants and traders, along with a scattering of officials—generally men who had come to Micronesia without families and expected to return to Japan after a few years. The South Seas Government, in its first annual report to the League, considered that few Japanese would want to emigrate to such "remote and lonely isles." But in the mid-1920s, the development of economic opportunities in the islands, particularly the sugar industry in the Marianas, began to attract an ever-increasing throng of Japanese, mostly permanent settlers who brought their families with them. Reproducing at a dramatic rate —women came to constitute over forty percent of the total immigrant community—the Japanese population in the islands rose from less than four thousand in 1922 to not quite twenty thousand in 1930 and more than sixty-two thousand by 1937. In Palau, the Japanese outnumbered the Micronesians two to one; in the Marianas they were ten to one; and throughout Micronesia as a whole, the Japanese population was larger than that of the indigenes by twenty percent.[82]

If there were no official directive behind this flood of Japanese who shouldered their way into the islands, neither was there any attempt to halt or even reduce it, a fact noted with increasing alarm by the members of the Permanent Mandates Commission in Geneva, particularly in view of the marginal increases in population among indigenous Micronesians. Though the Japanese government tried to deflect criticism by assurances that Japanese immigration was largely concentrated in the Marianas,[83] the stark fact of the matter was that the increasing number of new Japanese arrivals, whether by boat or by birth, threatened to swamp the Micronesian population. Outnumbered, unable to compete economically, their language, customs, and cultural identity submerged beneath those of the Japanese, the Micronesians on many of the islands might not have survived the century as an identifiable ethnic group had not the Pacific War brought a sudden and dramatic end to the Japanese presence. The point was noted by a number of foreign visitors to Micronesia during the 1930s. "The natives will soon pass on to silence and pathetic dust," remarked Alex Hume-Ford, director of the Pan-Pacific Union. "They are going down before the efficients." Willard Price, no less convinced of eventual Micronesian extinction after his visit to the islands in 1935, wrote that "on all the Micronesian islands the final solution, long-delayed perhaps, will be amalgamation. The brown man must disappear into the veins of the yellow. And he will disappear so completely as to leave hardly a trace of his color behind, it will be diluted in so large a sea."[84]

What was particularly injurious to the future of the indigenous population was that, from a purely economic perspective, there appeared to be no compelling reason for the Japanese government to rescue the Micronesian people from obliteration. Because the immigrant population came to provide most of the labor, production, and consumer demand in Micronesia, the economic role of Micronesians came to be of little importance in the development of the islands. Just as the mounting tide of Japanese immigration drained away official energies and resources that might have augmented programs in public health and social welfare, which in turn might have strengthened the Micronesian population, it also provided the Japanese government with the option of simply allowing the Micronesian population to be submerged.

As usual, Yanaihara Tadao saw the problem more clearly than his contemporaries. In his major work on the mandate, published in 1937, Yanaihara noted that even the most rapacious colonial governments usually considered the welfare of the indigenous population to be an essential concern, if only because that population was itself a resource essential to the exploitation of a colony: without native labor and native purchasing power, the trade and industry of most colonies would stagnate. No such economic considerations existed in the case of Micronesians. They provided the labor for only one industry, mining, and their purchasing power was slight compared to that of the swelling immigrant population. Far from being an economic resource, they were, for the colonial government, an economic burden. Nor, from the official Japanese perspective, were there any redeeming cultural affinities that might offset this economic inutility. Far from being the legatees of a great classical civilization, Micronesians represented a primitive culture, and were therefore viewed as inherently childish and indolent.

After consideration of these views, Yanaihara raised a disturbing proposition concerning the growing demographic imbalance in Micronesia:

> The last question left for our consideration is whether there is a necessity to put forth all these efforts for the protection and increase of a people so backward and uncivilized as the South Sea Islanders, who have been decreasing for many years past. . . . Viewed from a realistic, utilitarian point of view, it may seem more profitable for the government to leave the natives to dwindle naturally and let the Japanese immigrants fill their place. Some might even support this policy on the ground that it will provide an outlet for the expanding population in Japan and allow the more vigorous exploitation of the natural resources of the islands.[85]

One instantly recoils at this apparent piece of social-Darwinist racism. But Yanaihara linked the statement with the assertion that if the protection of the indigenous population could not be based on economic considerations, then it would have to be based on humanitarian ones. Moreover, Yanaihara wrote at a time of increasing government censorship and his statement is really a veiled indictment of a racial policy that the government seemed to be undertaking. His whole career, his established humanitarian convictions, and the tenor and depth of his sensitive research on Micronesia support this contention, I believe.[86]

Ultimately, the failure to stem the flow of Japanese immigration into Micronesia was the most important single breach of the trust that had been placed upon Japan by the League of Nations in 1921. Certainly, no one at the Versailles peace conference in 1919 when the mandate idea was conceived, or at the Permanent Mandates Commission in Geneva where the progress of the mandates was monitored, had imagined a situation in which the indigenous population, whose welfare the mandatory was supposed to guarantee, would be engulfed by immigrants from the mandatory power. Considering the positive encouragement given by the Japanese government to the limitless emigration to Micronesia of its citizens, it is hard to escape the conclusion that Japanese policy in the islands, in nearly every instance, was framed to suit the interests of its own nationals.

Japan's initial commitment to the mandate ideals of the League of Nations was nowhere written into the laws or formal administrative procedures by which the mandate was governed. The heavy bureaucratic cast of Japan's administration of Micronesia was manifest in the omnipresence of legal statute; almost every kind of human activity that took place within the mandate was hedged in by law. Yet nowhere in the multitude of executive ordinances, laws, and regulations having to do with the internal administration of the mandate was there any mention of the origins of Japan's mandate authority under the League Covenant or the mandate charter, of the responsibilities and limitations they imposed. The failure to incorporate the language of either the Covenant or the charter into the imperial ordinance that established the South Seas Government or into any subsequent executive ordinances or regulations issued from Koror, meant that Japanese bureaucrats in both Japan and Micronesia were never reminded of the conditions of the trust under which Japan held its mandate. Conscious only that Japan had been given the right to administer Micronesia as an integral territory of the empire, they had no reason not to press Japan's advantage to the utmost.

In sum, whatever noble task of advancing the well-being and development of the island peoples may have been assigned to Japan by the League of Nations, it was eventually set aside, less by a conscious shift in policy than by the pursuit of opportunity that absorbed the energy and attention of those who governed the mandate. For the twenty years or more of Japanese rule in the South Seas, Japanese, not Micronesian, interests remained paramount. And by the mid-1920s, the prime Japanese interest was to make the islands turn a profit.

CHAPTER 5

Making Paradise Pay
Japanese Development and Exploitation of Micronesia

BECAUSE OF THE outstanding vigor and humming economic success with which Japan eventually transformed the scattered outposts of its tropical colony into small but active participants in the Japanese economic machine, one is inclined to think that there was a well-conceived scheme, a ready blueprint for the economic exploitation of Micronesia from the start of the Japanese occupation of the islands.

In fact, the opposite seems true. Having acquired the islands for essentially strategic reasons in 1914, the government did not at first know what to do with them, particularly after it appeared that their military use was to be prohibited under international agreement. The initial and embarrassing failures of certain entrepreneurs who came to the islands in the early wartime years, as well as the mounting expenses of stationing naval garrisons there, caused not a few men of influence in Tokyo to wonder what sense their government had shown in acquiring the islands in the first place. Indeed, if we are to believe a persistent rumor, some, like old Itō Myōji, adviser to the Privy Council, advocated simply returning Micronesia to the League of Nations.[1] In the end, the navy insisted on retaining them for the same reason that they were first occupied—their potential strategic value.

If the economic beginnings of Micronesia under the Japanese seemed shaky, if some business pioneers through recklessness, ignorance, or lack of preparation, went bankrupt in these tropics, others, with greater skill, persistence, and preparation, founded economic empires in trade and industry. Seeking ways to redeem some economic value from the islands, the government nurtured their maturing enterprises with funds and favorable economic policy. By the end of the 1920s, Japan's mandate was no longer a net drain on the imperial treasury and had been transformed into a small but growing economic asset to the home economy. For the most part, private enterprise led the way, but it did so

118

under conditions most businessmen would relish: near monopoly, absence of outside competition, and generous government support. The subsequent economic development of Micronesia under the Japanese represents an interplay of private initiative and government capital, a combination that had first been successful in the homeland and had been replayed in each of Japan's colonial territories. Monopolies and subsidies provided the incentive for private enterprise, as well as the means to reduce the formidable obstacles to economic success in the tropical Pacific: distance, small land area, and the limited scale of the Micronesian market.

Copra and Commerce: The South Seas Trading Company

Trade came first, of course. The foundations of Japanese commerce in Micronesia had already been laid in the decades of German rule by pioneer entrepreneurs like Mori Koben—weather-beaten, island-wise men who had sailed south in flimsy boats across great ocean distances, struggling against isolation and a hostile colonial environment to put down roots in the islands, ultimately achieving commercial influence out of proportion to their tiny numbers. Several of these small ventures had merged in 1908 to form the Nan'yō Bōeki Kaisha (South Seas Trading Company)—Nambō or NBK, as it was known for short among Japanese and Islanders alike. By World War I, with a handful of men and small schooners, the company had woven a network of trading posts, commercial fishing enterprises, interisland mail, freight transportation, and passenger services that gave it a near monopoly of what modest trade existed in the Marianas and the Carolines. Only in the Marshalls was it kept out by German commercial competition.

As it did for Japanese commerce and industry everywhere in Asia and the Pacific, World War I provided a windfall for the NBK. Not only was the company placed under the protection of the Japanese navy as soon as Japanese warships entered Micronesian ports, but it fell heir to most of the German commercial holdings in the islands and was effectively shielded from all other competition when the navy embargoed foreign shipping in Micronesian waters. Yet the greatest fortune of all was the navy's award in 1915 of the exclusive contract for freight, passenger, and mail service, both interisland and to Japan. With these guaranteed earnings the company augmented its shipping capacity. For the next two years Nambō's fleet of four steamers and five sailing vessels plowed back and forth across the sea-lanes, hauling provisions, equipment, mail, and personnel to and from Micronesian ports.

With the total monopoly of shipping in Micronesia in its grasp, the company reached out for new ventures. It bought out the ships and warehouses of the Kōshin Sha, its last competitor in the islands, and

opened an office on Jaluit, a base from which it was able to take over
the commercial dominance of the Marshalls, formerly the domain of the
defunct Jaluit Gesellschaft. With the permission of the British, it
opened up another office in the nearby Gilberts (now part of Kiribati),
and soon established commercial bases at Manado and Makassar (now
Ujung Pandang) in the Celebes. By 1917 some of its vessels were carrying cargoes as far as San Francisco.[2]

In its aggressive drive to dominate the trade of Micronesia, Nambō
was also aided by having in place the most experienced commercial
agents in those seas, old Micronesia hands like Sekine Sentarō on
Ponape, Tanabe Kintarō on Saipan, and Miyashita Jūichirō in Palau,
men who had lived for decades in the islands, who had long-established
contacts in the local communities, who knew the best sailing routes, the
weather, reefs, and shoals of every island group, and whose collective
expertise helped this company to succeed where others failed.

Most other Japanese who entered the islands after 1914 in search of
quick and easy profit soon wasted their energies, and resources, or were
run out of Micronesia by the navy for shoddy practices. A few, with
brass, cash, and luck, gained fortune and position. Tanakamaru Zenzo,
a wealthy civilian contractor with the navy in Sasebo, was one of these.
Shortly after the navy had dispatched its squadrons south to Micronesia
in September 1914, Tanakamaru chartered a steamship and, with a few
friends, headed for Micronesia, intending to muscle in on the South Seas
trade by staking claim to whatever valuable German territory he could
find. Touring Micronesia that October and November, Tanakamaru and
his confederates put ashore at a number of islands in the Marianas and
Carolines where they put up signs declaring that these were now his
property. When the navy caught up with him he was threatened with
deportation, but luck was with him. The director of the Nan'yō Bōeki
Kaisha, recognizing that the firm was on the edge of major economic
opportunity in the islands, had been eagerly seeking venture capital.
Tanakamaru, abandoning his own freewheeling effort, offered to put
up ¥350,000 to help the company expand its merchant fleet and commercial properties. In grateful appreciation of his largesse, the directors
voted him president of the company and within a few months the Navy
Ministry, which had been ready to throw him out of Micronesia, had
awarded his firm the lucrative shipping contract that put the seal on its
success.[3]

But NBK was obliged to operate within certain limits. The first of
these were imposed by the government which, if it provided protection,
also insisted on asserting a degree of direction. The shipping contract
between Japan and Micronesia was too profitable not to attract the
attention of bigger, more influential, and more cost-efficient firms. And
in 1917 Nambō was ordered to turn the route over to the giant Nippon

Yūsen Kaisha (Japan Mail Steamship Company)—NYK—though it was able to retain its interisland shipping contract with the navy. Moreover, despite government support, NBK was not immune from the economic stresses of the postwar period. Financially overextended in a number of areas, it was hit hard by the global depression of 1919 and was only saved from collapse by an infusion of capital from the Kawasaki Bank, whose board of directors assumed virtual direction of the company.[4]

After shipping, the single most profitable activity for any commercial firm in Micronesia was trading in copra, that versatile product of the coconut used in soaps, livestock feed, and a dozen other products throughout the industrial world. The great advantage of copra was that coconut palms were found on most Pacific islands and the indigenous inhabitants, accustomed to using the coconut as a daily subsistence item, were easily brought into the processing of copra as producers, harvesters, and laborers. The copra trade had begun in German times, dominated by the Jaluit Gesellschaft, but Japanese traders had already elbowed their way into it by 1914. After the naval occupation of the islands, the copra business of Micronesia simply fell into their laps.

Here again, the Nan'yō Bōeki Kaisha was able to get a giant head start. From its new base on Jaluit, Nambō took over from the German firm, inheriting its warehouses, contracts, trade routes, and plantations. Management of the last, some seventy-two thousand acres spread throughout Micronesia by the 1930s, became one of its principal activities and helped the company to garner over seventy percent of the copra trade. With the acquisition of the Tokyo Oil Press Company and its facilities in Yokohama in 1936, Nambō obtained a virtual monopoly of the manufacture of coconut oil in Micronesia.[5]

Copra was produced in all the major island groups. Inevitably, there were hundreds of collection points throughout the islands—nearly seventy in the Marshalls alone—where copra would be gathered and stored to await shipment in NBK interisland ships. Usually, but not always, the storage facilities were managed by a Japanese agent for the NBK. As often as not, the local village producers took their payment in Japanese goods—sundries, foodstuffs, and tools—sold by the NBK agent himself. Thus was born the trade store, of the type that dots so many of the atoll maps dating from the Japanese period. In the Marshalls, the typical station was located at or near the best landing place, on the lagoon side of the atoll (Photo 14). Sometimes it was approached by a stone jetty or wooden dock, but more often the beach had to serve as the loading and unloading place. Typically, the station consisted of a combination house, store, and warehouse, with a customhouse and a bathhouse in the rear. The building usually sat on a concrete foundation just inland from the beach, its walls of whitewashed lumber, its corrugated tin roofs painted red, and "NBK" emblazoned in large letters on the side

Photo 14. Nan'yō Bōeki (South Seas Trading Company) store, Wotje Atoll,
Marshall Islands, c. 1920.

facing the lagoon. From the shelves of this tiny emporium came miso
paste, soy sauce, rice, biscuits, flour, cigarettes, clothes, watches,
towels, pots, pans, dishes, tobacco, kerosene lamps, sewing machines,
fishing gear, sugar, tea, hardware supplies, and all manner of wares
that came to shape the tastes and lifestyles of the villagers whose palm-
thatched houses clustered nearby.[6] Once every three months—every
four on some of the remoter atolls—the Nambō steamer would drop
anchor off the beach to unload a fresh supply of such goods and to pick
up the waiting cargo of copra, dried bonito, trepang, and tortoiseshell
—a trade cycle that seldom varied.

On the larger islands, the company's retail commerce was a good deal
more sophisticated, since the import trade catered to the Japanese
immigrant population. In Koror, the colonial capital, for example,
NBK operated a spanking big department store with tiled front and col-
umned entranceway and, inside, long glass cases crammed with all the
commodities—knickknacks, dolls, figurines, stationery supplies,
cloisonné vases, cakes, confectioneries, condiments, bean curd, pressed
seaweed—that were a daily part of Japanese life at home. Behind the
counters of such emporia on Saipan, Palau, Yap, Ponape, Truk, and
Jaluit, NBK was annually doing over one million yen's worth of business
by the eve of the Pacific War.

From its base on Koror, Nambō branched out into a myriad of other
enterprises. On Ponape, Truk, and Saipan it managed fishing fleets and
fish processing plants. Its subsidiary firms in the Dutch East Indies pro-

duced phenomenal profits from the refrigeration business, from the canning and processing of marine products, and from the sale of Japanese cotton cloth, foodstuffs, and pottery, in return for maize, cotton, coffee, tannin, and cocoa. Another subsidiary, the Nan'yō Bōeki Kisen, KK (South Seas Trade Steamship Company), specialized in marine transportation and handled the company's interisland routes, as well as maintaining a tramp service between Japan and Micronesia. Nambō also acted as agent for both NYK and the Nan'yō Kaiun, KK (South Seas Maritime Transportation Company) for exports, imports, and freight between Micronesia and the Celebes, and NBK buses jounced over the narrow roads on Saipan, Tinian, Rota, and Palau under the name of the Palau Transport Company.[7]

Other companies were engaged in the interisland trade. In addition to some larger firms, like the Taiyō Shōten and the Sōsei Shōji, KK, hundreds of independent traders set up their tiny tin-roofed stores in all the island groups. But they competed over commercial scraps; NBK, with its plantations, shipping lines, wharves, canneries, and above all, its subsidies from the government, maintained a virtual throttlehold on the trade of the Japanese tropics. Its interisland steamers ceaselessly plowed their lonely routes, carrying hardware to the Marshalls, trepang from the Mortlocks, and copra to Saipan. From Koror to Jaluit its three-striped flag surmounted the company's stores and warehouses, and its agents, who, as a group, probably knew more about Micronesia than anyone else, year in year out exploited the island trade with skill and determination.

Sugar as King: Matsue Haruji and the South Seas Development Company

In the beginning, the development of Japanese industry in Micronesia was far more unsteady than that of commerce. The first industrial ventures represented a dismal picture of corporate greed, mismanagement, and callousness. The misconduct of a few speculators seeking to exploit the phosphate deposits on Angaur, in Palau, that early in the war resulted in the takeover of the mines by the navy had its parallel in the Marianas. There, the focus of speculation was the potential of the islands for the cultivation and processing of sugarcane. Sugar seemed a particularly attractive industry to Japanese businessmen in these years. It had been grown with great success in Taiwan where it had invigorated the colonial economy, and the hot moist climate and fertile soil of the larger, flatter islands of the Mariana group seemed ideal for its cultivation. During World War I, moreover, the soaring price of sugar on the international market held the lure of quick fortune for the bold entrepreneur. Such were the reasons behind the formation of two companies in the initial years of the Japanese occupation, the Nishimura Takushoku (Nishimura Development Company) and the Nan'yō Shokusan (South Seas Production Company), neither of which had the slightest experience in the sugar business.

With little knowledge of either sugar cultivation or sugar refining (information carefully hoarded by Japanese sugar companies in Taiwan), and without adequate investigation or planning, both companies established themselves on Saipan, Nishimura Takushoku at the southern end of the island, Nan'yō Shokusan in the north. Each brought in Korean laborers, tenant farmers from Japan, and poor fishermen from Okinawa to serve as a labor force. After several years of dismal failure due to technical ignorance, corruption, and a sudden fall in the price of sugar brought on by a postwar economic depression, both firms were on the verge of collapse. Reluctant to put more money into the abortive ventures, their business leadership in Japan simply pulled out, leaving a thousand or more Japanese and Korean employees to fend for themselves.[8] Already discouraged, ignorant as to how to survive in the tropics, or how to deal with the heat and humidity, and without funds to return to their homelands, these immigrant victims of corporate mismanagement and cowardice soon faced disaster. Exhausted and apathetic, their clothes in rags, they barely survived the next few years by bartering eggs and coconuts for small quantities of rice and cooking oil at the local NBK station on Saipan. By 1920, their situation presented the civilian administration with a major humanitarian challenge. Anxious not to give persons of influence in Tokyo any further reasons to urge Japanese abandonment of the mandate, Tezuka Toshirō, the chief of the Civil Affairs Department, hastily cast about for economic opportunities that would rescue the derelict Japanese community. He invited the Tōyō Takushoku, KK (Oriental Development Company), a firm renowned for its exploitation of Korea, to investigate the possibility of starting some sort of industrial enterprise to employ the castaways. Reluctantly, that company sent to the island two investigators who returned with tepid recommendations for the planting of cotton.[9]

At this juncture there arrived on Saipan an entrepreneur possessed of determination, integrity, and technical skill who not only put the sugar industry in the Marianas on a solid foundation, but did more than any other Japanese to transform Micronesia into a valuable economic asset. Matsue Haruji (Harutsugu, 1876–1954), trained at Louisiana State University (then renowned for its work in sugar cultivation), apprenticed to the Spreckles Company, and destined to be nicknamed the "Sugar King" of the South Seas, had already made his name and fortune in the sugar business in Taiwan (Photo 15). He came to the Marianas in 1920 to look into the possibility of growing sugarcane on Saipan.

Photo 15. Matsue Haruji, 1876–1954. (Matsue Hiroji)

The first challenge Matsue faced was finding out what sort of competition existed and what it was doing to develop the island for sugar cultivation. He quickly concluded that it was doing very little. In addition to the Nishimura Takushoku and Nan'yō Shokusan, a number of sugar firms on Taiwan, seeking to take advantage of soaring world sugar prices and looking for new plantation sites outside that island, had for several years been interested in the development of the Marianas. The initial investigations by their representatives on Saipan had led them to conclude that the topography and jungle cover of the island would impede agricultural development there. But those agents had scarcely ventured outside Garapan Town on the western coast, choosing instead to relax in the company of Chamorro women and to spend lavishly, entertaining local traders and bureaucrats. Few had explored the interior of the island and fewer still had crossed the Tapotchau ridge to reach the eastern coast. Matsue found them no help at all in his investigations, while for their part, as he set off into the interior with a few Chamorro guides, they wrote him off as an impractical dreamer.

For ten days Matsue struggled through undergrowth, crawling on hands and knees behind his guides, who hacked a way through with their machetes. More than once he was caught in a sudden downpour and soaked to the skin; once he fell into a huge hole and was badly bruised. At last, one afternoon he stood atop Mt. Tapotchau, the highest point on the island, and saw the level land stretch east, south, and west to the coasts; to the north the ridge plunged suddenly from the awful cliffs of Banaderu to a broad plain that flanked the ocean. Fingering the rich soil while he surveyed the magnificent panorama, Matsue realized that the island possessed the essential and natural conditions for the cultivation of sugarcane: broad and fertile plains, plenty of moisture and warmth, along with moderate intervals of dry, hot weather. All that was needed was human ingenuity to exploit the conditions nature had so lavishly provided. In the weeks that followed, Matsue became convinced that with care and skill, with the application of the latest agricultural techniques, with up-to-date refining equipment, with adequate transport systems—a railway to carry the cane to the mills, and port facilities to service the freighters shipping the sugar to Japan—and above all, with concerned and rational management, a sugar industry could be developed in the Marianas. It would outproduce Taiwan acre for acre in cane and even rival the splendid plantations of Hawaii, whose latitude and climate the islands more closely resembled.

If we are to believe Matsue's autobiographical account of his pioneer venture, it was not only the prospect of financial profit that inspired his vision of waving fields of cane on the flatland of Saipan, but also his determination to redeem the terrible human cost of corporate incompetence and indifference wrought by the earlier failures of Japanese business. These, he told his readers, he had held to be an outrage and an international humiliation, which Japan should spare no effort to erase. Whatever his reasons, Matsue completed his survey on Saipan resolved to throw his energies and resources into building an enterprise that would transform the economic future of the islands.[10]

No one was more interested in Matsue's arduous investigations on Saipan than Tezuka Toshirō, charged with bringing into the Marianas some sort of economic activity that would rescue the castaways of the failed efforts of the Nishimura Takushoku and the Nan'yō Shokusan. Through Tezuka, upon arriving in Tokyo, Matsue met Ishizuka Eizō, president of the Oriental Development Company, who had expressed mild interest in backing the plan for the cultivation of cotton in the islands. Bursting with enthusiasm about his plans for the development of Saipan, Matsue persuaded Ishizuka that the economic future of the Marianas lay in sugar, not cotton. Backed by Ishizuka, Matsue returned to Saipan in August 1921 to work out the details, which centered on the purchase of the assets (such as they were) of the Nishimura Takushoku and the Nan'yō Shokusan along with their debts, which largely consisted of back wages owed to the employees left stranded on Saipan. Out of the ashes of their ruination rose a new firm, the Nan'yō Kōhatsu, KK (South Seas Development Company)—"Nankō" or NKK—which was to become the dominant economic enterprise in Micronesia. The final arrangements, worked out in Tokyo, made Matsue executive director of the new firm and provided for substantial assistance from the South Seas Government, most importantly, the use of government land on Saipan, rent free, for the cultivation of sugarcane. Armed with this support and determined to succeed, Matsue returned once again to Saipan in the late autumn of 1921 and set to his plans with a will.[11]

Considering the planned scale of his enterprise, Matsue's most essential requirement (after financial backing) was labor. To those destitute and abandoned immigrants already on Saipan, who now were employed by his firm, he assigned the task of clearing the jungle from the broad coastal plains on which they and others would plant cane. These laborers were augmented during 1922 by several thousand low-income farmers from Okinawa, who were brought to Saipan as tenant cultivators and housed initially in the former Nishimura Takushoku barracks in the southernmost village at Chalankanoa.

In recruiting the poorest of Okinawans under such arrangements, Matsue showed his determination to break with the usual patterns of emigration to Japanese overseas territories. These usually involved either contract laborers from Japan proper who were placed under the direct management of Japanese business, or individual farmers who were required to pay all the costs of transportation and settlement themselves and thus, inevitably, were largely middle-class emigrants. In contrast, Matsue made a conscious decision to turn to Okinawa for labor to cultivate the new crop and, in his account of the sugar industry on Saipan, set down four reasons for doing so: there were already over a thousand Okinawans on the island and this would minimize the possibility of friction among immigrant groups; Okinawans were used to a semitropical climate; they were familiar with the cultivation of sugarcane, which was grown on their own island; and recruitment of Okinawans for work overseas would lessen the problems of crowding and unemployment in the Ryūkyūs.[12]

Recognizing that poor farmers were unlikely to have the funds to emigrate on their own, Matsue arranged for his company to pay all the costs of emigration, from outfitting allowance and transportation to maintenance stipends while they cleared the land. Because of the repeated failure of contract labor under direct management in the sugar enterprises in both Taiwan and the Marianas, Matsue turned initially to a system of tenant farming under which the farmer signed a three-year tenancy contract. This provided that the tenant would grow cane and sell it only to the NKK, which thus guaranteed a market for the small grower. Once the land was cleared, it was divided into rectangular plots of about thirty acres, each bordered by a break of unfelled trees about six yards deep and crossed by farm roads running north and south. Within these boundaries each tenant farmer was assigned a smaller plot of about ten acres. In this way most of the central and eastern coastal plains of Saipan were cleared and planted with cane under company instructions.[13]

While the new immigrants toiled in the heat with machete and spade to clear and cultivate the land, others worked under Matsue's direction to construct a narrow-gauge rail line running up the eastern and western coasts of the island, a system designed to facilitate the transportation of cane from the fields to the mills. The distances were not great and the completed line did not represent a brilliant feat of engineering, but it was difficult enough; it encountered numerous gullies and ridges and surmounted some fairly steep gradients—challenging obstacles for a man who was not a civil engineer and did not have vast sums for construction at his disposal. Months in completion, the line soon became a significant and unanticipated drain on the company's resources and at one point caused its builder serious injury.[14]

During 1922 and 1923, other difficulties and setbacks arose one after the other to threaten Matsue's enterprise.[15] Because of labor problems in Germany, he encountered delays in obtaining refining equipment he had ordered from that country. His tenant farmers failed to prune the cane sprouts correctly, and due to the depredations of insects—particularly the cane borer, which destroys maturing cane stalks—much of his first crop was damaged. When at last, in August 1922, he had enough sugar processed for a small shipment to send to Japan, disaster struck. Unloaded in Yokohama later that month, the shipment was placed in a warehouse in Tokyo. Several days later, warehouse and sugar were consumed in the terrible fires that swept the city immediately after the Great Kantō Earthquake. Worst of all, the world price of sugar, a commodity always subject to dramatic fluctuations, suddenly plummeted. The capital at Matsue's disposal began to run perilously low, and Japanese government and business leaders, shaking their heads at this reconfirmation of the unsuitability of Micronesia for large-scale industrial ventures, signaled their disinclination to provide further support. On Saipan, the old fears of abandonment and destitution began to run through the immigrant community once more, and Japanese children along the dusty streets of Garapan and Chalankanoa took to repeating a jingle sung by the despairing workers of the Nishimura Takushoku some years before:

> Listen, Mr. Manager,   *Senmu, yoku kike yo*
> Your end will come,   *Omae no matsu wa*
> Starving on Saipan.   *Saipan no atari de notarejini*

The catalogue of discouragements and failures that brought Matsue's enterprise to the brink of disaster would have defeated most men. Yet, doggedly and resourcefully, with his last funds he undertook a series of measures to overcome these difficulties. To eradicate insect blight he had all the cane fields burned and from Hawaii he imported the tachinid fly to destroy the cane borer. He also planted a new, hardier strain of cane, which had been developed on Taiwan. In order to insure greater attention to proper pruning among his tenant farmers, Matsue introduced a system of cooperation and competition in which groups of tenants were made responsible for pruning, with each group member helping out the others and the best group being given an award (Photo 16).[16]

In these ways, the quality and quantity of the cane was greatly improved and with arrangements for more immigrants, many from the Tohoku region (northeastern Honshu) as well as from Okinawa, to speed the process, Matsue had over three thousand acres under cane by 1924. As the price of sugar began to climb once more, he began to ship his crop to the home islands again. In 1926, to rationalize his industry further, he eliminated waste by constructing a factory on the island to distill alcohol as a by-product from the quantity of molasses obtained in the process of milling (Photo 17).[17] That same year the South Seas Government began work to improve the anchorage and docking facilities at Tanapag Harbor on the western side of the island, north of Garapan

Photo 16. Award-winning group of sugarcane farmers, Saipan.

Photo 17. Sugarcane and sugar refinery, Chalankanoa, Saipan, mid-1920s.
(Kaigun Bunko)

Town, an effort designed to greatly increase the capacity for bulk shipments of sugar to the home islands. Through these means and through
the resurgence of the world price of sugar, the Nan'yō Kōhatsu at last
justified the energy, resources, and hopes that Matsue had invested in it.
By 1928, Nankō was processing twelve hundred tons of sugar a day on
Saipan, and in Japan the company was paying substantial dividends to
its stockholders. The next year Nankō had begun to clear and cultivate
Tinian, just to the south of Saipan and by the early 1930s most of that
island was covered with fields of tall, waving cane, sugar mills, rail-
ways, and distilleries that duplicated the success achieved on Saipan. In
the early 1930s, Nankō expanded its sugar enterprises to Rota, the
southernmost of the Japanese Marianas.[18] By 1930, sugar had indeed
become king in the Marianas. It had brought in thousands of new immigrants to the islands and, along with the phosphate industry, had
become the economic underpinning for the Japanese mandate government. The sugar-related industries of the Nan'yō Kōhatsu accounted for
more than sixty percent of the revenues of the Nan'yō-chō, largely
through port clearance fees for its products leaving Micronesia.[19]

Matsue Haruji's great contribution to Japan's colonial history was to
recognize that the opportunity offered by a single successful industry in
the Mariana Islands could become the basis for the economic development of the Japanese mandated territory as a whole. Although limita-

tions of soil and climate restricted the glittering success of the sugar industry to the Marianas (though sugar was eventually grown elsewhere in Micronesia, particularly on Ponape) its example convinced the doubters among Matsue's compatriots that Japan's small and fragmented Pacific colony could not only pay for itself, but become a net asset to the empire. Bureaucrats, bankers, and entrepreneurs were now persuaded to support the numerous industrial, commercial, and agricultural initiatives that followed. Encouraged by that support and seeking economic opportunities of their own, farmers, fishermen, shopkeepers, and small entrepreneurs of various kinds, were coming to Micronesia in increasing numbers by the 1930s. By this time, Matsue Haruji had returned to Tokyo a prosperous and honored elder statesman. His advice on economic development in the tropics was sought by his government, as well as by Japanese business, his influence was felt on a dozen or more major economic boards and trusts, and his memory honored on Saipan by a larger-than-life bronze statue in a park in Garapan.[20]

Matsue's account of his triumph by hard work and determination over the most discouraging obstacles illustrates how much of the old Meiji entrepreneurial spirit clung to him, in particular the idea of the concurrence between public service and private enrichment. Not content with mere economic success, Matsue viewed the growth of his sugar business in the far-off Pacific as a contribution not only to the prosperity of his nation, but to its prestige as well. Similarly, he saw the award of the Nan'yō to Japan as a League of Nations mandate as a divine indication that the nation's future course (and his future profits) pointed southward. The Nan'yō, Matsue believed, was important not just in itself, but as a base for economic penetration even further into the Pacific, to Melanesia, and beyond, to Southeast Asia. It was thus a valuable asset for the further advantage and prestige of his country.[21]

To the student of Meiji industrialization, moreover, there is something very familiar about the whole process of economic development in the Nan'yō in the 1920s, for if Matsue was an echo of the Meiji entrepreneurial spirit, the mutual interest and economic support between the Nankō and the Nan'yō-chō reflected arrangements typical of the interaction of private industry and government in mid-Meiji times. Matsue's most heroic individual efforts would have been fruitless without major support from the colonial government, for the rapid growth of the Nan'yō Kōhatsu was due in large part to the aid and favors it received from the Nan'yō-chō: nearly rent-free use of land in its early years; subsidies to support the necessary ground breaking, land-clearing, and planting; a favorable tax policy; and a virtual monopoly on sugar production in the Nan'yō. With government backing, Nankō began moving out to the other Micronesian island groups and ultimately into Melanesia and the Dutch East Indies, diversifying its efforts as it went along, into such enterprises as tapioca and coconut cultivation, marine products, phosphates, and warehousing. In return for its support, the South Seas Government closely monitored Matsue's company and obliged it to cooperate in the development of the mandate; by the mid-1930s the company was a substantial investor in the colonial government's own industrial enterprises.

The Nan'yō Takushoku Kaisha: Government Takes a Hand

The Nan'yō-chō was the third partner in the economic development of Japan's Pacific mandate, its chief economic activity being the operation of the phosphate mines at Angaur. There, the never-ending clank and rattle of refining and loading machinery proclaimed Japanese success in the exploitation of the island's single important resource. The powdery white chunks of phosphate were shoveled by Micronesian workers out of shallow open-pit mines and loaded directly into small dump cars that ran along the island's twelve miles of railway to the refinery at Saipan Village on the western shore. Crushed and refined, it was then brought by conveyor belt to an enormous automatic loading arm extending over the anchorage, where a channel had been cut to allow large steamers to come alongside, and funneled with a roar into the holds of waiting freighters ready for the long haul up to Yokohama (Photo 18). By the 1930s, an average of thirty-five hundred tons of phosphate a day were being shipped from Angaur to Japan. There it ended up in agricultural fertilizers or, later in the decade, in explosives for Japanese armies on the Asian continent. By mid-decade, phosphate was the second largest money-maker for the Nan'yō-chō, after sugar and before copra, and, along with those exports, contributed substantially to the net surplus of the colonial administration.[22]

But by the mid-1930s, from the Tokyo perspective, the financial profit turned by any particular Japanese colony was less important than the contribution it could make to the economic strategies and self-sufficiency of the empire as a whole. After 1931, amid a growing national sense of beleaguered isolation, provoked in part by its own military adventures in Asia, Japan had moved to a semiwar economy and the creation of a self-sufficient industrial base. Each overseas territory was to be harnassed more closely to the economic priorities of the colonial power, through more intensive planning, more thorough exploitation of the colony's resources, and greater regimentation of its economy.

These policies formed the background to the initiative undertaken in 1935 by Colonial Minister Kodama Hideo in forming a blue-ribbon commission to suggest means to accelerate the colonization and settlement of Micronesia, to intensify planning for the development and exploitation of Micronesian resources, and to promote tropical indus-

Photo 18. Loading phosphate, Angaur, Palau Islands. (Kaigun Bunko)

tries there. Among the commission's recommendations was one favoring the establishment of a state-run enterprise that could contribute to all these objectives. Thus, in 1936, was born the Nan'yō Takushoku, KK (South Seas Colonization Corporation)—"Nantaku"—with headquarters in Koror and a branch office in Tokyo. In theory, it was an agency of the Colonial Ministry, and on its board of directors sat a suitable mix of illustrious figureheads from both business and government, as well as persons of real authority and influence, including Matsue Haruji, the Nan'yō-chō governor, and a representative of the giant Mitsui conglomerate. The Nan'yō Kōhatsu, the NYK Line, Mitsui Bussan, Mitsubishi, and the Tōyō Takushoku were all important investors in its stock, but the majority interest in the company was held by the Nan'yō-chō. Nantaku, in its first several years, not only took over the direct management of the phosphate mines at Angaur and Fais (in the Yap District), but also funded and indirectly managed subsidiary companies which undertook a whole range of new industries: the South Seas Electric Company (Nan'yō Denki, KK), South Seas Aluminum Mining Company (Nan'yō Arumi Kōgyō, KK), South Seas Refrigeration Company (Nan'yō Seihyō, KK), Ocean Pearl Company (Taiyō Shinju, KK), Nantaku Pineapple Company (Nantaku Hōri, KK), Tropical Products Company (Nettai Shōsa, KK), and a good many others.[23]

Nantaku also took a hand in a number of activities—from hotel management to marine transportation—that stimulated economic development in nonindustrial sectors. As more intensive colonization of Micronesia was a primary concern of the corporation's founders, it sponsored several settlement projects in the mid-1930s on Palau and Ponape. Like those of Nambō and Nankō before it, the range of Nantaku's activities soon spread beyond Micronesia. Amid rekindled Japanese interest in southern lands and seas, the firm moved to establish economic footholds in Melanesia and Southeast Asia. Even the symbols of the corporation heralded the tide of Japanese ambition: its logo displayed the stars of the Southern Cross around the edge of a many-rayed sun; its company song was replete with references to coral strands, the glories of commerce, "heroic mission," and "southward advance." And when the Pacific War came, Nantaku would act as a principal agent of the Japanese military for the management of the resources of the occupied territories of Southeast Asia, as well as assisting the South Seas Government in the accelerated economic mobilization of Micronesia.[24]

These three institutions—Nambō, Nankō, and Nantaku—formed the economic triumvirate that dominated the development and exploitation of Micronesia during the Japanese period. Their roles in the economic development of the mandate were envisioned by the colonial government as being complementary rather than competitive, though the favored position of the Nan'yō Takushoku was often resented by the two private firms.[25] Their relationship with the colonial government evolved in a typically Japanese pattern of economic symbiosis: although their interests obviously weighed heavily in the policy decisions of the Nan'yō-chō, at the same time, encouraged by government subsidies and favorable policies, and held in check by a formidable array of government regulations, all three firms, even the two founded by private capital, tended to shape their economic activities to the overall priorities of the colonial government.

Agriculture: The Fruits of Research

The phenomenal success of the sugar industry in the Marianas was unique. It was unlikely that any other Micronesian crop could produce similar profits, since there was a greater demand in international markets for sugar than for any other product of the Pacific Islands. Encouraged by the success of Micronesia's first agriculturally based industry, the Nan'yō-chō worked with private firms to develop commercial agriculture on the larger Micronesian islands. This was a formidable task, since conditions of climate, soil, and rainfall varied widely from group to group. Moreover, few indigenous crops other than copra offered commercial prospects, and plants such as rice and coffee that had proved profit-makers elsewhere in the Pacific, or in Southeast Asia, usually failed to live up to expectations. Temperate zone vegetables, which were enjoyed by the Japanese at home and hungered for by Japanese communities in Micronesia, rarely flourished under tropical conditions. How to develop a thriving commercial agriculture, adapted to the difficult conditions of the mandate, was a major challenge that required the most informed judgment of agricultural specialists backed by government funds and given time and careful experimentation.[26]

Here the colonial government, true to the historical Japanese tradition of assiduous information-gathering, led the way. The Tropical Industries Research Institute (Nettai Sangyō Kenkyūjō) was established at Palau in 1922 to be an agricultural experiment center for the study of plants, livestock, fertilizers, and pest control programs suitable for commercial farming in the Pacific. Four years later, a branch experiment station was established on Ponape, and a third near Magicienne Bay on Saipan in 1930. Each station was staffed with trained experts, many of whom were graduates of the leading schools of agriculture in Japan, and each was involved in a variety of research activities: the introduction and testing of imported plant species possibly suitable to the tropics; the hybridization of different plants to improve their productivity or their resistance to heat, humidity, or insects; the testing of various fertilizers in the different soils of Micronesia; and the study of insect pests and their control. Each center devoted itself to particular agricultural problems. The Palau center investigated the development of upland rice, pineapples, raw cotton, coffee, and bananas. On Yap, Japanese vegetables previously unknown in Micronesia were grown on demonstration farms, and on Truk another model farm specialized in the cultivation of other vegetables and fruits.[27]

But by the 1930s the finest research work was being done at the Ponape station, largely through the efforts of one man, the distinguished agronomist Hoshino Shūtarō, who came to the island in 1927 and set about making Ponape the center of Japanese agricultural research in Micronesia. A tireless researcher who traveled widely, Hoshino scoured the world's tropics for plants, including medicinal varieties, judged to be potentially useful in Micronesia. Through his efforts the Ponape experiment station became one of the foremost world centers for the study of tropical agriculture. There the visiting American journalist Willard Price found him in the mid-1930s, "bluff, hearty, and rubber booted," presiding over a small agricultural kingdom on which he grew cloves and nutmeg from the Celebes, rubber trees from Malaya, vanilla, pepper, and cinnamon from Java, cashew nuts from India, and a multitude of other thriving ground plants, as well as grasses, shrubs, and trees, many of which were the product of his skillful crossbreeding.[28]

While the experiments carried out by Hoshino and his colleagues at other experiment stations around the mandate were of help to individual farmers and entrepreneurs who came to Micronesia, the primary value of this research was to the large private firms and the subsidiaries of the Nan'yō Takushoku. Tapioca provides an example. Using Javanese cassava plants, which tests at the experiment station had shown to have a higher yield of starch than other varieties, the Tapioca Flour Company (Tapioka Denpun Gōshigaisha) started a milling business on Ponape to produce tapioca starch for the cake and confectionery industry in Japan, an enterprise that employed a considerable number of the immigrants at the government-sponsored agricultural colony at Matalanim on the eastern side of the island. On Palau, the pineapple business benefited from the colonial government's agricultural research. Blending Jamaican and Hawaiian varieties, Japanese agricultural scientists were able to produce a better-tasting, more fragrant, richer-colored fruit. Raised on the broad uplands of Babelthuap Island and processed and canned by the Japanese agricultural communities there, the hybrid pineapple was exported by the Nantaku Pineapple Company (Nantaku Hōri, KK) to Japan, to Japanese military garrisons in Asia, and to other Asian countries.[29]

By the outbreak of the Pacific War, the Japanese cultivation of the islands had wrought a minor agricultural revolution, which, although it had but small impact on the empire as a whole, contributed to the general prosperity of the colony and changed the landscape of the larger islands. Where tangled jungle growth had covered Saipan at the time of Matsue Haruji's arrival, a decade later green swathes of cane waved beneath the sun, broken up here and there by smaller patches of coffee or cotton tended from nearby farmhouses. On Tinian, nearly all the island was taken up with agriculture. In Palau, Japanese agriculturalists on Babelthuap cleared the broad uplands and set out row on row of pineapples, and on all the larger islands, the jungle was increasingly cut back and more land turned over to the fruit tree, the coffee shrub, or the rice paddy. Had the war not scourged the islands, Japanese Micronesia might have become the agricultural showplace of the Pacific. But the bomb, the bullet, and the neglect of Japan's plantations and experimental farms by an indifferent Micronesian population all but eliminated the work of Matsue, Hoshino, and other Japanese agricultural pioneers.[30]

The Environmental Price of Colonial Development

The Japanese exploitation of Micronesia also left scars and noxious legacies. In their scramble to promote commercial agriculture, neither the colonists nor the companies were concerned with the conservation of the islands' meager resources. The forest cover of the larger islands was seen only as an impediment, to be stripped away as quickly as possible. Within twenty years, Saipan, Tinian, and Rota in the Marianas, as well as Babelthuap in the Palaus, which had had good stands of timber, were denuded; the Japanese on those islands were obliged to import lumber for construction, fuel, and charcoal. Though the colonial government eventually enacted timber-cutting restrictions, and began reforestation projects after 1938, those measures were too little and too late. They were quickly overwhelmed by Japan's wartime needs, which, if anything, accelerated the destruction of the native forests. Nor were the hardwoods the only victims of Japanese colonization. On Saipan, the coconut and areca palms that had covered much of the eastern lowlands and a large part of the southern plateau during the German period, were, by the early 1930s, almost entirely gone—cut down to make way for sugarcane or destroyed by the ravages of the coconut beetle. Even cultural artifacts were not safe from the spade and the plow. On Saipan and Tinian many of the *latte* stones, the ancient foundation pillars for Chamorro dwellings, were destroyed by agricultural operations (though the largest ruins, the House of Taga on Tinian, were preserved by the colonial government).[31]

The daily needs of a growing, alien population on the larger islands served to damage the Micronesian environment in numerous other ways. On the high islands of the Carolines, such as Truk, mangrove forests protected the low-lying coastal areas from wave action. But mangrove wood was valued by Japanese colonists for its charcoal, since it burned with a particularly hot flame, and the mangrove forests were soon attacked with axe and saw. In consequence, places that were completely denuded of mangroves were without protection and began to wash away rapidly. The search for construction materials also altered the landscape for the worse. On Ponape, which had few good beaches to begin with, the wholesale removal of sand for use in concrete badly damaged the barrier reef protecting the southwestern part of the island.[32]

In some cases the Japanese unwittingly altered the ecological balance of the islands by introducing plant or animal life for domestic use. To feed the cattle they were trying to raise on Ponape, Japanese farmers brought in "paddle grass," a tough prolific plant that eventually broke out of its confines and became a great nuisance, since it was thick and very difficult to kill. In importing the tachinid fly from Hawaii to prey upon the sugarcane borer, Matsue Haruji may have added to the maddening number of flies already swarming about the sugar mills. On other islands the Japanese imported toads to combat crop-damaging insects, and these places were in consequence soon overrun with toads.[33]

Of all the pests brought into Micronesia by the Japanese, without doubt the Great African snail was the most noxious. Relished by Okinawan settlers as a delicacy (in soup), the snails were originally kept in boxes and small plots bounded by wire mesh in which they were fed leaves and bits of sweet potato. However, in nearly every case they eventually made their slow slithery escape and found their new island habitat to be ideal. With its abundant vegetation, ample coralline lime for shell growth, and the absence of natural enemies, they proliferated horrifically. Loathed by the Micronesians, who were disgusted by the idea of snails as food, and devouring any plant life they encountered, the gastropods spread everywhere and became a serious menace to Japanese agriculture, as well as to the natural vegetation. No successful remedy was found while the Japanese remained in Micronesia, other than destroying the creatures on sight. On Ponape, children were instructed to collect the snails in buckets and dump them in the ocean on their way to school, but the pests continued to infest a number of the larger islands for many years into the American occupation.[34]

Bonito and Pearls: Commercial Fishing in Micronesia

While the development of commercial agriculture required time, planning, and considerable preparation, the richest harvests lay just off the reefs that girdled most of the islands, available for anyone with a boat, nets, and lines. Micronesian waters were inhabited by nearly two thousand kinds of fish, one tenth of the world's known species. Among them were varieties prized by fishermen around the globe: the strong, fast-moving Thunnidae—tuna, bonito, skipjacks, and albacores—as well as mackerel, mullet, herring, sardines, sea bass, and snappers. Prized above all by the Japanese were the bonito, which, dried to rock-like hardness, became *katsuobushi*, used for flavoring soup, and the yellow-fin tuna, which yielded the rich red flesh sought by *sushi* shops and canneries alike.

As in everything else it did to develop Micronesia after the establishment of the mandate, the Nan'yō-chō approached the exploitation of Micronesian waters with considerable research and planning. Following a comprehensive eight-year survey of the character and extent of Micronesian marine resources, the colonial government began to encourage commercial fishing by providing direct subsidies for the purchase of boats, fishing gear, and processing equipment. In 1931, to complement the successes achieved in agricultural research, the government established a Marine Products Experimental Station (Suisangyō Shikenjō) at Palau in order to investigate oceanic problems and to perfect the catching, processing, and canning of fish and shellfish. Encouraged by the prospect of huge catches in largely unfished waters, and by the information and assistance furnished by a friendly colonial government, Japanese fishermen and fishing companies began entering Micronesian waters in ever-increasing numbers in the early 1930s.[35]

Small-scale commercial fishing had been underway for some time before then. Unlike agriculture, modern commercial fishing offered relatively easy opportunities for the individual fisherman, particularly if he had a few partners to share the investment and the work. All that was needed was a small diesel-powered boat, some nets and lines, and a simple processing plant ashore. Even more than farming, these prospects appealed particularly to fishermen from Okinawa, who came to constitute the largest group engaged in commercial fishing in Micronesia. Operating out of Garapan on Saipan, Malakal in Palau, Kolonia on Ponape, and Dublon Town in Truk, they headed for the best fishing grounds far out at sea, fishing from their small craft in most kinds of weather, even the storms of late spring and early summer. Their crews of up to thirty fishermen often traveled for days, watching for flocks of terns hovering over schools of sardine and herring, a sure sign that bonito were nearby. When a school was located the men would scramble to put out long lines baited with sardines. If the school was big, a catch of several thousand bonito within half an hour was not unusual; often there were so many that the boats could hold no more and would head for home. As each boat entered harbor it would run up large colored flags emblazoned with Japanese characters to signal the size of the catch, or would give successive blasts on its horn, one blast for each hundred fish.

Once the cargo was brought ashore some of it was sold in the fish market of the local town, but the far greater portion of it was processed for export to the homeland as *katsuobushi.* The making of *katsuobushi* was a laborious process which, for the average Okinawan fisherman, who had little else but his boat and his fishing gear, had to be undertaken without the aid of machinery or refrigeration facilities. By organizing a flexible labor supply, usually composed of their wives and children, individual fishermen were able to process even the largest bonito catches before the fish started to spoil. By the time their boats had docked their relatives had assembled and recruited casual laborers in numbers sufficient to begin work immediately. Standing in simple sheds with concrete floors, the traditional *hachimaki* around their sweating brows, the workers moved with machine-like speed and precision to cut the heads off the fish, to open and clean them, often laboring far into the night, if the catch was large (Photo 19). Cleaned, boiled, and boned, the fish were then taken to drying sheds for several weeks of drying and smoking until each became hard as wood, after which it would be packed for shipment to Japan, where housewives would scrape its shavings into the family soup. Soon famed in Japanese households for its quality, Micronesian *katsuobushi* was the single greatest money-maker in the mandate's fishing industry. By 1937 nearly six thousand tons of it were being shipped annually to Japan, making it the fourth largest commodity by volume exported from Micronesia.[36]

Given the profits to be made in commercial fishing in Micronesia, it was inevitable that the big companies would soon enter it, bringing with them economies of scale. By the mid-1930s Nankō and Nambō had

Photo 19. *Katsuobushi* workers at Nan'yō Suisan factory, Truk.
(Yamaguchi Yoji)

come to dominate the industry in Micronesia and to employ the largest
number of fishermen and processing workers. Through its subsidiary
Nankō Marine Products Company (Nankō Suisan), Nankō ranked first,
with fishing fleets, refrigerator plants, drying sheds, and canneries on
Saipan, Palau, Truk, and Ponape. Nambō was second, and after that
came a string of smaller, regionally based firms like the South Seas Products Company (Nan'yō Bussan), which operated in the Marianas. So
lucrative was commercial fishing in Micronesian waters that there were
also a number of companies that dispatched larger boats of sixty to a
hundred tons, based at ports in southern Japan, to fish in Micronesian
waters, returning directly to their home ports without touching at any
of the islands.[37]

A host of other commercially valuable marine products from the
island waters had been sought by Japanese fishermen long before the
mandate period: the slippery trepang (bêche-de-mer), which was dried,
packed, and shipped to the Chinese market; shark fins and shark-liver
oil; the great hawksbill turtle, sought for its flesh and its beautiful
translucent shell; and a whole series of commercially valuable shells—
trochus shells, white oyster shells, and mother-of-pearl—all gathered by
Japanese divers.[38]

The most dramatic surge in the fishing industry in Micronesia during
the 1930s came from pearl fishing. Discovering that pearls could be cultured in Palauan waters in three to four years (a considerably shorter
period than in Japan, where the water was cooler), the Japan Pearl

Company established pearl farms in the lagoons surrounding Koror and Malakal. Kept in wire cages suspended at shallow depths, Palauan oysters produced pearls of unusual size and luster, and the company was soon doing a thriving business in Palau. Other companies soon followed suit, and the four biggest formed the Palau Pearler's Association.

It was then discovered that oysters in the Arafura Sea, between Australia's Arnhem Land and Dutch New Guinea, were even more adept at forming pearls. Japanese had been fishing these waters for some years, either as employees of Australian pearl companies or as poachers and smugglers along the lonely stretches of coast between Darwin and the Great Barrier Reef. In 1931, to the consternation of Australian pearlers, a Japanese discovered enormously rich pearling banks off Bathurst Island, near Darwin, but well outside the Australian three-mile limit. The discovery led to the dispatch of a small army of experts from Palau to investigate the find and determine the best way of working it. Within a few years more than a hundred Japanese pearl luggers, diesel-powered and radio-equipped, of about thirty tons each, were combing the waters five to fifty miles off the coast. They were served by mother ships of about one hundred tons each, which brought supplies from Palau and carried the pearl shells back to Koror. Each lugger carried approximately five divers working in shifts, so that from dawn to dusk there were always three men in the water. By the mid-1930s the Japan Pearl Company alone was employing over one hundred sixty boats in the Arafura Sea and sending some seven hundred tons of pearl shell back to Palau each month, a fact that infuriated Australian pearl fishermen.[39]

The divers were well paid for their work, since it was both dangerous and monotonous. Sharks, the deadly stone fish, and razor-sharp coral were among the daily hazards they encountered and, since Darwin was a hostile port and frequent return trips to Koror were uneconomical from the companies' point of view, the Japanese pearlers were obliged to remain in the Arafura Sea from six months to a year. When they at last returned to Koror to spend their accumulated wages, the divers stimulated a phenomenal boom in the hotel, restaurant, and entertainment business of the town during the latter half of the decade. The fishing industry, especially pearl fishing, and the demands it made for goods and services, transformed Koror from a drowsy colonial capital into a thriving small city.[40]

Dredges and Wharves: Harbor Improvement in the Mandate

It would have been difficult for fishing fleets to have been based in Micronesia or for commercial vessels to have called at Micronesian ports without reasonably safe and secure harbors. Fortunately, these existed at all the main ports of call in the mandate: Tanapag at Saipan, Malakal at Palau, Tomil at Yap, Eten anchorage at Truk, Ponape Harbor, Lele (Lelo, known nowadays as Lelu) at Kusaie, and the lagoon at Jaluit. Most of these were excellent anchorages for smaller vessels, but the needs of expanding commerce and industry led both the government and business to undertake several major efforts to improve port facilities in the mandate. In the lesser ports this usually meant simply setting out buoys to mark the anchorage, perhaps blasting away a few coral heads, or building jetties, piers, and warehouses to accommodate the unloading of fish and imported goods and the loading of copra and processed marine products. However, at the two most active harbors, Tanapag and Malakal, the scale of Japanese economic enterprises required extensive engineering projects and a considerable outlay of funds by the colonial government.

At Tanapag on the west coast of Saipan, north of Garapan Town, the needs of the sugar industry necessitated the work. Though the harbor provided an ample anchorage, naturally protected by the barrier reef offshore, it was too shallow to permit the entrance of larger vessels, which had to anchor at a considerable distance in the deeper waters of the outer Saipan Harbor. Beginning in 1926 therefore, the Japanese began to dredge an anchorage and a deep-water channel to the shore and to construct, between Garapan and Tanapag, two concrete jetties, fifteen hundred feet long, with a depth of twenty-eight feet alongside, and to provide one of these with a rectangular stone wharf parallel to the shore. Connecting with the pier were narrow gauge railway lines that brought the processed sugar from the refineries at the southern end of the island. By the time the work was completed in 1932, amid considerable international controversy and suspicion, Tanapag Harbor was able to handle ships up to three thousand tons and had become a major commercial asset to Japan.[41]

The transformation of Malakal (Palau) Harbor at Koror as a fishing base and as the principal shipping point for the mandate cannot be understood without glancing at a map of the area around Koror (Figure 3). It is a mapmaker's nightmare, a jumble of curving crooked islands, narrow channels, coral reefs awash at low tide, and hundreds of mangrove-covered islets spread everywhere like pebbles. Koror, on which was located the small capital city of the same name, initially had no berthing facilities because of the shallows along its waterfront. Malakal Island, which thrust into Malakal Harbor with its splendid deep-water anchorage, was without docking facilities or land connections to Koror. The third island, Arakabesan, potentially valuable for commercial purposes, was also limited by lack of land links to Koror, as well as by intervening shallows and coral reefs. Beginning in 1927, the government began to dredge a channel through to the southwestern side of Koror

Figure 3. Palau Harbor. (UK Naval Intelligence Division 1945, 369; British Crown Copyright, reproduced with the permission of the Controller of Her Britannic Majesty's Stationery Office)

Island, where land was reclaimed for wharfage, and to build on the north side of Koror a thousand-foot wharf that thrust out into the deeper waters of Koror Harbor. Concrete causeways were also constructed to connect Malakal and Arakabesan islands with Koror.

The major engineering effort was devoted to Malakal Island, which was to become the nucleus of the commercial port. Extensive landfills along the island's shore provided level space for the construction of docks, wharves, warehouses, and factories. Oil depots, water storage tanks, coal dumps, and cranes were erected for the refueling and replenishment of arriving ships. With the development of the fishing industry, fishing companies built their own facilities on the eastern side of the island, including a concrete wharf, a refrigeration plant, and a large cannery, all constructed by Nankō Suisan, and by the late 1930s the influx of Okinawan fishermen had promoted the growth of a Japanese fishing village on Malakal, the only one in Micronesia. By the opening of the Pacific War, Koror was the mandate's unrivaled entrepôt for general commerce, its waters sheltering passenger liners, freighters, and fishing craft—almost all, of course, Japanese.[42]

Shipping and the Links of Empire

By the time it had assumed control over the islands, Japan had a vigorous shipping industry able not only to tap the islands' commerce, but to contribute to their economic development through freight and passenger services at rates that were relatively low because of government subsidies.

The major maritime enterprise in the opening of Micronesia to Japanese colonization, investment, and development was the Nippon Yūsen Kaisha (Japan Mail Steamship Company)—NYK—the largest steamship line in the empire, which had taken over the government contract to act as the principal shipping agent between Japan and the main ports of Micronesia. At first, NYK assigned to the Micronesian run vessels it considered could be spared from the more lucrative routes in the Orient —passenger-cargo ships like the *Yokohama Maru*, the *Shizuoka Maru*, the *Yamashiro Maru*, and the *Yawata Maru*, each of some four thousand tons and all built in 1912 (Photo 20). Heavily subsidized (as was most Japanese shipping), the NYK put together two main routes in the South Seas: an eastern line from Kobe to Jaluit Atoll in the Marshalls, by way of Yokohama, Saipan, Truk, Ponape, and Kusaie; and a western route from Kobe to British North Borneo by way of Yokohama, Saipan, Yap, Palau, Angaur, Davao in the Philippines, and Manado in the Celebes (Figure 4). In the early 1920s NYK vessels steamed out of Kobe Harbor for the new colonial territory once every six weeks, swinging southward with a cargo of foodstuffs, building materials, machinery, coal, and

Photo 20. *Omi Maru*, NYK Lines.

sundries, along with a few passengers—mostly government officials and business people traveling first class and perhaps a few immigrants in steerage. NYK steamers heading back to Kobe from Jaluit or the East Indies would be loaded with copra, sugar, Manila hemp, charcoal, coconut oil, and assorted marine products, along with a handful of passengers—officials on leave or returning for reassignment, a copra broker or two, and maybe a few missionaries.

They seem to have been comfortable, these older NYK steamers on the South Seas routes, even if they lacked the glamor or appointments of the great ocean liners. Contemporary photos of the old *Yawata Maru*, for example, show dining rooms, smoking lounges, common rooms, and staterooms that are modestly proportioned but elegantly paneled in teak or mahogany, with only the graceful *bonsai* on the long tables in the dining room to hint that this was not a P & O steamer in a Somerset Maugham short story (Photo 21). Willard Price, who took a first-class cabin in the elderly *Yokohama Maru* in the mid-1930s, recalled with approval the comfortable arrangements, the availability of both Western and Japanese menus, and the affability of the ship's officers, most of whom spoke English. Third-class accommodations, those occupied by the vast majority of Japanese immigrants bound for Micronesia, were a good deal more crowded and spartan, of course—plain-walled cabins floored with tatami matting, and only low oilskin-covered tables for furniture.[43]

Year in, year out, the old faithfuls of the NYK South Seas service, members of a sisterhood of 1912, plowed their stately way along their

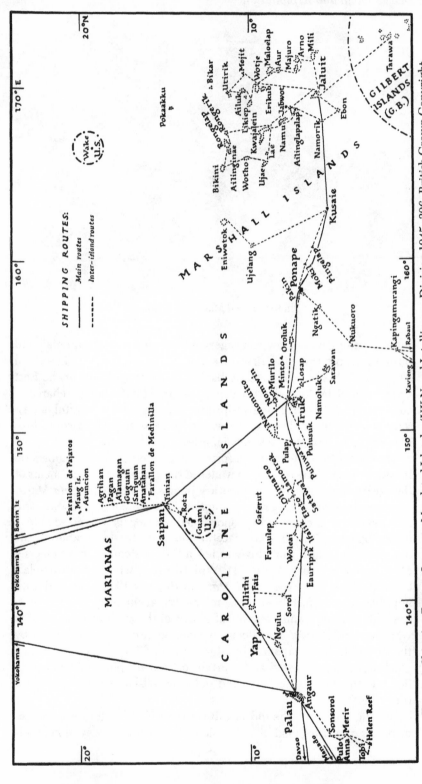

Figure 4. Shipping Routes, Japanese Mandated Islands. (UK Naval Intelligence Division 1945, 306; British Crown Copyright, reproduced with the permission of the Controller of Her Britannic Majesty's Stationery Office)

Photo 21. First-class dining room aboard *Yawata Maru*, NYK Lines.

routes in the Pacific tropics, constituting a vital economic artery that transported people, goods, and profits through the colonial economy in Micronesia.[44] From about 1925, NYK vessels became ever more frequent visitors to Micronesian ports. With the surge of immigration, and with Japanese commerce and industry at full swing in the islands, the company stepped up its service on the existing runs to once every three weeks, which meant that most Micronesian ports of call greeted an NYK vessel, either outward or inward bound, every ten days or so. NYK also inaugurated two new sailing routes: an east-west line from Kobe to Jaluit by way of Palau, Woleai, Truk, Ponape, and Kusaie, and a Marianas run from Kobe to Rota by way of Saipan and Tinian (Figure 4). But the grandest recognition of the heightened place of Micronesia within the economic concerns of the company was the construction of two fast, forty-five-hundred-ton cargo-liners, the *Palau Maru* and the *Saipan Maru*, built specially for the South Seas service. These were fast ships, up-to-date in equipment and appointments, with tastefully decorated staterooms, libraries, cocktail bars, movie theaters, and other amenities. Umesao Tadao, who accompanied the Kyoto University expedition to Ponape aboard the *Palau Maru* early in 1941, noted with approval the pristine condition of the ship, as well as its steadiness, a quality that made him feel as if he were on a cruise through Japan's Inland Sea. To the novelist-turned-bureaucrat Nakajima Atsushi, who took the same ship westbound toward Jaluit in the autumn of that year, the *Palau Maru* offered a luxurious haven from the scarcities and war jitters of Palau, his duty station. A phonograph and well-stocked library, mah-jongg, movies, decksports, and spectacular tropical sunsets provided an almost-cruise-ship environment, while the menus offered delicacies—duck, oxtails, bread, cakes, and fruit from Japan—to be found nowhere ashore in the mandate.[45]

Along with the steady increase in sightseers from Japan in the late 1930s, the establishment of a number of reasonably good hotels in Koror, and the appearance in Japan of a spate of travel books with titles like *Nan'yō wa maneku* (The South Seas call), these amenities aboard NYK passenger ships in the Micronesian service are indications that, just before the Pacific War, the Japanese had begun to add tourism to the burgeoning economy of Micronesia. Had not the militarization of the islands and the war itself intervened, it is possible that the mandate, or at least the Marianas and the western Carolines, might have blossomed earlier into the winter vacation lands for affluent Japanese that they have become in recent years.

While the NYK monopolized the shipping lanes between Japan and Micronesia, the Nan'yō Bōeki Kaisha, under NYK contract, was the principal carrier between the main ports of Micronesia and the outlying islands of the mandate. Just as the NYK routes pumped the economic lifeblood of Micronesia to and from the heart of Japan's colonial empire, the NBK lines kept alive the commercial extremities of the mandate. There were six of them, each servicing the remoter islands of the principal island groups. The Marianas route ran seventeen times a year from Saipan south to the territory of Guam by way of Rota, and five times to the northern Marianas (Anatahan, Sarigan, Alamagan, Pagan, and Agrihan). The Yap route ran four times a year to the eleven atolls of Yap. The Palau run went south four times a year to Tobi Island—the southernmost atoll of the mandate, only two hundred miles or so from Halmahera in the Dutch East Indies—by way of such specks of land as the Sonsorol Islands, Pulo Anna, Merir, and Helen Reef. One of the two Truk lines serviced the islands within the Truk area and touched at the Mortlocks, while the other ran twice a year southward all the way out of the mandate to Rabaul.[46] The Ponape line touched at the easternmost atolls of the Carolines, plus Kusaie and Rabaul, twelve times a year. And, finally, two lines circuited through the Marshalls seven times a year each, one through the Ralik Chain, the other through the Ratak Chain, with extended runs south to the British Gilbert Islands three times a year.[47]

The ships that made these runs were either small steamers of some four hundred tons, or even smaller one-hundred-ton schooners equipped with auxiliary power. Outward bound from their home ports, they carried the sundries and supplies that stocked the shelves of the traders' stores on the remoter landfalls; homeward they were loaded with copra, dried bonito, tortoiseshell, and dried trepang. Their passengers were few in number, mostly Micronesians who rode on deck for half the fare charged the occasional Japanese who rode in the cabins below. Disembarking from these small vessels onto islets on the far horizons of Japanese authority, the official stopped for a day or two to inspect, admonish, and depart; the trader for several years to try to wrest a meager profit from his tiny emporium near the beach; and the artist and poet Hijikata Hisakatsu, in 1929, to spend a decade of self-chosen exile on Satawal Atoll east of Yap. More than mere cargo or passenger carriers, the NBK ships were the outriders of the Japanese presence, bringing to the remote island communities they serviced, mail, medical service (there was usually a doctor aboard), and the assurance that neither those communities nor the small contribution they made to the economic prosperity of the empire were forgotten by those who kept its ledgers.

Aviation Comes to Micronesia

By the third decade of the Japanese occupation of Micronesia it remained only to bring commercial aviation to the islands. Given the generally rapid development of long-range commercial aircraft in the 1930s and the great strides of the Japanese aircraft industry in particular, it was inevitable that the Japanese should seek to link the mandate with the metropole by air. The oceanic environment, as well as the technology of the day, dictated that the flying boat should be the trail-blazer of commercial aviation in Micronesia, just as the clippers of Pan-American and the flying boats of British Imperial Airways had inaugurated American and British trans-Pacific services. Any sheltered body of water near a population center offered a potential landing area, a fact that contributed to charges at the League of Nations in the early 1930s that the development of Japanese aviation in Micronesia was motivated by military considerations.

The Japanese navy, using its twin-engined flying boats, pioneered Micronesian air routes largely because there were no civilian aircraft large enough to undertake the task. In 1929 two such flying boats made a training flight from Yokohama to Saipan, and in 1933 a single aircraft from a Japanese carrier flew to that island. Thereafter, the navy undertook regular training flights to the Marianas from seaplane tenders or from land bases outside the mandate, but there is no evidence that for most of the 1930s the Japanese maintained any air facilities for exclusive naval use. Although a commercial air route had been projected through Micronesia as early as 1933 by Great Japan Airways (Dai Nippon Kōkū), the pioneer flight from Yokohama to Palau was undertaken in 1935 by a Kawanishi flying boat leased from the navy, flown by a navy pilot, and carrying ten other navy personnel (who were hired temporarily as employees of the Nan'yō-chō) along with top officials of the Nan'yō-chō and their wives.[48] Not until 1939 did Great Japan Airways inaugurate the first regular Micronesian run from Yokohama to Palau, using a giant Kawasaki 97-type flying boat which, with its four 1080 horsepower engines and range of over two thousand miles, was the pride of the Japanese aircraft industry and the equal of any similar airplane in the West. The next year the line was extended westward from Palau to Dili (Portuguese Timor) in the East Indies, and eastward to Jaluit Atoll in the Marshalls by way of Yap, Truk, and Ponape.[49] But in this dawn of commercial aviation in the islands, with only eighteen passengers on each flight, the Micronesia route was obviously more a matter of prestige and strategic interest than of profit. Its Micronesian service did not operate regularly until 1941, and then not for long. Like the American and British air routes in the Pacific, it was quickly consumed in the flames of war.

Summing Up: Making Paradise Pay

It has been said of the Japanese colonial empire that its rulers tended to evaluate it with the eye of an accountant. If so, they could not have been very pleased with the ledgers for the Japanese mandated islands in 1922. Compared to its size and economic assets, the mandate seemed to require a good deal of administrative expenditure: subsidies from the imperial Treasury accounted for the bulk of its revenues, its imports considerably exceeded its exports, and the first major efforts of private capital to turn a profit in the islands had resulted in ignominious failure. To a number of Japanese in business and government, the acquisition of the nation's tropical colony seemed to have been a very bad bargain.

Yet, within a decade, a combination of vigorous private initiative and active government encouragement had completely reversed the situation. Within three years revenues from the fast-growing sugar and phosphate industries had made possible a sharp reduction in the subsidies from Tokyo. By the late 1920s the mandate was enjoying a favorable balance of trade, by 1932 government revenues were sufficient to obviate the need for all grants from the home government, and by 1937 the Nan'yō-chō had a reserve of almost three million yen in its accounts (Figures 5 and 6).[50]

In the process of creating this success the Japanese had shown considerable energy and imagination. Of the four principal exports from the islands—sugar, phosphate, dried bonito, and copra—only two, phosphate and copra, were produced during the German period. In developing the other two, private enterprise had led the way, while government had created a favorable economic environment: rent-free use of government land, generous subsidies for the purchase of facilities and equipment, and, for a few big firms, the guarantee of monopolistic or near-monopolistic conditions across a range of economic activities.

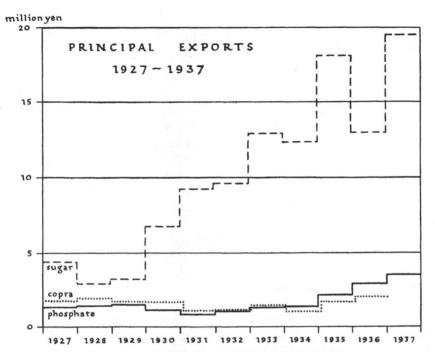

Figure 5. Principal Exports from the Japanese Mandated Islands, 1927–1937. (UK Naval Intelligence Division 1945, 355; British Crown Copyright, reproduced with the permission of the Controller of Her Britannic Majesty's Stationery Office)

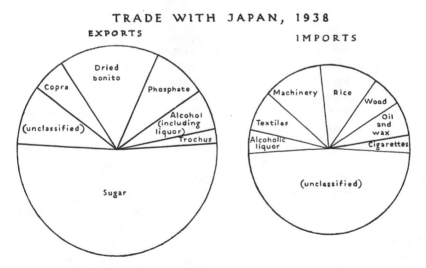

Figure 6. Trade of the Japanese Mandated Islands, 1938. (UK Naval Intelligence Division 1945, 355; British Crown Copyright, reproduced with the permission of the Controller of Her Britannic Majesty's Stationery Office)

The government also provided virtually total protection from foreign competition. Unable under the terms of the Versailles settlement to obtain free trade conditions in the other Pacific mandated territories, Japan sought to keep the shipping and trade of the Anglo-American maritime powers out of Micronesia. This policy was realized less by outright and provocative prohibitions (which would have created an immediate international outcry) than by a series of discouraging restraints on foreign trade within the mandate, including the requirement that all foreign vessels seeking to dock at Micronesian ports first obtain permission from the Japanese government. Not only did such authorization often take an inordinate amount of time, but it was valid only at certain specified ports and only for limited periods. Combined with the monopolies of trade and industry awarded to Japanese firms, such barriers to foreign commerce and shipping meant that no foreign company even attempted business in the Japanese mandate after World War I.[51]

Careful preparation was the final element in the successful Japanese effort to make their mandate turn a profit. While there was certainly no blueprint for the exploitation of the islands at the outset, no other mandate powers between the world wars devoted as much study and effort to the creation of favorable conditions for business and colonization in any territory under their charge. Certainly, in Micronesia, one cannot understand the economic boom in the third decade of Japanese rule without understanding the preparations that were made in the second. The fishing industry is a case in point: without the improvements in equipment and harbor facilities begun in the late 1920s the phenomenal growth of commercial fishing in the 1930s would not have been possible.[52]

Of course, within the larger imperial scheme of things, the economic contribution of the mandated islands counted for little. Not only did they collectively constitute Japan's tiniest colony, but their share of the total production of the empire was minuscule: one half of one percent in 1929 and only one percent in 1935.[53] To the government this hardly mattered, as long as the economy of the mandate grew as fast as it did. Yet no matter how zealously Japan promoted trade and industry and pursued the goal of self-sufficiency for its mandate, its greater interests in the islands were strategic, not, originally, in the immediate military sense, but in the sense that the islands expanded the southern horizons of the Japanese people in terms of settlement, as well as commerce. The colonization of Micronesia was thus to be the companion of trade. Undirected, and given only casual attention by the colonial government in the twenties, its flood-stage proportions by the thirties seemed to be the dominant fact of the Japanese presence in the islands just before the Pacific War.

CHAPTER 6

From Ripple to Riptide

Japanese Immigration into Micronesia

IT IS AS DIFFICULT today as it would have been in 1918 to conceive how dramatic was the transformation of the island landscape wrought by the great numbers of Japanese who swept into the high islands of Micronesia between the world wars. Forty years after the repatriation of nearly all the Japanese from Micronesia it is as astonishing to realize that the present number of Micronesians is scarcely five thousand more than the total population (Japanese and Micronesian) of the region on the eve of the Pacific War.[1] Even with this increase, most of the islands seem to the postwar visitor to have a strangely empty look. There is overcrowding, miserable in aspect, in certain places in the Carolines and the Marshalls, of course. One can hardly visit Ebeye islet on Kwajalein, tour the eastern end of Majuro, or drive along the western shore of Moen in the Truk group, and not see it. But these scenes represent as much the economic disequilibrium and the social tragedies of bureaucratic neglect or mismanagement as the pressures of an exploding population straining against the narrow confines of the island. For the most part, as one passes through the park-like expanses of Saipan, the lonely broad uplands of Rota, the hilly grasslands of Babelthuap, or the forested interiors of Ponape, the land seems unused, untrodden, and generally unpeopled. Yet half a century ago these areas were a checkerboard of cane fields, pineapple plantations, and rice paddies, dotted here and there with tidy village clusters, and (in the Marianas) laced with roads and railway lines. Even the present district centers seem oddly disjointed in arrangement, loose collections of buildings separated by vacant areas of weeds, grass, or trees. The effect is not always unpleasing to the eye, but is somewhat desultory in prospect, scarcely conveying the purpose, planning, or rhythms of a town. It requires some effort to imagine that most of these were once boom towns where government buildings, hospitals, factories, warehouses, radio stations, and newspaper offices competed for space with homes and shops densely packed along the crowded streets where handcart peddlers, bicycles, and an occasional automobile shared the way with parasol-carrying house-wives in white cotton yukata shopping for groceries and housewares, fishermen trudging to their boats, knots of giggling schoolchildren, knapsacks on their backs, postmen and policemen on their rounds, the bells on their bicycles ping-pinging peremptorily as they passed.

Little is left to remind us that these scenes ever existed. The blast of bombs, the near total evacuation of the once-thriving immigrant com-munities, the passing of four decades, and the understandable indiffer-ence of the present populations in these places to the preservation of the relics of a bygone colonial era, have obliterated almost every trace of the Japanese colonial presence. Scattered stone foundations, a rusting railway engine, an occasional stone marker half-hidden in the weeds, its feathery characters chipped and scarcely legible even under the tropical sun, are all that remain to certify that a vigorous, aggressive, and pro-lific people passed this way.

The Islands before the Immigrant Tide

In 1918 the high islands of Micronesia lay like an empty stage awaiting the appearance of a crowd of extras. Germany had never peopled the islands and its scant colonial population—a small band of officials, some traders, and a scattering of missionaries—had been packed off some years before. The German administrative centers were mere clus-ters of isolated buildings. Garapan had several thousand civilian inhabi-tants—Chamorros mostly, and some Carolinians—and its buildings, mostly wood and thatch, were strung out along the western shore of Saipan. Tinian was essentially uninhabited and Songsong Village on Rota was a collection of a few palm-thatch houses. Koror Town in the Palaus was surrounded by woods and grassland, and Jabor Town on Jaluit in the Marshalls centered largely on the stores and warehouses of the Nan'yō Bōeki. Only Kolonia, on the gently sloping heights around Ponape Harbor could boast of buildings—including a church and a gov-ernor's residence—sufficiently numerous and imposing to satisfy the conception of a true center of colonial administration.

The island landscapes themselves showed little human handiwork. Except for pockets of subsistence gardens, the Marianas still lay under primary jungle cover, their forests as yet untouched by axe or saw, their soil unturned by spade or plow. Sword grass still covered the uplands of Yap and Babelthuap, as forests covered those on Truk, Ponape, and Kusaie. Only the rows of coconut palms in the Marshalls and the white slashes of the open-pit mines on Angaur displayed the ordered workings of planter and mine operator.

The Japanese population—not counting the members of the navy's temporary garrison, the Provisional South Seas Defense Force—still numbered only a few hundred souls throughout Micronesia. To the original handful of traders, schooner captains, and fishermen who had come to dominate the commercial life of the islands during the last decade of German rule, the Japanese occupation brought a growing number of civilian officials, as well as a scattering of opportunists of varying shades of rascality. The first sizable numbers of immigrants, some two thousand all told, had arrived in the Marianas between 1916 and 1918, under contract to such ill-fated enterprises as the Nishimura Takushoku and the Nan'yō Shokusan; by 1920 there were approximately three thousand Japanese civilians in Micronesia. But so complete were the initial Japanese corporate failures in the Marianas and so abject the condition of those who had emigrated there, that the latter were survivors rather than settlers. For its part, the government, which had acquired the islands for their strategic advantage rather than their prospects for colonization, in these years showed little inclination to promote immigration.

Nankō and the First Immigrant Wave

Five years later, the success of Matsue Haruji's sugar enterprise turned a ripple of emigrant interest in Micronesia into a riptide migration over the next fifteen years. Heartened by the success of the first wave of Nankō employees and by the conditions of settlement in the Marianas offered them by the company, a growing number of Japanese, at first mostly poor farmers, signed up to cultivate the cane or work in the mills in the three major islands. By 1925 more than five thousand Japanese were settled in the Marianas, out of a total Japanese population in Micronesia of seven thousand. Five years later, the total number was nearly twenty thousand, of whom fifteen thousand were in the Marianas.[2] This was the beginning of an upward curve of Japanese immigration into Micronesia, the sweeping line of which was not to be broken until the approach of the Pacific War.

Despair and hope both played their part in creating this migratory surge into the Marianas during the 1920s. Despair was the natural result of a series of economic calamities in Japan: the joblessness in Tokyo in the years following the Great Kantō Earthquake of 1923, the heavy blows to the national economy by the world crisis later in the decade, and a series of ruinous crop failures in northern Japan. By decade's end, there were large numbers of landless, jobless, and discouraged men and women, largely from rural Japan, crowded together with too little land or opportunity; many of them welcomed a chance to start over—anywhere. Since Meiji times, emigration had offered such a hope. But by

the mid-1920s, doors once open to the prospective Japanese emigrant—
in the United States and the British Commonwealth particularly—were
closed. Others remained ajar: Brazil, parts of Southeast Asia, Manchuria, Karafuto (Sakhalin), Korea, and Taiwan. Although thousands went
to those places, to many Japanese each of those areas seemed flawed as a
prospective home. Brazil was too distant, Southeast Asia meant living as
an alien in an alien land, life in Manchuria and Karafuto were too harsh
and bitter, Taiwan and Korea were too crowded. In contrast, Japan's
new possessions in the South Seas seemed the ideal compromise: islands
over the horizon, yet not half the globe away, places of perpetual summer where a farmer wouldn't break his hoe on the frozen ground,
national territories where a Japanese could become an accepted, secure
citizen. Finally, there were the beneficial arrangements offered to those
who hired with the Nan'yō Kōhatsu to work in its sugar enterprises in
the Mariana Islands. More than any other single factor, the lure of these
benefits set in motion a mounting tide of immigration that was to
Japanize Micronesia. In the Marianas, this was not an uncoordinated
movement of individual families to a wild jungle frontier that they
cleared and cultivated on their own, but rather an infusion of great
numbers of Japanese, recruited by a large company to work its lands
and factories under a strict, but generous, paternalism.

Nankō provided for two different kinds of contract immigrants coming to the Marianas under its auspices: tenant farmers *(kosakunin)*, who
cultivated sugarcane under contract to Nankō, and laborers *(sagyōfu)*,
who worked on farms and in mills directly managed by the company or
on land managed by tenant farmers. Upon arriving in the Marianas,
each tenant farmer was given a lease on about five or six hectares of
company land, which usually had already been cleared. The agreement
usually stipulated that they were to cultivate at least four hectares each
year with cane (the remaining land being theirs to do with as they
pleased) under the strict supervision of the company. At harvest time, 12
percent of the cultivated crop had to be delivered to the Nan'yō
Kōhatsu; the rest would be sold to it at a price set by the Nan'yō-chō.
Though the farmers had no choice in the matter of the sale, at least they
had a guaranteed buyer at a fixed price, no matter what sugar sold for
on the international market. Moreover, if their crop in any particular
year was meager, the farmers were exempt from turning over any portion of it to the company. Laborers under contract to the company
worked for wages on a scale set by the Nan'yō-chō. Most came to the
Marianas in this capacity until they had saved enough to go into business for themselves, either as tenants or even independent farmers, or as
tradespeople or artisans, depending on their skills.[3]

Independent farmers were also permitted to emigrate to Micronesia,
but they never figured largely in numbers or in the economic develop-

ment of the Marianas. Few of those who sought to emigrate had the capital to pay for the passage, for outfitting, for livestock, tools, and the other requirements necessary to farm in the islands on their own, let alone the ability to maintain themselves on the modest profits from growing cane there.[4] In contrast, each emigrant under contract to Nankō was provided by the company with rail fare to Yokohama from the place of recruitment and with third-class passage to the Marianas aboard one of the NYK vessels. They were also given money for agricultural tools and livestock, for the construction of a small wood-framed, zinc-roofed farmhouse, and for living expenses for the first year. Having landed at Tanapag on Saipan, Tinian Town, or Songsong Village on Rota, the new arrivals would be housed for several weeks in company dormitories where they were instructed in the company's agricultural techniques, imbued with its ethos, and admonished to work with diligence and in harmony with their fellow immigrants. Their daily necessities of rice, *miso* paste, and the rest could be bought cheaply at the company's canteens; medical care was furnished to them free of charge by the company, and their recreation—mah-jongg, *shōgi*, table tennis, singing, and various group activities—took place in the company's clubhouses.[5]

For laborer and tenant farmer alike a contract to work for Nankō in the Marianas provided no sinecure. It required long months of backbreaking labor in the fields or in the mills under a glaring sun, their recompense coming literally from the sweat of their brows. But for thousands, and soon tens of thousands, from the most impoverished prefectures of Japan it was a welcome new start, a life often better than they had known in the homeland, one that required only the smallest amount of cash to start with, the minimum of economic risk, and the prospect of modest profit within a few years.[6]

The Patterns of Immigration

For Japanese from the Ryūkyū Islands, Okinawa in particular, Micronesia seemed to hold the greatest hope for new beginnings. Among the poorest of the nation's prefectures, with a population density greater than most of the rest of Japan, a great surplus of labor, and too little land, the Ryūkyūs had begun to experience intolerable economic and population pressures even before 1900. Physically isolated from the Japanese mainland and victims of social discrimination for their rustic ways and dialect when they traveled there, Okinawans could not hope to find a place in Japan proper. What was worse, they were not even masters in their own land. Beginning in the late nineteenth century, after Japan had annexed their islands, Japanese from the mainland had arrived to form a new elite that filled the ranks of local government, monopolized the trade and business of the Ryūkyūs, and jibed at the country bumpkin speech and bizarre manners of the indigenes. To escape these miseries and humiliations, emigration seemed to be the best answer. By 1907 more than ten thousand Okinawans were scattered throughout the Pacific, from New Caledonia to Peru, working largely as field hands and unskilled labor. For the most part they were *dekasegi*, emigrants who worked abroad in the hope that they would one day return to their homeland and, in the meantime, sent remittances to their families and relatives who had remained behind.[7]

To the unfortunate peoples of the Ryūkyūs, the Japanese movement into the South Seas seemed to open new doors. To the Okinawans, neither the distance nor the climate of the Marianas appeared to present any great change from their home islands, and they were quick to take advantage of the opportunities available in the seemingly empty new territories. The first Okinawans, a group of seventeen fishermen, arrived in Saipan in 1915, but it was the sugar industry that attracted the first real wave of immigrants from the Ryūkyūs. Victimized by the recklessness and neglect of Japanese business, they were rescued by the energies and concern of Matsue Haruji in the early 1920s. Possessing traits of solidarity, hard work, and frugality that made them ideal settlers, they were recruited heavily by the Nan'yō Kōhatsu, and their numbers increased substantially in the years that followed. Year after year, they came southward on the steamers of the NYK to the Marianas and the Palaus, some eventually eastward into the central and eastern Carolines, and a very few into the Marshalls. After 1925, Okinawans came to constitute not merely the largest bloc within the Japanese colonial population, but an absolute majority of Japanese settlers, whose growth outran even the ballooning rate of overall Japanese immigration into Micronesia.[8]

If Okinawa furnished the major supply of Japanese immigrants into Micronesia in the interwar years, by virtue of proximity and economic opportunity, the Marianas became their chief destination. In the three major islands of the southern half of the Marianas—Saipan, Tinian, and Rota—Japanese congregated in the greatest numbers, constituting 67 percent of the total colonial population in the 1920s, and 75 percent by the early 1930s. By 1939, however, a little less than 57 percent of the colonial population lived in the southern Marianas, almost 27 percent in the Palaus, about 10 percent in the central and eastern Carolines, and a negligible percentage was scattered throughout the rest of the mandate. By the end of the 1930s, the increase in the immigration into the Marianas had slowed somewhat, while that into the Palaus had increased (for reasons I shall mention shortly), but the Marianas maintained their dominant place in the demographic profile of Micronesia.[9]

Within the Marianas, agriculture remained the most important single occupation of the Japanese settlers, specifically agriculture related to the Nankō sugar enterprise, though those engaged in farming by no means represented an absolute majority. As the islands rapidly became settled, other businesses, heartened by the successes of the NKK, began to establish themselves there and to provide employment for willing hands. At the same time, other immigrants, less tied to the soil—shopkeepers, artisans, dealers, vendors of various kinds—took up residence and offered a range of goods and services sought by the burgeoning agricultural communities (Photo 22). But throughout the entire span of the Japanese presence in Micronesia, sugar was always king in the Marianas, the commodity on which all other economic activity, and thus all livelihood, depended, directly or indirectly.[10]

If the Ryūkyūs, the Marianas, and agriculture, each in different ways, continued to dominate the patterns of Japanese migration into Micronesia by the late 1920s, there was one important change in the demographic pattern of the immigrant communities there. The first arrivals earlier in the decade had been groups of single men who had come as laborers in the *dekasegi* tradition, bachelors or men without their families who viewed Micronesia as a temporary workplace and who hoped some day to return to their homeland, their labor, perseverance, and thrift rewarded with a modest fortune. Toiling in the sugar mills and cane fields of Saipan, the men from Okinawa sang the

Photo 22. Kikuchi Shōten, general store, established in 1921, Garapan Town, Saipan.

quavering melody of the *"Nan'yō kouta"* 'South Seas Air', written by one of their own, and the words gave voice to their longing and their hope:

> Leaving my folks and brothers and sisters back home,
> I've come to live in the South Seas of my dreams
> Some day, in early spring, when the blossoms are in bloom
> I'll go home with fame and fortune.[11]

The *dekasegi* tradition never entirely died out during the Japanese period in Micronesia, particularly among the Okinawan communities. Yet, as colonization of the islands was an objective shared by both Nankō and the Nan'yō-chō, and as colonial settlement is an activity that can hardly be sustained by single men who plan to pull up stakes and leave, it was inevitable that they were increasingly replaced by hardy young immigrant families willing to put down roots. Encouraged by business and government, the family became the cooperative production unit for the Japanese development of Micronesia and the proportion of women increased—marked by a shift in the male-female ratio from five to one in 1920 to three to two in 1935. Family workers were replacing the male labor battalions of the early 1920s.[12]

This demographic change had two important consequences. First, the immigrant society throughout Micronesia, but particularly in the Marianas, took on greater permanency, giving Japan a greater stake in Micronesia than ever before. To the profit and strategic advantage the islands provided, was now added responsibility for the lives and welfare of tens of thousands of Japanese families, an additional reason to view the islands not as mandated territories on loan from the League of Nations, but as an integral part of the empire. Second, the increasing number of Japanese women of childbearing age meant that a vigorous increase in the number of births each year added to the rising number of Japanese in the islands. That number was now more than doubling approximately every five years: there were nearly 20,000 in 1930 and over 50,000 (of whom nearly 40,000 were in the Marianas) by 1935, the year in which the Japanese population shot past the nearly static number of Micronesians (Figure 7). As a process of Japanization, this flood of immigration from Japan—Willard Price, visiting the islands at mid-decade called it a riptide—was more devastatingly effective than any government policy of assimilation could ever have been. In the largest of the Marianas, the indigenous population moved or was pushed to the margins of land occupied and tilled by Japanese settlers.[13] And still the flood came on. By 1940 the total Japanese population had climbed to 77,000; by 1941 it had surpassed 93,000; and, in 1942, it reached a high watermark of over 96,000. Had not subsequent disaster overtaken Japan and its empire, there is little reason to believe that the numbers would have halted at 100,000.

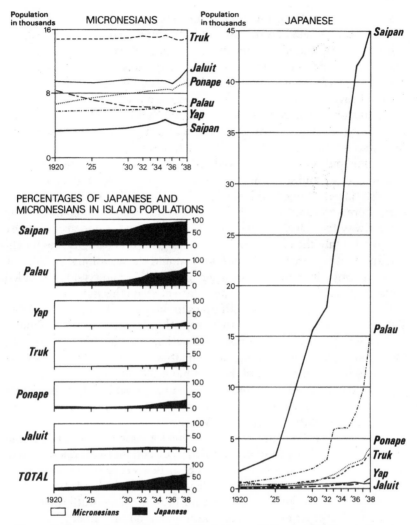

Figure 7. Comparison of Growth of Japanese and Micronesian Populations in the Japanese Mandated Islands, 1920–1938. (Redrawn by Noel Diaz from UK Naval Intelligence Division 1945, 324)

The Changing Face of the Marianas

By the mid-1930s this migratory flood had radically transformed the landscape of Saipan, the home of some three thousand Chamorros and Carolinians and more than twenty thousand Japanese. Except for the central mountain core, most of the island was now laid out to sugarcane, according to the original arrangements prescribed by Matsue Haruji: rectangular plots of about thirty-six acres, each bordered by breaks of trees and crisscrossed by narrow farm roads. Here and there were small plots of vegetables and fruit trees neatly tended. Coffee and pineapples flourished on the slopes of Mt. Tapotchau and in the southern part of the island the marshlands around Lake Susupe were converted to rice paddies (Figure 8). Beneath the towering smokestacks of the refineries at Chalankanoa, diminutive engines at the head of long trains of sugar-laden flatcars chuff-chuffed up the western shore of Matsue's narrow-gauge railway to the waiting freighters at Tanapag Harbor (Photo 23). On the way, they passed through Garapan, which had become a boom town of over fifteen thousand, mostly Japanese, its streets laid out in grid fashion and its blocks of densely packed, box-like wooden houses and stores all but submerging the occasional hacienda of Spanish times or stone building of the German period. Dotting the landscape here and there were small Japanese hamlets, some connected by the railway that circled three-fourths of the island, some accessible by dirt road. Only the clusters of poorer indigenous housing at the northern and southern extremities of Garapan and the occasional farmhouse of a wealthy Chamorro landowner around the countryside provided evidence that Micronesians had any place at all on this island.[14]

On Tinian, just two and a half miles to the south of Saipan, Micronesians did not even exist. More than any other territory in the mandate, Tinian was the island that Japan—or rather Nankō—built (Figure 9). With only a handful of indigenous inhabitants, second in area of the Japanese-held Marianas, and the least mountainous of all the chain, the island had been lived on by only a dozen or so Japanese after the failure of Japanese enterprises there had caused it to be abandoned by the first immigrant population after World War I.

Then, in 1926, Matsue, having obtained a lease on the entire island from the colonial government, decided to extend his sugar operations to Tinian. The first few laborers and tenant farmers, most of them from Saipan, arrived late in that year to begin clearing the land, but money, immigrants, and engineers did not pour into the island until the following year. The experience and techniques learned on Saipan, as well as the more level contours of the land, meant that the sugar enterprise developed much more rapidly than it had on the larger island. Since only a handful of the indigenous inhabitants remained on Tinian, Matsue could arrange his population centers, factories, and communications networks much as he chose. At Songsong, on the southeastern coast of the island, he directed construction of a town, with refinery and warehouses placed parallel to the shallow harbor where the bottom was eventually dredged and docks built to accommodate the freighters that would haul the tons of bagged sugar to Japan. On the gentle slope leading up from the shore, railway sheds, offices, a clubhouse, dispensary, canteen, and nearly seventy neat little company houses went up between 1927 and 1929. As on Saipan, the land was divided up into

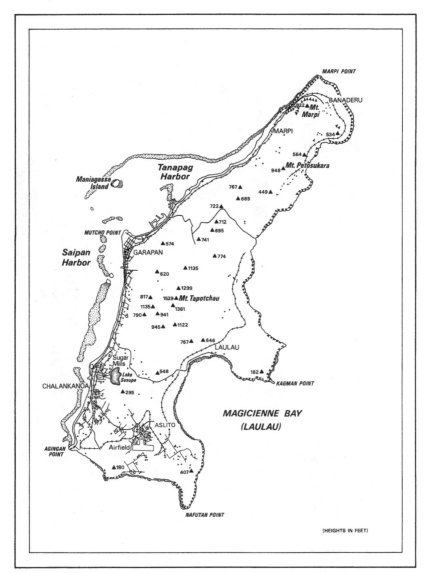

Figure 8. Saipan, Mariana Islands, c. 1938. (Drawn by Noel Diaz)

rectangular plots of cane that collectively covered more than eighty percent of the island, so that it functioned as a huge plantation. Roads, following the regular arrangements of the fields, crosshatched the gentle surface of the land and a narrow-gauge rail line from the town ran up the center of the island to its northern terrace, with spur lines connecting the small hamlets that sprang up as Japanese immigrants began to flood in at decade's end.[15]

Photo 23. Narrow-gauge sugar train railway, Saipan. (Yamaguchi Yoji)

With virtually no Micronesian population to contend with, the Japanization of Tinian was rapid and thorough in the years that followed. By 1930 there were nearly six thousand settlers on the island and by 1935 there were almost fourteen thousand.[16] In 1933, the Saipan Branch Government established a district office (headed by a *shochō*, appointed by and responsible to the branch governor) and changed the name of Songsong Village to Tinian Town, to follow the town-village system of rural Japan.[17] The first school was built in 1931, a community shrine went up that same year, and the usual array of local civic and community organizations quickly followed. While Tinian Town developed as the island's population and industrial center, small hamlets— Marpo, Kahi, and Churo—grew up about the island, their wood-walled, zinc-roofed houses clustered about the principal road crossings. In its human aspect Tinian had become as Japanese as any place in the home islands. Yet the brilliant green that blanketed the island from Lalo Point in the south to Ushi Point in the north, the relentless sun, and the dramatic blues of the surrounding waters proclaimed that this was Japan in the tropics.

Rota was the last of the three largest of the Marianas to be developed and colonized. Slanted generally northeast-southwest, the island was roughly rectangular in shape and divided between Sabana, an elevated plateau in the western half, and Sinapalu, a lower tableland to the east (Figure 10). A narrow peninsula extended from the southwestern edge of the island, ending in a ridged promontory, called Taipingot, which formed one side of curving Sosanjaya Bay. On the flat, narrow penin-

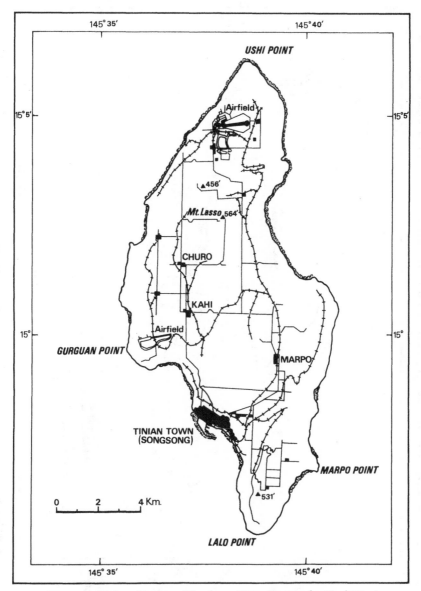

Figure 9. Tinian, Mariana Islands, c. 1938. (Drawn by Noel Diaz)

sula between Sabana and Taipingot was Songsong, a village of less than five hundred Chamorros and Carolinians who supported themselves largely through subsistence farming. The largest building in the village was a church dating from Spanish times and adjacent to it a convent and the old Spanish government office. Its three dusty streets formed a rough H, above the crossbar of which were the former German and

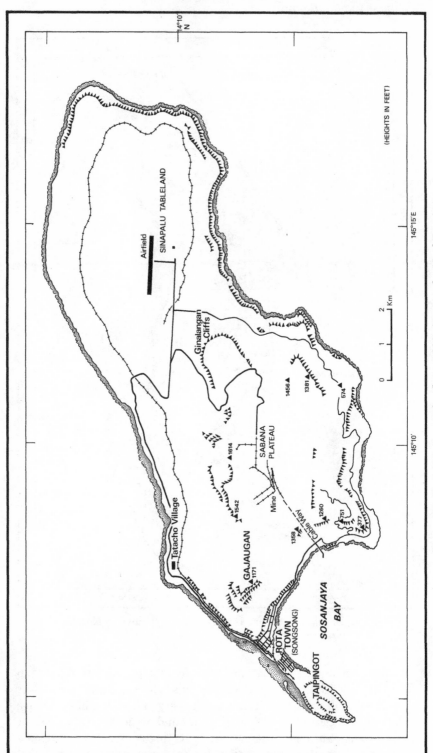

Figure 10. Rota, Mariana Islands, c. 1938. (Drawn by Noel Diaz)

now Japanese government offices (Figure 11). Like the other two larger islands in the Marianas, Rota had been the site of the abortive commercial effort of the Nishimura Takushoku which had brought over some eighty Japanese laborers in 1918 to assist in various agricultural schemes, only to evacuate them three years later, after the enterprises failed. Over the next decade less than a hundred Japanese drifted onto the island, mostly as farmers or fishermen.

In 1930, the transformation of Rota began when the Nan'yō Kōhatsu turned attention to its development. In September of that year, after surveying the island, Nankō cleared away much of the primary growth, laid out regular lots on the Sinapalu Tableland in anticipation of the arrival of Japanese cultivators, tested various varieties of cane, and began construction of a large refinery on the Taipingot Isthmus. A narrow-gauge railway was constructed from Songsong Village up the northwest coast to the cane plantations at Sinapalu. Phosphate having been discovered on the Sabana Plateau, mining operations were begun there, and an aerial lift was constructed to transport the excavated material down the steep cliffs to a loading facility on Sosanjaya Bay.[18]

Meanwhile, arriving ships began to offload laborers and settler families in ever-increasing numbers: over 300 in 1932, 500 the next year, over 1800 the year after that, and over 2000 in 1935; at mid-decade, the island had an immigrant population of nearly 5000 Japanese, a number that overwhelmed the indigenous population of less than 800. Songsong became a booming sugar-mill town, with paved streets, electric lights, telephone facilities, and trolley cars on the Nankō railway. Just to the south, along the isthmus, there emerged a new town—eventually called Rota Town—entirely Japanese in composition, with stores, bars, and restaurants that catered to the workers in the nearby refinery (Figure 12).

Even this new center was not large enough to hold the swelling numbers of Japanese who arrived. To make way for the needs of the Japanese, the colonial authorities decided, the Micronesian villagers in Songsong would have to move out. One day in 1936, the villagers were brought together in a public assembly by a clutch of white-uniformed officials, including the branch governor of the Marianas, and told that they were being moved to a newly laid-out village, Tatacho, about two miles up the coast. Similar forced removal of Micronesian farmers from their traditional lands had already been carried out in the interior of the island. Though they were given monetary compensation and deeds to the new properties, the best land was now turned over to Japanese agricultural families, who moved onto the island in force.[19] Within six years the somnolent peace of the island had been shattered by the aggressive energies of Japan, and Rota had become another Japanese island, in character as well as title.

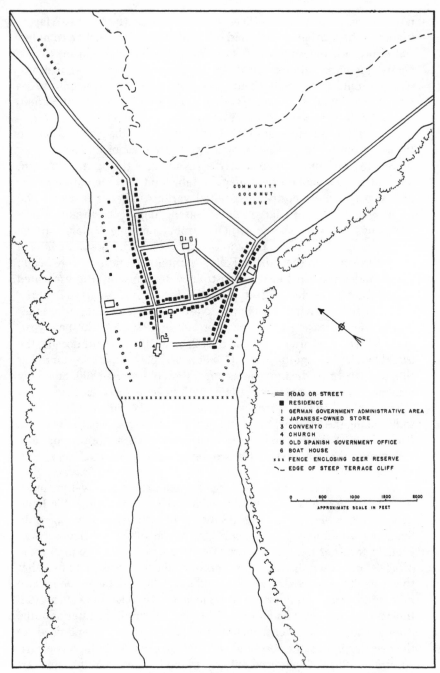

Figure 11. Songsong, Rota Island, 1913. (Reproduced from Bowers 1950, 108)

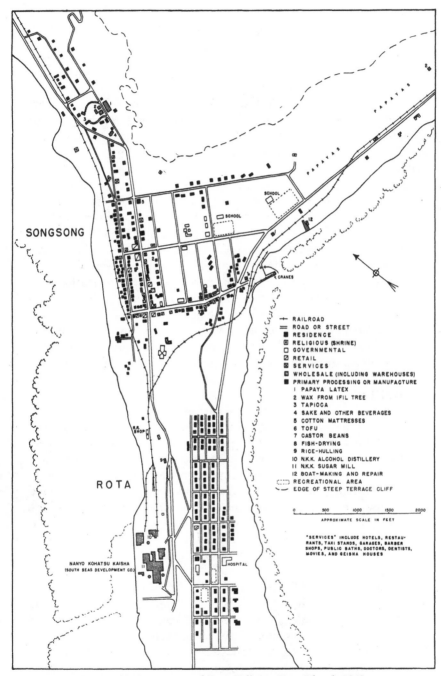

Figure 12. Songsong and Rota Village, Rota Island, 1943.
(Reproduced from Bowers 1950, 109)

Rural Japan in the Palaus

While industry-based agriculture furnished the dominant element in
the colonization of the Marianas, in the Palau group—Koror, Babelthuap, Pelelieu, and Angaur (Figure 13)—the impulses were more varied. To begin with, Koror, the largest of a cluster of islands (Koror, Arakabesan, Aluptagel, and Malakal), which collectively enclosed Koror
(Palau) Harbor, had been, since 1922, the administrative center of the
mandate. In that year, the Nan'yō-chō had begun setting out in Madalai
—the yet uninhabited western end of Koror—the streets and buildings
for a suitable capital for the new colonial government. The centerpiece
of this administrative town (known by the same name as the island on
which it was located) was the stately Nan'yō-chō headquarters building, adjacent to which were constructed the essential facilities for housing: family residences for married officials, dormitories for single men.
On Ngerbeched, the promontory southeast of Madalai, were the governor's residence, the high court for the mandate, a weather station, and
a biological experiment station. A half mile or so along the northern
shore to the east, a handful of Japanese quietly carried on their trading
and commercial activities as they had in German times. Through the
1920s, Koror was still a sleepy, if competently organized little town,
with no industries, no significant immigrant population, no hotels, few
places of business or entertainment, and a population composed largely
of colonial bureaucrats.[20]

North of Koror Island, across a narrow channel, lay Babelthuap,
largest island in the Palaus (nearly thirty miles long with a maximum
width of about ten miles) and shaped like a whale whose square head
pointed south and whose elongated tail thrust eight miles northward,
the whole animal being surrounded by a fringing reef. Much of the interior of the island was grassy, savanna-like country, with scattered
palms; elsewhere woods grew thick in the many gentle valleys where
small rivers made their way through mangrove swamps to the sea.
Though Palauan villages dotted the landscape here and there, most of
the two hundred or more square miles of Babelthuap appeared to lie
open and empty.

For this reason, in 1924, the Nan'yō-chō chose Babelthuap for a colonization scheme designed to bring Japanese immigrants to Micronesia
under arrangements and for purposes markedly different from those
undertaken by employees and tenants of the Nan'yō Kōhatsu. Whereas
Nankō had promoted large-scale farming of a single crop in order to
supply a particular industry, the government now proposed to establish
a network of agricultural settlements on Babelthuap, composed of families who would undertake small-scale farming, particularly the production of fresh vegetables, along with a little fishing, partly for sale in
Koror, but mostly to sustain themselves. In this way, the government

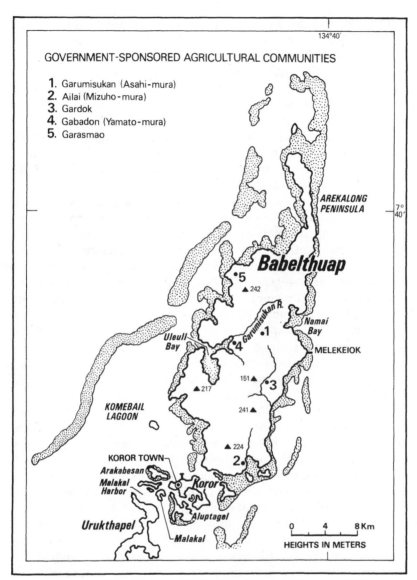

Figure 13. Babelthuap and Koror Islands, Palau Group, c. 1938.
(Drawn by Noel Diaz)

hoped to establish a network of self-sufficient agricultural communities throughout Babelthuap and so provide a testing ground for Japanese agricultural colonization in the tropics.[21]

In 1926, in pursuit of this scheme, a site was selected for the first settlement, an area on the banks of the Garumisukan (Ngarumisukang) River at the approximate center of the island. Eventually, three additional sites were colonized: at Ailai on the southern coast in 1931, on the

Gardok River in the southern interior in 1933, and on the Gabadon River near the western coast in 1937. Other settlements were developed in the early 1940s.[22]

From the beginning, however, the government's directly managed colonization program in Micronesia, unlike similar projects undertaken later in Manchuria, was ill conceived and mismanaged, one of the few lapses in Japanese efficiency in the development of Micronesia. In Japan, despite the existence of a recruiting plan (developed by the Nan'yō-chō) the government failed to turn up large numbers of Japanese farm families eager to move to the distant South Seas. In part, this was because in the mid-1920s no desperate economic crisis had developed in Japan to cause the impoverished end of the agricultural population to seek opportunities overseas, and in part it was apparently the result of inadequate publicity for the program. But undoubtedly, the real reason behind the failure of large numbers to respond to the program was that the terms offered by the Nan'yō-chō for settlement in the Palaus were far less generous than those offered by Nankō in the Marianas. Prospective immigrants, who were to be between twenty and fifty-five, to have farming experience, and to be robust in health and determination, were expected to pay the cost of their passage to Palau, to put down a substantial deposit, and to have on hand sufficient funds for each family member for the first year. Under these obligations, it is not surprising that there were few takers anxious to share benefits and risks that the government took little trouble to explain.[23]

Eventually, eight families were recruited as settlers for the first agricultural colony on the Garumisukan River, most of them from Hokkaido (which was to furnish the greatest number of immigrants in this government colonization program during the course of its existence in Micronesia). They arrived in December 1926 to find that a worse site could scarcely have been chosen. Land that was not covered by thick forest was generally sloping, the soil was poor, and the river itself was a swamp that furnished a home for dozens of crocodiles. Once inhabited by Palauans, the district had been abandoned because of its inhospitable environment. Nevertheless, the new immigrants, equipped only with hand tools and a few building materials, set about creating the new settlement with a determination and energy that astounded the nearest Palauan villagers, who, with the accustomed hospitality of their island, brought food and water to the immigrants during the early days following their arrival. Starting with the most primitive of shelters, often just a sheet of tin tilted against a tree, the settlers began to build simple frame houses laid out along a dirt street, to cultivate vegetable plots, and to put up a few stores. Then, in May 1927, just as the tiny community was beginning to show signs of permanence, a massive typhoon struck the Palaus with full force, tearing apart houses and devastating fields. Defeated, half the settler families soon left; the rest held on for a few years, but by 1930 the site was deserted.[24]

Garumisukan was started up again that year when a resourceful man from Hokkaido, with experience as a commercial farmer in the Philippines, arrived with his wife and three children to begin the cultivation of pineapples. As economic depression tightened its grip on Japan, other families came to the settlement to join in the enterprise, and within three years the village had a contract with the South Seas Pineapple Company, which set up a small canning factory nearby. With a commercial base, the settlement grew quickly over the next few years, with stores, a town council, a clinic, a school, and a steady stream of official visitors, for whom it became a required stop on any tour of the mandate.[25]

In 1938, as part of the strident nationalism that had come to color the purposes of all of Japan's overseas administrations, all the agricultural settlements on Babelthuap had their Palauan identity submerged beneath Japanese names. Garumisukan became Asahi—Rising Sun— Village, reflecting the fact that many of its inhabitants came from the Asahigawa District in Hokkaido, as well as Japanese hopes for the dawn of a new era of expansion in the South Seas.[26] To the villagers of Asahi Mura there was at least modest reason to believe in the latter view. By 1940, the settlement contained nearly one hundred families, whose town meetings, shrine festivals, and agricultural cooperatives reflected the activities and institutions of a typical community in rural Japan. During the 1930s the modest commercial successes of the government's agricultural settlements on Babelthuap justified the laying out of all-weather gravel roads, over which produce could be trucked to the piers and docks at selected points along the eastern and western coasts, where freighters could carry it down to Koror or even straight back to Japan.[27]

Yet while the Nan'yō-chō in its public relations made much of these enclaves of rural Japan in the tropics, in general they failed to live up to the hopes that had originally been invested in them. Conceived as self-sufficient communities, they were soon obliged to turn to commercial farming, but the poor soil, the small plots, and the narrow markets for their products demonstrated that small-scale commercial farming in Micronesia was only marginally successful, unless related to the production of raw materials—pineapples, tapioca, and such—for larger industrial enterprises like Nankō.[28] Even then, the future of the smaller Japanese agricultural settlements in the Palaus was tied to the whims of Japanese industry, often with seriously adverse results.[29] When arbitrary decisions by Japanese firms ruined or seriously limited the market for the principal commercial crop on which a village depended, it was inevitable that some villagers would drift down to Koror, where they became storekeepers or worked in the aluminum factory there, while

others simply packed up and returned to Japan, where wartime industrial and agricultural production had revived the sagging economy.
Most discouraging of all, the government's colonization program in
Palau failed to produce any significant immigration into the islands. By
1940, less than three hundred families had moved to Babelthuap. Considering that in the meantime many had given up and moved away, that
figure seems even less significant.[30]

Koror as a Boom Town

If the government's agricultural settlement programs in the uplands of
Babelthuap failed to stimulate substantial emigration to that island,
government subsidies to the fishing industry triggered a gusher of immigration into Koror, beginning early in the 1930s. In comparison to the
Marianas, the numbers on Koror (from less than seventeen hundred in
1930 to over three thousand in 1935) constituted a freshet, not a flood.
As the largely Okinawan fishing community began to swell in size,
other Japanese came south to open shops and provide a variety of services, setting off a building boom in Koror. After 1930, construction
barely kept pace with the demand for housing and business needs.
Under this pressure of population Koror rapidly spread eastward along
the northern shore of the island, as houses, hospitals, dormitories,
hotels, schools, radio stations, and commercial shops went up one after
another. From Koror the population spilled over to the adjacent islands
of Arakabesan and Malakal, the latter becoming the site of a village of
Okinawan fishing families. At the same time, the Palau Branch Government was able to control the quality as well as the quantity of most of
Koror's growth. It provided for open spaces, carefully positioned the
sites for all government buildings, saw to it that the streets were paved
and provided with adequate drainage, and that houses rested on concrete pads, foundations, or pillars.[31]

From a small village, by mid-decade Koror had become a tidy but
vigorously expanding colonial city. In his travel account, *Pacific Adventure*, Willard Price, who visited Koror in 1935, provided a sense of the
gold rush excitement in the city at this time:

> We slipped into the car . . . and whirled up through a half-mile of ris-
> ing houses, attractive little homes they would be, all in Japanese style, in
> plots roomy enough for plenty of shrubbery, with a romantic view of the
> island-studded bay. Then we drove through a fine old residential section
> (old in the boom-town sense, built three or four years ago) past the exten-
> sive buildings of the South Seas Government. . . . Past great radio towers
> . . . . Then just as we expected the town to peter out into the jungle, it
> only began to get serious. Schools, hospital, post office, steamship offices,
> and a typical city park. Then stores, a mile of them, all Japanese, some of

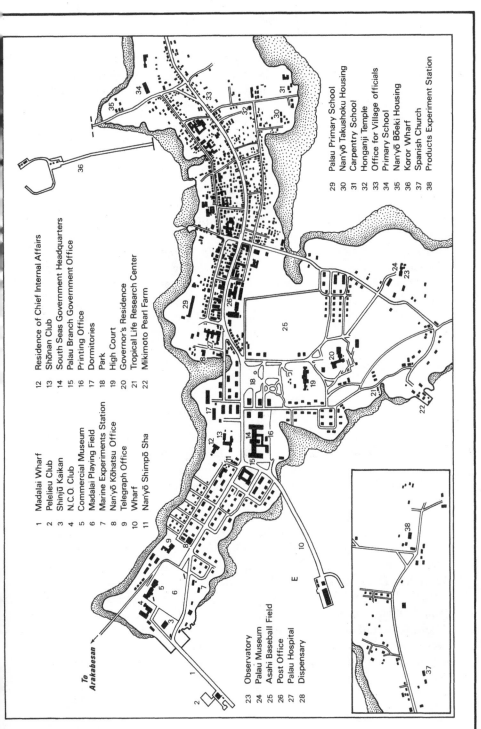

1 Madalai Wharf
2 Peleliu Club
3 Shinjū Kaikan
4 N.C.O. Club
5 Commercial Museum
6 Madalai Playing Field
7 Marine Experiments Station
8 Nan'yō Kōhatsu Office
9 Telegraph Office
10 Wharf
11 Nan'yō Shimpō Sha

12 Residence of Chief Internal Affairs
13 Shōnan Club
14 South Seas Government Headquarters
15 Palau Branch Government Office
16 Printing Office
17 Dormitories
18 Park
19 High Court
20 Governor's Residence
21 Tropical Life Research Center
22 Mikimoto Pearl Farm

23 Observatory
24 Palau Museum
25 Asahi Baseball Field
26 Post Office
27 Palau Hospital
28 Dispensary

29 Palau Primary School
30 Nan'yō Takushoku Housing
31 Carpentry School
32 Honganji Temple
33 Office for Village officials
34 Primary School
35 Nan'yō Bōeki Housing
36 Koror Wharf
37 Spanish Church
38 Products Experiment Station

To Arakabesan

Figure 14. Koror Town, Koror Island, Palau Group, 1938. (Redrawn by Noel Diaz from a map issued by the Nan'yō Guntō Kyōkai)

them department stores of considerable size. Here and there . . . was a
lone thatch hut with the elbows of Japanese shops in its ribs . . .[32]

The Koror building boom took another quantum leap after 1937,
when the pearl and mother-of-pearl industries began to yield substantial profits. During the winter months the presence of well over a thousand divers returning from long stretches of hard and dangerous work in
the Arafura Sea, their wallets thick with pay, fueled an economic boom,
particularly in the central districts of the city, where most of the inns,
restaurants, and entertainment business were located (Figure 14).
Koror's restaurants were booked solid every evening and its inns and
hotels filled to capacity. Bars, cafes, geisha houses, and brothels did a
roaring business and the twang of the shamisen and the sounds of raucous laughter, singing, and rhythmic clapping carried over the calm
waters of Koror Bay each evening the divers were in port. Although the
pearling population was a transient one, its regular appearance and the
economic opportunities it had created set off a migration into Koror
that lured so many Japanese away from Saipan, as well as from Japan,
that it sharply curtailed the swelling immigration into the Marianas.
Eventually, as military and naval units poured into the Palaus, the
number of Japanese in Koror increased still further, until by 1941 the
small city had become a boom-town and naval base, as well as a thriving port and colonial capital.[33]

The Transformation of Ponape

Because of its size—one-tenth of the total land area of Japanese
Micronesia—and because of the relative fertility of its soil, Ponape was
the locus of the third largest immigrant population in the mandate. Pro-
portionally, however, by the end of the 1930s that community was only
a third of the size of the Japanese population in the Palaus and a mere
fraction of the numbers that filled the Marianas.

After the withdrawal of the navy garrison in 1922, the Japanese on
Ponape numbered less than one hundred fifty government officials and
traders, mostly living in Kolonia, the administrative center since Spanish times. Their number grew slowly until the 1930s (about seventy new
arrivals between 1923 and 1930) and then, early in the decade, the
island began to feel the eastward surge of the Japanese migration into
Micronesia, much weaker in force and impact than in the Marianas or
western Carolines, but significant nonetheless.

Once again, fishing and farming were the principal impulses and
Nankō the specific agent of the movement. Nambō had possessed coconut plantations on Ponape since German times and its copra trade, as

well as its general merchandise business, had furnished the livelihood of a small group of Japanese traders. But fishing spurred the first significant population increase on the island. The first Okinawans to enter Ponape Harbor were independent fishermen and their families, but they were soon outnumbered by those working for the Nankō Suisan, whose *katsuobushi* factory continued to draw in fishermen and laborers, thereby setting off a booming industry along the waterfront. As on the other islands, the needs of a fast-growing fishing community stimulated a demand for a variety of goods, services, and housing. Other Japanese immigrants were attracted to Kolonia, which quickly spilled beyond the limits of the old German administrative center on the heights; the buildings dating from that era became submerged among the homes, stores, offices, and warehouses of a distinctly Japanese town.[34]

Industry also contributed to the economic growth and population increase of the town: tobacco, fertilizer, and pulp companies were among some thirty firms that had offices and warehouses along the waterfront, along with various light industries, boat builders, and canneries. Inland from the waterfront, schools, a hospital, and government offices gave employment to many more. By late 1941, the town covered half the promontory that jutted into Ponape Harbor and contained a population of around three thousand, about half the Japanese living in the Ponape branch district (Ponape, Kusaie, and adjacent atolls) (Figure 15).

By the mid-1930s, moreover, Kolonia was not the only population center on Ponape. Early in the decade, government and private enterprises sought to develop the hinterland of the island, each working separately to create a rural community. On the southeast coast, at Matalanim near the mouth of the Lethau River, Nambō had managed extensive coconut plantations since the early 1930s. In 1933, near the same place, Nankō started up cassava cultivation for the production of tapioca starch. Clearing away the dense growth, constructing a mill, and setting up company housing, the company brought in a thousand or more workers. Inevitably, as small businesses moved in to provide goods and services, tradespeople and shopkeepers arrived by the hundreds. The result was a company boom town at Matalanim (known alternatively as Sapalap or Lethau) which struck Willard Price with its frontier vigor when he stopped there in 1935. "We walked through a well lighted street of stores half a mile long where there were only dark woods a year ago," wrote Price in his travel account. "On this Ginza of Ponape we dropped into a lively department store, sat in arm chairs, and listened to phonograph records from Tokyo." From tapioca, the effort at Matalanim turned to sugar. Nankō set out cane fields, built a

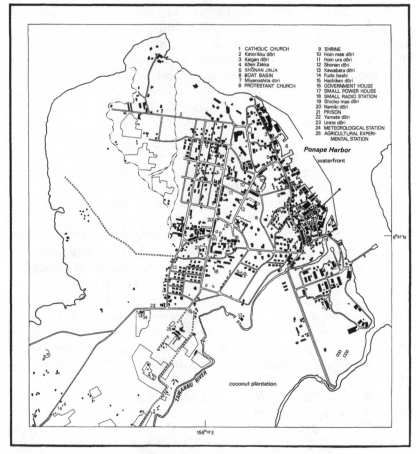

Figure 15. Kolonia (Ponape Town), Ponape, Caroline Islands, 1944.
(Redrawn by Noel Diaz from Air Target Map, Joint Intelligence
Center, Pacific Ocean Areas, 1 April 1944)

refinery, constructed a narrow-gauge railway to connect the two, and put up housing for the workers, mostly Okinawans and Koreans, who came flooding in. By the end of the 1930s Matalanim was the second largest community on Ponape, with a population of nearly three thousand.[35]

On the northwest coast, the government tried its hand at colonization when, in 1931, it established a settlement at Palikir, a small valley in the Sokehs district (Figure 16). Conceived as an important experiment in the suitability of Ponape as a place for Japanese settlement, Palikir (written in kanji by the Japanese as Haruki 'coming of Spring') was designed to be a self-sufficient counterpart to the government settlements on Babelthuap. Certainly its early years appear to have been no

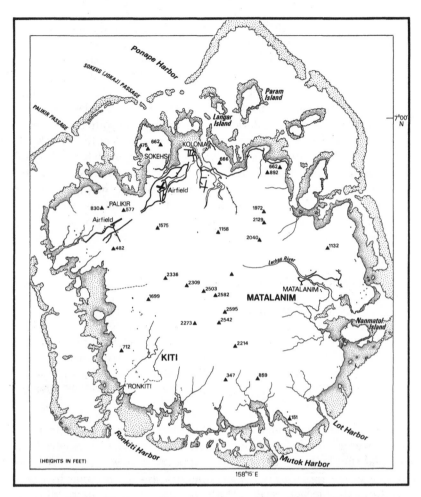

Figure 16. Ponape, Caroline Islands. (Drawn by Noel Diaz)

less difficult for its founding settlers, twenty-four farm families from Hokkaido who struggled to make a living by growing vegetables to sell to the townspeople in Kolonia, some five or six miles distant.[36]

As the road between Palikir and Kolonia was poor, no vehicles could get to the village, and the first settlers, rising while it was still dark, had to make the trip on foot, carrying their produce on their backs. At first, there was often not enough to eat in the village, let alone to sell. There being no doctor in the community, some who became ill died without medical attention. The rain, heat, and humidity must have tested the strength and endurance of even the hardiest sons and daughters of Hokkaido. Yet somehow, with persistence and dogged effort, the settlers at Palikir put down roots and began to establish a firm economic basis for their community. By mid-decade Palikir was producing an abundance of vegetables that were transported by truck over a substantial government road and sold in Kolonia through the Palikir Agricultural Cooperative. The villagers soon began to lay out rice paddies as well as vegetable plots; nearby, Nantaku leased land for the cultivation of pineapples; and on the southern edge of the settlement the Wakamoto Company started a cassava plantation.[37] By the time the young anthropologist Umesao Tadao visited Palikir with other members of the 1941 Kyoto South Seas observation mission, its appearance was idyllic. Climbing the ridge that separated Palikir from Kolonia, the visitors were greeted by a woman, clad in the traditional loose trousers of the Japanese farm wife, who escorted them to the settlement. Umesao and his companions felt as if they had come upon a mountain village in Japan, yet the lush mountains, the ferns, and the pandanus palms all spoke of the South Seas:

> From the ridge Palikir Village lay spread out before us, a small, isolated world unto itself, in a basin enclosed on the east by a range of mountains and on the west by the lower hills of the Nan Palikir. Here and there patches of fern lay scattered like green velvet from the ridge to the edge of the hamlet. Between them, unexpectedly for the red soil of this volcanic island, were rice paddies. Pineapple fields, laid out in narrow rows, formed plots of a somewhat different shade, and behind the paddies, surrounded by a grove of ivory palms, one could see the roofs of typical Japanese farm houses.[38]

Though the government effort at Palikir, like those in the Palau group, was undoubtedly out of proportion to the returns it received, the eventual success achieved at Palikir appears to have been part of an attempt at the Japanization of Ponape, just as the Marianas had been transformed a decade earlier. With over six thousand immigrants on Ponape by 1941, with Japanese fields and farms rapidly encroaching on the wooded interior of the island, with Japanese villages in the hinterland blossoming into towns, and Kolonia on the verge of transformation from a town to a small city, there is little reason to doubt that had the war not intervened, Ponape would have come to rival Saipan as a Japanese population center.[39]

The Lesser Settlements: Yap, Truk, and Kusaie

Except for Koror, none of the other high islands in the Carolines developed any significant immigrant population. Despite its earlier reputation as a source of international controversy, Yap did not develop a sizable Japanese community until the years just prior to the war (around two hundred seventy-five in 1931, not quite six hundred in 1935, and

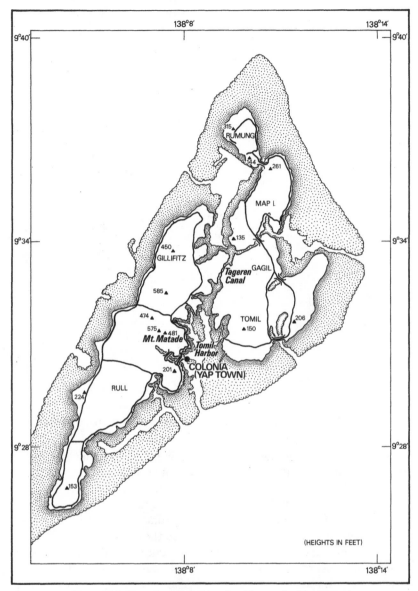

Figure 17. Yap, Caroline Islands. (Drawn by Noel Diaz)

over fourteen hundred early in the war). Most of the Japanese were concentrated at Colonia (alternatively known as Yap Town), the administrative center, located on a peninsula extending from the western shore of shallow, reef-filled Tomil Harbor (Figures 17 and 18). Tomil was a reasonably good anchorage, and a good set of roads skirted the adjacent islands that made up the Yap group, but the generally hilly topography

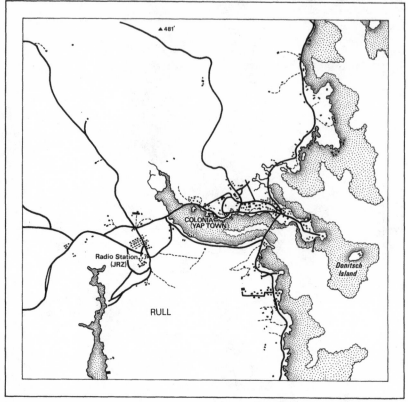

Figure 18. Colonia (Yap Town), Yap, Caroline Islands. (Drawn by Noel Diaz)

of Yap meant that neither agriculture nor industry found much of a
footing. On the main island, the government established an agricultural
settlement for the production of pineapples and tapioca, and Nantaku
organized a pioneer unit of youths from Saitama Prefecture for the
development of Yap, but little apparently came of these initiatives and,
by and large, the tide of immigration passed the islands by.[40]

Existing as the tops of great drowned mountains, the islands of the
Truk group, locked within the huge triangular reef, scarcely had any
level terrain that could have supported large scale agriculture (Figure
2). But to these peaked islands, clothed in coconut palms, hibiscus,
mangoes, and bougainvillea, came groups of Okinawan fishermen and
some traders—over seven hundred by 1935—who settled mostly on
Dublon in the eastern group of islands, or on Tol, largest of the islands
on the western side of the huge lagoon.[41] Shaped like the head of a dog
facing east with its jaws open, Dublon had been the administrative center for Truk since German times (Figure 19). The branch government
building, the post office, hospital, and a few other government build-

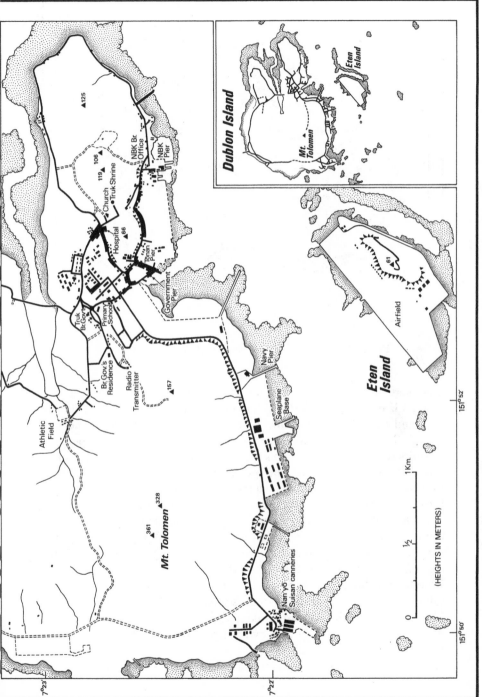

Figure 19. Dublon and Eten Islands, Truk Group, Caroline Islands, c. 1938. (Drawn by Noel Diaz)

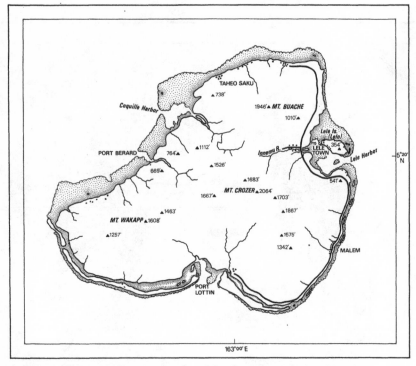

Figure 20. Kusaie, Caroline Islands. (Drawn by Noel Diaz)

ings were located halfway along the lower jaw. Clustered around
Dublon Harbor, a small indentation on the underside of the jaw, fishermen and traders came to build piers and sheds, shops and canneries,
though there were scarcely eight hundred Japanese in the little port by
the mid-1930s.[42] Dublon Town's most robust growth awaited the immediate prewar and early wartime years, when the navy returned in force,
putting up barracks, pouring concrete for seaplane ramps, and flooding
the island with construction crews and naval personnel.

On Kusaie, two hundred miles southeast of Ponape and in some ways
the most beautiful of all the high Carolines, the Japanese community
was even smaller. Positioned at the edge of a pocket in the encircling
reef on the east coast of the lush and mountainous main island, Lele
Island—low, luxuriant, and fringed with dazzling white beaches—contained the only significant colonial settlement at Kusaie (Figure 20).
There, on the southern shore flanking the snug harbor, not more than a
hundred Japanese, mostly Okinawan fishermen and a handful of traders, created a tiny community of houses and stores, which added to the
existing church, hospital, police station, and the NBK branch office
(Figure 21).[43]

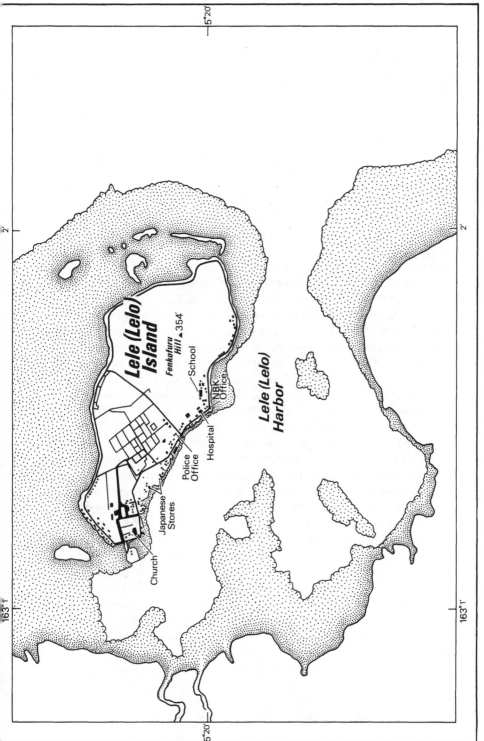

Figure 21. Lele (Lelo), Kusaie, Caroline Islands, c. 1938. (Drawn by Noel Diaz)

Migration's End: The Marshalls

In Micronesia, starting from the west, everything diminished by the time one got to the Marshall Islands: land, vantage point, population, daily tempo, and a sense of frontier. With a total area of seventy square miles between them, and without any piece of land more than a dozen feet above sea level, the thirty-three atolls of the Marshalls had little to attract the immigrant farmer, being composed of coral, sand, and the thinnest of topsoils, on which little besides palms, scattered shrubs, and grasses could grow. The copra and general merchandise trades, along with some commercial fishing, were about all that the Marshalls had to offer. Not surprisingly, their small Japanese population was divided about evenly between traders, fishermen, and colonial administrators.

Since German times, the center of that population, as well as of administration in the Marshalls, had been Jaluit, a roughly lozenge-shaped atoll at the southern end of the Ralik chain. The atoll consisted of a dry land area of little more than four square miles, distributed among approximately eighty-four islands and islets spread along the reef, which enclosed a lagoon some two hundred sixty square miles in area (Figure 22). Three ship passes pierced the atoll's rim, the most commonly used among them being the southeast pass between Enybor and Jabor islands. On the northern tip of Jabor the administrative center, the branch government office, was located, along with the wharves and copra warehouses of the NBK (Figure 23). Around these a town grew up, as a ripple of Okinawan fishermen, followed by small traders and storekeepers, drifted into Jaluit in the late 1920s and the 1930s. Along with the small corps of government officials at Jabor, these made up a Japanese community of a little over two hundred fifty by 1930, less than twice that five years later, and probably under a thousand by the end of the decade, sharing the atoll with some two thousand Marshallese. In the early thirties, the buildings of the town were ranged along two principal streets of sand and gravel, wide enough for cars, one of which ran along the lagoon shore and around the tip of the island, while the other intersected it at right angles just north of the main pier and crossed the island to the outer beach. North of this principal transverse street were the buildings of the Jaluit hospital, a small Shintō shrine, some small stores, and the wooden buildings of the Boston mission. South of it were a public school, more shops, the Jaluit Branch Government office and government dormitory for single officials, residences, the police station, the post office, and the houses of the Okinawan fishing families. At the southernmost edge of the town was the radio transmitter by which Jaluit kept in touch with Truk, Ponape, and Palau.[44]

For the rest of the Marshalls, indeed for the other Micronesian islands I have not mentioned—the smaller, northern islands of the Marianas

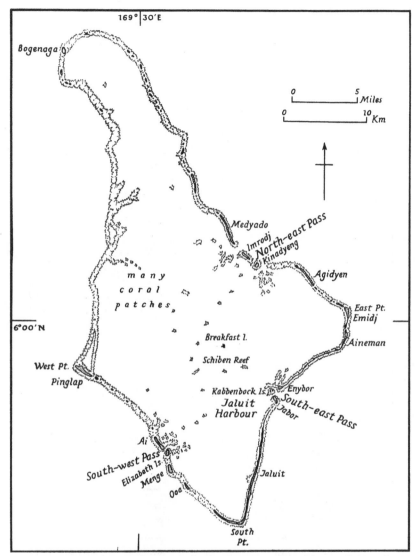

Figure 22. Jaluit Atoll, Marshall Islands. (Reproduced from UK Naval
Intelligence Division 1945, 420)

and all the low islands of the Carolines—one cannot really speak of a
Japanese population. Immediately before World War II there were
probably not more than two hundred Japanese civilians, almost entirely
traders (and most of them connected with the NBK) scattered among
these distant landfalls, eight or ten at the most on any one atoll, and
usually only one or two. They lived out the cycle of months and years
amid the shimmering beauty and monotony of their surroundings.

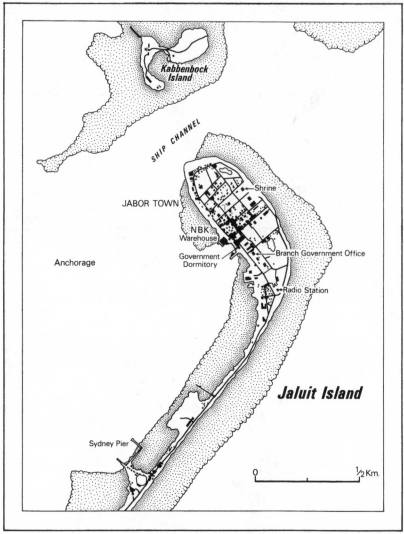

Figure 23. Jabor Town, Jaluit Atoll, Marshall Islands. (Drawn by Noel Diaz)

Names on the Tide

Until now I have spoken of the Japanese in Micronesia only in terms of island groups, occupations, and regional origins. I have generalized about the motivations for emigration among the largest immigrant class, the Okinawans, and have provided rough figures for the distribution of Japanese communities among the various island groups.

But the Japanese who came to Micronesia—traders, farmers, fishers, homemakers, shopkeepers, laborers, bar attendants, and officials—

were not a faceless mass; they were individuals, each with a history—ambitions and hopes, human strengths and human frailties. Admittedly, we know far too little about far too many of them. The collections of biographic sketches that fill the back pages of contemporary guidebooks and official reports tend to concentrate on "worthies," successful men, honored by government or business and standing as exemplars to their colonial communities or administrations. The adulatory purpose of such summaries tends to attenuate their individuality, to leach them of the colorful anecdote or critical judgment. In part, the problem lies in the tradition of Japanese biography, which has been to honor those with whom it deals; in part in the Japanese cultural character, which rarely gives an honored place to the dominant personality or the colorful eccentric; and in part in the Japanese communities overseas, where even the wealthiest and most powerful never constituted a separate elite of affluence, influence, or social prestige. Just as there were no individual officials of awesome reputation in the Japanese mandate, there were no lofty taipans, no Rajah Brookes who personally presided over great estates or vast plantations. We know even less, of course, about individuals at the lower end of the economic and social scale. In Japanese Micronesia we hear of no legendary beachcombers or drifters, nor, with one remarkable exception, do we learn of resident expatriate writers or artists like Stevenson, Gauguin, or Frisbee. We can be certain that there were more than a few failures, men and women who eventually gave up the struggle to carve out a new life from volcanic soil or atoll trade and returned to Japan, but their individual tragedies are not remembered.

We are left with a most incomplete record, confined almost entirely to men who succeeded, and presented in a style that is all too often blanched of color. Yet, even a sample from this fragmentary evidence, allows us to see the Japanese presence in Micronesia as an aggregate of individuals, not as a mere population whose contours are shaped only by statistics.

We may select, for example, the leading hotelier and restaurateur of the Marianas, one Yamaguchi Momojirō, from Shinjo in Yamagata, who came to Saipan in November 1914, the first from his prefecture to emigrate to Micronesia and one of the first to do so on his own. Yamaguchi started running a dry goods store in Garapan for two years before he sent for his wife and opened a small restaurant in the town. Five years later, the couple opened the Saipan-kaku, the first inn-restaurant on the island, but with too few Japanese as yet visiting the Marianas, the venture folded. Undaunted, Yamaguchi started a general merchandise store and a papaya canning business, both of which did so well that he was able to turn back to innkeeping. In 1929, with the inward flow of compatriots at full tide, he opened the Yokarō (Leisure Mansion) which became the best inn in the Marianas throughout the 1930s. By the end of that decade he was a wealthy man, the owner of a large house on the western coast, and a leading figure in Garapan. In 1943, a year before the disasters of war destroyed the polished floors of the Yokarō, Yamaguchi sold it and returned to Yamagata.[45]

Tanabe Kintarō, a nephew of Murayama Sutekichi, founder of the Nan'yō Bōeki, probably contributed more to the development of the Mariana Islands than anyone else except Matsue Haruji. His photograph, in a prewar book on Japanese pioneers in the South Seas, shows him to be a big square-jawed man, with a look in his eye that would surely cause the dishonest and incompetent to quail. In his early career he apparently dealt swiftly with both. In 1903, at the age of twenty he was sent to work at the faltering Guam branch office of his uncle's company. He quickly uncovered an embezzlement scandal by the office accountant and encountered the hostility of the branch manager, who refused to take any action in the matter. Tanabe singlehandedly exposed the case and took over the Guam operation himself, turning it into a major success and earning praise from the Japanese community. In 1908, he was sent to the Saipan office and forced the resignation of the incompetent senior company official there. When Japanese naval forces occupied Saipan, he organized the Japanese community to aid in the administration of the island. During the next few years Tanabe was everywhere, developing maritime communication routes between the Marianas, heading relief and recovery work following a disastrous typhoon, and organizing the nascent municipal government of Garapan. By the eve of the Pacific War, Tanabe Kintarō was without doubt the leader of the Japanese community on Saipan, a worthy among worthies.[46]

Other Japanese are more interesting for their individual accounts of how and why they came to the South Seas. Yamaguchi Yusaburō, for example, had graduated from Nihon University before World War I, had worked for the South Manchuria Railway Company, and had been an employee of the Home Ministry in the early 1920s. But life in Tokyo was difficult after the Great Kantō Earthquake, and in May 1925 he transferred to the Nan'yō-chō. Years later, Yamaguchi was to recall the voyage south to Palau aboard the old *Chikuzen Maru*, plowing through mountainous seas. He could feel once again the awful seasickness as, prostrate in a cabin lit by one dim porthole and located at the stern, he felt the ship shake violently each time the propellers lifted out of the water. He remembered, too, the rapture of going ashore on Saipan, his first tropical island, where the palms stretched out along the beach, the sky was a brilliant blue, and the roads of crushed coral dazzled the eyes. When Yamaguchi arrived in Koror it was still a village and the Nan'yō-chō was but three years old, a fledgling organization where an ambitious young bureaucrat could make his mark. Yamaguchi did exactly that, rising through the colonial administration to become branch governor of Palau.[47]

Miyashita Juichirō was one of the true pioneers of Japanese Micronesia. In his youth he worked for a doctor in Japan and learned some paramedical skills. In 1908, at the age of twenty-one he got a job as a medical assistant aboard a Nambō vessel plying the interisland trade. Several passages later, he got off the ship at Koror, where, with brief interruptions, he was to spend the rest of his life. Soon after his arrival, he met and married a mixed-blood Palauan woman, the daughter of a Japanese who had been trading in Palau since Spanish times. After his father-in-law hired him, he and his wife took up residence in a small wooden house on Malakal, where he was one of the first Japanese to settle. Miyashita's knowledge of the islands and his web of Palauan contacts made him invaluable to the Japanese navy when it occupied Palau in 1914. Hired as liaison and interpreter, he became an invaluable counselor to the naval occupation and, by the beginning of the mandate administration, was already the single most influential and successful entrepreneur in the western Carolines. In the succeeding years he became a quiet but ever more powerful voice in the economic development of Koror.[48]

Other Japanese who came to Micronesia are of at least passing interest because they represent the variety of commercial endeavors in the islands, or because their fortunes demonstrate how the range of opportunities in Micronesia enabled an individual to shift from one calling to another. Takahashi Akira, from Hachijō Island, south of Tokyo, for example, had hunted and traded on Iwo Jima, the Bonins, and the northern Marianas. He had been hired by the ill-fated Nan'yō Shokusan to raise sugarcane on Saipan, but suspicious of the contract (one of the few immigrants who was, apparently), he took passage for Ponape, where he became a partner in a fishing company and cannery. The business did not flourish and Takahashi turned to charcoal manufacture, a common enterprise in the islands during the Japanese period. With financial backing from a charcoal dealer in Osaka, he soon had two hundred fifty Ponapeans working for him to cut mangrove wood and twelve Japanese to burn it. The business was a thumping success, though he eventually sold it and turned to an even more lucrative sugar enterprise near Palikir.[49]

Ishiyama Mantarō, a roof thatcher from Yamagata, was one of those recruited by the Kita Gōmeigaisha to assist in the company's projected coconut plantation on Tinian in 1917. He cultivated land between Songsong Village and Marpo and tried planting palms, but like those of other immigrants, his young trees withered and died. When the company collapsed, Ishiyama, along with some compatriots from Yamagata, crossed over to Saipan, working first as a laborer in the cane fields, then as a tenant farmer for Nankō. One of the first on the island to use oxen to plow his fields, Ishiyama eventually did quite well, and became one of the most prosperous farmers on the island. Sadly, however, history records that he was one of the many blown to pieces in the American naval bombardment of Saipan, on 8 July 1944.[50]

Yoshikawa Tadao from Hokkaido was the leading figure in the entertainment business in Micronesia. As a young actor, known as "Fatso" (Debu) to his friends, Yoshikawa had toured Japan, Manchuria, and Korea with a variety troupe. In 1927, he had become involved with a film tour in Micronesia, sponsored by the government most probably, of a documentary on the state funeral of the late Emperor Taishō. Encouraged by the prospects for the commercial film business in the islands and by the obvious hunger for entertainment in the Japanese communities he visited, Yoshikawa opened the first movie theater on Saipan in 1929 and went on to manage a string of theaters in the Marianas, as well as becoming a prosperous impresario for theatrical troupes touring the mandate.[51]

One of the most interesting Japanese in Micronesia during the interwar years was Captain Konishi Tatehiko, who served from 1934 to 1937 as the head of the Imperial Japanese Navy's liaison office in Koror, the only representation allowed the Japanese navy under the terms of the mandate. A graduate of the Japanese Naval Academy in 1913, Konishi had been a member of the navy's occupation force during the war years and afterward had become interested in the study of the weather of the Pacific. In 1933, he was given command of the navy's small survey ship *Kōshū*, the only IJN vessel permanently stationed in Micronesia until the late 1930s, and spent much of his time at sea gathering data concerning weather, topography, and soundings of various islands in the Carolines. Ashore, he acquired a legendary reputation for being able to hold his liquor, and when not on duty could usually be found quietly drinking at his favorite Japanese restaurant in Koror. During the course of his duty in Micronesia, he acquired considerable expertise in the strategic and economic development of the mandate, a knowledge that he undoubtedly put to work when he was reassigned in 1937 to a research position in Tokyo. When he retired in 1940, Konishi kept his hand in, being much sought after as a speaker and writer on Japan's role in the South Seas, and was a frequent contributor to the *Nan'yō Shiryō*, a series of scholarly monographs on Micronesia, Melanesia, and Southeast Asia, issued by the prestigious South Seas Economic Research Institute.[52]

The most singular character in this short, random list of Japanese in Micronesia was neither settler, trader, nor government official. Yet he is of interest, in part because he was one of the very few Japanese in the interwar years who found fulfillment in seclusion among the island peoples, and in part, because of this, one of the very few who took the trouble to observe and appreciate Micronesian life and culture.

Painter, sculptor, poet, and folklorist, Hijikata Hisakatsu (1900–1977) was born to an upper class Tokyo family that fell on hard times. The son of an army colonel married to the daughter of a baron and admiral, Hijikata attended the prestigious Gakushuin Middle School, where he displayed the artistic interests that were to shape his career. After his father became ill, the family fortunes declined and Hijikata was compelled to abandon his education to care for his father. His own health was ruined in the process, and he was obliged to enter a sanatorium in 1917. His father died two years later, and Hijikata, having recovered, began five years of training in sculpture at the Tokyo University of Fine Arts. His first works, in metal, being rejected for exhibition, Hijikata began working in wood and in 1927 held an exhibition at the Maruzen Gallery with modest success. The next year, his mother died and Hijikata, depressed and alienated, decided to try his hand in the South Seas. In March 1929, he pulled out of Yokohama aboard the *Yamashiro Maru*, headed for Palau. He spent two years there, immersing himself in Palauan life and taking down much of what he heard of the oral history of the islands (Photo 24).[53]

Then, in the autumn of 1931, in the same way that Gauguin had abandoned the colonial atmosphere of Papeete for the remoteness of the Marquesas, Hijikata, looking for an island untouched by industrial civilization, departed Palau aboard the *Chōmei Maru*, a Nambō schooner, bound for the low islands east of Yap. At Satawal, halfway between Palau and Ponape, and the turn-around point for the schooner's run, he disembarked.

Prewar descriptions of the place do not make it sound inviting. A crescent-shaped island, half a mile long by perhaps a quarter of a mile at its widest point, surrounded by a fringing reef unconnected to any other land mass, and without a safe anchorage, Satawal was one of the lonelier landfalls in the Pacific. Thickly wooded on its western side, the island was rocky and covered with low scrub and coconut palms on its eastern. In the 1930s there were approximately three hundred Micronesians on Satawal; a British naval intelligence survey mentions an NBK store and three Japanese there in 1935. "The sanitary conditions are bad," according to the 1938 U. S. Hydrographic Office *Sailing Directions*, "and flies and mosquitos are numerous."

Nevertheless, Hijikata was to call Satawal home for seven years. He set up house with a Satawal woman and took a deep and intelligent interest in his surroundings and the people among whom he lived. From the day he set foot on the island, whose circumference he could walk in an hour, he began keeping a diary. It was a record, not of his personal life, but of the life of the island, a transcription of everything he saw around him: the daily activities of the islanders, their folklore and customs, the natural surroundings, the seabirds, the hermit crabs, the sunsets, and the surf pounding relentlessly on the reef. Published in 1943,

Photo 24. Hijikata Hisakatsu (1900–1977), on Palau.
(Hijikata Keiko)

under the title *Ryūboku* (Driftwood), the diary is terse rather than literary, but it shows Hijikata to be a keen and sensitive observer, whose
knowledge of Micronesian life was unrivaled among his compatriots,
though his work has largely been ignored in Japanese academic circles.[54]

Hijikata's most delightful insights into Micronesian life were expressed as a sculptor and painter. On Satawal he cast aside the formalism of the Japanese art world in which he had been trained in Tokyo
and plunged into the natural environment in which he lived. As there
was no clay at hand, he was obliged to work in wood, and only that of
the coconut palm was available to him. He worked it with a locally
made adze, but found it so resistant that he found it best to carve reliefs.
His sculptures of Satawalese subjects, taken from island life and legend,

convey a primitive vigor, as do his paintings, done in bold, water-based colors. They hardly match the haunting beauty of Gauguin's work, but they have a simple charm and directness, nevertheless. Perhaps their greatest importance is that they are the only substantial Japanese effort in the plastic arts to deal with the South Seas.

In 1939, Hijikata returned briefly to Japan, bringing back with him a collection of Micronesian artifacts, which he eventually donated to the Department of Anthropology at Tokyo University. He returned that same year to Palau, where he was employed by the South Seas Government as a sort of cultural adviser. In 1942, following the Japanese conquest of Southeast Asia, he was hired as a civilian by the Japanese army and sent to Borneo to head a research team that was to advise the military administration there on policy toward Indonesian peoples. Falling ill, he was hospitalized and repatriated to Japan in 1944. After the war, he became a respected figure in the Japanese art world, where his works were frequently and successfully exhibited.[55]

Mori Koben, Again

Although all of these persons, whether by virtue of example or inherent interest, deserve a place in this short list, perhaps no Japanese in the history of the mandate came to command as much attention, respect, and even awe, as did Mori Koben (see chapter 1). By the time Japanese warships dropped anchor in the huge lagoon at Truk in the autumn of 1914, Mori, by character and exploit, was already a legend among the small Japanese community there. Fluent in Trukese, married to the daughter of a local chief, possessed of numerous contacts throughout all the islands within the group, Mori, like Miyashita Juichirō in Palau, was invaluable to the new naval administration, which quickly took him on as civil affairs adviser. So respected was his expertise concerning the islands that, in 1916, the commander of the naval garrison asked him to prepare a detailed briefing paper on Trukese society. The result was a pioneer scientific study, *Torrakku shotō fūzoku shūkan gaiyō* (An outline of the customs and culture of the Truk Islands). Demonstrating a grasp of the subject possessed by few scholars in Japan or the West, it was to inform official policy toward the Trukese throughout the navy's administration of the islands.[56]

By the early 1920s, Mori's success as a planter and trader had made him one of the wealthiest men in the Carolines. An ardent booster in the development of Truk, he was generous with his fortune as well as his energies in furthering this effort and took a leading role in the improvement of schools, communications, transportation, and commercial facilities throughout the Truk group. Inevitably, his name led the lists of a dozen Japanese boards and associations in Truk. His standing among his wife's people was equally high, a fact demonstrated in the late 1920s when he was elected by the Trukese community on Tol to the position of chief of that island, an honor that appears to have been unique in the annals of the Japanese in Micronesia.[57]

Considering the enervating climate of the Carolines, in which it was common for immigrants to give way to lassitude—*Nan'yō boke*, the Japanese called it—the persistence of Mori's intellectual vigor as he approached old age was remarkable. An avid, reader, he maintained an interest in mathematics, the physical sciences, and the Chinese classics. In his commodious study in his home on Tol, surrounded by books and encyclopedias ordered from Japan, he spent his evenings reading quietly beneath a kerosene lamp. He was also an enthusiastic photographer, taking countless pictures which he developed in his own darkroom, no doubt a priceless visual record of the era, as well as of his personal saga.[58]

As the years went by, Mori acquired an appearance and a persona fitting to his legendary reputation. A flowing white beard swept down from his chin in two magnificent forks. He strode about in Japanese attire, though photographs show him pith-helmeted as well, and he often went barefoot, according to local custom. His countenance and manner were not the least elements in his dominating personality: his gaze was piercing, and local lore had it that "when he was angry wild animals would quail, and when he laughed he could charm the smallest child."[59]

By the 1930s, Mori's name, in both Japan and Micronesia, was inevitably bound with Truk's. No branch governor, no hospital functionary, no school principal or company representative took a post in the islands without first paying his respects to the old man at his home on Tol. Transient visitors of every kind—scholars, newspapermen, businessmen, ship-captains, and naval officers—came to his sturdy zinc-roofed house. All were affably received and regaled with stories of the far-off days when he first came to the lagoon or instructed in the lore and customs of the island people. Often, hearing that a visiting vessel had on board a person of interest, he would have himself taken out in a launch to meet him, without waiting for the visitor to land. Sometimes he entertained the entire crews of Japanese training ships that put into port.[60]

By the start of the Pacific War, Mori Koben had, in a sense, attained the exalted position he had dreamed of as a young man. He was indeed, "King of the South Seas" *(Nan'yō no ōsama),* as the Japanese press referred to him. The capstone of his long and adventurous life came one spring morning in 1940 when, as part of the ceremonies for the opening of a splendid new athletic field on Dublon, Mori was publicly honored by his government. Not only was he awarded the Order of the Sacred

Photo 25. Mori Koben upon his award of the Order
of the Sacred Treasure, Dublon Island, Truk, 1940.
(Kochi Shimbun)

Treasure (to add to his other decorations), but a stone marker was
erected at the edge of the field so that future generations might appreciate the half century of his contributions to Japanese progress and
Micronesian welfare.[61] The photograph of the occasion, sometimes
reprinted in Japanese books on Micronesia, shows the old man standing
next to the monument, ramrod straight, his decorations proudly spread
across his coat (Photo 25). It was a fitting tribute, no doubt, for Mori
Koben represented the best of all Japan had done in Micronesia, and he
was, at all events, the most remarkable of all the thousands of his people
to come south to the tropics.

CHAPTER 7

Japan in the Tropics
The Varieties of Colonial Life

DESPITE THE FACT that Micronesia was ruled by Japan for three decades, it remained a relatively remote place, unfamiliar to most Japanese intellectuals, as well as to the Japanese public. There were exceptions, including not only the ethnologist Matsuoka Shizuo (see chapter 3), but also the ethnomusicologist, Tanabe Hisao, who spent more than a month in the islands in 1934 and wrote an extensive account of his observations. Most important was Yanaihara Tadao, the great scholar and humanist who succeeded Nitobe Inazo in the prestigious chair of colonial studies at Tokyo University. Yanaihara, who surpassed his mentor as a specialist in Japanese colonialism, based his scholarship upon extensive travel and observation of each of the component territories of the empire, as well as on wide reading in the field. His research brought him to the mandate in 1933 and resulted in a comprehensive survey of Micronesia in all its aspects under the Japanese. Published in 1935 as *Nan'yō guntō no kenkyū*, it was translated into English as *Pacific Islands Under Japanese Mandate* (1940), in which form it constituted until World War II the single most important English language source on Micronesia under Japanese administration—and it has informed much of my own understanding of the subject. As the Pacific War neared, a team of scholars from Kyoto University under the eminent biologist and anthropologist Imanishi Kinji, was sent by the government to gather information on Micronesia, with particular emphasis on Ponape. Included in the group was a young student, Umesao Tadao, who went on to a distinguished and versatile academic career, and whose personal account in the massive study that resulted from the expedition is a superb and illuminating piece of travel literature, which I have cited frequently in these pages.

From a literary perspective Micronesia failed to stir great interest among Japanese writers. The islands were never the setting for any major piece of fiction, in large part because there was no resident Japanese counterpart to Robert Louis Stevenson, Pierre Loti, or Louis Becke. Nevertheless, some Japanese writers were concerned with the South Seas: Ando Sakan (Sei), Nakagawa Yoichi, Ishikawa Tatsuzō, and Nakajima Atsushi. Of these Ishikawa and Nakajima, both of whom were in Micronesia just before the Pacific War, were the most important.

Ishikawa Tatsuzō (1905–1985) had made his mark with two novels, one based on the life of Japanese emigrants to Brazil, which earned him the Akutagawa prize, and the other, a sensational account of the horrors of the China War based on interviews with Japanese troops shortly after the Rape of Nanking, which earned him a brief prison sentence. In May 1941, on the spur of the moment, he set out to visit Palau, via the Marianas, largely out of curiosity to see an out-of-the-way place. The result of his trip was a short but marvelously crafted travel account, "Akamushijima" (Red Insect Island) published in 1943. The work is divided into three sections: a description of the sea voyage south to the Marianas; impressions of Rota, Yap, and Palau, with most attention to the last; and a description of six days that he spent with several employees of a Japanese pearl company on a tiny uninhabited island (Ngchus, at the southwest tip of Urukthapel Island) in the Palau group where the company cultivated artificial pearls. Together, the pieces evoke both the pristine remoteness of the South Seas and their rapid and not always visually edifying transformation by Japan.[1]

Nakajima Atsushi (1909–1942) was a frail, bookish young man with romantic tastes, born into a family with traditions of scholarship, particularly in the Chinese classics. After graduating from Tokyo University in 1933, he became a high school teacher in Yokohama and, despite a chronic asthma condition, traveled several times to China, as well as to the Bonin Islands in the 1930s. In early 1941 he wrote his first major work, *Hikari to kaze to yume* (Light, wind, and dreams), a semifictionalized account of the life of Robert Louis Stevenson, which revealed Nakajima as a gifted and sensitive writer. His research for this work on Stevenson, a writer he had long admired, stirred his interest in the South Seas. In the summer of 1941, hoping perhaps that a tropical climate would ease his physical condition, as Samoa had helped Stevenson to lead a comparatively active and productive life, Nakajima sought and obtained a position in the education section of the Nan'yō-chō; he was charged with compiling and revising Japanese language textbooks for use in the government schools in Micronesia.

Nakajima's brief sojourn in Micronesia from August 1941 to March 1942 was an administrative failure and a personal disaster.[2] His official mission for the Nan'yō-chō was blighted from the start. He got on badly with the older colonial officials and soon realized that the administration, caught up as it was in the mobilization of indigenous populations to aid in the Japanese defense effort, had little interest in anything as marginal as the genuine improvement of textbooks for Micronesian children. Far more serious, his physical condition, rather than strengthened, was weakened by the hot, damp climate of Palau. Struck with dysentery within weeks of his arrival, Nakajima then contracted dengue fever. By autumn he had recovered sufficiently to go on a series of official observation tours that took him to all the major island groups and were to furnish a wealth of material for a short collection of beautifully written essays and travel accounts of Micronesian scenes. Together they provide a rich sense of what Micronesia was like just before the war—a contrast between the natural beauty of the South Seas and the ugly scars inflicted by Japan's rapid militarization of the islands. On Palau he was befriended by Hijikata Hisakatsu, who introduced him to a small circle of Japanese and Micronesian friends. From these acquaintances, as well as from Hijikata, Nakajima gleaned material on which he based several oddly haunting fictional sketches that were published in a posthumous work, *Nantō dan* (South Sea island tales). In March 1942, Nakajima's asthma so wracked his thin frame that he felt obliged to relinquish his appointment and return to Japan. Shortly afterward he contracted pneumonia, which, in his weakened condition, proved fatal before the year was out.

Micronesia: An Environmental Balance Sheet

All these writers had something to say about the varieties of Japanese colonial life as they observed it in the tropical Pacific. In terms of privilege and sacrifice, acculturation and isolation, the Japanese who lived in the South Seas had much in common with colonials elsewhere in the tropics. To begin with, their environment was exotic, extreme, and remote—qualities that admittedly presented less of a challenge to the Okinawan majority in the islands than they did to main island Japanese. For the latter, the almost continual summer, the truly insular nature of their surroundings, and the distance from their homeland presented a radical change from the familiar. But, for nearly all of the Japanese in Micronesia, the new environment offered advantages and risks, privileges and sacrifices, in almost equal proportions.

The climate, of course, had held a common attraction for all who had left Japanese shores. At its best, in the Marianas, the Micronesian climate could be delightful, not merely perpetual summer, but better than the summers in much of Japan, where the rainy season of June and July could bring suffocating heat and humidity, often without the benefit of sunshine. Moreover, the absence of extreme shifts in temperature meant that clothing and housing were more easily managed than in Japan.

The availability of land was another attraction. Despite the insularity of their new surroundings, the Japanese in Micronesia often had more living space than in the villages and cities of their homeland (although this advantage would diminish as the islands filled with immigrants). One has the impression that the crowding together of houses and stores in the Japanese towns in Micronesia was due more often to custom and habit than to necessity or ordinance.

When they troubled to notice it, there was also the beauty of the natural environment, particularly in the high islands where the majority of the Japanese population resided. They were surrounded by colors of intense brilliance—emeralds, turquoises, and dazzling whites. On the high islands, particularly, the flora of the tropics delighted the eye and added to the exoticism of the surroundings. Coconut palms clustered in groves provided welcome shade or stretched out along the shore; flame trees dotted the coastal plains on Saipan; hibiscus spread down the slopes of Mt. Tolomen on Dublon; and bougainvillea ran riot along the roadsides of Kolonia on Ponape. In their backyards Japanese occasionally grew papayas, guavas, mangoes, and other tropical fruit.

As well, the Japanese in Micronesia lived as members of a privileged class whose welfare and security were prime concerns of their government, whose economic activities were in large part subsidized by the colonial administration, and whose interests had come to take precedence over those of the indigenes. Like colonials everywhere, they sometimes acquired comforts they had not enjoyed in the homeland. Not a few, for example, hired Micronesians to work in their homes, to aid them in their office chores, or to provide the manual labor at their warehouses and docks.

Many Japanese who came to the South Seas recognized that while there might be initial toil and hardship, emigration meant new beginnings, a chance to break free from the restraints that economic or social circumstances imposed at home. Added to the enticing languor of the tropics, this recognition held in check their natural nostalgia for their homeland. As one former Nan'yō-chō official recalled in later years:

> Compared to Japan, where one works hard enough in this short life of ours, the life and surroundings of the tropics required extraordinary effort, but there one felt liberated in a way that one could only dream about in Japan, as well as feeling an indescribable sense of ease. For the first two or three years one yearned to return home, but after the spell of the South Seas began to take hold, the years stretched out until, before one knew it, twenty or more had passed.[3]

For all this, Micronesia was hardly a paradise for the average Japanese immigrant. Besides the initial years of hardship and toil that were the lot of many of them, the tropical Pacific, for all its beauty, presented an array of hazards and miseries that could overwhelm those less determined or more easily discouraged. While moderated to an extent in the Marianas, the heat and humidity of most of the other island groups often crushed the energy and initiative of the newcomer. There were also the debilitating effects of climatic monotony in the tropics—the absence of seasons, the predictable appearance of the trade winds, the regularity of the sudden, dense showers—which even the most dramatic sunsets and brilliant ocean colors could not offset. As the colonial administration readily informed its prospective recruits, these were problems that could mentally unhinge the irresolute or unresourceful.[4]

When the weather was not monotonous it could be awesome. Umesao Tadao, visiting Palau for the first time, was stunned by the sheer violence of a Micronesian cloudburst that caught him and his party in an open launch heading for the Koror docks. Most terrible were the occasional hurricanes. Typhoons, often spawned in the central Carolines, were no stranger to Japanese, especially Okinawans. But when the winds reached more than one hundred fifty miles an hour and created mountainous seas, they were the terror of Japanese communities on all but the largest islands.[5]

The fauna of the islands held its share of hazards and nuisances. Sea snakes were a constant threat to wading fishermen along the shores of the Marianas and crocodiles were found in the swamps of the Palaus. Scorpions and centipedes lay in wait for the unwary householder in the Carolines, and the lagoons of the Marshalls held a good number of poisonous, as well as edible fish. Dysentery and dengue fever were endemic to most of the islands, and the common housefly, carrier of a variety of diseases, was the most ubiquitous and dangerous insect in all of them.

Colonial Life: Housing, Food, and Entertainment

To deal with these problems, the Japanese in Micronesia did what most colonials in the tropics attempt to do—to recreate a world familiar to themselves. Being among the most cohesive and exclusive of peoples, the Japanese carried this tendency to an extreme, creating, at least in the larger communities of the mandate, "little Japans" that existed quite isolated from their surroundings. By the 1930s, they were able to surround themselves with all the amenities of Japanese life, from foodstuffs to phonograph needles. In all the larger population centers there were electric lights, telephones, ice, restaurants, bakeries, and all manner of goods ordinarily available in towns of comparable size in the home islands. News from the homeland might be a few days to a few weeks old, but it was at least regular by the late 1930s. In the Marianas, at least, radio programs were received directly from Tokyo, as were the latest samurai movies. The major metropolitan dailies had a very small circulation, but throughout the islands there were a number of regional papers, of varying circulation and quality.[6]

Many of the inhabitants of the larger Japanese settlements seem to have been content to exist in their isolated colonial environment and rarely moved beyond the narrow confines of the towns. To Umesao Tadao, so Japanese in aspect and outlook was Kolonia on Ponape that there were times when he felt as if he were not on Ponape at all. In some exasperation he wrote that "the Japanese [on Ponape] live a life completely isolated from the island and its people . . . . Though they live in the South Seas, they know absolutely nothing about it."[7]

Nevertheless, the environment inevitably imposed special circumstances that affected Japanese life in Micronesia. Like most colonials in the tropics, the Japanese were inconsistent in their adjustment, sometimes adjusting their daily living arrangements to the conditions imposed by their surroundings, sometimes stubbornly clinging to Japanese customs and habits that were really unsuited to the tropics.

The arrangement and construction of Japanese housing in the mandate was a case in point. To begin with, Japanese immigrants, unlike Micronesians, were averse to sequestering their houses among whatever trees they found at the building site. They usually succumbed to the immemorial urge of the pioneer to clear the land, to cut away the surrounding vegetation (though often they took the trouble to landscape the houses with attractive gardens). In the tropics, where people need as much shade as possible, this made little sense, and the absence of large trees often left their homes exposed to the ferocity of the elements. Yet, in many ways, the average Japanese bungalow in Micronesia was highly utilitarian. It was a box-like structure of modest size, usually raised three or four feet off the ground on pillars of stone or concrete, in part to provide coolness and dryness, but more importantly to minimize the ravages of termites, which otherwise could reduce the foundations of a wooden building to powder in six months. In the first decade or so, as the Japanese cleared away the forests of the high islands for agriculture, lumber was readily available, and wood was the common building material. Later, as the forests were depleted, cement construction was increasingly substituted.[8]

The roofs of Japanese homes in Micronesia were usually made of that ubiquitous building material of the modern tropics, the corrugated metal sheet—of iron, tin, or zinc. This covering was at once useful and uncomfortable: down its grooves sluiced the rain that beat upon it during the regular downpours, to be funneled by gutters and piped into a cistern that provided for the daily needs of the household (a matter of no little import since ground water on many of the islands was unpleasant to the taste and often brackish); but bare to the unrelenting sun, the corrugated metal roof also raised the temperature of the rooms below far higher than that of a thatched house.[9]

Around the structure there often ran a covered veranda on which, in the evenings, seated on rattan chairs, the owner—administrator, plant manager, or trader—and his family or friends would smoke and talk over the day's events. Inside, the house was usually a mixture of Western and Japanese styles; the walls of the more affluent homes were usually of plaster, across which the ever-present geckos chased mosquitoes and night crawlers. Though tatami matting was rarely used because of the humidity, tatami covers were usually tacked down over the hardwood floors. The use of the traditional sliding doors—wooden *fusuma* and paper shoji—permitted cross ventilation and helped to reduce the temperature during the day. However, R. V. C. Bodley, staying at a Japanese inn on Saipan, noted with distress that the inn maids, following the custom in the home islands, closed all the *fusuma* at night, rendering the rooms inside unbearable. By the late 1930s, the better Japanese homes in Micronesia were constructed of concrete, their deep-set windows shielded by double shutters that swung outward, significant steps toward making household living more comfortable. Yet, oddly, neither doors nor windows held any screens, a surprising oversight in the tropics where the torment of flies and mosquitoes can be a frequent misery.[10]

In any event, this box-like structure formed the general architectural style for Japanese dwellings in Micronesia. Single men employed by the Nan'yō-chō, Nambō, or Nankō lived less well, being housed in dormitories provided with individual Japanese-style rooms, but sharing common washroom facilities, and taking their meals in a common dining room where, not surprisingly, the food was generally unappetizing.

In matters of clothing the average Japanese immigrant adjusted easily to the tropics, since summer apparel in Japan proved easily adaptable to the South Seas. Coats and neckties were abandoned (except, it appears, when posing for formal photographs) and, by the time Asai Tatsurō visited Ponape with the Kyoto University research group, men were wearing shorts to work, though at home they often donned the casual *yukata*,[11] the informal wraparound worn in summertime in Japan. On the street women wore *yukata* or simple Western-style dresses; at home almost always the former. The heavier layered kimono was not a practical piece of clothing in the tropics (though, again, it appears in formal group photographs of the period). Even the traditional finery of the Japanese geisha had to be adjusted to the heat and humidity. As perspiration ruined expensive silks, geisha in Micronesia usually wore unlined rayon kimono. In rural settlements on Palau and Ponape, men generally wore long-sleeved shirts and long trousers of sturdy material, but often went barefoot in keeping with Micronesian custom; women in these places wore the loose trousers and scarf of the traditional Japanese farm wife.[12]

Only officialdom held to a punctilious dress code, at least until 1940. Throughout most of the period, the standard uniform was a white linen jacket with stand-up collar, buttoned to the neck, with trousers to match, white shoes, epaulettes, and a pith helmet. By 1941, this uniform had been relaxed sufficiently to permit administrators the comfort of wearing white shorts. But the most sensible tropical uniform was brought in by naval personnel in the early 1940s: light-green denim shirts, open at the neck, and shorts of the same material.[13]

It was in their eating habits that the Japanese in the South Seas were the most unaccommodating to their environment. With a wealth of local foods to choose from—breadfruit, taro, yams, coconuts, bananas, pineapples, papayas, mangoes, guavas, chicken, and pork—and surrounded by an ocean teeming with fish, the Japanese communities remained curiously and obsessively dependent upon foods familiar to them—pickles, miso paste, seaweed, and rice—and available only in cans, jars, or bags imported from Japan. This phenomenon of Japanese colonial life was remarked upon by every thoughtful visitor to the islands, Japanese or Western. Ando Sakan observed that Japanese in the Marianas and Palau refused to try island dishes or to prepare meals using local ingredients. In Japanese restaurants where he was entertained he never encountered sashimi, and the fish he was served always came out of a can. As Ando sailed south from Koror to the East Indies, the Nambō steamer stopped at Sonsorol Atoll south of the Palaus to offload *eleven tons* of Japanese foodstuffs—a year's supply—for the six Japanese *katsuobushi* workers who lived on the atoll amid a Micronesian population of nearly two hundred. On Ponape, Umesao Tadao, strolling among the stores and bustling markets on Kaigan Dori in Kolonia, noted that nearly all the foodstuffs for sale, groceries along with canned goods, seemed to be imported. Even the vegetables trucked in from the Japanese agricultural settlement at Palikir Mura were sold in relatively small quantities (which may help to explain why the government's agricultural communities were seldom an economic success). It was Umesao's opinion that while Japanese colonials in Micronesia tended to blame all their physical and mental ailments on the effects of the climate, their health would have improved if they had taken advantage of the food resources at hand.[14]

Such dependence on food imports from Japan had serious consequences. The importation of food contributed to the dramatic rise in the cost of living in the islands; by 1940 food costs in the Carolines were nearly twice what they were in the homeland. Inevitably, too, with the approach of war, food from Japan not only increased in price, but also major items, such as miso paste, soy sauce, salt, and beer, were swiftly rationed and became available only at designated stores. The dietary predicament of the Japanese soon came to contrast with the nutrition of the Micronesians who were self-sufficient in food (except for a small elite class who had adopted Japanese tastes). It would take the exigencies of war, utter isolation, and the possibility of mass starvation to change the eating habits of the colonists.[15]

Because the burgeoning Japanese population in Micronesia was overwhelmingly rural in origin and agricultural in occupation, there was little of the grand colonial style in the Japanese presence in the South Seas. Without a social or economic elite within the colonial population of the mandate—no great commercial taipans who maintained themselves in the grand manner, no individually wealthy planters who presided over great estates, no group of bored but affluent expatriates of the sort found from Bombay to Shanghai—the Japanese colonial lifestyle in Micronesia lacked the glitter and magnificence of the European colonies in East Asia or the South Pacific. R. V. C. Bodley noted, for example, the absence of those recreational facilities—the club, the polo grounds, the race course—by which European expatriates diverted themselves and sorted out the social status of their compatriots. Touring the mandate, Bodley was hospitably entertained by his Japanese hosts, but came away with the impression that it was a rare indulgence, not a mere pretext for warding off the monotony of the tropics.[16]

Yet an organized social life of a more traditional Japanese sort did exist in the mandate, though it largely involved colonial officialdom and the upper echelons of Japanese business in the islands, particularly Nankō. For the latter, the Kōhatsu Club, a social facility established on the larger islands, became an important center of leisure activity, a place where company employees could gather in the evenings to drink a glass of beer, read back issues of *Kingu*, *Kaizō*, or *Jigyō no Nippon*, play mah-jongg or *shōgi* 'chess', or discuss the day's events.[17]

The center of social life in Koror was the Shōnan ("Prosperous South") Club, a low, modestly proportioned building across the street from the headquarters of the South Seas Government. There, weary administrators could gather at the end of the day to relax, read old newspapers, play billiards, or gossip, an activity that not only provided diversion in all insular communities of the day, but was the only source of information that was not already weeks old. For many years, the central focus of activity at the club for aspiring junior officials was the polished surface of the *gō* board, since that Japanese game of strategy was the particular passion of Yokota Gōsuke, the longest serving of the Nan'yō-chō governors, and a frequent visitor to the Shōnan. Indeed, so avidly were the fine points of the game pursued by the more ambitious club members, that the chief of the communications section of the Nan'yō-chō owed his appointment to the fact that he held the third rank in *gō* and could double as the club's instructor.[18]

In the early years of the Nan'yō-chō, when there was no hotel worthy of the name in Koror, the Shōnan functioned as the guest house for distinguished visitors to the mandate. With the installation of beds and mosquito netting it could be transformed into a satisfactory hostel in a twinkling. Through its low portico walked navy fleet commanders, Diet members, imperial princes, and various other VIPs. In later years, the prominent visitor was taken to the Nan'yō Hotel, a sprawling building of tasteful landscaping and shaded verandas, before which an enormous nipa palm spread its fronds like a peacock's tail.[19]

If there was one gala event in the official life of the islands it was the annual celebration of Administration Day *(Shisei kinembi)* on 1 July, to mark the establishment of civilian rule in Japan. In Koror, the festivities took place at the Shōnan Club in the form of a large garden party, bringing together colonial officials, the most important citizens of the town, and the leading Palauan chiefs. Refreshments included a buffet of Japanese delicacies, along with *oden* (a Japanese stew with vegetables), and *sekihan* (rice boiled with red beans), all washed down with beer and cold sake. A stage was usually set up for various performances, which in the early years usually comprised classical dance, Chinese poetry recitation, and other traditional Japanese performing arts. These were regarded as a bore by the majority of younger club members who eventually voted in entertainment of a livelier and more raucous variety, including lotteries, juggling, magic tricks, and female impersonation. For the colonial community, invitations to the club on that day were regarded as a mark of status, and the day was anticipated months ahead of time by Palauan chiefs as one of the few occasions on which they were permitted to drink liquor.[20]

The Emperor's Birthday was a more prestigious and significant occasion, but it appears to have been marked with somewhat more solemn ceremonials, at least in Koror. At some of the branch government headquarters, however, it was the occasion for general festivities. On Jaluit, for instance, it was marked by baseball games, sumo wrestling, and kendo contests. A festive occasion at any time was the appearance of a Japanese naval vessel, usually a training ship, which not only hosted shipboard visitors and parties, but also provided for concerts ashore, the ship's band thumping out old navy favorites like "The Battleship March" and "Commander Hirose," to the delight of the populace (Photo 26).[21]

For the majority of Japanese in Micronesia, mostly Okinawans engaged in farming or fishing, leisure and companionship were generally found within the family circle. In the larger Japanese communities, movie theaters and variety halls *(yose)* provided most of the entertainment needs of the immigrant. Sports facilities, usually a baseball diamond and track, were built at Madalai on the western end of Koror, in the suburbs of Kolonia, Ponape, on the level ground behind Dublon

Photo 26. Navy band concert, Garapan Town, Saipan, c. 1938.

Town, Truk, and at Jabor Town, Jaluit, and were the sites of frequent ballgames, track-and-field competitions, and other athletic events. For more leisurely recreation on the larger islands there were excursions to places recognized by the Japanese community to be of scenic beauty. On Ponape, such sites included several waterfalls, large pools in the mountain streams, or mountain vantage points, as well as the great cave of Pahn Takai in the U district. To such places schoolteachers would take their pupils on excursions, and visiting officials and other travelers would be brought or make their way to rest awhile, amid the coolness of splashing water and lush foliage.[22]

For single males, both government workers and company employees, such innocent pastimes were less likely to hold appeal. Without a home life, housed in dormitories where the food was often monotonous, lacking any cultural amenities, it was inevitable that in their off-hours they found their principal pleasures in women and strong drink.[23] By the 1930s there were plenty of both available in the mandate. For the relatively impecunious, such as Okinawan field laborers and factory workers, there were the bars and pothouses where, amid fairly dingy surroundings, patrons knocked back glasses of *awamori*, a fierce brandy made from millet, served to them by barmaids *(shakufu)* who derived the greater portion of their income from prostitution. For those on higher pay scales, there were the *ryōriya*, or restaurants, an often-ambiguous term which sometimes meant simply a place where food and drink were served and geisha were present to entertain and converse with guests, but which could also mean establishments where geisha not only sat with customers, but were available for sexual diversions as well.

When the navy was running Micronesia, prostitution had been strictly forbidden, a simple edict, since the profession was generally unknown to the indigenes and Japanese were still insignificant in number. With the rising tide of immigration in the 1920s and 1930s, however, it became an inevitable accompaniment. In 1924, the Nan'yō-chō instituted a licensing system patterned after the regulations governing the practice in Japan.[24] By the 1930s every Japanese town in Micronesia had its *hana machi* 'flower quarters'—rather shabby little buildings with incongruously poetic names where men could eat, drink, and enjoy the company of women for an evening. There were usually seven or eight women to each *ryōriya*, though the largest of them, in Koror, employed some sixty geisha and barmaids.[25] Advertisements in local newspapers and pamphlet guides usually provided the prospective customer with a selection of female companionship. In Tinian Town, for example, women from the Japanese mainland graced the rooms of the Nantei (Southern Mansion), the Hassensō (Eight Thousand Grasses), and the Shogetsurō (Shining Moon Mansion); those who felt more at home in the company of Okinawan women could drop in at the Miharashi (Beautiful View), the Komatsu (Small Pine), or the Nangetsu (Southern Moon). In Dublon Town, which by the early 1940s was increasingly frequented by naval personnel, there were the Maruman, the Yamagata, and the Nankai—all first-class establishments—but the elegant Tokiwa (Evergreen) was reserved for navy officers, particularly the senior officer ashore.[26]

The term *geisha* thus took on a rather sordid meaning in the mandate. Not only were most geisha engaged in prostitution, but apparently most were in the yellow leaf. The accounts of a number of visitors to Micronesia in the 1930s mention the faded aura of the geisha encountered at dinner parties arranged by their Japanese hosts. R. V. C. Bodley asserted (on what authority is not clear) that the superannuated geisha encountered in the South Seas were those cast off when no longer in demand in Tokyo, moving ever eastward through the mandate and downward in their social function as their charms gave way over the years, so that the geisha of the Marshalls were mostly wizened prostitutes. True or not, geisha in Micronesia seem often to have occasioned more sadness than delight for those who sat across the restaurant tatami from them. To Ando Sakan, sitting in a *ryōriya* in the Marianas amid the heat and mosquitoes, the faded entertainer before him in her cheap rayon kimono filled him only with an overwhelming sense of the transience of all human existence—hardly the kind of thoughts inspired by the traditional Japanese geisha party![27]

The Japanese Town as a Colonial Type

The generally commonplace quality of the Japanese colonial presence in Micronesia was manifest in the arrangement and appearance of the towns. To many Western eyes, the Japanese town is inherently unattractive in composition and arrangement—streets narrow, box-like houses and stores crowded together, too often unrelieved by shade trees, parks, open spaces, or gracious vistas, colors usually an unrelenting blend of grays and browns. The transfer of this style to Micronesia did little to alter these prospects, and solely from an aesthetic point of view, there is little to regret in its passing from the Micronesian scene following World War II.

Garapan, for example, was the largest town in the mandate, but had little to recommend it in terms of beauty. Indeed, Ishikawa Tatsuzō, visiting Garapan in the spring of 1941, thought its appearance even more dreary than its homeland counterparts: "Built by labor and industry, the town contains none of the flourishing consumer culture of Japan. It stretches flat and squalid, its streets, unadorned and mean-looking, lie sweltering side by side . . . ."[28] Photographs from the time confirm Ishikawa's impression and convey something of the sunbaked appearance of the closely packed houses (e.g., Photo 27).

Both the materials employed and the arrangement of the usual Japa-

Photo 27. Aerial view of Garapan Town, Saipan, c. 1938. (Yamaguchi Yoji)

nese commercial buildings often contributed an air of impermanence to the whole town. Of Tinian Town, wedged in between the coral beach and the edge of a sugar plantation, Willard Price recalled that

> the buildings were typical Japanese structures, light and thin, looking as if they had been thrown up in an afternoon. They stood elbow to elbow down the street with no space between—Japanese stores, school, hairdressing parlor, cinema, photograph shop, hardware shop, fishmongers . . . and Buddhist temple.[29]

Umesao Tadao, visiting Dublon Town on Truk in 1941, thought it a rustic, mean-looking little place where only the main street was paved and the side streets, intersecting the bedraggled row of stores along the shoreline, were churned into bright, glue-like mud after a heavy rain.[30] Traveling on to Ponape, Umesao, like others who approach Ponape Harbor by sea, was awed by the grandeur of Sokehs rock, which plunges sheer some nine hundred feet to the bay. But he was distressed by his initial impression of Kolonia, as he approached the shore by launch. To the east of the town, the Chikunami (Dewannu) River emptied in a brown flood into the harbor, which was also the recipient of the town's sewage and of the discarded viscera of thousands of bonito from the nearby *katsuobushi* factory. Passing along Kaigan Dōri, where part of the harbor had been filled in to make space for the bars, restaurants, geisha houses, fishing companies, small stores, and businesses that crowded in, Umesao considered that the waterfront looked jumbled and unfinished.[31] Only when one left it and walked up to "Government Hill" on the modest heights above, did Kolonia assume any gracefulness. Proceeding up Hachiken Dōri, a wide street flanked by rows of palm trees, one passed a pretty park and came to the Ponape Branch Headquarters of the Nan'yō-chō, a rather dumpy building with a heavy and ungainly front portico, but suitably authoritative in its elevated setting, overlooking the entire town. Namiki Dōri—Tree-lined Street (which photographs suggest belied its name)—seemed pleasant enough, but the tightly packed rows of wooden stores and shops with covered entrances extending to the street, hardly conveyed that imposing air of privilege and economic power associated with other colonial towns in the Pacific (Photo 28).[32]

Of the Japanese population centers mentioned, only Koror seems to have approached the dimensions and arrangements of a European-style colonial city. By the end of the 1930s, it stretched halfway across the north shore of the island, from Madalai and its sports field on the western shore, past the veranda of the South Seas Government Headquarters and the Shōnan Club, through the bustling business and entertainment district, out to the eastern suburbs, beyond which lay the terraced ground where the grand Shintō shrine for the South Seas was built.

Photo 28. Street scene, Kolonia, Ponape, 1930s.

Most of the side streets in the center of the town were narrow, with stores along their edges, giving an appearance that was not much different from a suburb of Yokohama. But as a whole, Koror appears to have been a place of open spaces, attractively situated and landscaped government buildings, and broad, tree-lined avenues leading into the city (Photo 29). To Umesao, approaching the city by car in the dusk just after a rainstorm, the beauty of the place seemed magical:

> The wide, even asphalt road, wet with rain, reflected the light of the street lamps placed at intervals along it, like the lighted surface of a canal. The car's headlights caught the brilliant red of the hibiscus flowers which grew up along the roadside hedges and on either side of the road stretched a row of lovely palms . . . their broad fan-shaped leaves rustling in the wind, imparted a dream-like quality after the rain. The streets were otherwise dark, but the buildings—airy, modern, and handsome—seemed appropriate to the capital of the Japanese South Seas.[33]

Elsewhere in the mandate the natural setting, if anything, lent beauty to the places where the Japanese had chosen to congregate. Colonia, on Yap, for example, was not much of a town (Photo 30), but, as Willard Price approached it from the harbor entrance, it seemed trim enough and preserved, if faintly, the ambience of the old Spanish settlement it once had been:

> From a distance it looks like a strip of white adhesive tape neatly stuck to the edge of the lagoon. It boasts four dozen resplendent sheet iron roofs

Photo 29. Street scene, Koror Town, Koror, Palau Islands, c. 1935.

Photo 30. Colonia, Yap, c. 1920.

and is ashamed of a dozen thatched roofs. . . . The Japanese government office is just where the Spanish office was, perched on a walled mound, suitable in case of native rebellion. The jail is still called the calaboose and the sound of bells still comes down from the old Spanish mission.[34]

Lele Village at Kusaie was even less consequential, but to Price, approaching it at dawn, the harbor was "as beautiful as an Italian lake [whose] still surface reflected the mountains that stood in a semi-circle around the little port where thatch houses nestled among the palms,

Photo 31. Japanese freighter entering Lele Harbor, Kusaie, Caroline Islands,
c. 1935. *(National Geographic)*

canoes lined the shore, and beyond stood a little white church, as
primly as if cut out of cardboard"[35] (Photo 31).

To the eye, the physical manifestations of the Japanese colonial presence rarely matched the vividness of their exotic settings. As the territo-
rially smallest, administratively least significant, and by distance, the
most remote component of the empire, the mandate never saw the construction of official buildings, monuments, or public works on the scale
of those in Taiwan or Korea, where massive stonework and wrought
iron were used to fashion governmental headquarters designed to over-
awe subject peoples and impress foreign visitors. Yet the administrative
offices of the mandate, nearly always encompassed by verandas, as befit
the tropics, were usually the most prominent structures in the islands by
location, if not always by scale or design. The Yap Branch Government
building sat on a high artificial embankment surrounded by shrubs and
bougainvillea; that of Truk was positioned amid lush greenery and scar-
let poincianas on a hill overlooking Dublon Harbor (Photo 32); the one
at Jabor Town on Jaluit Island dated from German times, and was only
a small bungalow in a palm grove, but it stood proudly behind its two
little stone gateposts. The approach on Saipan led to a wooden, cupola-
surmounted structure that stood on a hill at the back of Garapan (Photo
33). It was a welcome sight to Yamaguchi Yusaburō, passing through on
his way to pick up his new administrative assignment in Koror. "On
either side of the road leading up to the headquarters flame trees
bloomed in a riot of color," he recalled years later. "Two large [latte

Photo 32. Branch Government Headquarters, Truk, c. 1932.

Photo 33. Branch Government Headquarters, Garapan Town, Saipan.

215

stone] columns stood at the bottom of a flight of stairs leading up to the building. Climbing them I looked up and was swept with profound emotion to see, dazzling at the top, the chrysanthemum crest . . ."[36]

Yet none of these buildings were as distinguished in design as their counterparts in Penang, Noumea, or Suva. The sprawling, veranda-sheltered wings of the largest of the administrative centers, the South Seas Government Headquarters Building in Koror, were graceful enough, but its wooden construction and plain bungalow style scarcely qualified it as a structure in the grand colonial manner.

Race Relations in Japanese Micronesia

Historical judgments on the relations between two races are always a slippery business, involving as they do, differing perspectives not only on each of the races, but also on the nature of the evidence, as well as a shift, over time, in the general moral position of the historical profession. Although any assessment of Japanese attitudes toward Micronesians is based on generally fragmentary evidence, it is clear that those attitudes were influenced by a number of elements. How the average Japanese colonists treated Micronesians—when they came in contact with them—or thought about Micronesians—when they thought about them at all—was shaped in part by popular perceptions of Micronesia in Japan, by the size of the Japanese community in which the colonists lived, by their own sense of superiority as members of a materially advanced society, and by the general passivity of the indigenous populace in the face of aggressive Japanese intrusion into the islands. All of these elements combined to produce in the attitudes of ordinary Japanese colonists a patronizing, yet generally tolerant attitude toward the gentle people whom they were rapidly displacing.

To begin with, the average Japanese arrived in Micronesia devoid of any understanding of the islands other than that arising from the Japanese popular culture of the day, which served up an image of the South Seas through pulp magazines, comic strips, and cheap novels. Micronesia was viewed as a distant paradise, conceived as being literally in the South Pacific, and inhabited by primitive peoples not much different than "savages" anywhere—naked, ignorant, sensuous, and dark skinned. In the words of a popular song of the 1930s:

> My sweetheart is the daughter of a village chief
> She's pretty dark, but in the South Seas, she's a beauty
> In the Marshall Islands, below the equator [sic]
> She dances slowly in the shade of the palm trees.[37]

After arriving in Micronesia, most colonists, who usually settled in one of the larger Japanese communities in the islands, had little opportunity to alter this stereotype, since they made scant effort to break out of their colonial boundaries. The most cohesive and exclusive of peoples, the Japanese on the high islands often simply failed to take notice of the Micronesians around them. But, as Umesao noted:

> This is not because Micronesians are not in evidence. Indeed, one often sees more Ponapeans on the streets of Kolonia than Japanese. Some have houses in the town; many others come to town from all over the island to have a good time. Yet, except for some officials and missionaries, the Japanese colonists generally ignore them. They are treated like children who are to be indulged, but who are not really qualified to participate in the life of grown-ups.[38]

Such complacent indifference went hand in hand with the steady increase in the Japanese population, making the Micronesian peoples decreasingly important from an economic standpoint (as I have written in chapter 4). As the indigenous people on the larger islands were not seen as having a productive future in Micronesia, it was possible simply to look through them. The passivity of the Micronesians in the face of Japanese prejudice also facilitated this complacent indifference. Discrimination took place not only in terms of education, employment, and official policy, but also in terms of insensitive treatment by ordinary Japanese. Umesao noted, for example, that in coffee shops and tea-houses, Japanese and Micronesians were often seated at different tables. Older Micronesians today recall offensive Japanese gestures in public places, such as holding their noses against the odor of the coconut oil often used by the Islanders. Yet none of this appears to have sparked any serious incident between the two races. To Japanese, even to perceptive observers like Umesao, this apparent absence of rancor on the part of the indigenous population under these conditions was explained by the fact that Micronesians didn't really perceive that they were being discriminated against.[39]

Today, one is inclined to write off such an idea as fatuous. Certainly, in the half century since, Micronesians have on numerous occasions voiced their resentments when recalling the many indignities of the colonial past under the Japanese. Yet, it seems to have been true that during the Japanese period Islanders accepted with relative equanimity situations of social and economic discrimination that any Micronesian would find intolerable today.

To the extent that one can generalize, Japanese civilian attitudes toward Micronesians seem to have ranged between amicable tolerance and insensitivity and indifference. At least, that is the conclusion one reaches from the random comments of Micronesians during the postwar decades. As one Palauan recalled after the war:

> Japanese officials looked down upon us Palauans, but the ordinary Japanese was friendly. Yet, even with them there was the unspoken distinction

—they were Japanese, an advanced, civilized people, and we were
natives, backward and primitive. Nevertheless, they tried to maintain
good friendship.[40]

Sometimes, such assumptions of superiority even among intelligent
Japanese, shaded off into explanations that can only be called racist.
Matsue Haruji, for example, could write that the decrease in intimacy
between Japanese and Saipanese as the former became more firmly
established on the island, was attributable to a "biological principle"
relating to the regression of an inferior species in relation to a superior
one when the two were in close proximity.[41] Other commentators were
flattered by real or imagined manifestations of Micronesian desire to
become more Japanese. Gondō Seikyo, visiting Micronesia in the late
1930s, was delighted by demonstrations of respect, obedience, and loyalty on the part of Micronesians toward Japan, such as conscientious
efforts to fly the Japanese flag, and he cherished the notion that
Micronesian women yearned to marry Japanese, since it gave their families social prestige. In a similar vein, after visiting Sonsorol in 1935,
Ando Sakan wrote that the women on the atoll were very passionate
and gave themselves eagerly to Japanese.[42] Decades removed, one is at a
loss as to how to judge whether these statements bore any semblance of
the truth; but they do indicate a Japanese state of mind toward the
island peoples.

Even sensitive Japanese observers like Nakajima Atsushi brought to
their observations of Micronesian life certain judgments which, though
sympathetically expressed, are oddly jarring today. On Palau, Nakajima came to know and admire a highly educated Palauan woman who
was a friend of Hijikata Hisakatsu. But his impression was that her cultural attainments, which included fluency in Japanese and English,
were incongruous with her ample figure and the tropical environment,
and created a humorous, slightly pathetic effect. In Nakajima's view,
when Palauans tried to emulate Japanese they only looked silly. Seeing
Palauan women attending a Spanish church on Koror he thought them
ludicrous in appearance because of their Japanese finery, red lacquered
geta, and the heavy makeup they wore over their dark complexions.[43]

If it is difficult to generalize about Japanese attitudes toward
Micronesians, to attempt the reverse is even riskier, except for those
Micronesians who had actively cast their lot in with the Japanese. On
most of the high islands there was an elite group of Islanders (not in the
sense of the traditional culture, but in a modern economic sense) who
prospered economically, held positions in the Japanese administration,
or were married to Japanese, and who identified themselves and their
future with Japan. For these persons, living in or adjacent to the major
Japanese population centers, emulation of Japanese became a symbol of
respectability. Palauans in Koror, for example, adopted Japanese dress,

began to eat Japanese food, and, if they were affluent, built Japanese-style houses. Chamorros in the Marianas developed an interest in *chambara eiga* 'samurai movies' and other Japanese arts. Marshallese, on Jaluit atoll at least, took up baseball and the boisterous activities related to Japanese shrine festivals. Umesao Tadao noticed that among those Ponapean women who wore lacquered geta, carried parasols, and bowed when greeting friends, even their facial expressions began to take on that self-conscious quality of the Japanese.[44]

It was usually from among members of these newer elite groups, as well as occasionally from the older traditional elites, that marriages and liaisons between Japanese men and Micronesian women took place. (As in most colonial situations, such arrangements rarely took place between Japanese women and Micronesian men.) The colonial administration tended to favor these connections, since the families which resulted from them were more Japanese in character than they were Micronesian. Yet the children of mixed Japanese-Micronesian parentage, while they possessed certain privileges, such as a *shōgakkō* rather than a *kōgakkō* education in the mandate, nevertheless paid a price. Minoru Ueki, son of a Japanese engaged in the lumber trade and a Palauan mother, recalled that though he was raised as a Japanese and spoke the language fluently, he encountered considerable discrimination from his Japanese schoolmates in addition to slighting comments from his Palauan friends and relatives of his age group. The same dilemmas were faced by other mixed-blood children, such as Kazuo Miyashita, son of the pioneer trader Miyashita Jūichirō and his Palauan wife.[45]

Among Islanders who stood outside this elite circle of Japanized or semi-Japanized Micronesians, feelings toward ordinary Japanese varied from island to island, with no apparent pattern. Most Micronesians seem to have been ambivalent in their feelings. In some circumstances they held Japanese in awe for their energy, organization, and purpose. On Babelthuap, for example, the first Palauan visitors from nearby villages, bringing food, seeds, and plants to the government agricultural communities, were astonished by the accomplishments of the pioneer Japanese settlers who worked with only hand tools and a few building materials. Each time the villagers returned, they saw the increasing results of Japanese industry and enterprise: houses, cultivated fields, roads, and small stores.[46] Similar admiration was undoubtedly provoked by the agricultural communities on Ponape.

Contemporary accounts of visitors to the islands provide conflicting evidence concerning Micronesian fear or familiarity in regard to the Japanese. While on Yap, Willard Price observed the way in which the Islanders not only deferred to Japanese traders, but seemed to be afraid of them. Yet Umesao Tadao was impressed by the relaxed attitude of the Micronesians he and his party encountered: "Even when we visited

Micronesian homes, our hosts didn't seem rattled, but, seated on the straw matting of their houses received us simply but amiably. Toward us, indeed toward all Japanese, they seemed to display genuine familiarity." Most probably, these different attitudes were in large part based on the degree of contact between the two races. One can imagine that on the remoter parts of Yap the appearance of a nonresident Japanese trader, particularly if he was a bully, might create uneasiness among the Islanders. But in the larger Japanese population centers, where Umesao and his group spent a good deal of their time, Micronesians had greater opportunity to become used to Japanese customs and manners.[47]

Such familiarity occasionally provoked among Micronesians the feeling that, in some ways, the Japanese immigrants were beneath them. On Ponape, for example, Japanese eating habits, especially their predilection for snails and frogs, were the object of concealed derision by the Islanders. Many sneered at what they regarded as the unkempt attire of Japanese laborers they encountered in the street, and older Ponapeans were shocked when Japanese men took island women as mistresses. Certain Japanese occupations, moreover, were revolting to Ponapeans. Among the successful Japanese entrepreneurs in Kolonia, for example, was a tough old Japanese named Ogata, who went from house to house, dressed in simple shorts and shirt, collecting night soil from cement-lined outhouses for processing and sale as fertilizer to farmers and agricultural companies. The business made him quite wealthy; but to Ponapeans it was a disgusting trade, unworthy of any self-respecting individual.[48]

The anomalies involved in the social ranking of three fairly distinct classes that had emerged in Micronesia by the 1930s—main-island Japanese at the top, Okinawans and Koreans in the middle, and Micronesians at the bottom—served to increase the ambivalence of the indigenous populations toward the Japanese immigrant communities. While Okinawans and Koreans were granted a position superior to that of the Islanders, by occupation or education they often seemed suspect in the eyes of the island peoples. Many Okinawans, for example, performed some sort of manual labor, an occupation regarded with mild contempt by high-born Micronesians. Younger Micronesians who spoke Japanese reasonably well were astonished when they met Koreans from remote mountain areas who were less cultured and spoke Japanese badly. Perceptive Micronesians were sometimes struck by the contrast between what they perceived as traits of cultural inferiority among Koreans and Okinawans and the privileges they enjoyed as immigrants that were denied to Micronesians. An Okinawan could swill *awamori* until blind drunk, but most Micronesians were never allowed to touch a drop of liquor. A Micronesian couple might be considerably more Japanized than most Koreans in the islands, but their children could not enjoy the better *shōgakkō* education available to Korean children.[49]

The Okinawan Underclass

To touch upon these matters is to take note of the subtle fissures that existed within the Japanese colonial population. Japanese histories and official surveys of the time say nothing about the prejudices held by main-island Japanese against the Okinawan majority and the sprinkling of Koreans in the islands. Koreans had long been the object of a good deal of Japanese prejudice, an attitude that went far back into the histories of both countries, but Okinawans had barely entered the consciousness of the average Japanese.

For this reason Japanese in Micronesia encountered Okinawan manners and speech with some shock. For some Japanese, the initial contact took place on board the NYK steamer taking them to the South Seas. Gondō Seikyo, for example, recalled looking in on a noisy party in the third-class cabins and seeing Okinawans drinking *awamori* and dancing to the accompaniment of a *jamisen,* an Okinawan version of the shamisen. He was surprised to find their songs unintelligible and their dancing coarse, since he had not imagined that differences existed between main-island Japanese and Okinawans. Ishikawa Tatsuzō, visiting an Okinawan variety hall in Garapan was absolutely bewildered by the speech of the actors and patrons. Others were aghast at the poverty of the Okinawan condition in Micronesia. In his book, *Sekidō o sen ni shite* (With the equator at my back), an account of a trip through Micronesia, Nonaka Fumio graphically described the griminess of an Okinawan cafe he visited in Tinian Town. [50]

Umesao Tadao, walking around Koror in 1941, concluded that behind the stately avenues, modern buildings, department stores, and hotels there was another face to the capital. Visiting the sidestreets of the city, where the Okinawans lived, one had the impression of walking into the confusion and poverty of a Chinatown. There the shops were small and dirty, naked children played in the streets, and one encountered half-dressed Okinawans, their skins blackened from exposure to the sun. Yet at the same time, Umesao was filled with admiration for the tenacity of this underclass, which was struggling to succeed on Japan's tropical frontier. In his view, the staunch contribution of this lowest socioeconomic level of Japanese society to the nation's southward drive demonstrated the basic human strength of the Japanese effort to develop the South Seas, a fact seldom understood by Japanese in the homeland. [51]

By the 1940s, the government itself had become disenchanted with the character and conduct of the Okinawan population in Micronesia. Supposedly, the government's principal concern was with the increasing tendency of Okinawans, who had come to the islands under contract as tenant farmers or farm laborers, to break their contracts by taking up more lucrative and less arduous activities, such as the charcoal business or shopkeeping, as a sideline. This trend developed just as the colonial administration was attempting to increase agricultural production as part of the effort to promote the self-sufficiency of the colony. In late 1941, the Nan'yō-chō moved quietly to reverse a twenty-year trend: it passed the word to the home islands that further immigration of Okinawans into Micronesia was not desired and, further, began a campaign to deport from the colony all immigrants—mostly Okinawans, presumably—found to have more than one means of support.[52]

It is difficult to say what the long-term implications of this policy would have been, for the coming of war in late 1941 soon made further immigration of any sort impossible. It was, however, part of a pattern of hardship and misfortune that makes up the story of Okinawans in Micronesia. For years, Okinawan immigrants, scorned at home and abroad, had struggled on in the tropics, enduring hardship and difficulty in the expectation that they would some day return to their home islands with money in their pockets and a proud sense of accomplishment. With the coming of the Pacific War the fate of the overwhelming majority was shatteringly different. Aerial bombs and naval shells brought death to many (including, one sadly notes, the young Okinawan who wrote the *Nan'yō kouta*) and siege and isolation brought privation and suffering to the rest. Ragged and starving, their homes reduced to rubble, those who survived at war's end were shipped home in American vessels to cities no less ravaged by the war.[53]

"Southward Advance" and Its Discontents

Usually, though not always, the settlement of an overseas territory reflects attitudes and pressures within the home country, as the case of Japan's Micronesian colony illustrates. In the first five years after the assumption of civilian rule in the islands, far from generating much interest as a place of settlement, Micronesia was written off as worse than useless by not a few in the upper reaches of the Japanese government. But within a few years, the success of Matsue Haruji's enterprise in the Marianas proved the worth of the islands in economic terms and eventually led to an expanding torrent of immigrants from Japan in the second half of the 1920s and the beginning of the 1930s. During this middle period, the settlement and development of the islands were seen largely as ends in themselves, by both business and the government.

By the 1930s, however, the growing sense of national crisis and militancy that gripped the political and military leadership in Japan had led to a series of adventures on the Asian continent. These, in turn, had reopened the debate as to the proper direction for Japanese expansionism. Opposed to the insistence of the military that Japan should move aggressively in northeast Asia, many Japanese—businessmen, pol-

iticians, and journalists—with increasing clamor began to support the
navy's contention that Japan's vital interests lay instead in the "South
Seas," a term that had come increasingly to mean Southeast Asia and
Melanesia. Thus was rekindled in the decade before Pearl Harbor the
idea of a *nanshin* 'southward advance', whose origins I have traced in
chapter 1.

Under these circumstances, Micronesia came to be seen as valuable
not just in itself, but as a "southern lifeline" *(minami no seimeisen)*, in a
favorite phrase of navy propagandists. In this view, the colonization of
Micronesia was increasingly seen as a preliminary to the movement of
Japanese colonists into Melanesia and Southeast Asia. Academic writers
and commentators now studied the experiences of the Japanese immigrant communities in the mandate for whatever clues they might yield
for the long-range future of Japan in tropical Asia.[54]

Not surprisingly, given the expansive mood of the day, Japanese commentators tended to view the role of Japan in the tropics with a good
deal of optimism and to frame their judgments within assumptions concerning race and climate that would not be given much credibility
today. Some attached considerable importance to the fact that so many
Japanese had managed to find a new home in the tropics and that Japanese labor had come to play such a major part in the sugar industry,
showing the adaptability of Japanese to the Micronesian environment.
Others, using flimsier evidence, favorably contrasted the allegedly
inherent capacities of Japanese to adjust to a hot and humid climate
with the supposed inability of Caucasians to do so.[55]

Renewed public interest in a southward advance took some years to
develop, but it was encouraged by the expansive statements of certain
navy spokesmen and by the publication of a number of popular com-
mentaries like Murobuse Koshin's *Nanshin ron* (On the southward
advance, 1936). Yet, given that Southeast Asia appeared to lie firmly in
the grip of the Western colonial powers, the seeming lack, in the 1930s,
of an immediate means to effect the Japanese penetration of the region
gave a certain unreality to all the *nanshin* arguments. Then, in 1940,
just as had happened in 1914, a sudden shift in international events presented Japan with a golden and wholly unanticipated opportunity: the
collapse of France and the Netherlands suddenly left their Asian colonies virtually unguarded, and, with Britain now besieged and beleaguered, its Asian colonies were only slightly less vulnerable.

Prepared by the heated *nanshin* rhetoric in the mass media in recent
years, the Japanese public was quick to believe that the wealth of the
Indies was now suddenly within the range of Japanese ambitions and
that vast, underpopulated, and underdeveloped areas like Borneo and
New Guinea now lay open to Japanese commerce and settlement.
While these visions may have excited certain enthusiasm in some busi-

ness circles, among expansionists, and within various special interest groups in Japan, they produced an absolute fever in the Japanese communities in Micronesia. In his travel account, Umesao makes frequent references to conversational and written examples of this obsession among Japanese in Micronesia who believed that their personal horizons, as well as those of their nation, would soon be unlimited. Everywhere, there was talk of the new opportunities that awaited enterprising Japanese in the Netherlands East Indies. South Seas study clubs and volunteer labor groups for the exploitation of "southern areas" sprang up in Koror.[56] In Kolonia, Ponape, Umesao came to the conclusion that the operations of the more than thirty firms whose offices were ranged along Kaigan Dōri were merely trial runs; the firms had established themselves in Ponape not to exploit the meager resources of the island, but to prepare themselves for entry to the far richer markets of Southeast Asia, once the path to the exploitation of that area lay completely open.[57]

Ishikawa Tatsuzō saw this fixation as the culmination of an inherent rootlessness in the Japanese communities in Micronesia. In Koror he found himself oddly bored and impatient with the half-modernized character of the city, where everything—the houses, the furniture, the people in them—seemed temporary, waiting for some great change, some onward movement. The cause of this unsettled atmosphere, Ishikawa concluded, was the pervasiveness of the *nanshin* mentality of Koror's colonial population. The attention of the city's inhabitants was constantly fixed on Java on Indochina or New Guinea or some other wider shore in the Asian tropics, in a way that fused personal frustrations and the nation's current priorities. In consequence, he noted, their mood seemed continually dependent on the tide of events in other places. Was there heady talk today in the shops and cafes of the latest Japanese advance into Indochina? Tomorrow, the streets would be filled with the bitter news that the government had failed to press its demands on the Dutch East Indies. In the summer of 1941, the Japanese in Micronesia had assumed the outlook of transients, waiting for some decisive break in international currents, for some national signal that would start yet another migration to seek glittering opportunities even further south. Micronesia no longer represented the terminus of personal and national aspirations, but was merely a station on the way to more distant and more golden shores. A whole community was now marking time, Ishikawa felt, and in doing so, it had created its own stagnation. "Life in Koror," he wrote, "is like the prolongation of life aboard a steamer bound for the South Seas and the tedium that one feels in the streets is like the collective weariness of a family on such a passage."[58]

The Sun at Apogee: Establishment of the Kampei Taisha
Nan'yō Jinja

Although in physical appearance, in lifestyle, and in reputation, there was little in the Japanese presence in Micronesia that captured the magnificence of European tropical empires—or even the occasional splendor of the larger Japanese colonies in Asia—one brief event did bring to Micronesia the mysterious aura of the national cult, accompanied by the majesty of the imperial throne. In doing so, it marked the proud meridian of the Japanese sun in the tropical Pacific. This was the enshrinement ceremony held in February 1940 to establish the state Shintō shrine at Koror, the Kampei Taisha Nan'yō Jinja.

Because it was at once the most ancient element in the Japanese cultural tradition and, by the last decade of the nineteenth century, a form of secular worship that supported the state, Shintō was very much part of the Japanese colonial scene. Wherever Japanese gathered in the empire, the Shintō shrine, with its sweeping torii gateway, was a fixture of the overseas community, bringing to it more than just a faith, but a sense of stability and security, no less one supposes than the way in which the Anglican parish church or the Catholic église in a hundred exotic and imperial sites brought temporal as well as spiritual assurance to the British and the French around the globe. Even more than the European church or the Asian Buddhist temple, the Japanese Shintō shrine was also the suprareligious symbol of a society and, more than that, of a theocratic state centered on a divinely descended dynasty. In this sense the shrine could, in its grandest manifestation, symbolize the power and authority of the Japanese nation.

These varied functions of Shintō meant that its shrines throughout the empire came in all sizes and settings. In the rugged fastnesses of Taiwan and Korea small shrines were often sited on the tops of mountain peaks where they could be seen from afar. In colonial towns they were more easily accessible to the faithful and were sited within or near the town limits. In the great colonial cities they served to make a statement to inhabitants and visitors as to the transplanted majesty of the Japanese state. In Taihoku (Taipei), for example, the Taiwan Grand Shrine, erected on a commanding site overlooking the Keelung and Tamsui rivers and the city, housed symbols of Shintō deities held to be special guardians of the colony.

In Micronesia shrines were distributed throughout all the islands where Japanese had settled. There were three on Saipan, the largest within the city limits of Garapan, and the two others sequestered in the mountains. On Koror there were two rather nondescript shrines of concrete, one behind the Nan'yō-chō headquarters and the other in the rear of the Japanese *shōgakkō*. At Truk there was a small shrine on the upper edge of Dublon Town. However, the smallest shrine in the islands was the object of veneration of the tiny Japanese community on Lamotrek Atoll in the central Carolines, where, complete with miniature sanctuary and torii, it sat amidst a sheltering palm grove.[59]

By the late 1930s, some on the upper levels of the Nan'yō-chō concluded that, in light of the renewed national concern with Japan's southward expansion, it was time to establish in Koror a suitably prestigious Shintō shrine for the divine protection of the nation's southernmost territory.[60] The guiding hand behind this project was Dōmoto Teiichi, who had made a name for himself, first as a hard-driving colonial bureaucrat in Korea, and, since 1936, in the economic development of Micronesia as private secretary to the Nan'yō-chō governor. In the summer of 1939, with the governor's blessing, Dōmoto met in Tokyo with the members of the august body that usually decided such matters, the Association for the Dedication of Shrines, composed of priests from the greatest shrines in Japan and various high-ranking bureaucrats, including representatives from the Imperial Household Ministry and the Colonial Ministry. Dōmoto's proposal for the establishment of a state shrine at Koror was approved, and the association decided to establish a state shrine there that would be second in rank only to the Great Shrine at Ise. A committee was set up to study a suitable site, the architectural style and arrangement of the shrine buildings, and, most important, what particular deity should be enshrined. It was a mark of the importance with which the government contemplated the project that, after extended deliberation, it was decided that none other than Amaterasu Omikami, the sun goddess and divine progenetrix of the imperial family would be worshipped at the shrine. The site selected, in keeping with immemorial tradition, was a place of great beauty, on the crest of a ridge on the eastern end of Koror overlooking Songel-a-lise Bay. While construction got underway, the priests who had been selected to serve at the shrine were sent to Palau for a special training course that focused on the Micronesian environment, on the Japanese and indigenous populations of Palau, and on the supervision of an overseas shrine of state rank. Among the instructors in this special two-month program were officials from the Nan'yō-chō, officers of the Imperial Japanese Navy, and, not surprisingly, Hijikata Hisakatsu.

By autumn 1940, construction of the shrine, designated the Kampei Taisha Nan'yō Jinja (literally, Shrine of the Second Rank, South Seas) was essentially completed. Its buildings, arranged on two levels from which all foliage had been cleared, were constructed in the timeless Shintō form, rectangular in shape, steeply gabled, and fashioned entirely of natural wood. Access to the upper level, where the inner sanctuary was sited, was up a wide flight of stone steps, flanked at the bottom by two huge stone lanterns and surmounted at the top by a large torii, which opened grandly onto the shrine courtyard.

The enshrinement ceremonies for the edifice spanned three days, beginning on 1 November with the arrival in Malakal Harbor of the official representative of the emperor, an imperial prince who had sailed in retinue from Japan bearing the reliquary considered to contain the spirit force to be lodged at the shrine. Met at dockside by a throng of resident priests, navy officers, colonial officials, including the minister of colonial affairs, leading Japanese citizens, and Palauan chiefs, the princely retinue swept majestically eastward through the streets of Koror in a cortege of nine black limousines (Photo 34). It was a procession of mystery and solemnity rather than jubilation and magnificence. No dogs barked as it passed (they had all been destroyed lest they mar the august majesty of the event) and the crowds that lined the route stood silently with bowed heads so that few actually witnessed its progress.

Arriving at the shrine, the officiating priests carried out the initial rites of purification at the *honden*, the upper sanctuary, while others, with some twenty of the most important civil and military officials in attendance, and joined later by the chief priest, performed additional rites sanctifying the buildings on the lower level (Photo 35). In solemn procession the enshrinement party then carried the reliquary and a box of sacred offerings to the upper level. There the sacred boxes were opened and the spirit of Amaterasu was enshrined in the main sanctu-

Photo 34. Procession bearing the reliquary for the Kampei Taisha Nan'yō Jinja, Koror, Palau Islands, 1 November 1940. (Yamaguchi Yoji)

Photo 35. Opening ceremonies at the Kampei Taisha Nan'yō Jinja, Koror,
1 November 1940. (Yamaguchi Yoji)

ary. The ritual over, congratulatory speeches were read by the highest
civilian and naval representatives and toasts were drunk in sake by the
assembled dignitaries. For two days the ceremonies continued—
respectful devotions at the shrine by the general public, along with solemn performances of classical music and dance on the precincts. On the
third day, the celebrations took a pagan, festive air. A zigzagging procession carrying a *mikoshi*, a sacred palanquin containing a symbol of
the shrine spirit, moved out from the shrine along the road to Koror, to
the accompaniment of rapid, rhythmic chanting, banging drums, and
tootling flutes. Composed of representatives from all islands and districts in Palau, the boisterous parade gathered members as it passed
through each hamlet, until it formed a large throng winding its way
through the streets of the capital. Concurrently, festivities were held
throughout Koror: pictorial displays of Japanese naval and military
might, demonstrations in the martial arts, baseball games, and all manner of athletic competitions.

The establishment of the Kampei Taisha Nan'yō Jinja in November
1940 was the greatest and grandest event in the history of Koror, indeed
in all of Japanese Micronesia.[61] It was celebrated that year amidst a
blaze of national fervor and determination which swept the empire. In
the superheated nationalism of the day, the year had been given mystical significance in government propaganda as the legendary (but histor-
ically spurious) twenty-six hundredth anniversary of the founding of
Japan. By 1940, too, the rhetoric and ideology of the new expansionism
had transformed the definition of Japanese dominion overseas. No
longer might one speak of the colonies and the metropole—colonialism

was a corrupt and outmoded European system that was to be swept away—there was only the inner territory (Japan) and the outer territories, all part of an expanding, coprosperous bloc of East Asian (and by inference, Pacific) peoples, under the guidance and benevolence of the emperor.

Yet if, as 1940 ended, Japan looked southward and saw horizons of glittering opportunity, it seemed that in moving toward them the nation was heading into uncharted waters that held great peril. As the new year opened, it was possible for Japanese to speak of both the inevitable expansion of their nation and the danger of encirclement by its potential adversaries in East Asia and the Pacific. The establishment of the grand shrine at Koror had focused all these concerns. While it was seen by the government as marking "a step forward in the sacred task of constructing the New East Asian Order," it was not without significance that the resplendent dress whites of the Imperial Japanese Navy had been in evidence at the ceremonies. By 1940, in Japanese eyes, Micronesia was no longer a mandate territory held with the acquiescence of the League of Nations (from which Japan had withdrawn seven years before), but was an integral part of a "national defense state," an advance base for the extension of Japanese naval and military power south across the equator.

CHAPTER 8

A Question of Bases
The Japanese Militarization of Micronesia

It is a matter of historical record that, in the first forty-eight hours of Japan's hostilities against the United States in December 1941, powerful Japanese naval and air forces based in Micronesia launched swift and crippling attacks against American territories in the Pacific. To many Americans in the 1940s, this sudden outward thrust from Japan's tropical islands was unarguably part of a grand scheme of conquest that had been several decades in the making.

Specifically, part of the popular American conviction as to this long-standing Oriental perfidy was the presumption that, from the beginning of its occupation of Micronesia, Japan had planned to use the islands as bases for aggression in the Pacific. Long decades after the fires of the Pacific War have burned out, that charge has lain over the history of Japan's endeavors in Micronesia like a trail of acrid smoke. To test its substance and to render a reasoned judgment on the pace and process by which Japan transformed its Pacific islands in order to strike at the United States requires closer attention to geography and historical chronology, more concern with Japanese intent, greater awareness concerning the international environment at given points between the world wars, and above all more insistence on hard evidence, than were brought to it by American journalists, politicians, and naval commanders prior to, during, and immediately after World War II.[1]

The Strategic Dimensions of Japanese Micronesia

To begin with, one must weigh the relative strategic value of the Micronesian islands—both in terms of the various groups and in the aggregate—to Japan and to the United States. I speak here of their natural strategic value, that is, to what extent, by topography or by geographic location, they lent themselves to military or naval use.[2]

If one studies the natural features of the individual island groups of Micronesia in terms of classical maritime strategy and of early twentieth century military technology, they appear to have been of varying worth to any nation that possessed them. The Marianas north of Guam, devoid as they were of any good harbors or an abundance of natural inland strong points, would seem to have had little inherent value as bases. Much the same could be said for the principal islands of the western Carolines—Yap, Palau, Pelelieu, and Angaur. However, the three high islands of the central and eastern Carolines—Truk, Ponape, and Kusaie—possessed such strong natural features as to make them the most important islands in the western Pacific, except for Guam. Of the three, Truk was undoubtedly the most formidable. Its far-flung triangular reef, the entrances to which could be easily mined, enclosed a huge lagoon in the midst of which were clustered several groups of high islands of volcanic origin. Truk provided a natural harbor and refuge with numerous superb anchorages, and its inner islands, rising steeply in places, could be effectively fortified. Ponape and Kusaie were also strategically valuable, if only in defensive terms. Each had several reasonably good anchorages, but more important, their rugged interiors offered excellent defensive possibilities, particularly in the positioning of coast defense artillery. The Marshalls, in the classic maritime sense, would have had little value. While undoubtedly submarines and light naval forces could be based there, the islands were too low, too minuscule in land area, and too devoid of natural food supply to sustain any garrison, and their high water table complicated the construction of deeply entrenched fortifications.

It can hardly be said, therefore, that Micronesia was plentifully endowed with natural military or naval fortresses. In terms of classical maritime strategy, there was only one potentially superlative base among the islands: Truk. Yet, from 1931 to 1941, a period that marked the emergence of the air age, the strategic profile of Micronesia changed dramatically. By the early 1930s, the advent of the flying boat, the land-based bomber, the carrier-borne dive-bomber, and the fighter-interceptor, raised the military and naval value of some islands and diminished that of others.

The Marshalls, for example, during those years took on vital importance. Their flatness and their friable coral soil made for easy construction of airfields; most of their thirty-three atolls included at least one island of sufficient size to be used by land-based bombers and fighter-interceptors. Allowing for the removal of any obstructing coral heads, all had lagoons that could be used almost immediately by flying boats. The military value of the southern tier of the Marianas was also enhanced in the air age. The terraced tablelands of Saipan, Pagan, Tinian, Agiguan (Aguijan), and Rota made them suitable for use by bombers and fighter planes. The same could be said of the Palaus—Babelthuap, Pelelieu, and Angaur—but Yap would require more leveling to make it suitable as an air base. Conversely, the three high islands of the central and eastern Carolines were rendered somewhat less formidable. The mountainous interiors of Ponape and Kusaie offered fewer level areas for airfields than did some of the other island groups, and the potential sites for coastal batteries were now vulnerable to attack from the air. Truk's vast lagoon was still an asset, for it provided ample room for ships to maneuver under aerial attack, but none of the high islands in the center and only one or two of the islets on the surrounding reef were level or large enough for quick adaptation to military aviation.

There is no doubt that the air age enhanced the potential value of most of the principal island groups of Micronesia. But their utility in a military or naval sense must also be assessed in terms of their strategic location. In the aggregate, the islands of Micronesia lay like a barrier across the western Pacific, and their acquisition by Japan in 1914 infinitely complicated the central strategic problem for the United States. In the event of war with Japan, the dilemma that had haunted the United States Navy ever since 1905 was how to relieve or reconquer the Philippines. In the event of a Japan–U.S. war the location of the principal island groups gave them varying degrees of importance. The Marianas lay squarely in front of the most probable course for a westward-moving American fleet, and the ocean interval between the Marianas and the Bonins, the widest passage through which American ships might try to force their way, was only three or four hundred miles. Should the Japanese be able to develop Tanapag Harbor at Saipan for fleet use, the Marianas could become a dangerous obstacle to an American advance. Naturally, too, the islands so fortified could most immediately threaten American-held Guam.

The chief value of the Palaus in terms of their location lay in their proximity to the Philippines, Koror being less than seven hundred miles from Davao. The three principal islands of the central and eastern Carolines lay not in the path of any westward-advancing American fleet, but along its flank. In the Japanese naval scenarios of the 1920s and early 1930s, however, neither Truk nor Ponape nor Kusaie figured greatly in the destruction of American forces. In those plans the Japanese battlefleet was not based on Truk, but much closer to the home islands, from which position it could strike south at the advancing enemy. In prewar Japanese naval thinking the Marshalls, which lay close to no important land mass (the British-owned Gilberts, atolls like the Marshalls, were their nearest neighbors), were more important. From the Marshalls, which flanked the course of any advancing American fleet, the navy would launch attacks by submarines, light naval forces (and, in much later scenarios, by land-based bombers) to whittle down the size and fighting power of the enemy fleet.[3]

Japanese Restrictions, American Suspicions

The consensus view among American navy brass at the end of World War I was that it was less important who held legal title to the former German Pacific islands north of the equator than whether or not they were militarily developed. Recognition of that fact caused American naval advisers at the Paris Peace Conference to work for international agreement on their neutralization. From the Japanese point of view, this was an acceptable concession to keep the islands away from further American interference. Yet Japanese as well as American navy men recognized that, unfortified, they were vulnerable to American assault in the event of war. Once lost to Japan, the islands, particularly the Marianas, would become a perilous strategic threat to Japan.

The compromise formula—Japanese retention of the islands under a solemn pledge to refrain from using them for military or naval purposes—was worked out (as I have written in chapter 2) in three basic agreements between 1920 and 1922: Article Four of Japan's mandate charter, issued on 17 December 1920 and based upon Article 22, Part 1, of the League of Nations Covenant; Article 19—the nonfortification pledge—of the Washington Naval Limitations Treaty of 1922; and the United States–Japan Convention of 11 February 1922 and its explanatory notes, by which the United States specifically recognized Japan's mandate and Japan reiterated the pledges it had given not to fortify the islands. The wording of these pledges was brief and, in retrospect, fatally ambiguous. They provided merely that Japan would establish no "fortifications" or "military or naval bases," but left these terms undefined. Most probably, in the minds of those who drafted these agreements and those who signed them, the categories of military and naval facilities and fortifications forbidden to the Japanese in Micronesia were conceived as being within a classical, pre–air-age context and would have centered on defensive fortifications, weapons, and combat troops, along with ammunition, equipment, and supplies to support them. That, as we shall see, was certainly the interpretation that Japan, particularly the Japanese navy, chose to give to the treaties.

At the time of their signing, in any event, these arrangements had avoided a confrontation over the islands. Yet suspicion and resentment in the upper naval echelons of both countries smoldered on. Adding to the mutual distrust was the fact that none of the agreements provided any means for insuring that Japan would not militarize the islands. Indeed, without Japanese permission, neither the League nor the United States could even inspect the islands to assure themselves that

Japan was still in compliance with the treaties. The American nightmare was that Japan would secretly fortify Micronesia in violation of its
written pledges. Conversely, Japan feared that, should Micronesia be
opened to any and all outside observers, in the event of a U.S.–Japan
war, the Americans could quickly seize the islands, based on a detailed
knowledge of the strategic value of each of the groups.

Had they known it, each side, by 1922, could have pointed to evidence indicating that these fears had some tenuous validity. We know
from official Japanese naval records, for example, that in 1918 the Provisional South Seas Defense Force made numerous surveys of each of the
island groups to evaluate their general value as potential naval bases.[4]
More than this, there is evidence that the Japanese navy had plans for
Micronesia that were to be in effect well after the withdrawal of the
defense force and the establishment of civil administration in the
islands. Even after the navy was reconciled to the withdrawal of its
ships and men under the terms of the mandate, its conviction that
Micronesia would remain a vital strategic area led it to plan for the
rapid militarization of the islands in the event of war with the United
States. Specifically, the navy concluded that in the event of a Japan–
U.S. war it would be to Japan's great advantage to have already in
place plans for deployment of naval forces in the islands, as well as for
the rapid construction of naval facilities there. Based on these conclu-
sions, the naval high command in Tokyo on 12 April 1921 sent an en-
crypted telegram to the commander of the provisional South Seas
Defense Force, instructing him to make an urgent survey of the problems and requirements in converting Palau, Japan's new administrative
center for Micronesia, to military use in a wartime emergency. Eight
months later, shortly before the withdrawal of the defense force, Tokyo
sent another message pointing out the importance of drawing up plans
for the wartime use of various islands while Japan was still at peace.
Further, it suggested the possibility of establishing within the Nan'yō-
chō a special office that would be responsible for such preparations.[5]

These communications make clear the continuing importance the
Japanese navy placed on Micronesia as a strategic area. Specifically,
they demonstrate that it was the navy's intention in peacetime to plan
for the rapid militarization of Micronesia in time of war. They are also
clear evidence that the Japanese navy, possibly with the collusion of the
civil government, at least considered the possibility of circumventing
the *spirit* of Japan's international pledges on the nonfortification of its
new mandate, as early as the beginning of the 1920s.

But the cautious researcher is compelled to note that *planning* for the
military use of the mandate in the event of hostilities was not specifically forbidden in any of the international agreements which Japan had
signed in 1921–1922, and that even the establishment of an office

within the Nan'yō-chō to help formulate such plans (if such an office did indeed exist in the 1920s) did not itself violate the letter of Japan's agreements. More important, there appears to be no evidence in the relevant naval archives in Tokyo that between the autumn of 1914, when the Japanese navy first occupied Micronesia, and the spring of 1922, when it was compelled by the terms of the mandate to withdraw, the navy constructed any fortifications in the islands that could be considered a direct violation of its international pledges.

On the American side, there were certainly some American officers who were pondering ways and means to wrest Micronesia from Japan. Chief among them was the erratic, imaginative, and ultimately doomed Marine Corps officer, Colonel Earl H. ("Pete") Ellis. In 1920, based on his observations and ruminations while stationed on Guam in 1914–1915, Ellis wrote a thirty-thousand-word tactical plan for the seizure of Japan's newly acquired islands, specifically the Marshalls. His "Advance Base Operations in Micronesia," adopted by the Marine Corps as Operations Plan 712, brilliantly prefigured the tactical, logistical, and communications requirements for the conquest of Micronesia, and rightly earned him posthumous acclamation as the progenitor of American amphibious warfare. But like Japanese thinking on how best to defend their Micronesian territories in case of a Japan–U.S. conflict, Operations Plan 712, designed to seize the islands in the same eventuality, represented contingency planning—a set of tactical hypotheses—rather than a strategic plot.[6]

Even without knowing of these initiatives, there were individuals in government and public life in each of the two naval powers who kept alive the embers of mutual mistrust in the Pacific. Basic to the origins and intensification of these suspicions during the twenty-seven years between 1914 and 1941 was the mystery with which Japan obdurately chose to cloak its occupation and administration of Micronesia. Given both the sensitivity of the issue of fortification and the publicity given in the West to the furtive nature of Japan's presence in Micronesia, it is surprising that neither Japanese naval nor civilian authorities ever drew a connection between their secrecy concerning what was happening in Micronesia and the efforts by Americans to penetrate it, either openly or clandestinely. (For their part, American naval and civilian officials failed to appreciate the fact that these attempts only provoked tighter Japanese restrictions against foreigners prying about Micronesia.) Out of this secrecy and mystery, there arose in the West the specter of a vast, hidden stronghold in southern seas, from which Japanese militarists plotted the conquest of the Pacific. Shaped by rumor, guesswork, and speculation in the 1920s, for many Americans it had hardened into accepted fact by the 1940s.[7]

Just as furtiveness and reticence had marked the beginning of the Japanese occupation of Micronesia in 1914, Japan had also made it plain to its wartime allies that it wished no assistance in the occupation of the islands and wanted no Allied warships to enter Micronesian waters. Together, these attitudes appear to have stemmed from a desire to provide no opportunity for Allied opposition or protest before the Japanese navy was in effective control of all of Micronesia. Once in control, the Japanese navy extended its prohibitions to foreign commercial shipping through a series of ad hoc restrictions. One by one, Western firms that had been trading in Micronesian waters were effectively excluded. In 1915, the Atkins Kroll Company, island merchants in copra and sundries throughout the Marianas, were refused entry to that group; in 1916, the British freighter *Mawatta* was refused anchorage at Jaluit atoll. Only in the Marshalls, where it had traded for years, was Burns, Philp & Company able to hang on until 1921, solely because the Japanese had reasons for allowing it to do so; that year, giving up the struggle to trade in the islands under discouraging Japanese restrictions, it, too, was gone.[8]

In 1917, possibly in response to the protests from Allied governments concerning these restrictions, the Provisional South Seas Defense Force issued its *Nan'yō Guntō sempaku torishimaru kisoku* (Regulations concerning control of commercial shipping in the South Sea Islands). But the regulations themselves threw up a thicket of obstacles to Western access to Micronesia, since they required that only such ships as had received permission from the Japanese Navy Ministry in Tokyo or the defense force headquarters in Truk were to be allowed entry into Micronesian ports. Vessels that obtained such permission were to be allowed to touch only at certain designated ports and then only for a limited period. Similar restrictions applied to individuals; foreigners seeking access to Micronesia discovered that such permission required numerous formalities, paperwork, and delays. Permits were rarely refused; they were merely not granted.[9]

As I have suggested in chapter 5, the purpose of these restrictions, frustrating as they were, probably had less to do with the concealment of military or naval activities in the islands than with establishing a Japanese commercial monopoly in Micronesia. In this they were highly effective, particularly since no Western government cared to challenge them,[10] and by the end of World War I Western commerce had been driven out of Micronesia. But whether their purpose was commercial or military, during these early years Japan's active efforts to severely restrict foreign access to Micronesia provided fertile ground for rumor and speculation. Missionaries of long residence in the islands brought out word of newly constructed barracks and other installations; commercial travelers, such as they were, "had it on good authority" that radio equipment and heavy guns were being installed on the larger islands.[11]

American Intelligence Efforts in Micronesia, 1915–1936

It was not long before this hearsay information drifted into U.S. Navy headquarters in Washington and began to set off alarms of doubt and concern, particularly in the corridors of the Office of Naval Intelligence (ONI), which began seeking means to find out what the Japanese were up to in the South Seas. American surveillance of Japanese activities in Micronesia began with the urgent request from the chief of the ONI to the naval governor of Guam to supply any and all intelligence on what the Japanese were doing in the Marianas, Carolines, and Marshalls. But such a request would have been a daunting task for the U.S. Navy as a whole, let alone for the handful of navy men on Guam: the vastness of the area to be covered (over three million square miles), the Japanese restrictions on foreign access to Micronesia, and Japan's silence about its activities in the islands, were all formidable obstacles.[12]

During the wartime years, the United States attempted to circumvent these problems through an essentially passive, low-level intelligence effort that involved interviews of businessmen, travelers, missionaries, and Islanders coming out of Micronesia, conducted by its consular agents in Asia and its intelligence personnel in Hawaii. The results of this effort, a series of reports prepared by the ONI from 1915 to 1919, turned up very little information, except for further accounts of Japanese secrecy and vaguely worded references to "communications facilities" on some of the islands.[13]

After World War I, Secretary of State Charles Evans Hughes suggested a more open method of gaining information about Japanese activities in Micronesia. As part of his short-lived hope that an era of trust could be inaugurated in the Pacific, Hughes proposed an exchange of inspection visits, including those areas subject to the nonfortification restrictions of Article 19 of the Washington Naval Treaty. Surprisingly, he met with adamant opposition from the American Navy and War departments, which rejected any notion of inspection of American territory, ostensibly because such inspection would be an infringement on American sovereignty (essentially the same argument that the Soviet Union has used in the postwar period to prevent international inspection of its territories). In reality, the opposition stemmed from the belief of American army and navy brass in the 1920s that Japan had more to gain from such observations than the United States.[14]

Yet the United States Navy apparently believed that the scraps of intelligence it had collected from 1915 to 1919 justified a more active clandestine effort to probe Micronesia. In pursuing that effort, the ONI, in an era when there were few technological means to gather intelligence, was obliged to rely on such human agents as it could recruit. Of the small number of Americans who were able to visit Micronesia in this period, scientists were of greatest interest to the ONI, due to their care-

ful, analytical observation and because their research often required
them to visit a wide range of islands. Between 1920 and 1926, a number
of such persons, either on individual research of their own, or as members of scientific expeditions, were able to obtain Japanese permission to
putter about the islands, principally the Marianas, where they collected
impressions as well as specimens.[15] During the first few years of this
effort, which coincided with the last years of the Japanese naval administration in Micronesia, the American investigators seem to have been
courteously and even cordially received by Japanese naval commanders
at ports where they stopped. Indeed, as we saw in chapter 3, Japanese
naval hospitality led visitors like Henry Crampton and William Hobbs
to heap unreserved public praise on the Japanese administration in
Micronesia upon their return to the United States.

But by 1924 the succeeding Japanese civilian administration had
begun to take a quite different attitude, perhaps due in large part to the
obvious connection of the U.S. Navy to some of these American travels
around Micronesia. The navy often provided vessels for the research
and transportation of these American civilians, thus providing a con-
venient pretext for sending its ships to poke about in Micronesian
waters, to the growing irritation of the Japanese. When the cruiser *Mil-
waukee* made an unscheduled and unannounced stop at Truk in 1923,
the Japanese reacted with anger and protested the unauthorized visit
through official channels. By the time Hans Hornbostel, the naturalist
and former Marine Corps associate of Earl Ellis, was traveling through
the Marianas, the Japanese authorities were highly suspicious and even
hostile.[16]

But Crampton, Hobbs, and Hornbostel were all bona fide scientists
with legitimate research interests in Micronesia; they had merely agreed
to keep their eyes and ears open and to report what they saw and heard
when they returned to the United States. But in 1922, the U.S. government had dispatched to Micronesia an agent of its own—the legendary
Colonel Earl Ellis himself. Much has been written about the curious, ill-
conceived, and ultimately futile odyssey of Earl Ellis through the Japanese mandate from July 1922 to May 1923. Although there are puzzling
aspects about its denouement which may never be resolved, the general
outlines of his abortive mission have been covered elsewhere, sufficiently that they need not detain us long.[17] Dispatched at his own sug-
gestion by the commandant of the Marine Corps to survey the islands
for topographical and hydrographic information that might aid in their
capture some day, as well as to search out possible Japanese fortifications, Ellis traveled "incognito" through the Marianas, Marshalls, and
Carolines, ending up on Palau, where he died in May 1923, most probably of acute alcoholism. Romance and intrigue have for years covered
the Ellis legend, but as a spy, he cut a preposterous figure: he was an

alcoholic who was sober scarcely half the time; he was a Caucasian traveling among Micronesians and Asians, and thus attracted the immediate attention of the police, who kept him constantly under surveillance; his notes and drawings were quickly and easily discovered by the Japanese; and most incredible of all, on the last day of his life, in an alcoholic daze, he blubbered openly to his Palauan acquaintances the real purpose of his travels! There are no indications that he discovered any evidence of Japanese skulduggery in the mandate;[18] what he did accomplish was to put Japanese authorities in Micronesia on their guard against further espionage in the islands.

Having attempted surveillance by human agents and obtained little to show for it, the American government tried another clandestine means to find out what was going on behind the reefs of Japanese Micronesia: communications intercepts. This involved monitoring Japanese radio traffic in the islands, an effort begun in the mid-1920s and continued through the 1930s. From what little scholars now know of this program, it seems that, while it retrieved millions of dots and dashes from the airwaves over the Pacific, it turned up little significant information about Japanese activities in Micronesia.[19]

In 1929, the U.S. Navy attempted a direct approach to the problem. Reversing its earlier opposition to the idea, it sought the assistance of the State Department in gaining visitation rights for American warships to stop at various Micronesian islands. In April of that year the American chargé d'affaires in Tokyo informed the Japanese Foreign Ministry that the United States proposed sending the cruiser *Asheville* to visit Angaur in the Carolines and six atolls in the Marshalls and asked the Foreign Ministry to convey this request to the Nan'yō-chō through the Colonial Ministry. The response of the Nan'yō-chō arrived some weeks later, relaying the willingness of Japanese authorities to have the *Asheville* call at Angaur, which had been declared an open port, but not at the atolls in the Marshalls, where most of the anchorages were not open to foreign ship traffic. The Nan'yō-chō explained that visits to such remote landfalls were not possible because there were no resident Japanese officials there, no pilots available, and the anchorages were "difficult of approach and dangerous." In June, the American embassy submitted a similar request for six destroyers collecting hydrographic information to touch at Jaluit, Wotje, and Kwajalein in the Marshalls. Back came the response from the Nan'yō-chō: the destroyers could stop at Jaluit, which was an open port, but not at the other atolls. In the meantime, the embassy was informed, the Japanese navy would prepare charts and tables providing American commanders with the hydrographic information they sought.[20]

In vain, the embassy tried to deal with this "dangerous harbors" ploy, assuring the Foreign Ministry that U.S. warship captains could handle their vessels with sufficient caution to navigate the waters surrounding the islands they wished to visit. In December 1929, in pursuing the matter with the vice foreign minister, the American chargé d'affaires encountered a new Japanese pretext for refusing American ship visits to out-of-the-way islands in Micronesia. The vice foreign minister confided that the Japanese government was by no means unified on the general question of such calls and admitted that some of the branches of the government were "obsessed with notions of secrecy." The principal objection, he informed the chargé d'affaires, came not from the navy, but from the Nan'yō-chō, whose officials were convinced that such visits of foreign warships were disturbing to the Islanders, since Micronesians associated such vessels with wars and with changes in the governments over them and thus tended to become excited. At open ports—those islands where Japanese officials were already on hand to explain the situation—the indigenous populations would be less likely to be disturbed, or so Japan's colonial spokesman blandly asserted.[21]

In the mid-1930s, a different American administration was to make one more open attempt to gain access for its vessels to call at Micronesian ports, noting pointedly in representations to the Foreign Ministry, that the United States had provided Japanese vessels with facilities in Alaskan harbors not normally open to foreign commerce. The Foreign Ministry once more referred the question to the Colonial Ministry, but never received an answer; several months later the Foreign Ministry indicated it could do nothing more. Similar requests by the British navy also met with refusal, the British naval attaché in Tokyo being told that such calls would be "inconvenient for some time to come."[22]

By the end of the 1920s, all the U.S. Navy had to show for its fifteen years of trying to look and listen in on the Japanese in Micronesia was a handful of suspicions. Since the end of World War II and the opening of Japanese archives, one can say with reasonable certainty that in the 1920s these suspicions were unjustified. When the Japanese navy pulled out of Micronesia in 1922, it left only a single resident liaison officer *(kaigun bukan)* stationed at Palau. Usually concurrent members of the Naval General Staff and the Yokosuka Naval Base, the officers who occupied this position (like the hard-drinking Konishi Tatehiko whom we encountered in chapter 6) seem to have had few responsibilities in the 1920s and early 1930s other than a minor liaison function and the collection of hydrographic and meteorological information.[23]

Japanese Secrecy Considered, 1915–1930

Yet, if the navy's liaison officer at Palau constituted the total Japanese military presence in Micronesia through the 1920s, the inevitable questions arise: why were Japanese authorities so secretive and why were they so reluctant to open the islands to foreign observation? As one later eminent British visitor to Palau was to remark about the restrictions with which Japanese officials hedged his movements on the island: "They are too intelligent a people to make mysteries about nothing and their attitude was designed to make us wonder just what it was they needed to hide."[24]

There is a logical explanation for Japanese behavior during this period. During World War I, as I have indicated, it seems to have stemmed initially from a desire to establish control over the former German colonies without outside interference and, once in firm occupation, from a quite ruthless decision to shoulder out all foreign commercial competition from the islands. But after the war, the reasons for Japanese secrecy in the Pacific undoubtedly had more to do with Japanese security. Although the Japanese navy physically withdrew from Micronesia in 1922 its strategic concern for the islands was undiminished, along with its suspicions that the United States continued to harbor designs upon them. From the Japanese perspective, what other explanation could there be for the insistence by American "scientists" and "copra merchants" on taking sightings, soundings, and various notes on topography and weather? To the Americans who gathered such information, the natural qualities of Micronesia showed how easily it could be fortified; to the Japanese, the collection of information concerning the islands demonstrated evidence that their future conquest was being planned. Another possible explanation for Japanese secretiveness in Micronesia (suggested first by the American embassy in Tokyo, in its correspondence with Washington concerning the abortive ship visit proposals of 1929) was that the Nan'yō-chō was extremely sensitive to the possibility of adverse criticism of its administration in Micronesia being circulated abroad.[25] If so, this anxiety may have stemmed from the questionable nature of Japanese labor practices on Angaur, though this does not seem to square with the willingness of Japanese authorities to let U.S. vessels visit that island.

Lastly, we must consider the remark of the vice foreign minister in 1929 that some branches of his government were "obsessed with notions of secrecy." He was undoubtedly speaking of the Japanese navy which, if it did not administer the mandate, nevertheless retained ultimate authority in matters relating to access to the islands. And the navy, obviously, wanted them closed. In his memorandum to the department reporting the vice foreign minister's remark, the American chargé d'affaires in Tokyo commented that "The [Japanese] navy wants to keep the islands segregated, if possible, not because there is anything much there, but out of a habit of secrecy to no very great purpose."[26] In any event, as now seems plain, such secrecy to no purpose was injurious to Japan's wider interests. It heightened the conviction within the United

States Navy, specifically, that Japan was preparing the islands for war, and it helped to perpetuate suspicion of Japan's overall intentions among Western nations in general, at a time when Japan was becoming increasingly isolated in the world.

But the American position on free access to the Japanese mandate is also difficult to understand. While it may be true that the United States had no unassailable legal ground for demanding the right for American warships to visit Japan's Micronesian islands (the American right to transit Micronesian *waters* never being in doubt) still, during the 1920s and early 1930s, there was a curious passivity and reticence in Washington's attitude toward access to the islands. Not once did the United States Department of State protest to the Japanese Foreign Ministry about restricted access to Micronesia; not once did the United States take the matter to the League; and not once did the American government choose to make public its concern or its communications on the subject.

In the decade following the Yap controversy, the Nan'yō rarely became a subject of international discussion. Year after year, the Japanese delegate to the Permanent Mandates Commission filed his government's annual reports on the mandate, but the members of that body seldom probed beyond the colorless phraseology and clusters of statistics. Though they raised occasional queries concerning Japanese immigration into Micronesia, the few in the international community who even cared that Japan had a mandate in the Pacific saw no reason to believe that Japan was either violating its mandate charter or planning to disturb the peace of that ocean.

Suspicions Deepen, 1930–1937

By the end of the 1920s the winds of international controversy began to ruffle the relatively calm waters of international opinion concerning the Pacific. In 1930, delegates of the world's three great naval powers met at London to revise and update the naval arms limitation agreements concluded at Washington eight years earlier. At the conference, Japanese proposals for a more equitable distribution of naval tonnage allowed under the Washington system met with the combined opposition of the American and British delegates. After an intense struggle, followed by a series of compromises, the Japanese representatives— members of the more moderate "treaty faction" within the navy— signed the agreement. Although it more nearly matched Japanese than Anglo-American desires, the treaty produced furious denunciations in Tokyo, particularly from the hard-lining "fleet faction" within the navy, the leading proponents of which called, with increasing vehemence, for Japanese withdrawal from the naval treaty system. Since that treaty system, and its limitations on naval tonnage, was intimately linked with nonfortification of Japan's Pacific mandate, such arguments in Japan rekindled speculation in the West as to how Japan might choose to use its Micronesian territories in the future.

The following year these conjectures were suddenly infused with a sense of immediacy by the violent shift of events in East Asia provoked by Japan's sudden thrust into Manchuria. By 1932, all of Japan's overseas activities and policies were being subjected to rigorous scrutiny by increasingly hostile powers. China, the United States, the Soviet Union, and the leading nations of Western Europe, all came to look askance at resurgent Japanese imperialism.

Inevitably, suspicion touched upon the Japanese administration of Micronesia. It began with unsubstantiated accounts in the American press that improvements being undertaken by the Nan'yō-chō at Tanapag Harbor, Saipan, were actually part of preparations for the construction of a clandestine submarine base on the island. By the autumn of 1932, when the Permanent Mandates Commission took up Japan's annual report on its mandate, the Western press was in full cry, though it traded entirely in rumors, not evidence. Displaying laborious courtesy, but an incredible ignorance of geography, the chairman of the commission requested the Japanese delegate, Itō Nobumi, to provide the commission with assurances from his government that rumors concerning the establishment of a naval base "in the Western part of the Archipelago in the direction of Hawaii [sic]" were indeed unfounded and that Japan had no plans for fortifying the islands. Several weeks later the answer came back from the Foreign Ministry: no, the Tanapag Harbor improvements were not for a naval base, but only for the enhancement of commercial facilities on the island; and no, Japan did not intend to construct any such base in the Pacific.[27] The commission adopted Ambassador Itō's report and, in turn, the council of the League adopted the report of the commission without comment. No League member raised any question as to Japan's good faith in the administration of its mandate, so removed from the fluctuations of world opinion was the League.

Then, in May 1933, the Japanese government undertook a dramatic initiative that provoked a new and unprecedented level of controversy over its presence in Micronesia. That month, the abrupt and theatrical walkout of Matsuoka Yosuke, Japan's delegate to the United Nations, signaled his nation's determination to quit that organization permanently two years later. This action prompted heated debate between legal scholars, as well as statesmen the world over, on the question of Japan's legal right to administer the mandate once it had withdrawn from the League. These arguments, extended, involved, and ultimately futile, need not detain us,[28] since the Japanese government made it clear that Japan had no intention of relinquishing its mandate, though it stopped short of declaring that the islands had been formally absorbed into the empire. Speaking in response to questions put to him in the Diet, Foreign Minister Hirota Kōki explained that Japan's status as a legal mandatory in Micronesia had nothing to do with its membership in the League. It had come about, not as a gift from the League, but as a result of negotiations with Japan's principal allies in World War I. Hirota did not claim the islands as formally part of the empire, but only insisted upon the legality of its status as a mandatory power (which, as we have seen, practically amounted to the same thing). For that reason the government felt duty bound to continue to make annual reports to the Permanent Mandates Commission as before.[29] Japan held to this policy until the outbreak of World War II, when the disappearance of the League made it possible to drop the pretense that Japan remained in Micronesia to fulfill its obligations as a mandatory power. For its part, the League was unwilling as a body to challenge Japan's interpretation of its mandate charter and no member nation rose to speak against it. After 1933, for all practical purposes, Japan's position in Micronesia was whatever Japan said it was.[30]

Considering that Japan's departure from the League coincided with an ominous increase in tension between Japan and the United States, it is not surprising that Japanese intransigence on the mandate question was stiffened principally by the Japanese navy. Navy spokesmen, including Navy Minister Admiral Ōsumi Mineo (who had served in the navy's occupation force in World War I) not only began issuing policy statements insisting on the Japanese right to remain in Micronesia, but also took the increasingly hard line that the navy was ready to defend its rights by force.[31] This harsh rhetoric paralleled the beginning of a publicity campaign to convince the Japanese people that the islands were vital to the nation as a "life-line" *(seimeisen)* for Japanese security and Japanese expansion.[32] Once more, there was vague but urgent talk of the nation's destiny in the "South Seas," though the term came increasingly to include Southeast Asian lands and waters. Navy enthusiasts of a "southward advance" and the civilian publicists who supported them now began to frame those geopolitical concepts of self-sufficiency, Asian cooperation, and colonial liberation that were to spring forth a decade later under the banner of "East Asian Co-prosperity." By the early 1930s, naval and civilian advocates saw Micronesia, now termed the Inner South Seas *(uchi Nan'yō)* as a base to prepare the "advance" (the exact meaning of the word was usually left unclear) into Southeast Asia, now designated the Outer South Seas *(soto Nan'yō)*.[33]

Throughout the 1930s, these attitudes, combined with the increasing reluctance of the Japanese government to open Micronesia to foreign observation, heightened the suspicions among the Anglo-American naval powers that Japan was engaged in clandestine militarization of its mandate in violation of its international pledge. The announcement in November 1933, by Governor Hayashi Hisao, that the Nan'yō-chō had constructed an airfield at Saipan for commercial purposes merely provoked a fresh round of speculation about Japan's warlike preparations in the Pacific.

In 1934, these rumors once again caused the Permanent Mandates Commission to question the Japanese representative closely about a possible violation of Japan's mandate charter. Once more, the Foreign Ministry came back with the response that no fortifications had been built in Micronesia (though a close reading of the ministry's statement showed that it contained no assurance that they would not be constructed in the future).[34] This time, Japan's answer satisfied no one, but the League found itself unable to probe further, lacking the will, the means, and the established legal right to inspect the mandate.

In 1935, at London, the leading naval powers of the world made one last attempt at continuing the faltering naval arms limitation system. But when Japan's representatives stalked from the conference and announced Japan's intention to abrogate the existing treaties by the end of 1936, the system collapsed. On 1 January 1937, the great powers would enter a treatyless era, each free to construct whatever naval strength it felt necessary to its security. Japan would turn to building those monster battleships, the *Yamato* and *Musashi*, and Britain and the United States would start work on their own upgraded battleship designs. By New Year's Day 1937, moreover, Article 19 of the now defunct Washington Treaty would become a dead letter. Japan's pledges on nonfortification of its mandate would now rest largely on its own interpretation of its mandate charter and on the U.S.–Japan convention of 1922.

Nevertheless, in the early 1930s Japan recognized the advisability of reducing the increasingly hostile suspicion of the West concerning its occupation of Micronesia—if only to delay a buildup of American military and naval forces in the Pacific. For this purpose, the Japanese government continued to grant permission for a number of Western observers—military professionals, as well as civilians—to travel the islands. The Japanese expectation was that these persons would convey their impressions to reading publics in the West that Japan had undertaken no aggressive preparations in the Pacific. That Japan was willing to grant such access, even for a limited number of foreign visitors, is evidence that as late as 1935, it considered that it had little to hide.

In any event, the accounts and reports of this handful of outside observers, including those of the British journalist R. V. C. Bodley, the British writer and long-time Japan resident R. A. B. Ponsonby-Fane, the Stanford University zoologist Albert Heere (all of whom visited

Micronesia in 1933)—Paul Clyde, professor of political science at the University of Kentucky, who made a wide-ranging tour of the islands in 1934—and the globe-trotting American Willard Price, who toured Micronesia in 1935, constituted the main outside judgments at the time on the enigma of the Japanese mandated islands.

Some of these visitors wrote of the elaborate and even ludicrous evasions, delays, and excuses thrown up by Japanese authorities concerning arrangements for travel to and within Micronesia,[35] as well as of the "unremitting curiosity" of the Japanese police while they traveled in the islands. Yet, to a man, they reported that there was no evidence that Japan was militarizing its mandate. Upon his return from the Pacific, Professor Heere, for example, asserted in the *Palo Alto Times* that "charges and insinuations . . . that Japan is secretly fortifying certain Pacific islands in the mandate group are just plain 'bunk'." In his *Drama of the Pacific*, Ronald Bodley wrote that "having visited practically every island in the Japanese Mandates in the Pacific [sic], I am convinced that nothing has been done to convert any place into a naval base." Nowhere, Bodley declared, did he see signs of airfields, moorings for seaplanes, or fuel depots.[36]

In 1934, the Japanese government invited Paul Clyde to make an extended voyage through Micronesia. According to Clyde's *Japan's Pacific Mandate*, the most detailed and unbiased analysis of the Japanese administration of Micronesia published before World War II, he was afforded every opportunity to see and examine Japan's administration and his activities and itinerary (Saipan, Tinian, Rota, Yap, Palau, Truk, Ponape, Kusaie, and Jaluit) were restricted only by the sailing schedules of the commercial vessels he traveled on. In his book, Clyde devoted an entire chapter to the fortification question. After an extensive and thoughtful discussion of the subject, he declared flatly that there was "no evidence to indicate that Japan had violated Article 4 of its mandate charter or that it contemplated doing so."[37]

Willard Price traveled with his wife through the Marianas and Carolines—Saipan, Tinian, Yap, Palau, Angaur, Truk, Ponape, and Kusaie —in 1935, enjoying nearly complete freedom, though he was eyed continually by the police, and sometimes his requests to visit certain places encountered two or three days of official resistance or delay. Only when he asked to visit the island of Arakabesan, near Malakal Harbor in the Palaus—where Japan did later develop a seaplane base of moderate importance—was Price turned aside (by the redoubtable Captain Konishi Tatehiko). But Price left Micronesia with the firm conviction that there was no visible evidence that Japan had militarized its mandate. Nor did he know of any other outside observer who had seen such evidence. In his *Pacific Adventure*, published in 1936, Price asserted that "observers in the islands have been unable to discover firm ground for these suspicions. Foreign visitors are few, but two or three every year pass through the Mandate, calling at the most important islands such as Palau, Truk, and Ponape. Not one of these has ever reported the existence of fortifications." Moreover, Price noted that the small permanent missionary community in Micronesia was unanimous in declaring that there was no evidence of Japanese militarization of the islands.[38]

Willard Price was one of the last foreign visitors to travel in Japanese Micronesia and his observations did little to choke off the persistent stream of rumors about Japanese military preparations there. Indeed, those rumors were fed by the increasingly hostile relations between Japan and the United States, as well as by ever-tighter Japanese secrecy and reticence. Then, in 1937, the world was suddenly presented with a dramatic mystery that served to increase the intensity and urgency of American doubts about the Japanese mandate: Amelia Earhart's disappearance on her attempt to circle the globe. Earhart's fatal course across the Pacific from Lae, New Guinea, to American-owned Howland Island ended in oblivion. Within weeks her disappearance had generated a score of explanations, most of them sensational, many of them illogical, and few of them based on a coherent pattern of evidence. The unifying theme of most of these farfetched theories, many of which have been elaborated upon during the half-century since her departure from New Guinea, was that Amelia Earhart and her navigator, either inadvertently, or as part of a secret American espionage mission, flew over secret Japanese bases in the mandate, variously identified as Truk, Saipan, and Mili Atoll in the Marshalls, was shot or forced down by the Japanese, then captured and executed in order to prevent her from revealing to the world her knowledge of Japanese perfidy.[39] In the words of John Burke, author of one of the few responsible books on Earhart, such a cloak-and-dagger explanation "supplies a heroic ending, much more glamorous, than the possibility that [the] plane simply ran out of gasoline and went into the drink."[40] But even Burke's treatment fails to deal with the fundamental question of whether, in 1937, there were sufficient Japanese military and naval preparations in Micronesia to have necessitated such ruthless measures to preserve their secrecy. To deal with that question, one must turn to the Japanese record, paying close attention to chronology, intent, and evidence.

Suspicions Reconsidered, 1930–1939

The transformation of Japan's Micronesian islands for military purposes seems to have proceeded in four stages, from 1930 to 1941. The first of these, from 1930 to 1934 involved the construction of commercial and communications facilities by the Nan'yō-chō and the Nan'yō Kōhatsu; the second, from 1934 to 1939, after the naval limitations system had collapsed, saw the initiation of a limited construction program of air and communications facilities in the Marianas and Carolines, jointly involving the Nan'yō-chō and the Japanese navy; the third, from 1939 to 1940, was marked by an intensified effort by the navy alone to develop military and naval bases in the islands; and the last, from 1940 to 1941, saw the introduction of substantial numbers of naval units, aircraft, and personnel, as well as a desperate effort to finish certain bases before the outbreak of war in the Pacific.

The first substantial efforts at improving the commercial and communications facilities in Micronesia began in 1926 with the dredging of Tanapag Harbor on the west side of Saipan, and the deepening and improvement of Malakal Harbor at Palau, beginning in 1927. From evidence at the time and Japanese records available after World War II, there is no reason to believe that these construction projects were undertaken for purposes other than those given by Japan at the time: an improvement of the shipping facilities for Matsue Haruji's sugar enterprise on Saipan and the enhancement of Koror as a commercial port. With the establishment of air facilities in Micronesia, Japan's purposes become more ambiguous. In 1930, at the direction of Matsue, engineering specialists at the Nan'yō Kōhatsu made surveys for the location of airfields on Pagan Island and at Aslito on southern Saipan, and the construction of these facilities was completed by the Nan'yō Kōhatsu in 1934. That year, seaplane facilities (docks, ramps, refueling tanks, repair sheds, and such) were begun at Saipan, Yap, and Arakabesan in the Palaus. At the time, the Japanese claimed that all these facilities were for commercial use, and indeed, their establishment did coincide with the projection of a commercial air route through the mandate by Great Japan Airways.[41] Yet, there can be little argument that all these facilities *could* be (and eventually were) used for military purposes. The question is whether they were intended for such use at the time of their construction.[42]

In this regard, the postwar Japanese official history of naval operations in the central Pacific helps to illumine the gradual evolution of the Japanese navy's plans concerning Micronesia. In 1930, following the acrimony surrounding the London Naval Treaty, the Japanese navy began reassessing its capabilities in the Pacific. Part of this effort involved a reevaluation of the strategic potential of various Micronesian islands in the event of war with the United States. To this end, the Yokosuka Naval Base (which, ever since World War I, had been responsible for the navy's interests in Micronesia) sent a team of seventy-eight men to survey Truk and Saipan for possible fleet bases and airfields. In 1931 the same group made a similar survey of Palau. During 1933 and 1934 the navy dispatched several warships to make preliminary surveys of other Micronesian islands, and in 1936 more intensive surveys were made of the Marianas and Carolines by surface and air units of the navy. In 1933, as well, the Combined Fleet had held grand exercises off the Marianas in which it practiced repelling an attack by the enemy and tested plans for the rapid development of military bases in the Marianas, particularly Saipan and Pagan.[43]

Yet, it seems clear that these surveys and exercises, like those undertaken in 1918–1922, fall under the category of contingency plans: detailed surveys for suitable sites for airfields, gun emplacements, fuel dumps, communication facilities and the like, which could be rapidly completed *in the event of hostilities*. By themselves, however, such plans and maneuvers could not be said to have violated Japan's international pledges, though in retrospect one can see that they undercut the flat denials of intent by Foreign Ministry spokesmen.

From 1934 to 1939, in cooperation with the Nan'yō-chō, however, the Japanese navy did indeed begin a limited program of airfield construction in the Marianas and Carolines. At first, it appears that the navy merely assisted the Nan'yō-chō in selecting the sites and in providing logistical support, but increasingly during that five-year period, the Navy Ministry came to assume direction of the construction program. The first four major projects included expansion of the airfield at Aslito on Saipan, construction of the seaplane ramps at Arakabesan, and the construction of an airfield on Eten, a small island just south of Dublon Harbor, Truk—facilities reported to the outside world as airstrips for commercial aviation or drying flats for fishing nets. Communication centers and fuel storage facilities were also established at all four places.[44] Yet by the summer of 1937, about the time that Amelia Earhart departed on her mysterious flight, it still would have been difficult to have indicted Japan for a gross violation of its international pledges, even if its Micronesian islands had been fully open to international inspection. On the actual islands Japan had placed no weapons of war—no military aircraft, no military combat units, no defensive artillery. *Had* Amelia Earhart flown over any of the Marianas or Carolines, which she most assuredly did not, she would have seen only the same sort of facilities available to Pan-American Airways at its new commercial base at Guam; *had* she flown over the Marshalls, which most probably she did not, she might have seen Japanese warships at Jaluit Atoll (not forbidden by any of the agreements of the 1920s), but no sign of improvements for even commercial aviation.[45]

In the second half of the decade it is obvious that Japan, controlling Micronesia under only the most vestigial obligations to the international community, unrestrained now by any agreement limiting its naval strength, and drifting ever closer to a confrontation with the United States, was increasingly motivated to push forward with improvements in the islands that could be used in time of war. This hardening Japanese decision to prepare the islands for war was underscored by the navy's intensified involvement in expanding its air and surface facilities in Micronesia. By 1937, the navy was calling the shots and the navy, not the Nan'yō-chō, initiated construction of major improvements in air, sea, and land facilities in Micronesia. But, in the Japanese navy's view, the establishment of these facilities did not violate the terms of the earlier treaties, since those only applied to "fortifications" and "bases" and did not extend to the improvement of "available sites" for military and naval operations in time of war.[46] Because the wording of those agreements was ambiguous, it seems fair to say that in terms of the facilities it established in Micronesia, up almost to 1940, Japan could not be charged with flagrant violation of its earlier pledges. That Japan took measures to conceal the navy's hand in the facilities it did establish appears to have been due in part to the navy's general policy of strict security and in part to Japan's reluctance to expose to international criticism its own particular interpretation of its earlier agreements.[47]

For most of the 1930s the navy had considered that the Marianas and the Carolines would form Japan's first line of defense in the Pacific, and that, given their general location and topography, the Marshalls would be indefensible and of little use. But improvements in aviation technology during the decade, particularly the development of the heavy, all-metal, land-based bomber, not only influenced a change in Japanese naval strategy and tactics, but also caused a reassessment of the value of the Marshalls. Specifically, the demonstrated efficiency of the navy's twin-engined Mitsubishi type 96 bomber for long-range missions in China during 1938, made it apparent that similar aircraft based in the Marshalls could have a crucial impact on the course of any war in the central Pacific. Japanese bomber bases in the Marshalls would allow the navy to strike out against British and American islands in the central Pacific in the event of war; conversely, loss of the Marshalls and the establishment of enemy bomber bases there could imperil Japanese positions in the eastern and central Carolines.[48]

These considerations led, in 1939, to the dispatch of a navy survey team to gather airfield construction data for the Marshalls. Once it had this information in hand, however, the navy was faced with a major choice in priorities, since time was running out in preparing the islands for possible hostilities against the United States. The question was whether to rush a few fully equipped air bases to completion in the Marshalls (as well as in the Marianas and the Carolines) or to undertake simultaneous work on all the atolls so that each would have at least one serviceable airstrip. The decision was quickly made to pursue the former course, and an accelerated schedule of construction was initiated to complete airfields on Roi (on Kwajalein Atoll), Taroa (Maloelap Atoll), and Wotje.[49] This airfield construction program in 1939 by the navy marks a quantum jump in Japan's intent and preparations to use Micronesia for war purposes.

The year 1939 was also a turning point in the Japanese militarization of Micronesia because it was late in that year that the navy dispatched the Fourth Fleet to Micronesia, the first Japanese naval unit specifically assigned service in those waters since World War I. A modestly-scaled force with few major warships and no attack aircraft, its primary task at this point was military construction, principally of airfields, communication centers, and fuel dumps, throughout Micronesia.[50] Until the last months of 1940 there were still no permanent shore garrisons or land-based aircraft in the islands. Nevertheless, the organization of a major fleet unit to be assigned to Micronesia, along with the accelerated airfield construction program, leaves no doubt that by 1940 Japan had clandestinely embarked upon a major effort to militarize its Micronesian territories.

Building the Bases with Conscript Labor

In pushing forward construction of naval and air facilities in Micronesia the Japanese were hampered by the fact that, compared to the United States, civil engineering in Japan was woefully unmechanized and far more dependent on human labor.[51] The key to the completion of the air base construction program, therefore, was an adequate labor supply. But this raised major difficulties. Obviously, the navy's own personnel were too few in number and too essential to the task of technical supervision, to fulfill the need. The Nan'yō Kōhatsu could and did supply some labor from the resident Japanese population in the islands, but this was not enough. With passage of the Military Manpower Mobilization Law in 1939 it was possible to conscript labor elsewhere in the empire and during that year drafts of Korean coolies began to be shipped over from Japan and from Korea, the most regimented and exploited of Japan's colonial territories. But other sources were needed.

Inevitably, in this situation, the navy sought to exploit a labor source near at hand—the Micronesian population. Beginning in 1939 Micronesians in all three island groups were conscripted for heavy construction work, largely against their will. On some of the larger islands where Japanese civilians had long resided, the process of recruitment was softened to a degree. On Truk, for example, Mori Koben was able to persuade rather than compel young men to come forward to aid in the construction effort. On other islands, such as the Marshalls, labor recruitment was far harsher, whole villages being swept for adult males, who were then shipped from atoll to atoll as the navy's labor requirements dictated. Thus began the increasingly insensitive and ultimately brutal exploitation of the indigenous population by the Japanese military, an activity that was eventually to corrode whatever loyalties the Micronesians held toward Japan.[52]

But even the dragooning of island labor was insufficient for the pace of construction upon which the Japanese Imperial Navy was now embarked. Additional labor would have to be supplied from Japan, but the taxing conditions of the task in Micronesia—the heat, the humidity, the remoteness, the necessity for secrecy—made it unlikely that ordinary labor could be hired in Japan to do the work. For this reason the navy turned to the Justice Ministry for help. In October 1939, that ministry, in response to the navy's request, made available some two thousand Japanese convicts, the largest number coming from the Yokohama Central Prison. To infuse these unfortunates with an enthusiasm and patriotism that otherwise they could hardly have felt, they were organized into labor battalions that were given suitably zealous names (such as the Sekiseitai, "Sincerity Battalion") and provided with a rousing send-off at the Yokohama docks by representatives of the Navy and Justice ministries.[53]

The first shipments of these penal battalions, escorted under civilian guard, began in December 1939 and continued through the winter of 1940, the drafts being used principally for construction of airfields on Tinian, Wotje, and Moen Island in the Truk group. Once there, the Japanese prisoners encountered the most appalling conditions of heat, backbreaking labor—mostly pickax work—and the brutality of their civilian guards. Their suffering was intense. Of more than twelve hundred men assigned to Tinian, for example, more than twenty died of heat, exhaustion, and disease; on Wotje over thirty died. Of the majority who survived, most were shipped back to Japan in 1940, upon completion of the work, though some were kept on in Micronesia, where they were overtaken by the disasters of the Pacific War.[54]

Base Construction at Full Swing, 1940–1941

By resorting to all these measures, the Japanese navy was able to push forward work on its airfields and naval facilities in Micronesia during 1940. That summer and autumn, as Japanese military forces occupied Indochina and set the nation on a perilous new course toward southern lands and seas, the Fourth Fleet labored to consolidate its position in the islands. To expedite that effort, the navy divided Micronesia into four sectors, each with a "Base Force" headquarters under a rear admiral: Saipan for the Marianas, Koror for the western Carolines, Truk for the eastern Carolines, and Kwajalein for the Marshalls. In addition to the Base Force (*konkyochitai*, roughly a battalion in strength) each sector commander had a "Defense Force" (*bōbitai*, five hundred men), a communications unit, and a small air unit. Because of the number of key bases there, the Marshalls also received reinforcements in the form of three "Guard Forces" (*keibitai*), each composed of eight hundred combat-ready naval troops. By late 1940, the navy had also initiated research across a range of operational problems—flying boat operations in the Marshalls, heat acclimatization studies, take-off and landing techniques for island airstrips, and a number of other studies that would assure maximum effectiveness of the bases under construction.[55]

In February 1941, the Fourth Fleet commander arrived to establish headquarters at Truk, as the first warships and shore defense units began to take up positions at bases on Saipan, the Palaus, Truk, Ponape, and key atolls in the Marshalls.[56] In that month, too, the Fourth Fleet activated its Construction Division, which took over the last phase of the base construction program from the Yokosuka Naval Base. Its work force was largely composed of Korean coolies, unskilled and ill-trained laborers on whose straining backs the naval officers and civil engineers directing the construction program now placed a major share of the physical effort to prepare the islands for war.[57]

Throughout 1941, as the discussions in Washington between Secretary of State Cordell Hull and Japanese Ambassador Admiral Nomura began to founder on the shoals of misunderstanding and distrust, and the two nations drifted closer to war, the Japanese navy pushed forward with the militarization of the islands. In all the island groups the navy's needs took priority. In the Marianas civilian buildings were taken over for barracks and offices, in the Carolines choice land was appropriated for military use (on Dublon, for example, the newly completed athletic field where but a year before a bemedaled Mori Koben had stood proudly for his portrait, was expropriated as a navy drill ground), and on the atolls of the Marshalls whole palm groves were cut down for airfields without compensation to the villages that depended on them. Everywhere on the high islands one heard the sound of blasting, as dynamite became the ubiquitous leveler and tunneler. Nakajima Atsushi's ears rang with it during several depressing visits to Truk in the autumn of 1941.

The Militarization of Micronesia in Retrospect

At the Tokyo war crimes trials, Japanese witnesses for the defense were to claim that no bases or fortifications were established in Micronesia until the last month before the Pacific War. Further, their testimony appeared to validate the statement, in the Nan'yō-chō budget, that the large expenditures at eight key islands during 1940 were for "lighthouse construction." Yet, as Thomas Wilds demonstrated a decade later in his comprehensive and authoritative review of Japanese navy documents of the period (most of which were not introduced at the trials), both the testimony and the budget documents were fraudulent. Even by the navy's restricted definition of what constituted bases and fortifications, the Japanese had certainly commenced installation of antiaircraft guns, command posts, ammunition depots, barracks, and a variety of other weapons and military facilities on the islands by the end of 1940.[58]

In assessing this undeniable military buildup in Micronesia almost two years before Pearl Harbor, several points become clear. First of all, it is necessary to place Japan's militarization of the islands in historical perspective. By late 1940 the naval high commands in both Washington and Tokyo assumed that a collision between the United States and Japan was inevitable within the next few years. Given this fact, together with the collapse of the naval limitations agreements five years before, and the evaporation of any vestigial authority of the League of Nations, it is unreasonable to charge that the Japanese fortification of a strategically critical forward area in the last year or so before the war constituted a long-planned and treacherous violation of international agreements. Indeed, the American failure to strengthen its own possessions in the western Pacific in the late 1930s appears to have had less to do with national scruples than it did with the unwillingness of a parsimonious Congress to allocate funds for an adequate defense.

Second, there were those in the Japanese navy who were seriously concerned about the laggardly pace and mistaken direction of the buildup in Japan's Pacific territories. In January 1941, Vice Admiral Inoue Shigeyoshi, chief of naval aviation and one of the navy's most forward-looking officers, had urged accelerated progress in the fortification of key air and submarine bases in Micronesia as part of a radically different approach to Japan's national defense requirements. His recommendations and the brilliant plan that contained them were set aside, however, by the battleship-minded staff of the Navy Ministry, and Inoue himself was packed off to take command of the Fourth Fleet at Truk, where he could take orders, not challenge policy. In 1940–1941, that policy, given the limitations on even the navy's expanded budget, set a priority on maintaining a large mobile fleet and forward-based air power. For this reason, the navy high command considered it more important to prepare the Micronesian islands as bases for offensive air and surface operations than to transform them into heavily fortified bastions.[59]

Truk was a case in point. Long considered one of the greatest potential bases in the Pacific by both American and Japanese strategists (indeed, in the 1930s the United States Marine Corps had developed a plan for its capture, since its use as a fleet base had been deemed essential to the success of the American Orange Plan), it had taken on a mysterious and awesome reputation in the American press by the time the war broke out. Yet despite the frenzied work there in 1941, its defenses and fleet facilities were fairly modest prior to 1943. It contained no great dry docks or vast arsenals, sheltered no major fleet units, and supported no large number of aircraft, and its first defenses were limited to a few antiaircraft and coastal guns and light automatic weapons (Photo 36).[60]

Nor were the other islands better fortified. The defenses of the Marshalls, for example, were almost nonexistent in December 1941. In the previous summer Rear Admiral Takeuchi Kaoru, newly appointed commander of the Sixth Base Force at Kwajalein, made a tour of the Marshalls and was appalled by the lack of preparedness he found. "There are no defense systems or defense equipment at all in the whole area of the Marshalls," Takeuchi fumed to his staff upon his return. "I doubt the mentality of the high command and I am going to say that in Tokyo." It is said that word of his stinging memorandum to the navy brass demanding the hardening of the bases in the Marshalls echoed throughout the Fourth Fleet, but in December 1941, though the key atolls possessed runways, aircraft, and warships capable of offensive operations, work on their defenses had only begun.[61] Indeed, it was still being desperately pushed forward to completion when the American amphibious offensive guided by the tactical principles of Earl Ellis, overwhelmed the Marshalls two years later.

Photo 36. Dublon Town, Truk, as a naval base.

There is an irony in the clandestine preparations of the Japanese navy from 1930 to 1941. For the greater part of its rule in Micronesia, Japan did, in fact, abjure the construction of those largely defensive military and naval facilities that were most obviously prohibited to it by international agreement. Thus, Japan's "invulnerable fortress" in the Pacific was a myth whose origins lay partly in the mystery and secrecy with which the Japanese chose to veil the islands between the world wars and partly in the fevered imagination of the American press. But, as the later course of the Pacific War was to demonstrate most starkly, in an age of aerial bombardment and mobile amphibious operations the islands *as defensive positions* counted for little. Their true value was made brilliantly clear at the outset of the conflict. In the war's first few hours, it was the *offensive use* that Japanese ships and planes made of the airstrips, docks, fuel dumps, and seaplane ramps—some of which had been constructed years before, but none of which had been specifically prohibited under international agreement—that made possible the opening blows Japan rained down upon the hapless American and British territories in the Pacific.

CHAPTER 9

"Crushed Jewels"
and Destitute Garrisons
The Nan'yō Conquered, 1941–1945

IN THE EARLY HOURS of 8 December 1941, as the planes from Vice Admiral Nagumo Chūichi's strike force streaked toward the green hills of Oahu, Japanese naval and air forces based in Micronesia and other Japanese territories were moving toward predesignated objectives in the western and central Pacific. Japanese submarines that had rendezvoused at Kwajalein were already in position off Hawaii and prepared to support the attack on Pearl Harbor. Out from Palau moved a Japanese task force composed of a carrier, four cruisers, ten destroyers, and some two dozen transports carrying army units ready to make three of the six Japanese landings in the Philippines—at Davao, Legaspi, and the Jolo Islands. At the same time as an invasion force from the Bonins was approaching Guam, Japanese bombers lifted off airfields on nearby Saipan to strike at the American island, on which American resistance was overcome within a day. From Roi and Namur islands on Kwajalein Atoll a flight of Mitsubishi medium bombers of the Twenty-fourth Air Flotilla roared their way north to Wake, followed by an amphibious task force organized at Truk and dispatched from Kwajalein. The Japanese would find Wake a tough nut to crack, but after an initial bloody repulse, they would have the atoll in hand a little more than two weeks later. Far easier would be the conquest of Tarawa and Makin in the nearby Gilbert Islands, the objectives of a small attack force that had been organized at Jaluit. From Majuro Lagoon a detachment of flying boats lifted off to strike at America's Howland Island, as did others from Jaluit to bomb Nauru and Ocean islands.[1]

Within a few days, except for the epic resistance put up by the American marines at Wake, Japanese surface and air units were everywhere swiftly victorious in the Pacific. Within a few weeks Japanese forces had control of the western and central Pacific, and had overrun much of the Philippines, Malaya, and the Dutch East Indies. By late spring of 1942,

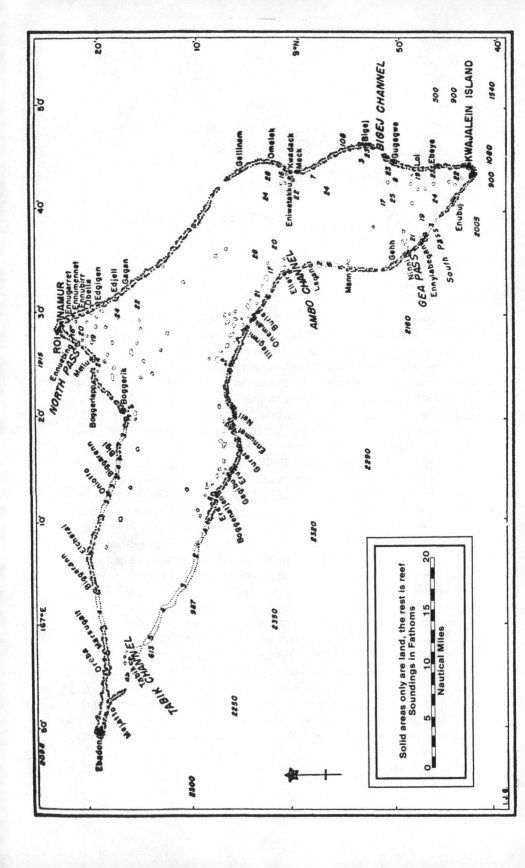

the boundaries of Japan's Greater East Asian Co-Prosperity Sphere took in most of Southeast Asia and Melanesia and from their powerful advance base at Rabaul, seven hundred miles south of Truk, Japanese forces were threatening Australia and the remaining Allied positions in the South Pacific.

The first Allied counterblows against the Japanese colonial empire were struck early in 1942 when naval and air units of the United States Pacific Fleet launched attacks against Kwajalein, Wotje, Jaluit, and Maloelap in the Marshalls. But these were light jabs along the periphery of the empire, designed to lift sagging American morale rather than expected to inflict crippling damage on Japanese defenses in Micronesia. For the next two years, as the Americans first halted the lightning Japanese offensives, and then turned the tide of battle in a series of decisive carrier engagements in which the Japanese lost the best portion of their naval air forces, the emperor's island territories remained inviolate. On the larger islands, life for civilians and military personnel alike did not change dramatically from the immediate prewar years, and military preparations continued at an almost leisurely pace.

Only in the Marshalls and the newly occupied Gilberts did the Japanese navy accelerate its effort to strengthen its positions, though even there the Sixth Base Force at Kwajalein gave priority to improving air and fueling facilities, and only secondarily to putting in fortifications, coast defense and antiaircraft guns, searchlights, and radar. Still, by the fall of 1942, Kwajalein, Jaluit, Wotje, and Maloelap had been substantially strengthened and Mili Atoll transformed from a lookout station to a major base. As the nerve center for the surrounding bases and as the funnel through which all shipments of men, weapons, and material flowed into the Marshalls, Kwajalein became particularly important. Roi and Namur islands at the northern tip of the atoll's vast lagoon, Ebeye on its southeastern side, and Kwajalein at its southeastern corner became jammed with barracks, runways, communications facilities, and aircraft of various types (Figure 24).[2]

Lacquer Trays and Band Music: The Combined Fleet at Truk

When Japan had acquired Rabaul on the northern tip of New Britain, Truk had become the rear area headquarters for the Japanese Combined Fleet.[3] Then, with the beginning of the American offensives in the Solomons in the late summer of 1942, Truk took on added importance. Approximately equidistant from Rabaul and Kwajalein, it was a key staging point for sea and air communications between Japan and its forward areas in the South Pacific. Although Truk never came to be the impregnable fortress American planners imagined it to be, it was greatly strengthened as increasing numbers of shore personnel were stationed on its principal islands. On their mountain slopes were placed heavy guns (none, contrary to myth, from the captured British base at Singapore), and at the same time the atoll's airfields and seaplane ramps were extended and improved.[4]

The arrival of the Combined Fleet in the summer of 1942 made Truk a wonder to behold. To that splendid natural harbor formed by the far-flung coral reef around the islands came Admiral Yamamoto Isoroku and the greatest battleships that the world would ever see, the *Yamato*, and later, its sister ship, the *Musashi* (Photo 37). Yamamoto had come south to plan and prepare for the decisive battle, long an article of faith within the Japanese naval high command, in which the eighteen-inch guns of his great battleships, together with the bombs and torpedoes of his carrier planes, at the right time and the right place, would trap and crush the enemy, winning the war in one thunderstroke.

The Combined Fleet riding at anchor at Truk must surely have been one of the greatest spectacles of Japanese imperial history. At its center, anchored in the waters just southeast of Dublon, lay the vast bulk of the *Yamato*, from whose bridge Yamamoto, alone resplendent in dress whites, presided over the fleet, while officers and men scurried about in khaki on the decks far below. Scattered about the enormous lagoon was an armada of lesser battleships, aircraft carriers, and heavy cruisers, shoals of destroyers, submarines and fleet auxiliaries, between which ships' launches dashed hither and thither like water beetles on important business. In those months, while the enemy and the thunder of war lay hundreds of miles beyond the horizon, it was still possible for the rhythms of the fleet's activities to be measured and ceremonial. Every morning at sunrise, when the navy's sunburst ensign was raised over each ship, and at sunset, when it was lowered, the band of each flagship played *Kimigayo*, the national anthem, and the melody was repeated around the fleet by ship's bugle. In those brief moments, the launches would cut their engines, their crews facing the flag as the solemn, dirge-like melody floated out over the water. At noon, the fleet band, standing on the after deck of the *Yamato*, would play various martial selections, perhaps "Umi yukuba," "Getsu-getsu-ka-sui-moku-kin-kin," or "Suishiei no kaiken." When major warships of the fleet entered or departed the lagoon, the band would strike up the "Battleship March" and the crews of all the vessels at anchor would line the railings to cheer and wave their caps.[5]

For those who served with the Combined Fleet staff at Truk during 1942 and early 1943, it was a time of leisure and comfort incredible for a navy at war. The ships usually anchored for a month or more, and their officers and crews spent at least a quarter of that time ashore. Officers had few restrictions on their shore liberty and the pleasures of Truk in those early war years were not inconsiderable. For many, there

Photo 37. Battleships *Yamato* (left) and *Musashi* (right), in Truk lagoon.
(Kaigun Bunko)

were the delights of liquor and women at the *ryōriya* and grog shops in
Dublon Town; others played tennis during the day and in the evening
quenched their thirst on cold beer, always in plentiful supply; some
went to see the Micronesian dances and sing-alongs arranged for their
benefit by the navy and the Nan'yō-chō; others tramped about the
islands, taking along a *bento* box of fish, rice, and pickles, or climbed a
mountain slope to watch the white-tailed tropic birds skim the island
waters.

None lived as regally, of course, as Admiral Yamamoto. When ashore
he would sometimes lodge at the branch governor's residence overlooking Dublon Harbor, there to dine on wild fowl and mangrove crab. Or
perhaps he would spend an evening at the Tokiwa, where the food and
the women were the best Truk had to offer. But most of his time he spent
in the comfort of his quarters aboard the "*Yamato* Hotel," as his flagship
was known around the fleet for its size and its luxuries. There, as the
weeks and then months slipped by, Yamamoto dined with his staff on
delicacies such as sea bream served on individual black lacquer tables
while they planned how to trap the Americans in decisive battle.

For all this mighty concentration of naval power, the sojourn of the
Combined Fleet at Truk, from the summer of 1942 to November 1943,
proved an exercise in futility. While Japanese battlefield commanders
on Guadalcanal sent desperate pleas to the navy to dispatch the *Yamato*
with its eighteen-inch guns to pulverize the American enemy in the
Solomons, the naval high command in Tokyo, still obsessed with the pri-

macy of battleships and unwilling to risk them in anything but the encounter of decision, kept the main units of the Combined Fleet at Truk. There Yamamoto waited in the splendid isolation of his quarters, dispensing Scotch whiskey, English cigarettes, and examples of his calligraphy to his staff, while awaiting the opportunity, which never came, to strike a decisive blow at the enemy. When at last Yamamoto decided to take an active hand in the combat being waged in the western Pacific, the decision cost the life of this most famous naval commander of Japan. Alerted by a decoded Japanese radio message outlining the route of his inspection trip to the Shortland Islands, American aircraft intercepted the bomber in which Yamamoto was a passenger and shot it out of the sky.

Yamamoto's successor as Combined Fleet commander, Admiral Koga Mine'ichi, suffered no better fate. With both the *Musashi* and the *Yamato* at his disposal, Koga kept the remainder of the fleet together at Truk for the realization of his "Z Plan," the annihilation of the United States Pacific Fleet. Twice Koga made sorties to Eniwetok in the Marshalls, and each time the failure of the American fleet to materialize forced him to withdraw empty-handed. When Koga moved his aircraft and lighter surface units to Rabaul in late 1943 to threaten American beachheads in the Solomons, they were torn apart in savage aerial attacks on the harbor. Now shorn of sufficient air cover should they sally forth, Japan's superbattleships sat virtually immobilized in Truk lagoon. By this time, the enemy had begun to carry aerial vengeance to the Marshalls, the front line of Japan's embattled empire, waging a war of attrition against Japanese air power there and threatening Truk and the eastern Carolines. Forced to pull back his command and his battleships to the Philippines, Admiral Koga perished with his aircraft when it went down in a storm during the withdrawal.

Holding the Line: Japan Strengthens the Central Pacific

Once the Americans went over to the offensive in the Solomons and New Guinea in the autumn of 1942, Japanese forces in the Pacific never regained the initiative, though it would be another year before the inferno of combat scorched their Micronesian bases. From the autumn of 1942 to the autumn of 1943 American air, sea, and land forces battered at Japanese positions in the southwest Pacific in a grinding war of attrition, while American submarines began to ravage Japanese shipping in Micronesian waters. Reviewing this situation on 30 September 1943, the high command in Tokyo decided on a major restructuring of Japanese strategy in the Pacific. Japan was now to abandon its futile offensives and consolidate its positions to a more manageable defense perimeter while gathering strength for a mighty counterstroke that would be organized behind an "absolute national defense sphere" *(zettai kokubō ken)* running from the Kuriles to the Bonins, the Marianas, the western and central Carolines, the Sunda Islands in the East Indies, and around to Burma. This greatly constricted strategic defense perimeter excluded the Gilberts and the Marshalls, but those islands groups were not to be given up without a fight. On the contrary, they were to be strengthened rapidly; when attacked, their garrisons would hold out as long as possible, wearing down and perhaps even annihilating the approaching enemy while Japan strengthened its new perimeter.[6]

The decisions of 30 September 1943, which shifted Japanese strategy in the Pacific from an offensive to a defensive posture, had two major consequences: they caused the introduction of considerable numbers of Japanese army troops and they necessitated a desperate attempt to build or strengthen fortifications on all the key islands of the Carolines and Marshalls.

Until the autumn of 1943, the defenses of the Pacific regions, such as they were, were the responsibility of the Japanese navy.[7] Traditionally trained and equipped for offensive air and sea operations, the navy had never given much thought to digging in on land. Moreover, the review of the requirements for the "absolute national defense sphere" had shown that the navy's island garrisons, though tough and combat ready, were far too few in number to withstand the enormous American forces that were now being gathered against them. It was time for the army to lend a hand. From various garrisons and units in Japan, Manchuria, and the Philippines some forty battalions were reorganized into amphibious brigades *(kaijō kidō ryōdan)* and South Seas detachments *(Nan'yō shitai,* of about two thousand men each) and hurried south to be redistributed through the central and eastern Carolines and the Marshalls, while the Fifty-second ("Oak") Division was formed in Kanazawa in the homeland for shipment south to Truk. To the Marshalls, the army sent some thirteen thousand men by the end of 1943. The two largest contingents were the First Amphibious Brigade, organized from units that had been on garrison duty in Manchuria, and the First South Seas Detachment, formed from troops in Japan and the Philippines. On the whole these were not first-line troops, and outside some of the veterans of the First South Seas Detachment, who had seen service in the conquest of Bataan in 1942, few had combat experience.[8]

With the arrival of these army units in the late autumn of 1943, the Japanese undertook their first major effort to fortify their principal bases in the central Pacific. On the high islands, Japanese construction crews and conscripted island laborers gouged out tunnels and caves and poured tons of concrete for communications centers, ammunition dumps, and gun emplacements. Some of the efforts to mount heavy guns on island peaks and promontories were prodigious undertakings.

Naval guns were hauled up the slopes of Mt. Tonachau on Moen Island, Truk, and placed in caves excavated there for their concealment. On the coast of Ponape, it took nearly a year to drag several naval cannon through the thick underbrush and up the slopes of Sokehs to place them atop the nine-hundred-foot rock. In the interior of Ponape, two vintage six-inch guns were wrestled to the top of a two-thousand-foot mountain overlooking the U Valley.[9] The effort was prodigious; the results were futile. Only once during the Pacific War did American warships stand off Ponape to bombard it, and even then they were at too great distance for Japanese guns to find their range.

In the Marshalls, the problems encountered by the Japanese were different, but no less difficult. The small land area, the high water table, and an elevation of no more than a dozen feet on the average atoll island, did much to determine the nature and arrangements of the fortifications built there. Since the islands did not provide room for tactical withdrawal, even had the traditional concepts of the Japanese army permitted it (which they did not), the Japanese insular fortifications at this stage of the Pacific War were generally limited to beach defenses, intended to annihilate the enemy at the water's edge.

In a typical arrangement for such atoll-island fortifications, antilanding obstacles—barriers of concrete and coconut logs—as well as minefields were placed along the shore. Behind these was a primary defense line of pillboxes just beyond the beach, sited so as to provide enfilading fire and fronted by antitank ditches. Behind this first line was a secondary defense perimeter of mutually supporting, bunkered strong points, sometimes constructed of ferroconcrete, most often of palm logs covered with corrugated iron, topped with sand and earthcover or sand-filled rice bags. None of the islands was fortified in depth, since the defenders were expected to defeat the enemy while he struggled out of the surf onto the beach, though on some of the principal island bases, dozens of concrete communication buildings, hangars, and barracks could serve as positions from which a bitter-end defense could be conducted.[10]

While the defense arrangements of any atoll island tended to be standardized, the Japanese were forced to modify their design, in large part because of the war's increasing exigencies. The most serious of these were the growing shortages of construction materials, particularly steel, concrete, and barbed wire, as American submarines and aircraft began to ravage Japanese transport to the islands. The ferroconcrete pillbox eventually gave way to ones constructed of palm logs, stone, and sand-filled fuel barrels. But lack of time more than anything else prevented the laying out of elaborate defenses. As the Americans came storming through the Marshalls in February 1944, the newly arrived troops on Eniwetok Atoll, for example, had neither time nor materials to construct strong points with firing slits. Instead they simply honeycombed the atoll's islands with webs of tunnels connecting well-covered and concealed foxholes for individual defenders.[11]

As the American seaborne offensive crashed into the Gilbert Islands in the late autumn of 1943, and took Tarawa and Makin atolls in the first bloody test of the U.S. Marine Corps' amphibious doctrine, Admiral Akiyama Monzo's Sixth Base Force at Kwajalein scrambled to complete the defenses of the Marshalls. But the real key to defending the atolls, or to defending these or any other Japanese positions in the Pacific for that matter, was the control of the waters around and the skies above them. By late 1943, the Japanese navy had lost command of both. Because of the rampaging attacks of American submarines, the feebleness of the Japanese antisubmarine effort, and the general inability of Japan's own submarines to retaliate in kind, Japan was rapidly losing the struggle at sea. Few Japanese vessels dared enter the waters of the Marshalls, and elsewhere in the Pacific scarcely a day went by without a transport or warship being fatally struck by American torpedoes.

Had Vice Admiral Yamada Michiyuki's Twenty-fourth Air Flotilla been able to provide effective air cover for the atoll bases, the American amphibious offensive might have been halted and certainly would have been delayed considerably. As the Marshalls had generally been written off by the high command, however, Yamada's force was able to muster only about one hundred aircraft by the time the enemy arrived in the skies overhead, though scratch reinforcements from Hokkaido and Rabaul were fed in after the battle began.

Even worse than the size of Japanese naval air power in the Marshalls was its poor quality, a condition that reflected the decline of Japanese air power everywhere in the Pacific by this time. Japanese planes, which, type-for-type, had been far superior to the American enemy in the first six months of the war, were now totally outclassed. Moreover, the core squadrons of trained Japanese aircrews had been shredded in the great carrier battles of 1942. Because of lack of fuel and time for training equally qualified successors, they had never really been replaced. Gone were the incredibly skilled pilots of 1941–1942 who had jinked about the skies, using their Mitsubishi zeroes like rapiers. Increasingly their places were taken by pilots with far less training, skill, and confidence.

Early Disasters: Loss of the Marshalls, February–April 1944

Inadequately prepared on the seas, on the ground, and in the air, the Japanese navy and army units on the five major atoll bases in the Marshalls—Kwajalein, Wotje, Jaluit, Mili, and Maloelap—braced to meet the American onslaught surging up from the Gilberts. In mid-November 1943, even as American marines poured ashore in the

Gilberts, American planes launched an aerial bombardment of the Marshalls to destroy Japanese air strength there prior to an amphibious assault. Initially, the large Japanese bases at Taroa on Maloelap and Mili on Mili Atoll bore the full fury of the increasingly destructive enemy attacks, which continued through December by both carrier planes and land-based B-24 bombers. Both bases threw up curtains of antiaircraft fire and thickets of interceptor aircraft, forcing the bomber crews to fight their way in and fight their way out. But, minus a few of their number, the bombers generally reached their targets, blasting the installations, strafing aircraft on the ground, gouging out the runways, and sinking the few small ships incautious enough to have anchored in the lagoons.[12]

Desperately, Akiyama attempted to keep the runways repaired and Yamada attempted to keep them reinforced with aircraft, but the numbers the enemy brought to this campaign of attrition doomed their efforts. In December, when the Americans began escorting their bombers with fighter aircraft, Yamada's inexperienced pilots were shot down in wholesale lots. Week after week, the incessant pounding continued; on several occasions, enemy bombers working in shifts remained over Mili all day long. By late January, Taroa and Mili were finished as bases, no aircraft rose to meet the attackers, and even antiaircraft fire was feeble (Photo 38). By January, too, the brunt of the attacks had fallen on Kwajalein, Wotje, and Eniwetok. Toward the end of that

Photo 38. Airfield, Taroa Islet, Maloelap Atoll, Marshall Islands, December 1943.

month, just prior to the invasion of the Marshalls, an American carrier task force raked all the islands, concentrating at Roi on Kwajalein, the center of Japanese air power. On 29 January, Admiral Yamada still had approximately one hundred thirty serviceable aircraft under his command. Two days later, so devastating was the American aerial attack, he had none.[13]

The amphibious assault on the Marshalls caught Admiral Akiyama on Kwajalein by surprise, since he had expected that the enemy would attempt to seize the outermost atolls, Mili, Jaluit, and Ebon, before attempting to thrust deep into the web of Japanese bases. But, leapfrogging beyond those atolls, in what was to become a standard American strategy for neutralizing Japanese positions in the Pacific, the enemy moved to seize Majuro, an atoll some two hundred sixty-five miles southeast of Kwajalein, occupying it without a shot. Unaware that the Japanese navy had abandoned this former seaplane base (except for a warrant officer left behind as custodian of Japanese property there) a combat-loaded destroyer transport slipped into the Majuro Lagoon on the night of 30 January and debarked its troops to take control of the atoll (capturing the warrant officer in the process). With this bloodless conquest of the first territory of the Japanese colonial empire (that is, territory formally held by Japan prior to 1931) the enemy secured an excellent advance naval and air base for the conquest of the Marshalls.[14]

In the meantime, because of his misreading of the American strategic plan, Admiral Akiyama had mistakenly shifted a good number of his troops from Kwajalein to Mili. Even so, the garrisons on Roi-Namur, the twin islands on Kwajalein's northern rim and Kwajalein Island at the atoll's southern end, were sufficient in men and defenses to put up formidable resistance (Figure 24). Yet their ultimate fate could not be in doubt when the American amphibious force, preceded by a fire-storm of aerial and surface bombardment, suddenly and simultaneously struck the northern and southern ends of the atoll on 31 January 1944.[15]

Roi-Namur was defended solely by navy troops, just under three thousand of them, but only the four-hundred-man detachment from the Sixty-first Guard Force was a combat unit; most of the rest were the aviators, mechanics, and support personnel of Admiral Yamada's Twenty-fourth Air Flotilla, now without a single plane to fly or service. The Americans quickly overran Roi, which consisted mostly of runways and air facilities, but the resistance of the naval combat troops on adjacent Namur was ferocious. Firing from scattered pillboxes, covered buildings, and the rubble of their gun emplacements, the defenders fought with light automatic weapons, mortars, and grenades against tanks, flame throwers, satchel charges, armor-piercing shells, naval broadsides, and aerial bombs until 3 February, when the last of them were killed.[16]

On Kwajalein Island, the struggle was even more frenzied, since there were a good many more combat troops to defend the position. In addition to the Sixth Base Force, under Admiral Akiyama—the overall atoll commander—the bulk of the navy's Sixty-first Guard Force under Captain Yamagata Masaji was solidly entrenched on Kwajalein, along with some twenty-six hundred naval service personnel. Since November, these naval forces had been reinforced by about one thousand army troops, the core of which was the Second Battalion of the First Amphibious Brigade, under Colonel Aso Tarokichi. For five days, from 1 February through the fifth, these men resisted the steel avalanche that roared down upon them, fighting from their rapidly crumbling positions, dashing out in small clusters in futile suicide charges, sniping from the palm trees, scrambling over enemy tanks to try to drop hand grenades down the hatches, their officers even beating their swords in helpless rage against the advancing machines. On 2 February, Admiral Akiyama sent a final message to his men from his bunker, calling upon them to die in their positions. Few needed encouragement. The fighting reached a crescendo during the Japanese resistance in the central blockhouse area in the center of the island, now reduced to a jumble of twisted girders and rubble. On the morning of 2 February Akiyama was blown to bits while inspecting the front lines. Two days later, most of the remaining troops had been compressed into the northern tip of the island. On the fifth the survivors, with Colonel Aso at their head, made a direct frontal attack on the American positions and were completely annihilated. From 2 through 6 February, the invaders then turned the weight of the offensive to Ebeye Island on the southeastern side of the atoll and the desperate resistance and subsequent slaughter was repeated until the island's last defenders were blasted away.[17] By the second week in February, then, the Japanese had suffered a fatal blow to their defenses in the Marshalls. With the loss of the nerve center of those defenses, it became impossible to mount a coordinated resistance to subsequent American landings in the islands.

In late February, the invaders turned their attention to Eniwetok, the last major Japanese base in the Marshalls as yet untouched by either American bombs or landing craft. A roughly circular atoll of some thirty-five islands and islets distributed around the second largest lagoon in the Marshalls, Eniwetok is the most northwesterly of that group (Figure 25). In American hands, it could block any Japanese attempt to reinforce their remaining bases in the Marshalls or reconquer those already seized. Though it had been used as a fuel depot for a few years before the war, the Japanese navy had been slow to recognize its potential value. Naval construction crews, 1942–1943, had built an undefended airstrip on Engebi, the largest island on the northern rim of the atoll, but the airfield itself had lain idle until pressed into service in

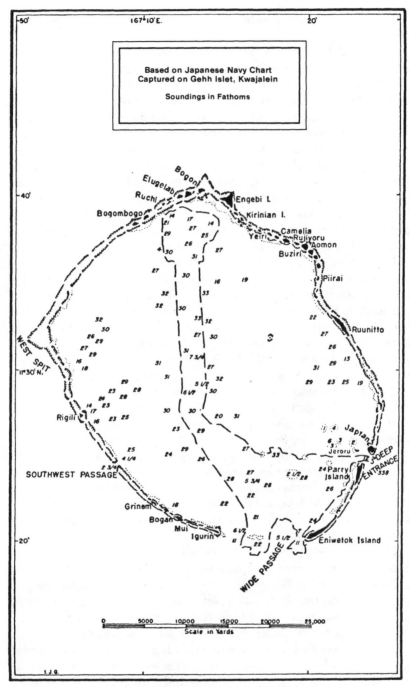

Figure 25. Eniwetok Atoll, Marshall Islands.
(Reproduced from Morison 1951, 284)

late 1943 as a ferrying point for aircraft passing through the Marshalls.[18]

Early in 1944, with the enemy's aerial assault on the Marshalls in full swing, the Japanese army rushed a garrison to Eniwetok, landing three battalions (over twenty-five hundred men) of the First Amphibious Brigade under Major General Nishida Yashima, hardy men from northern Honshu, who had most recently seen garrison duty in Manchuria. Under orders from Fourth Fleet headquarters at Truk to build permanent fortifications on Eniwetok as rapidly as possible, Nishida pushed his men furiously. He selected Parry Island at the atoll's southeastern rim as his command post and there concentrated his largest force, over one thousand men, equipped with some artillery and even a few tanks, while he sent approximately eight hundred men to Eniwetok Island, just to the south, and another seven hundred to Engebi, supplied with some artillery and three tanks, but supported by no aircraft.[19]

Dumped on the atoll only six weeks before its fall, overworked, on short rations, staggered by the unaccustomed heat—conditions that soon put scores in the base infirmary suffering from exhaustion—the garrisons on Eniwetok Atoll, despite their dogged efforts, accomplished little in the way of preparing permanent defenses. Without heavy equipment and, more important, without time for more elaborate defenses, the best they could do on Parry was to honeycomb the island with hastily dug foxholes, shallow bunkers covered with coconut logs and sand and connected by a web of trenches and tunnels. Their one advantage was that they were superbly camouflaged, so well, indeed, that Nishida's men deceived the enemy's reconnaissance planes into believing that neither Parry nor Eniwetok was defended.[20]

On 30 January, almost as an afterthought, the army flew in a pathetic packet of ten fighters to Eniwetok from Tinian, a flight not unlike that of moths to a furnace. The next day, as American landing ships approached Kwajalein, the first B-24s appeared over Eniwetok, catching six of the Japanese planes on the ground, and destroying the other four in the air. From that day, bombs rained down on the atoll for nearly two weeks, principally on Engebi, where half the garrison was killed, not directly by the explosions, but crushed under the collapsed palm logs and other heavy construction materials of their hastily prepared defenses. On 19 February, after occupying a half-dozen nearby islets, the Americans landed in force on Engebi, and after a brief but bitter struggle the thousand or more defenders were killed.[21]

Through captured documents, the invaders learned of the concealed presence of Nishida's forces on Parry and Eniwetok and turned to smash them. On 20 February, the marines stormed the beaches of Eniwetok Island, where the enemy resisted with deadly and accurate automatic-weapons fire until the last of them were confined to the island's northern tip. "We cornered fifty or so . . . on the end of the island where they attempted a banzai charge," an American participant recorded, "but we cut them down like overripe wheat and they lay like tired children with their faces in the sand."[22]

General Nishida's command on Parry was the last to fall. Assaulted on 21 February, the men of the First Amphibious Brigade fought with determined frenzy from their warren of foxholes and tunnels, until the last handful were blasted or roasted out with artillery, satchel charges, grenades, and flamethrowers. Somewhere and sometime in the carnage their commander died, but the chaos and destruction were so total that there was no time for any final messages, or diaries, from which a Japanese account of the garrison's final hours could be reconstructed. We know only that in the loss of Eniwetok Atoll, over twenty-seven hundred men fell and sixty-four were captured (mostly Okinawan and Korean laborers), in a resistance that was as bitter as it was doomed.[23]

In late 1943 there had been five major Japanese bases in the Marshalls —Kwajalein, Wotje, Jaluit, Mili, and Maloelap—with a sixth, Eniwetok, rushed into semireadiness in January 1944. In a little over three weeks of desperate combat, the enemy had ripped out the heart of the Japanese defenses in the Marshalls by taking Kwajalein and then Eniwetok, a setback so severe that the Japanese high command in Tokyo decided to keep it secret from the public.[24] The remaining four bases, which were simply bypassed by the Americans, no longer formed part of a cohesive defense of the Marshall Islands. No longer possessed of any ships or aircraft, or even effective communication between themselves or with higher headquarters, almost entirely cut off from supplies and reinforcements, and under continual aerial bombardment, the garrisons on Wotje, Jaluit, Mili, and Maloelap could do nothing to prevent the rapid seizure of all the rest of the Marshall atolls where Japanese garrisons were either minuscule or nonexistent. In the American mop-up of the Marshalls, some of these places were occupied peacefully, some after an hour or so of desperate but futile resistance (Figure 26). By April 1944, the Japanese flag no longer flew over any of them.[25]

In the years since the end of the Pacific War, the common virtue of the uncommon valor displayed by American marines who stormed the beaches and strong points of the Japanese islands in the Pacific has justly become a hallowed part of American history. Perhaps, it is time, after more than forty years, to pay equal tribute to the heroism of those against whom they fought. A Westerner does not have to sympathize with the cause of Japan in World War II to recognize that in the ferocious combat in the Pacific the odds against the Japanese fighting man in Micronesia were overwhelming, his situation usually hopeless, and the conditions in which he fought and died appalling. Consider the contrasts:

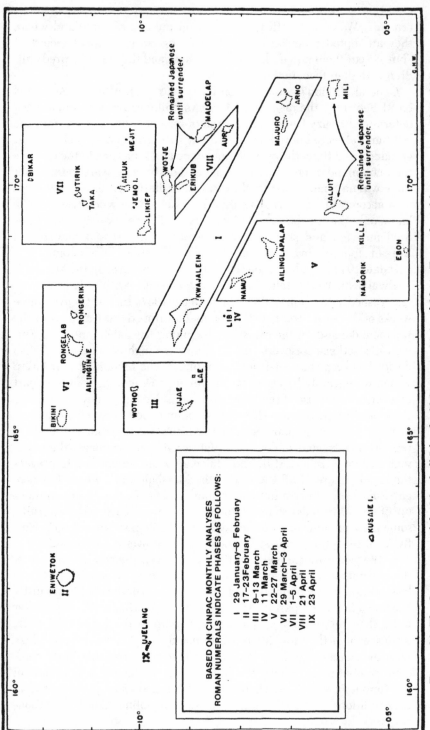

Figure 26. The Occupation of the Marshall Islands, 29 January–23 April 1944. (Reproduced from Morison 1951, 311)

Terrible though their ordeals might have been, American soldiers and marines after 1942 nearly always fought with a mighty armada of ships at their backs and an almost unchallenged protective umbrella of air power above them; they were usually well supported by tanks and artillery; thanks to both the immense forge of American industry and the brilliant effectiveness of American amphibious warfare and logistics, they were never long without an endless stream of food, ammunition, and medical supplies; and their wounded were never long without the best medical attention their nation could provide. Most important of all, they had the confidence and the reality that they were on the winning side and that every island they conquered brought them that much closer to Tokyo and final victory.

The situation of the Japanese defenders of Micronesia, 1943–1944, was almost the complete reverse. On islands that were totally blockaded by enemy warships and dominated by enemy air power, both of which poured an unending rain of explosives down upon them, supported by pitifully few guns and only rarely by any tanks, cornered in the rubble of their bunkers and strong points, which rocked with the force of explosions, compelled to rely on whatever ammunition, food, and supplies they had with them, struggling to care for the wounded with only rudimentary first-aid supplies, firing from embrasures only a few inches wide at approaching infantry, tanks, and artillery of whose movements they could know very little, Japanese troops in Micronesia during these months fought on without hope of reinforcement, without hope of victory, even without hope of survival. Those who were fortunate took a bullet to the brain, were smashed to a bloody pulp by satchel charges or armor-piercing naval shells, or took their own lives by holding hand grenades to the head; others lingered on for a while with hideous mutilations, were slowly suffocated in the dark when their tunnels collapsed or were sealed by the enemy, or suffered searing agonies wrought by American flamethrowers.

In pondering why, in Western terms, these men were not sensible, why they did not raise the white flag of surrender when all was apparently lost, it would be well to move beyond the opinion commonly expressed in American accounts of the campaigns in the Pacific that Japanese troops were motivated by insane fanaticism. It is unjust of Americans to award the laurels of heroism only to American fighting men in the Pacific while dismissing as simple fanaticism the sacrificial resistance of the Japanese who opposed them. "No nation has a monopoly on heroism," Richard Minear has recently written, "nor apparently is any nation backward in sanctifying the sacrificial deaths of young men." Americans at the Alamo and the French Foreign Legion at Dienbienphu, he correctly reminds us, are two examples of similarly legendary sacrifices unto death by fighting men of the West.[26] It must be understood, moreover, that from feudal times the Japanese military tradition had held surrender to be dishonorable and thus made immutable the concept of death before dishonor. There was a hallowed military term for the idea: *gyokusai.* Literally, it meant a "crushed jewel"; figuratively, an honorable death.[27] A unit that was annihilated, like those on Kwajalein and Eniwetok, was called a "crushed jewel" by the Japanese military. The term gained increasing currency in the Pacific War as battalions, regiments, and even divisions chose annihilation rather than surrender.

The Destruction of Truk

By February 1944, even as the American amphibious offensive was swamping the Japanese defenses in the Marshalls, the American high command in the Pacific had at last turned its baleful glare upon Truk, still conceived as a fortress of tremendous strength where armadas of aircraft jammed its airfields, antiaircraft and coast defense artillery bristled from every mountain slope, and battleships and carriers anchored in its vast lagoon. For their part, the brass in Tokyo knew Truk was not impregnable, but they remained optimistic about its ability to beat back any American attack. After all, Truk was not just a collection of coral patches, like the Marshalls, but endowed by nature with both mountains and reefs. Its entrances were mined and its principal islands and fleet anchorage could not be reached by naval gunfire from outside the reefs. There were over three hundred fifty aircraft on its airfields and while discretion dictated that it was unwise to leave major fleet units in the lagoon, it was possible to keep the base supplied by surface transports. The army garrison of more than eight thousand men, centered on the main force of the Fifty-second Division newly arrived from Kanazawa, was as stout as its name and could be expected to carry out a defense in depth should the enemy somehow land on the islands.[28]

The reality was far different. While there were indeed military installations on all the main islands, several hundred planes on its airfields, and a garrison that was the largest in the central Pacific, Truk's reputation as a fortress was a sham: the aircraft were no longer the equal of the enemy, nor were those who flew them; incredibly, most of the trained pilots were quartered on Dublon while the aircraft were parked on Eten and Moen; there were only forty antiaircraft guns in the entire archipelago, and all fire-control radar had gone down with the ship carrying them to Truk; aviation fuel was so scarce that it was difficult to fly regular patrols outside the islands; indeed all supplies, ammunition, and fuel were in short supply because of the endless attrition by American submarines.

Early in February 1944, after spotting an American reconnaissance aircraft, the last of the major warships of the Combined Fleet pulled out of Truk, falling back on the relative safety of the Palaus, though a large number of freighters and transports remained in harbor to unload desperately needed fuel, munitions, and food. Without any warships of its own to speak of, the Fourth Fleet was now a hollow shell. Its commander, Vice Admiral Hara Chūichi, listening to American radio broadcasts that referred to Truk as the "impregnable bastion of the Pacific" could only hope the enemy would not discover its true weakness.[29]

But in less than a fortnight the Americans would lose their awe of Truk. In Washington, the Joint Chiefs of Staff were forming a new strategy to complement the amphibious leapfrogging of Japanese bases. Truk was to be the precedent. Rather than attempting a costly direct seaborne assault to capture the archipelago, the Japanese defenses there were to be "neutralized" with an overwhelming burst of air power. At dawn on 17 February, waves of planes from the carriers of Task Force Fifty-eight came roaring in over the northeastern edge of the reef, the fighters clawing down thirty of the forty or fifty Japanese pilots who had been able to get into the air with only ten minutes advance warning; dive bombers and torpedo bombers then turned on shipping in the lagoon. Photographs of the raid show the hapless end of the numerous freighters and transports that had failed to clear the harbor (Photo 39). Here a listing freighter pours out a stream of smoke; there we see the thin wake of a torpedo streaking toward a transport; a tanker off Dublon is hit amidships and out of its ruptured belly the contents spread out like blood upon the water. When the oil from the stricken tanker caught fire, a Japanese observer on Dublon recalled later, it seemed to turn the entire harbor into a sheet of flame. That night, the attackers returned and hunted down the remaining ships and aircraft with radar. At dawn of the next morning they were back again. As the lagoon was now empty of ships, they turned on the airfields, hangars, storage tanks, and ammunition dumps.

When the raiding aircraft left at noon, Truk's awesome reputation, as well as its installations, lay in a smoking shambles. The loss to the Japanese merchant marine was unprecedented—thirty-one ships found a graveyard in the lagoon. The navy suffered considerable losses as well: ten warships took the plunge, including two cruisers and three destroyers, most of them caught outside the reef trying to flee westward; two hundred seventy aircraft were destroyed, along with barracks, two thousand tons of food, hangars, and three fuel tanks holding seventeen thousand tons of fuel oil. Six hundred military and naval personnel were killed, not counting those who went down with the ships in the harbor (Photo 40).[30]

In Tokyo, Task Force Fifty-eight's crushing assault on Truk came as a

Photo 39. Japanese freighter struck by aerial torpedo, American aerial
assault on Truk, February 1944.

profound shock to the high command. The "T Affair" *(T jiken)*, as it
was referred to in classified dispatches, produced recriminations between the two services that became so bitter that the navy sent an investigation team to Truk headed by Rear Admiral Ōmori Sentarō, respected head of the navy's torpedo school, to find out how the disaster
happened, who was responsible, and how to prevent its reoccurrence.
Ōmori returned with the general conclusion that given the overwhelming air power brought to bear by the enemy in relation to the relative
weakness of Truk, no commander could have done better in resisting the
attack.[31] But one thing was certain: Truk was finished as either an
advance base or a rear area headquarters. Though its runways could
and would be repaired and aircraft replacements flown in, and though
its military garrison burrowed ever deeper into the mountainsides,
blasting out tunnels and recesses for gun emplacements and ammunition depots, it now could serve only as a defensive outpost. Never again
did the Combined Fleet anchor in majesty at Truk.

If Admiral Ōmori had any recommendations as to how to turn aside
subsequent enemy raids on Truk, official Japanese histories do not mention them. In any event it matters not, for the islands were pounded
again and again that spring. On 6 and 7 April B-24s took a hand in
attacking the atoll, destroying one hundred thirty Japanese aircraft in
the air and on the ground, and then turned on Dublon Town and
incinerated half of it. For the rest of the month bombers ranged over
Truk on alternate nights carpeting the islands with bombs. On 28 and

Photo 40. Dublon Town and naval base after American attacks of
February and April 1944.

29 April, carrier planes raked the islands once more, knocking fifty-nine
Japanese aircraft out of the sky and destroying thirty-four on the
ground. The navy ferried in more aircraft and pilots to be slaughtered,
but the alternate night attacks continued through mid-May, were
halted for several weeks, and then continued again throughout June.
Wrack and ruin was everywhere on Dublon, Moen, and Eten. Truk was
dying as the tide of battle surged beyond it.[32]

Torpedoes and Bombs: The Neutralization of the Pacific

Long before this, by subsurface attacks on Japanese shipping the enemy
had begun to destroy Japan's ability to keep any and all of its Pacific
Island bases reinforced, supplied, or equipped. Singly or in wolf packs,
American submarines ranged the central Pacific, sometimes blockading
Japan's Micronesian ports and bases, sometimes assisting American
amphibious operations, but usually ravaging Japan's tropical sea-lanes
on their own war patrols. No ship, no convoy, and few harbors were
safe from their depredations, as slowly but inexorably Japan's merchant
marine was shredded. Among the seemingly endless roll of maritime
obituaries were many of the NYK reliables that had made the rounds of
the emperor's islands during peacetime. The *Palau Maru* had been
struck down early in the war. Steaming along unescorted toward Truk
near midnight on 8 May 1942, the ship was about a hundred miles
northeast of that atoll with over two hundred passengers aboard, when

it was struck on the port side by three torpedoes from the USS *Greenling*. The liner went down by the bow in twenty minutes, taking over a third of the passengers with it; the survivors spent several days in lifeboats before being picked up by a fishing boat and taken to Truk. The *Yokohama Maru*, which Willard Price had boarded in 1935, had already fallen victim to aerial bombs while unloading troops at Salamaua two months before. The USS *Haddock* caught the *Saipan Maru* loaded with troops north of Palau on 21 September 1943 and sent her quickly to the bottom. The *Taian Maru* fell beneath the torpedoes of the *Gar* off the northeast coast of Saipan a week later. The *Kasagi Maru* was closer to the home islands when it was run through by torpedoes from the *Swordfish*.[33]

And so it went, week after week, month after month, as Japanese freighters, transports, and tankers, sank with a roar or a sigh into the shallow waters and grand abysses of the Pacific, taking with them the troops, the planes, the tanks, the ammunition, the food—and the hope —that might otherwise have sustained Japan's beleaguered and desperate island garrisons.

Destruction of Japan's merchant fleet as well as its warships was not limited to submarines, of course. A significant number were sunk by American carrier aircraft, particularly those of the deadly Task Force Fifty-eight, and by land-based bombers, especially the B-24 Liberators of the Seventh Air Force, operating ever westward across the Pacific. In general, however, the heavy bombers concentrated on island targets and, increasingly, in the spring and summer of 1944, the newer objectives were the more populated and heavily garrisoned islands of Micronesia. American strategy toward these places followed the precedent set at Truk: they were to be rendered useless to Japan by eliminating whatever offensive capability they might possess, which meant, in brief, the destruction of their air strength and their naval facilities; their ground defenses were bombed as a matter of course. In this way, the larger Japanese islands of Micronesia came to feel the hot flame of war.

Ponape was the first to be torched, largely in response to a daring air strike—one of the few the Japanese navy was able to mount after 1943. On 12 February, six four-engine flying boats from Saipan, staged through Ponape, made a highly effective night raid on the newly captured American base at Roi-Namur, demolishing a large food depot and some very valuable radar equipment, and demonstrating the threat the island could pose to the American drive through the Marshalls. Four nights later, Ponape paid for its temerity. In four raids, from 16 to 26 February, B-24s from Tarawa struck the island and its bases with nearly one hundred twenty tons of bombs and thousands of incendiaries. The first raid hit the largest airfield and the seaplane base on Langar Island and demolished much of Kolonia's waterfront. This was followed by a series of highly destructive incendiary attacks, which consumed most of the nine hundred forty buildings in the town. By the end of the first series of raids Kolonia had been reduced to a ghost town and Ponape was finished as a base. Off and on, the bombers returned that spring, and in May six of the United States Navy's largest battleships stood off the island's northern coast and shelled it for over an hour in what amounted to little more than target practice.[34]

In late March of 1944 Task Force Fifty-eight—that floating nemesis of Japanese bases in the Pacific—assembled in Majuro Lagoon and headed west. On 30 March, planes from its three carrier groups came skimming over the intricate channels and reefs of Koror to attack the Japanese airfields, the shipping in the harbor, and the town itself. For a day and a half flights of fighters, dive bombers, and torpedo bombers shuttled back and forth over Koror and Babelthuap, bombing and strafing every conceivable target. Desperately, the Japanese navy flew in all the fighters it had on Yap and Pelelieu. They succeeded in downing a few of the invaders, but these Japanese pilots, like those throughout the Pacific by 1944, were totally outclassed. They seldom pressed home their attacks and more often than not were shot to pieces by an experienced enemy flying faster, better-armored, and better-equipped aircraft.[35]

To isolate Koror as a port the Americans dropped mines into Malakal Harbor, preventing the few ships left afloat from getting out and any vessels bringing supplies or reinforcements from getting in. In June, Task Force Fifty-eight was back again, shooting up Japanese aircraft replacements and those military installations the defenders had managed to repair. During July and August 1944, as the garrisons in the Marianas were being shattered in American aerial and amphibious offensives, the Palaus were given a respite. Then, toward the end of August, B-24s took up the ceaseless hammering of Koror and Babelthuap. In the process, Koror Town was hit repeatedly, and by the time the last of the bombers droned over the horizon in early September, Japan's tropical capital was no more.[36]

By the summer of 1944 the Japanese islands and atolls in the Marshalls and eastern and central Carolines that had been bypassed by the enemy now constituted an American rear area. Yet even as the course of the war swung west and north, the interdiction and neutralization of these places by the United States Army Air Force continued on a regular, though decreasingly frequent schedule. Jaluit, Mili, Wotje, and Maloelap in the Marshalls, and Ponape, Truk, and even occasionally Kusaie in the Carolines, still rocked with explosions, adding to the increasing torment of the wretched garrisons and civilian communities that were gradually succumbing to starvation and disease. In addition, some of the more recently established bases in the central

Carolines—Woleai, Puluwat, and Satawan atolls—all began to feel the hard hand of war as each was bombed in turn.[37]

By the autumn of 1944, the submarine and the bomber had made meaningless the furious energy that the Japanese navy and army had expended in late 1943 and early 1944 in fortifying these places. Their shattered garrisons isolated, stranded, starving, no longer contributed to Japanese strategy in the Pacific; they were, on the contrary, a net drain on Japan's dwindling resources, as the navy (and even the army) tried to keep them supplied by the occasional flying boats or submarines that could get through. The predicament of the Japanese in the Marshalls and Carolines by the summer of 1944 was put succinctly by Samuel Eliot Morison in his magisterial history of the United States Navy in World War II: "Island bases are useful only as long as striking forces can operate from them. When cut off through loss of sea command, they are a liability. And an airfield from which planes cannot operate is as harmless as a tennis court."[38]

"A Bulwark of the Pacific": Defeat in the Marianas

After the initial Japanese victories in December 1941, the Marianas had come to serve principally as a supply and staging area for troops, ships, and aircraft committed far to the south and east. Part of a rear area, their garrisons had been token sized, but with the loss of the Marshalls and the isolation of the eastern and central Carolines, the Marianas, along with the western Carolines, suddenly became the front line of the empire's defenses, a vital segment of the "absolute national defense sphere." Forced to fall back more rapidly to that line than they had anticipated, the Japanese navy and army reorganized their commands in the Pacific, while rushing men, weapons, and aircraft to bolster the Marianas and the Palaus.

The navy's responsibility for the defense of the Marianas, the Palaus, and the Bonins now fell to the newly organized Central Pacific Fleet with headquarters on Saipan under Admiral Nagumo Chūichi, commander of the carriers that launched the dazzling Pearl Harbor strike. But as far as ships were concerned, Nagumo's was a paper command. His fleet was, in reality, an assembly of shore-based naval garrisons. The real striking power left to the navy was based in the Philippines, where the newly organized First Mobile Fleet, composed of nine carriers, four battleships, five cruisers, and assorted lesser ship types under Admiral Ozawa Jisaburō awaited the ever-elusive opportunity to launch the decisive blow against any attempt by the Americans to break Japan's vital defense perimeter.[39]

Saipan was also the headquarters of a new military command, the Thirty-first Army under Lt. General Ōbata Hideyoshi, who was given

the same geographic responsibility as Nagumo, though he was technically Nagumo's subordinate. Almost immediately, these arrangements
produced a new flare-up of the animosity between the two services and
the wrangling was only lessened when Ōbata and Nagumo each agreed
not to attempt to exercise complete authority over the other—a ludicrous situation for a defense theater so soon to be under assault.[40]

How rapidly that assault might fall on the Marianas was made alarm-
ingly clear even as the Japanese struggled to retain the Marshalls. In a
devastating air raid in February 1944, the carrier planes of Task Force
Fifty-eight had crippled Japanese air power on Saipan, Tinian, and
Rota, destroying hundreds of aircraft that the high command was never
able to replace.

With that ominous proof of the ability of the enemy to reach the
Marianas, the Japanese government attempted to accelerate the evacuation, initiated in 1943, of the nearly forty-three thousand civilians in
the islands. By March of 1944 some twenty-one thousand of Japan's
noncombatants were still left in the Marianas, though about five thousand more departed before the American invasion in June. Yet, by the
spring of 1944, for the average noncombatant, the risks of putting out to
sea were as great as those of staying put. In March, one of the last convoys left the Marianas with a large number of evacuees, mostly women,
children, and old men, seventeen hundred of them aboard the incongruously named transport *Amerika Maru*. The convoy had not even
cleared the northernmost islands of the archipelago when every ship
was torpedoed. The *Amerika Maru* went down quickly, taking with it a
large number of the passengers aboard. A few days later two other
transports in another convoy from the islands suffered a similar fate,
with correspondingly heavy loss of innocent lives.[41]

Nearly sixteen thousand civilians remained in the Marianas; some
with resignation, some with fierce determination, now set about assisting the incoming military units in preparing the defenses of the islands.
By late May 1944, the army had rushed two divisions, two independent
brigades, and three expeditionary units to the Marianas Sector Group
under Ōbata's command, and the navy had sent in two of its guard
forces. Besides a division sent to Guam, the core of the Marianas Sector
Group was to be the Forty-third ("Glory") Division, under Major General Saitō Yoshitsugu, which was assigned the defense of Saipan. Composed of three infantry regiments and supporting elements, the Forty-
third, despite its nickname, was not an impressive division. It was
commanded by an aging cavalry officer who himself had no combat
experience and was composed of new draftees led by inexperienced officers. Moreover, it was less than a year old and had spent its brief life in
antiaircraft duty in the Nagoya area, service that hardly prepared it to
repel an American amphibious offensive.[42]

Assigned mediocre forces to begin with, Ōbata's Marianas Sector Group could not even count on those units arriving intact, since American submarines began taking a disastrous toll of the convoys bringing troops, weapons, and supplies to the islands. The Forty-third Division, sailing in two echelons from Japan, was itself fearfully damaged in such attacks. The first contingents, with General Saitō at their head, had landed safely in late May, but the convoy bringing the second echelon had lost five out of its seven ships, and with them a good number of the troops on board and all of their weapons and equipment. The division's 118th Regiment suffered the most: of its one thousand survivors, half were badly burned or wounded. Other units bound for other islands in the Pacific were similarly shipwrecked and turned up in the Marianas by circumstance not plan, so that Ōbata's command was increasingly burdened with a motley collection of weaponless units that washed up like flotsam to the shores of Saipan. Equally discouraging was the loss of vital materials for the construction of fortifications. As Ōbata's chief of staff fumed to Tokyo, "unless the units are supplied with cement, barbed wire, and lumber, which cannot be obtained in these islands, no matter how many soldiers there are, they can do nothing but sit around with their arms folded, and the situation is unbearable." The navy contingents, for their part, had sufficient construction materials for defenses, but, incredibly, refused to share these with Ōbata's men.[43]

Even though the material means were in short supply, Ōbata was determined to build an "impregnable fortress" on Saipan and, with the thirty thousand men at his disposal, to hold this vital sector of the national defense sphere against the western-sweeping tide of the enemy. In his welcoming address to General Saitō and the men of the Forty-third Division, it was Ōbata apparently, who coined the phrase used repeatedly by beleaguered and doomed Japanese commanders in Micronesia: "We must use our bodies to construct a bulwark in the Pacific" (*Ware mi o motte Taiheiyō no bōhatei taran*).[44]

Despite this ringing admonition, the defenses of the Marianas were fatally compromised by further weaknesses. The Japanese army at this point still clung obsessively to the idea of annihilating the enemy at the water's edge, a tactic that might have been inevitable on the flat and narrow atolls of the Marshalls (where it had nevertheless proved futile), but made little sense on an island the size of Saipan, with its rugged interior offering opportunities for defense in depth. Yet Ōbata concentrated his units along the western beaches of Saipan, the most likely approaches for an invading force, leaving only a feeble reserve in the interior. Should the enemy break through the beach defenses, it fell to a tank regiment to attack the salient and drive it into the ocean. For the defense of the interior, the garrison, short of time, construction materials, and engineer units, was to fall back on the rugged central spine of the island running from Mt. Tapotchau to Mt. Marpi and the Banaderu cliffs at the island's northern tip. But the plans and movements to make this withdrawal effective were still being worked on when the American invasion force smashed into Saipan.[45]

Even more disastrous than these imperfect defenses was the Japanese miscalculation as to the immediacy and direction of the American thrust against the Japanese strategic perimeter. The Forty-third Division had landed on the island only a month before the invasion, and for the first several weeks of its arrival the work on bunkers, gun emplacements, and communications centers proceeded at an almost leisurely pace, largely because the rank and file were not made aware of the imminence of the American attack. Convinced, moreover, that the first American blow would be struck at the Palaus, not the Marianas, General Ōbata was on an inspection tour of that southern-sector group in mid-June when the huge American invasion armada, preceded by a furious naval and aerial bombardment, approached Saipan's western shores. Unable to return to his northern command, Ōbata passes from our story, since tactical command now fell to the stodgy General Saitō, though Admiral Nagumo, without ships or aircraft, and with only a few troops, was technically the senior officer ashore.[46]

On 15 June, as Saipan rocked with the explosions of bombs and shells and the Americans stormed the beaches just above Chalankanoa, the thousands of Japanese infantry dug in along the shore opened a withering defensive fire, until, unit by unit, they were blasted out of their positions as the Americans fought their way inland (Figure 27). To the north, Garapan was deserted by its civilian population, which, fleeing the strafing and bombing of the town, made its way to the relative safety of the caves in the island ridge. By the end of the first day, the Americans had a firm beachhead, had entered Chalankanoa, and were advancing on Aslito Airfield. To try to regain the initiative, General Saitō, on the night of 16 June ordered an all-out counterattack by his tanks against the northern end of the enemy beachhead. Amid an inferno of tracers, flashing lights, and crashing shells, the attack was thrown back by American artillery, with heavy losses.[47]

Over the next several days, in desperate fighting, the Japanese were pushed eastward back to the slopes of the interior and away from Garapan and Aslito Airfield, but the defenders were sustained by the news that the Japanese navy in the shape of Ozawa's First Mobile Fleet was on its way to annihilate the enemy at sea, as well as his troops ashore. On learning of the American approach toward Saipan, Ozawa and his carrier group had indeed turned north from the Philippines, counting on both surprise and the support of five hundred land-based planes to gain a smashing victory. As it turned out he had neither. Despite his extravagant promises of support, Vice Admiral Kakuta Kakuji, com-

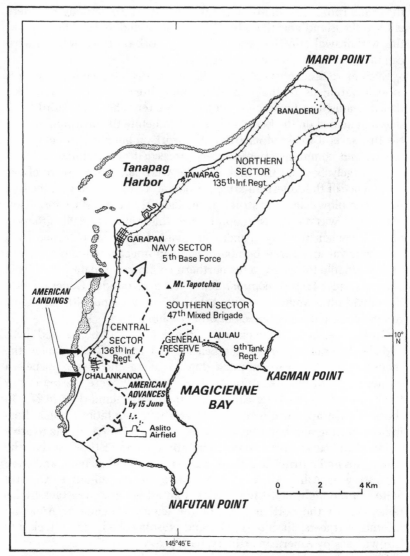

MARPI POINT

BANADERU

Tanapag
Harbor

TANAPAG

NORTHERN
SECTOR
135th Inf. Regt.

GARAPAN
NAVY SECTOR
5th Base Force

AMERICAN
LANDINGS

▲ Mt. Tapotchau

SOUTHERN SECTOR
47th Mixed Brigade

CENTRAL
SECTOR
136th Inf.
Regt.

GENERAL
RESERVE

LAULAU

9th Tank
Regt.

KAGMAN POINT

CHALANKANOA

AMERICAN
ADVANCES
by 15 June

MAGICIENNE
BAY

Aslito
Airfield

10°
N

0   2   4 Km

NAFUTAN POINT

145°45'E

Figure 27. The Defense of Saipan, 15 June 1944. (Drawn by Noel Diaz)

mander of the First Air Fleet on Saipan, contributed very few planes to
the battle and those few were completely ineffective in their attacks on
the American fleet. Task Force Fifty-eight, on the other hand, was
superbly supplied with an abundance of planes and battle-tested pilots,
as well as good intelligence on the plans and movements of Ozawa's
fleet. In the disastrous Battle of the Marianas (the Philippine Sea in
American naval annals), 18–19 June 1944, the slaughter of Ozawa's
inept and poorly trained pilots was so rapid and complete that jubilant

American airmen dubbed it the "Great Marianas Turkey Shoot." With this shattering defeat at sea Japanese naval air power in the western Pacific evaporated and, along with it, all hope that the navy could come to the aid of Saipan, now under attack by three enemy divisions.[48]

By the evening of 18 June, the invaders had captured three-fourths of southern Saipan and a bitterly contested struggle had begun for the island's central ridge, the Japanese fighting from every cave. Earlier that day Prime Minister Tojo had sent a radio message to the Thirty-first Army to steel its determination: "Because the fate of the empire depends upon the results of your operation, inspire the spirit of your officers and men and to the end continue to destroy the enemy gallantly and persistently, thus alleviating the anxiety of our Emperor."[49]

On 19 June in violent fighting, Mt. Tapotchau fell to the Americans and a few days later the Japanese were faced with a new landing on the eastern side of the island at Laulau (Magicienne) Bay. In a week of terrible fighting the enemy battered his way up the eastern side of the island toward Mt. Donnay, which up to now had been a rear area in the battle for the island. At the army field hospital near the slopes of Mt. Donnay, the chaos, the roar of exploding shells, the filth, the shrieks and groans of the wounded, the stench of the rotting dead, the utter inadequacy of the medical staff, the lack of anesthetics and drugs, had created unbounded horror. As the enemy approached, the chief surgeon was ordered to evacuate the hospital. For those who could not walk there was at least a quick release from their agony: hand grenades were passed out so that they could spare themselves the shame of capture.[50]

By 5 July the Japanese garrison on Saipan had been squeezed into the northern two-thirds of the island. There were now only two choices open to the defenders: to undertake a fighting withdrawal to Marpi at the island's northern tip, holding out as long as possible, or to hurl themselves at the enemy in one last annihilating charge. The navy commanders wanted to withdraw to Marpi, but staff of the Thirty-first Army and Forty-third Division, true to their traditions, insisted on a final counterattack, and their arguments carried the day. On the afternoon of 6 July, General Saitō drafted a last message to the remaining Japanese garrison, calling upon them to follow him in the assault. His words, a battlecry of tenacity and defiance, echo down across the decades: "Whether we attack or whether we stay where we are there is only death. But realizing that in death there is life, let us take this opportunity to exhalt Japanese manhood. I shall advance upon the Americans to deliver still another blow and leave my bones upon Saipan as a bulwark of the Pacific . . . Follow me!"[51]

In fact, however, Saitō and Nagumo had chosen a third course: self-destruction. Between nine and ten that evening, at Saitō's command post, a small cave north of Mt. Tapotchau, Saitō and Nagumo, along with two staff members, blew their brains out.

Just before sunrise on 7 July, some three thousand Japanese—the remnants of the Forty-third Division, some naval troops, reservists, and a large number of civilians—filtered down from the ridge to the northwest coast, just north of Tanapag, for the final assault (Figure 28). Preceded by a furious mortar barrage, the advance, led by the last five Japanese tanks, swept down toward the American positions, followed by a chaotic column of men armed with rifles, pistols, swords, and bamboo spears, and behind these, incredibly, hundreds of walking, weaponless wounded: some on crutches, others hobbling and staggering forward. Smashing into the enemy, this human wave swept over an opposing infantry regiment and drove in the American line. All through the morning the battle raged, but by noon the Japanese attack had diminished, its lifeblood drained. By the afternoon, the last remnants that had gone to ground were being cornered and annihilated. By nightfall, the Forty-third Division had become a crushed jewel.[52]

In small packets, the scattered survivors of the garrison made their way north to hurl themselves from the fearful Banaderu cliffs or to blow themselves up with hand grenades in the caves at Banaderu. Yet at Marpi Point, where the cliffs drop a hundred feet to the Pacific, an even more pitiful and useless tragedy took place. There, a huge throng of civilians—mostly women and children—had gathered to commit mass suicide. In vain, Japanese-speaking American interpreters in small boats just off the shore, pleaded with the terrified crowds to surrender and save themselves, but the ocean soon became so thick with floating bodies that the American naval craft were unable to steer a course without running into them.[53]

The majority of the civilian population—over ten thousand Japanese, twenty-three hundred Chamorros, thirteen hundred Koreans, and nearly nine hundred Carolinians—had either given themselves up or remained in hiding in Saipan's hills and caves. Gradually, they were captured or coaxed to surrender. Many of them ill, wounded, and shell-shocked, the refugees were confined to the American stockade built for them at Susupe at the island's southern end.[54] Of the prosperous island they had known, little was left. The once-emerald cane fields were blackened, the sugar refineries were a heap of twisted girders, and Garapan was nothing but gutted buildings and rubble-filled streets (Photo 41).

After the annihilation of the main garrison, a few small groups of Japanese soldiers managed to hold out in the hills around Mt. Tapotchau or among the caves at Kagman Point on the southeastern coast. Largest among these was a group composed of men from various units who came together under the command of Captain Ōba Sakae, Eighteenth Infantry Regiment. For eighteen months Captain Ōba's tiny force, constantly on the move in the dense underbrush which still

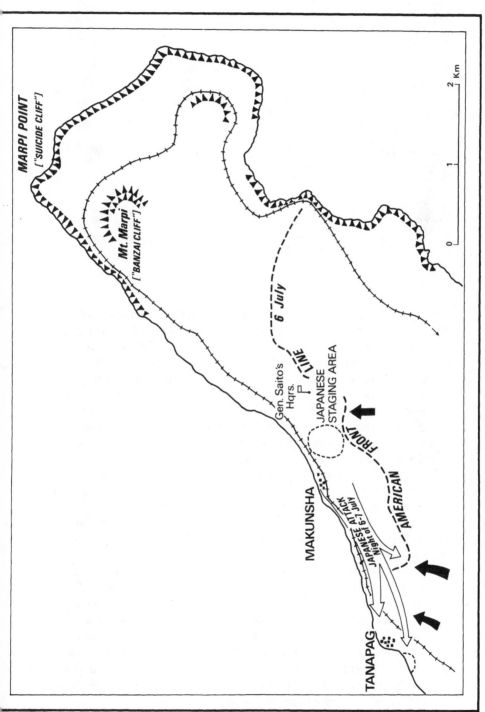

Figure 28. The Last Japanese Offensive on Saipan, 6–7 July 1944. (Drawn by Noel Diaz)

Photo 41. Garapan Town, Saipan, after the fighting of July 1944.

remained on the island, carried out raids against American facilities. But American patrols and operational sweeps across Saipan steadily reduced the numbers and effectiveness of such holdouts. By war's end, they were engaged less in raiding than in a struggle to survive.[55]

Once Saipan had fallen, the position on Tinian, three miles to the southwest, was hopeless. Even as American marines fought their way north on the larger island, the massed fire of some thirteen artillery battalions on southern Saipan added to the devastation visited on Tinian by American battleships and planes. Systematically, the island's railway junctions, airfields, bunkers, storage depots, and cane fields were ripped asunder, and on 19 July the island became the first victim of the searing horror of napalm, which the Americans used to scorch away all foliage and concealment (Figure 29).

Hunkered down in his cave command post on Mt. Lasso, Colonel Ogata Takashi, responsible for the defense of the island, planned his strategy to meet the imminent enemy attack. He had approximately thirty-eight hundred men in his command, centered on his own Fiftieth Infantry Regiment, newly arrived from Manchuria, plus an infantry battalion, a tank company, and a scattering of service troops. The senior navy commander on the island served an almost useless function. Vice Admiral Kakuta, commander of the now nonexistent First Air Fleet, had filled the air with promises not planes and thus had contributed to the rout of Admiral Ozawa at sea. Now without any planes of his own, he and his pilots could only sell their lives alongside the men of the navy's Fifty-sixth Guard Force on the island.[56]

Colonel Ogata, tough and resourceful, had planned a defense of the

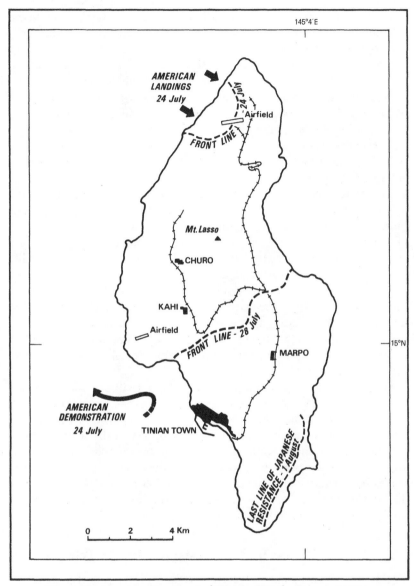

Figure 29. American Conquest of Tinian, 25 July–3 August 1944.
(Drawn by Noel Diaz)

island that differed dramatically from accepted Japanese doctrine. While each of his sector commanders had orders to annihilate the enemy at the beach, Ogata kept two-thirds of his force inland as a mobile reserve that could be shifted to meet any invasion.[57] Unfortunately for Ogata, the Americans brilliantly deceived him by sending an amphibious force to make a diversionary feint toward Sunharon Beach just north of Tinian Town. Ogata fell for the bait, rushing his men to the threatened sector while the real enemy landings were made against only light opposition along the white beaches at Ushi Point at the northern end of Tinian. Too late, Ogata's reserve turned to meet the invasion. Over the next three days, contested every step of the way by Ogata's men, the Americans moved southward across what had once been a pleasant and prosperous island. Tinian Town lay smashed and deserted, its remaining civilian population fleeing with what little they could take with them to the safety of caves along the southeast coast. By 27 July Ogata no longer had an organized command, the defenders having broken into little pockets of men fighting from the woods and caves in the southeastern corner of the island. On 2 August, trapped in an area only a few miles square, Ogata led a last annihilating charge of approximately one thousand men—civilian volunteers, as well as the remnants of his regiment. Nearly all, including the colonel, perished in the attack. Admiral Kakuta, far from the deck of a carrier, took his own life in one of the many cliffside caves.[58]

In the record of death and devastation in the fall of Tinian, only the fate of the majority of the surviving civilian population provides some happy relief. Responding to the leaflets and voice commands of American interpreters, they came out of their caves in hesitant small packets at first, then in larger numbers, waving white towels—hungry, thirsty, but alive.[59]

For those in the high command and those civilians who had some understanding of the strategic issues involved in the Pacific War, the fall of Saipan and Tinian pointed to the hopelessness of their nation's position. American capture of the Marianas[60] breached the strategic inner defense sphere, enabling the enemy to cut communications with the western Carolines, as well as providing bases from which Japan itself could be aerially bombarded. It was, indeed, from the airfield on Tinian that the bomber "Enola Gay" departed for Hiroshima in August 1945, with its load of terrible destruction.

The Last Battles for Micronesia: Angaur and Pelelieu

The attack on the Palaus in March 1944 by aircraft from the carriers of Task Force Fifty-eight had convinced Imperial General Headquarters that the next American amphibious blow would fall on those islands, a conviction in which both Tokyo and the Thirty-first Army persisted up to the very last days before the American invasion of Saipan. For that reason the Japanese army, scanning its maps and unit distribution charts, decided to shore up the defenses of the Palau Islands with the very best troops available. The fighting force selected, the Fourteenth ("Sunlight") Division, then on duty in Manchuria, was one of the best in the army. Its battle honors stretched back to the Russo-Japanese War and its three infantry regiments, the Second, the Fifteenth, and the Fifty-ninth, were all fine, battle-tested units.[61]

When Lt. General Inoue Sadae had arrived at Koror with the Fourteenth Division in April 1944, he concurrently assumed command of the Palau Sector Group—the Palaus, Yap, and Ulithi—responsible to General Ōbata and the Thirty-first Army in Saipan. Inoue's orders were to prepare the Palau Sector for imminent enemy attack and, when it came, to hold the Palau Islands, particularly their airfields, at all costs. To do so, Inoue dispatched the Second Infantry Regiment to Pelelieu, a battalion of the Fifteenth to Angaur, and the bulk of the Fifty-ninth Infantry to Babelthuap, while he remained with division headquarters on Koror.[62]

Within three months of these dispositions, the loss of Saipan and Tinian, which had taken both Imperial General Headquarters and the Thirty-first Army by surprise, completely changed the strategic picture in the Pacific. Not only had the "absolute national defense sphere" been ruptured at its center, but the apparent danger was that the enemy might simply bypass the Palaus and try to retake the Philippines. As this seemed increasingly likely during the summer of 1944, the Japanese high command decided to pull back to the Philippines, making the Palaus expendable. This decision, along with the difficulties of the Japanese strategic situation in the western Pacific by the late summer of 1944, fatally imperiled the Fourteenth Division. On the one hand, the Tokyo high command concluded that it could not spare more ships, planes, or troops to reinforce the Palaus, since these were now needed to defend the Philippines. On the other, it could not risk losing elements of the division by trying to evacuate it by sea, even if shipping were available to transport it. After July 1944, the Palau Sector Group was essentially on its own; after September, not even a barge got through to reinforce or supply it. Inoue's forces faced a hopeless situation: annihilation if the enemy launched an invasion, slow starvation if he bypassed the Palaus and cut off its supply routes.[63]

Confronted with this situation, Inoue determined to prepare as resourcefully as possible for a do-or-die defense of the Palaus. His decision incorporated an entirely new tactical scheme ordered by higher headquarters. The old doctrine that had dictated attempts to annihilate the enemy at the shoreline, a tactic that had failed utterly in the Marshalls, was now replaced by the concept of defense in depth. As before, the beaches were to be strewn with barbed wire, obstacles, and land mines, and a secondary defense of pillboxes and strong points was to be established behind it, but the main line of resistance was now to be located sufficiently far inland to minimize the effects of preinvasion bombardment, to be sufficiently elaborate to wear down the attacking force, and to be sufficiently garrisoned to provide sizable reserves for counterattacks against enemy salients.[64]

By a stroke of fate the islands of Angaur and Peleliu were the objectives of an offensive aimed at securing the eastern flank of the American drive to reconquer the Philippines. They were also the positions on which the Japanese army decided to put its new defensive tactics to the test. While neither island possessed features that would have made it valuable from the perspective of classical nineteenth-century strategy— no generous anchorages that could harbor great fleets, no mountains or forbidding cliffs where great guns could be mounted to command the approaches—they were superbly adaptable to the kind of defense the Japanese army now had in mind.

Peleliu, the southernmost island within the Palau reefs, was nearly six miles long and two miles wide, with a deep indentation at its northeastern end that created a thick promontory some four miles long, separated from a more slender peninsula by shoals and swamps. The southwestern base of the island was fairly level, but the northern arm was serrated by a series of tortuous ridges called, in Palauan, the Umurbrogol. To Western ears the word sounds vaguely sinister, like the name of some evil kingdom in a Tolkien fantasy, and indeed, the Umurbrogol was a witches' cauldron, a maze of peaks, cave-pocked cliffs, and rubble-strewn defiles. It was in reality an undersea coral reef that aeons before had been thrown above the surface, then covered with a thin topsoil and a thick cover of vegetation. It would be difficult to imagine a more natural fortress.

Angaur, the island whose rich deposits of phosphate had been worked for decades, first by the Germans and then by the Japanese, was ten miles south of Peleliu, and roughly triangular, approximately two miles long and one mile wide at its furthest points. It was a good deal flatter than Peleliu, but its northwest corner held an area of rugged terrain called the Ramuldo. A minor version of the Umurbrogol, the Ramuldo was a series of wooded coral ridges one to two hundred feet in height, also riddled with caves, and only somewhat less formidable than the Peleliu redoubt.

If the terrain of these two islands offered the Japanese advantages for preparing a formidable defense, the particular circumstances of time and place offered others as well. For the first time, the Japanese garrisons had time to prepare adequate defenses and to lay in plentiful supplies of ammunition, food, and water, all of which could be stored in deep subterranean caches. The nature of the terrain meant that few construction materials were needed, only dynamite and pick-axe labor to enlarge the existing caves and blast out new ones. And, unlike the Thirty-first Army in the Marianas, the garrisons on Angaur and Peleliu were not burdened by a noncombatant population, since all civilians had been evacuated from the two islands. Nor was Peleliu easily cut off from communication with the outside world. Unknown to the Americans, the garrison was linked by submarine cable to General Inoue's divisional headquarters on Koror, a communication system that was to offer information and encouragement to the defenders throughout the coming siege.[65]

Finally, the troops assigned to defend Angaur and Peleliu matched the island terrain. On Angaur, Major Gotō Ushio commanded approximately fourteen hundred men centered on the First Battalion of the Fifty-ninth Infantry, along with a number of artillery, mortar, and antitank units, all superbly trained and ready to defend their positions deep in the Ramuldo to the last man. On Peleliu, the garrison was larger and, if anything, even tougher. The Second Infantry Regiment was one of the army's oldest and its soldiers from Mito, northeast of Tokyo, among the army's best; the same could be said of the two battalions of the Fifteenth Infantry that shipped to Peleliu with the Second. Colonel Nakagawa Kunio, commander of the Peleliu Sector Unit, judging not only from his conduct of the defense, but his photograph in the Japanese official history of the campaign, seems to have been an officer of unflinching, perhaps even brutal determination (Photo 42).[66]

Photo 42. Colonel Nakagawa Kunio, defender of Peleliu.
(Japanese Defense Agency)

Upon arriving on Pelelieu, Colonel Nakagawa was quick to perceive that while its airfield might be the island's most valuable military facility, the key to Pelelieu's defense was the Umurbrogol, honeycombed with caves and raked with boulder-choked defiles. There, Japanese naval units already on the island had, with the aid of professional miners, developed the existing caves, excavated new ones, and connected the whole system with a maze of tunnels. Without help from the navy (incredibly, the naval commander on Pelelieu refused to share either labor or materials with the army), Nakagawa's men set about creating their own fortress, less commodious than that built by the navy, but, with its staggered levels, multiple passageways, and well-camouflaged and well-sited gun positions, even better prepared for an extended defense.[67]

On these two islands the Japanese garrisons were among the most solidly entrenched of any that defended the emperor's territories in the Pacific War. Determined, defiant, and confident in their ability to delay if not halt the enemy's advance, they waited deep in their coral bunkers for the worst the Americans could throw at them.

In mid-September the enemy's invasion fleets appeared, his landings preceded as usual by thunderous naval and aerial bombardment that smashed all buildings and facilities above ground and blasted away some of the jungle cover on both islands. The fight for Angaur lasted a month (Figure 30). There, in the thick, matted jungle, the Japanese and Americans fought it out through the latter half of September and into October, until the remnants of Gotō's force were compressed into the vine-covered ridges of the Ramuldo at the island's northwestern tip. From that fastness, in slowly diminishing numbers, they resisted with frenzy the attempts of the attackers to dislodge them. It was late October before the last of them were killed, blasted, or roasted in their caves. Two days before the last underground strong point was captured or sealed up, Major Gotō and one hundred thirty remaining soldiers had launched an abortive counterattack in which all were killed.[68]

Ferocious as it was, the Japanese resistance on Angaur hardly compared with the fight put up by Colonel Nakagawa and his men on Pelelieu. As the last rounds were being fired on Angaur, the death struggle for Pelelieu was just beginning, though the invasion had begun a day before the landings on the smaller island (Figure 31). It is said that prior to the landings, after having pounded Pelelieu for hours, the American battleship commander had complained that he had run out of targets and the Marine Corps general in command of the landing forces had claimed that the island would be in American hands in three days.[69] In reality, thousands of men and hundreds of artillery pieces concealed within the Umurbrogol would, for over two months, resist with incredible ferocity American attempts to dislodge them.

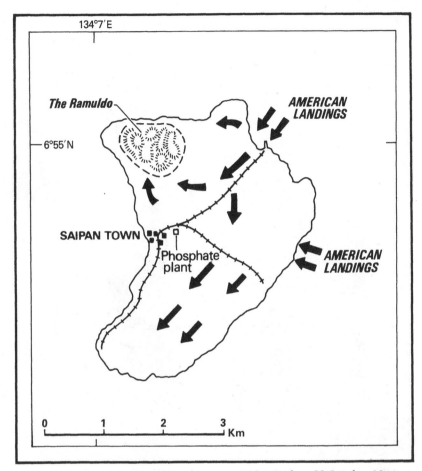

Figure 30. American Conquest of Angaur, 17 September–22 October 1944.
(Drawn by Noel Diaz)

As he had planned, Nakagawa had conducted a savage if unavailing defense of the base of the island, delaying the American capture of the airfield. By October he had been forced back to the Umurbrogol. But from the safety of that awful terrain where no tanks could penetrate and bombs and shells were unavailing, he could train his high velocity guns on the airfield or send out small parties of men armed with high explosives to blow up American facilities there. All through October 1944 and into November, the men of the Second and Fifteenth regiments, firing almost unseen from their maze of tunnels and caves, cut apart the small units of American marines who attempted to get at them over jumbles of rocks and boulders. In constant communication with divisional headquarters on Koror, the Pelelieu garrison was able to keep

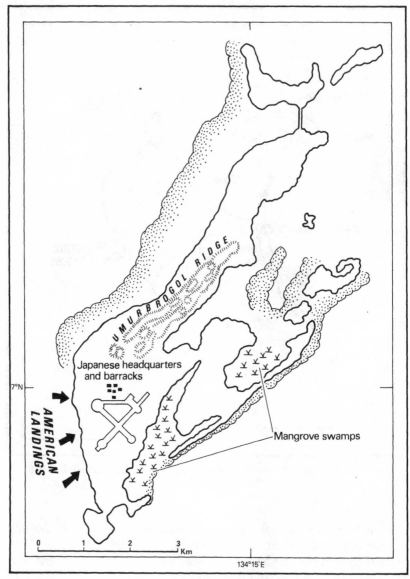

Figure 31. The American Assault on Peleliu. (Drawn by Noel Diaz)

the Japanese army informed of the progress of the battle, and the indomitable stand of Nakagawa's men was an inspiration to the nation. Messages of support poured in from various higher commands and even the emperor sent words of encouragement.[70]

Ultimately, of course, Nakagawa's position was doomed, since he not only faced superior numbers, but also the heroism of an enemy as unrelenting in attack as his men were in defense. By late November, crushed by high explosives, cremated by flamethrowers, or entombed when their caves were sealed up, the garrison was reduced to several hundred men. Only one ridge was left to the defenders. On the twenty-fourth, having been refused permission by divisional headquarters to make a final annihilating charge, Nakagawa, with his staff, committed suicide in the last cave command post. Two days later, all organized Japanese resistance came to an end, though it was not until February 1945 that the last five Japanese dug their way out and were induced to surrender. By this time over ten thousand Japanese had died defending this tiny slice of the emperor's domain.[71]

Pelelieu was the last of Japan's Micronesian islands for which the nation's military and naval personnel, fighting in desperate defense, laid down their lives in great numbers. In September 1944 the deserted atoll of Ulithi, northeast of Yap, had been occupied by the Americans without resistance. The last Japanese garrison in Micronesia to go down fighting was an eight-man detachment of the navy's Special Landing Party that was exterminated in brief and futile combat to defend Fais Island, southeast of Ulithi, in January 1945.[72]

Under Siege: The Japanese Communities at War

While these bloody and futile struggles by the Japanese army and navy form the central chronology of Micronesia during the Pacific War, the impact of the war upon the civilian communities there is a sad but important theme in the last chapter of the Japanese in the islands.

The coming of the war had brought increasing austerity to all the Japanese settlements, as we have seen: food rationing, restrictions on travel, and a drastic reduction in consumer goods coming into the islands. The sugar and phosphate industries came almost to a halt, along with interisland trade and commercial fishing. What comforts and recreations the colonial populace had come to enjoy were now sacrificed to the national defense effort. Schools were closed and the students organized into labor units for food production and military construction; in the towns there was drilling in the parks and school grounds; everywhere civilians went about in the *kokuminfuku*, the drab national service uniform. The gay festivities of the annual Administration Day garden party at the Shōnan Club gave way to a smaller briefer gathering of officials in front of the Nan'yō-chō headquarters to sing the national anthem and to listen to exhortations about inevitable Japanese victory.[73]

But the coming of the Japanese armed forces, in particular the army, with its voracious demands on labor, land, food, and housing, caused the most profound dislocations in the patterns of civilian life. On the larger islands, martial law had been in effect since the navy arrived in 1941, providing the military with virtually unlimited claim to local resources. Civilians, Japanese and indigenous, were now pressed into compulsory labor service, each household providing one person per day. Micronesians, particularly in the Marshalls, were often conscripted on one atoll for service on another. Uprooted from their families, the men were often unable to return for months and, after hostilities isolated the islands, many not for years.[74] The Micronesian women and children who were left behind were often compelled by the Japanese military to undertake heavy work in agricultural or construction projects, often to the neglect of their own fields.

On certain islands, such as Angaur and Pelelieu, the civilian populations, both Japanese and Micronesian, were completely uprooted and moved to other areas. Everywhere they set foot, the needs of the army and navy came first. Many choice lands—beaches, recreation grounds, and farm plots—were seized and given over to military purposes. The arrival of large numbers of troops also put a tremendous strain on housing, since new construction could not keep up with the army's requirements. Micronesians and even some Japanese were compelled to give up their homes to the army for use as billets, while they moved in with friends or relatives or into makeshift housing elsewhere.

As the war situation worsened and Japanese garrisons intensified their preparations to ward off enemy landings, their demands on local resources became ever more voracious and accelerated the damage to the island ecology and Micronesian culture. On Ponape, some forty thousand coconut trees were cut down to build bunkers, revetments, and gun emplacements, and many houses that had been confiscated were demolished for their wood. On Babelthuap the last of the great Palauan war canoes, built in the 1920s for the island races, was broken up for firewood. The Japanese need for sand for construction cement further weakened the shorelines of many islands, and in the Marshalls the practice of using hand grenades to kill quantities of fish irrevocably damaged the coral reefs. Everywhere on the high islands of the Carolines, roads and foundations for fortifications were hacked out of the hillsides without concern for drainage or erosion.[75]

By the autumn of 1943, as the gathering power of the United States cast a towering shadow westward across the Pacific, the government decided that it was time for Japanese civilian families to go. An evacuation program was begun for women, children, and old men, most in ships, a few in planes, and even some in submarines. Some of these refugees, traveling as they were through submarine-infested waters, never reached the homeland, but perished when their ships were sunk. In the Marshalls and Carolines, those generally left behind were the single men—company officials of Nambō and Nankō, along with officials of the Nan'yō-chō. In the Marianas, in contrast, a far greater number of families were trapped on the islands by the time of the American invasions.

On Truk, one elderly Japanese who stayed on was Mori Koben. Probably no one could have made him go, for the islands were his life and he would share their fate. He could have left much earlier, undoubtedly, but he had chosen to stand with his nation on its now imperiled southern frontier. Mori had little use for the aggressive bombast of Japanese propagandists, and he had genuinely feared the coming of the war. Yet, fiercely loyal to his country, he had actively assisted in the military preparations and had drawn upon decades of good will among his Trukese relatives and friends to help muster labor and support for the war effort. But he was an old man with failing powers, and by the time the war broke out he had suffered a stroke that paralyzed his right side and left him unable to walk. He became a convalescent at his home on Tol, cared for there by his family. In the summer of 1943, he began to have hallucinations in which he saw his country's utter defeat. His mind began to wander and, by the time American planes roared over the reefs to launch their devastating attack on Truk in February 1944, Mori had slipped into senility; late that year he was moved to his eldest son's home on neighboring Polle.[76]

Even as the defenders of Kwajalein and Eniwetok peered through the gun slits of their bunkers at the waves of approaching American landing barges through the spring of 1944, the bombs had begun to fall on one after another of the Japanese towns in Micronesia—first Dublon, then Kolonia on Ponape, Lelo Village on Kusaie, next Garapan on Saipan, Koror, and Colonia on Yap. Reducing them to smoking rubble usually took only a few hours, their populations forced to make their way into the jungles and hills, there to eke out an increasingly wretched existence for the rest of the war. After Koror was rendered uninhabitable, such of the Nan'yō-chō as remained moved to the Tropical Research Institute at Aimeliik Village on Babelthuap and the Fourteenth Division's headquarters to Gasupan (Ngatapang) Village on the same island. But orderly administration was now at an end on Palau, as elsewhere in Micronesia. The Japanese armed forces were the only organization that could have provided it and they had little time, resources, or inclination to look after the welfare of civilians, Japanese or Micronesian.[77]

Increasingly, the attention and energies of the refugee populations were devoted to food production, since, except for the occasional supply submarine, the islands were now entirely cut off by the enemy's submarine and air menace. The ocean offered the greatest source of food, but fishing was a risky business from islands under frequent attack from the air. In the Carolines, because of the regularity of the enemy bombing runs, fishing-boat crews learned to time their expeditions between raids, but off Rota and Pagan in the Marianas, they hardly dared put out from shore, so close were they after July 1944 to enemy airfields on Tinian.[78] On all the islands, efforts were made with increasing desperation to try to coax taro, potatoes, and vegetables from the soil. By the autumn of 1944 little livestock was left on any of the high islands. Indigenous tropical fruits—coconuts, breadfruit, mangoes, and bananas—were becoming scarce and the Japanese had begun to attack the palm trees to get at the hearts, an activity that inevitably killed the trees. Perceptibly, the physical condition of the civilian communities, as well as the military garrisons, went from malnourishment to outright starvation.

While the evidence of the worsening war situation for Japan was clear from the increasingly stark conditions of their surroundings, the Japanese communities on these bypassed islands, up until the last year of the war, continued to believe in the ultimate victory of their nation. News of the progress of the war elsewhere in the Pacific, served up with rhetorical flourishes and optimistic claims, came largely from radio broadcasts from the homeland. On Babelthuap, this meager informational fare was distributed to the members of the Japanese community through the hopefully named *Kaishō Nippō* (Rapid Victory Express), a mimeographed sheet printed in a shack. Efforts to keep up morale became more and more difficult. The 1944 commemoration of Administration Day at Aimeliik was grim indeed: no toasts, songs, or festivities, only a bleak address by the governor, Admiral Hosogaya, calling upon the participants to think of their comrades fighting and dying on Saipan. By 1945, the wretched community on Babelthuap was reduced to eating roots and leaves. Deaths from starvation and illness had begun to strike down a growing number of the enfeebled. By the summer of 1945, just getting to the annual Administration Day ceremonies, held in front of a small shed on Aimeliik and led by the wraith-like figure of Hosogaya, was an effort for the handful of officials who attended.[79]

On Polle Island, Truk, Mori Koben, drifting in and out of consciousness, probably did not catch the distant roar and thunder of the occasional raids on Dublon, Moen, and Eten. By August, he had slipped into a coma and on the evening of the twenty-third, surrounded by his family, he breathed deeply and was gone.[80] Eight days earlier, his nation, in ruins and utterly defeated, had surrendered.

The Micronesians Turn Away

The Pacific War was the turning point in relations between Japanese and Micronesians. It began with the generally passive and sometimes even willing acquiescence of the Islanders toward Japan and its war effort; it ended with the near total abandonment of the Japanese cause by these same peoples and, on some islands, with the eruption of active hostility toward the Japanese. Although it is difficult to generalize about the pattern, pace, and intensity of this disaffection throughout Micronesia, it appears to have had three basic causes: the insensitivity and, eventually, the brutality of the Japanese armed forces toward the Islanders; the miseries brought to the island communities by the war itself; and the recognition among many Micronesians by 1945 that the Japanese could not or would not effectively protect or govern them.[81]

At the outset of the war, decades of Japanese conditioning had gained the loyalties and affections of a small but significant number of Micronesian youth, many of whom had joined the *seinendan* and other associations organized by the colonial government to promote identification with Japan. These young men learned spoken Japanese reasonably well, revered the emperor, professed, as did Japanese, the need to make sacrifices on behalf of the nation *(okuni no tame ni)*, and believed, initially, in the certainty of Japanese victory. Many of them willingly served as messengers, military assistants, interpreters, and supervisors of indigenous labor. More impressively, a small number, some of the strongest and brightest of their communities, eagerly joined the volunteer units *(teishintai)* raised by the colonial government for noncombatant service alongside the Japanese army in the New Guinea theater in 1942–1943.[82]

The brief histories of these units were bitter and tragic. Usually raised by active or retired Nan'yō-chō officials and numbering twenty to forty men apiece, these units shipped out from Ponape and Palau in the early war years with a tremendous sense of bravado and adventure. Arriving in Rabaul or on the New Guinea coast, they were usually used as little more than laborers. Worse, they were often split up and assigned to individual Japanese infantry units locked in bitter combat with Allied forces for the control of eastern New Guinea. Serving in that capacity, all but three members of one Ponape volunteer unit were killed in the fighting around Buna in 1943. Another *teishintai*, the 104th Construction Detachment, was left stranded on New Guinea at the end of the war, unpaid, forgotten, and leaderless—their Japanese unit commander had committed suicide. It took them years to make their way back to Palau.[83]

For these young men the horrors of war on a distant shore and the indifference of the Japanese military must have destroyed all feelings of loyalty to Japan. For most other Micronesians, disillusionment set in soon after the military arrived in their islands. The confiscations, conscription for labor, and preemptions of Micronesian land and property were common to all the islands where there were substantial Japanese garrisons, and without doubt worked to corrode whatever sympathies the Islanders may have had toward the Japanese.[84] In the Marianas and the Marshalls, the antagonism of the Japanese military toward Micronesian Christians was a particular sort of abuse: military edicts made attendance at mass by Chamorro Catholics purposely difficult; in the Marshalls indigenous and European pastors were harassed and in some cases actually executed. On many islands that retained Japanese garrisons after 1944, Japanese treatment of the Micronesians became more abusive as the situation of the garrisons became more desperate.[85]

Even if the excesses of the Japanese military had not antagonized the indigenous communities on islands where Japanese bases were located, the suffering brought to nearby communities would have turned them away from Japan in any event. The same privations of misery and hunger as afflicted the Japanese garrisons obviously weakened the villagers on the same islands; each American bombing raid or naval bombardment exposed Micronesians as well as Japanese to death and destruction; and the ferocious combat on Kwajalein and Saipan between Japanese defenders and American attackers took a proportionately heavy toll of the local populations.

Finally, even if, at the outset of the war few Micronesians bore any deep-seated antipathy toward Japan, few had any strong attachment to it either. When war came, except for a small elite core of zealously patriotic youngsters, most Islanders hardly considered either the conflict or Japan's cause to be their own. When the tide of war turned sharply against Japan and the Americans landed on their shores, many Micronesians, having seen foreign rulers come and go, were quick to drop any connections or affiliations with the Japanese.[86]

On the atolls of the Marshalls bypassed by the Americans after the offensive of 1944—Jaluit, Wotje, Mili, and Maloelap—all these elements in Micronesian disaffection toward Japan played themselves out most clearly. As the conditions of the Japanese garrisons worsened and the abuse of the Islanders by the military became more extreme, the Marshallese living on those four atolls were tempted ever more strongly to escape to neighboring atolls now in the hands of the enemy, or to resist the Japanese war effort. Not surprisingly, such subversion—"disloyalty" in the eyes of the Japanese—provoked violent retaliation from the increasingly demoralized garrisons. Hundreds of Marshallese were tortured, machine-gunned, or beheaded.[87] The process of Micronesian resistance and Japanese reprisal is summarized succinctly in the volume of the official Japanese history that deals with this period in the war:

> At first the voluntary cooperation of the islanders with our forces was excellent, but after a few months of daily exposure to aerial leafleting and other subversive strategies by the Americans, the temptation among the islanders to go over to the enemy became stronger. As a consequence, the incidents in which they killed our men and stole our weapons and boats in order to accomplish their purpose, became more frequent. On their part, our troops meted out capital punishment to those who instigated escapes, killed members of the garrison, plundered weapons and boats, or acted as spies.[88]

Despite these draconian measures, by 1945 whole villages were responding to stealthy nighttime operations by American naval personnel for the evacuation of the Marshallese. (The Japanese official history refers to it as "kidnapping," *ratchi*). By rubber boat, patrol plane, or submarine, villagers were rescued from Japanese-held atolls, especially from islands along the atolls that were not closely watched by patrols. With the escape of these Islanders, the Japanese garrisons lost an important labor supply, and the American forces learned a good deal about the disposition and condition of the remaining Japanese garrisons.[89]

Destitute Garrisons

By the autumn of 1944, the tide of the American offensive had rolled past the Marianas and Palaus and on to the Philippines and by winter it had moved on to Iwo Jima and was pointing at the Ryūkyūs. The remaining Japanese military and naval forces in Micronesia, composed of not quite sixty thousand army and navy personnel, were now represented by two threadbare and utterly impotent commands, both with headquarters on the blasted bastion of Truk: the Thirty-first Army, under Lt. General Mugikura Saburō, who commanded his own Fifty-second Division and the other army elements on Truk and theoretically had command over General Inoue's forces in the Palaus and on Yap and garrisons on the Mortlocks, Puluwat, Woleai, Ponape, Rota, and Pagan; and the Fourth Fleet under Admiral Hara Chūichi, who on paper commanded not only the naval personnel on Truk, but also those forces on Kusaie and on the four atolls of the Marshalls that remained in Japanese hands.

In fact, these command structures were almost meaningless, so utterly isolated had each of these islands become. Cut off from reinforcements by surface and air units from the home islands and from any other Japanese base overseas, as well as from each other, no longer possessing any offensive capability, periodically subjected to heavy aerial and surface bombardment by American forces on patrol, these remaining Japanese islands became useless bits of real estate where the garrisons struggled merely to stay alive.[90] At first they worked to strengthen their defenses and kept a sharp watch out to sea awaiting invasion fleets that never appeared, but the soldiers and sailors on these isolated and beleaguered islands soon found starvation and disease to be their immediate enemies. By the summer of 1944, even with careful rationing, the supply stockpiles, foodstuffs and medicines in particular, had become perilously low on most islands.

Food was the greatest need, since few garrisons had anticipated the dire situation in which they now found themselves, or had taken any measures toward becoming self-sufficient. By the autumn of 1944, for-saking all pretense at military activity, the garrisons had turned their waning energies to growing small truck gardens, fishing the lagoons, and hunting what animal life existed. Occasionally submarines, flying boats, and fishing craft that successfully ran the gauntlet of enemy air, surface, and submarine patrols, were able to bring in small amounts of provisions and medicines, but these were proportionately thimble-sized supply loads and, in any event, ceased altogether in the late spring of 1945 as American forces approached Japan itself. Inexorably the hand of famine began to close around these forlorn and destitute contingents.

Only perhaps on Ponape, the largest island in Japanese Micronesia, with relatively abundant plant and animal life, did the food problem never really become serious for the eight-thousand-man garrison and fifty-seven hundred civilians. Yet even here the garrison was obliged to undertake stringent rationing and a major effort at agricultural self-suf-ficiency. On the other high islands, the situation was much worse. Strangely, Kusaie, which early in the war had been used as an agricul-tural supply point for the Marshalls, eventually faced a major food shortage that left the way open to malnutrition and disease. So seriously was the condition of the garrison weakened, that by war's end three hundred men had died there. On Truk things were far worse, since many more men, some thirty-eight thousand, were crammed onto a far smaller land space, and the islands were subject to far more frequent and demoralizing aerial and surface bombardment.[91]

By the summer of 1944, like the other garrisons in Micronesia, the armed forces on Truk had become primarily an army of weak and weary gardeners struggling with mediocre soil, infestations of insects, and frequent devastation from the air, to coax small patches of taro, sweet potatoes, and vegetables into life. On Babelthuap, General Inoue's men made similar efforts with somewhat greater success, but their agricultural produce was still pitifully inadequate and their condi-tion so weakened by war's end that over two thousand had succumbed to starvation and disease.[92]

On Rota and Pagan, the loss of life through privation was not so star-tling, largely because the ratio of people to land was slightly better and the islands were relatively well endowed with coconuts, breadfruit, bananas, mangoes, and other fruit. Yet, by the end of the summer of 1944 these had largely been consumed and the four-thousand-man gar-rison on Rota, along with as many Japanese civilians and nearly nine hundred Chamorros were in extremis. By early autumn the garrison commander had instituted a strict rationing system, and, with the aid of agricultural technicians from the Nan'yō-chō, had begun a food pro-duction program on the cool uplands of Sabana; but in the months before the crops came in, the enfeebled Japanese, like those on Pagan, were increasingly vulnerable to the ravages of malnutrition and disease.[93]

If the situation of the Japanese garrisons on the high islands was one of destitution, the condition of their compatriots on the atolls of the Carolines and the Marshalls was a living hell. From the continual attacks of the American B-24s there was almost no place to hide on land masses as small and flat as these. For the bomber crews these missions became boringly routine: the official American Air Force history speaks of "the monotonous task of neutralizing the by-passed Marshalls."[94] For those below, each raid was a shattering, shaking agony of explosions that blasted buildings, tore apart bodies, stripped away whatever shade-giving foliage existed, and brought nerves to the breaking point. On these tiny slivers of land, moreover, plant and animal life, slender to begin with, was soon devastated by the starving soldiers who were marooned upon them. After all edible livestock and edible fruit had been consumed, the garrisons often turned to eating grass and palm leaves and catching lizards, rats, and crabs. Attempts at vegetable farming were usually futile: the climate was inhospitable, the soil infertile, and the area available for cultivation steadily reduced by enemy bombardment. On Satawan Atoll in the Carolines, the men of the Fourth South Seas Detachment, trying to clear the underbrush for planting crops, were tormented by tiny red chiggers whose bites produced an agony of itching and incapacitated the sufferers from further work. Having consumed all the edible life on land, the troops in the Marshalls turned to fish-bombing the lagoons with hand grenades, but not knowing which fish were poisonous (some species familiar in Japan are highly toxic in Micronesia) not a few died in excruciating agony. Worn out by their exertions, weakened by malnutrition, burned by a pitiless sun, the men on these islands began also to succumb to a variety of diseases—amoebic dysentery, paratyphus, dengue fever, and beriberi —and had few or no drugs or medicines to treat them. The mortality rate of the garrisons on some of these atolls provides an indication of the horrors they faced. On Mili, for example, out of an original garrison of forty-seven hundred, nine hundred were killed in enemy raids and over a thousand died of starvation and disease. On Maloelap, by war's end, of the three thousand three hundred men who landed on the atoll in 1943, just over a thousand survived. On Wotje only one thousand of the nearly three-thousand-man garrison made it back to Japan.[95]

The Torment of Woleai

Of all the tales of privation and suffering among the helpless remnants of the Japanese army and navy in Micronesia, none is more appalling than that of the seven-thousand-man garrison on Woleai Atoll in the central Carolines.[96] Woleai (which the Japanese called Mariaon or Mereon) about halfway between Palau and Truk, was a small double atoll shaped roughly like a figure eight, around which were spread some twenty-one islands and islets. Like most other atolls of the Pacific, its islands were covered with coconut palms, breadfruit, and other trees. There had been some three hundred fifty Micronesians on the atoll before the war and the inevitable lone Japanese who ran the NBK store and collected copra for shipment. In 1942, the navy had built a small airstrip on one of the larger islands and the next year a small navy garrison had taken up its defense. Then in early 1944, the Tokyo high command had decided that the atoll's strategic location justified its transformation into a major base. Army units, material, and aircraft were rushed to Woleai that spring, so that by May there were some seven thousand men on the atoll, most belonging to the Fiftieth Independent Mixed Brigade under Colonel (later Major General) Kitamura Katsuzō, the overall garrison commander.

Even as the Japanese moved to strengthen the atoll's defenses it was subjected to fearful attacks by American carrier- and land-based planes that destroyed all its aircraft, severely damaged its facilities, and sank most of the transports bringing food, ammunition, and medical supplies to the garrison. By mid-June the supply situation of Kitamura's men was already severe, the per capita ration per day falling from seven hundred fifty to five hundred grams. After the fall of Saipan and Tinian and the interdiction of supplies from the home islands, the situation of the garrison sharply worsened, for the natural resources of an atoll that had supported six hundred persons in peacetime could hardly sustain ten times that number in combat. Throughout the summer of 1944, as the garrison weakened, the mortality from disease, usually amoebic dysentery, began to climb at an alarming rate. In August, the B-24s bombed and strafed "this negligible island" (the words are Samuel Eliot Morison's) almost daily. Hospital facilities for those wounded in these attacks consisted of an open concrete trench and a nipa-palm hut in which the men lingered on without medicines or anesthetics until they died. Although there were building materials on a number of the islands for the construction of bomb-proof shelters and other fortifications, the bombing attacks and the enfeeblement of the garrison slowed the work and then halted it permanently. In August too, the daily ration dropped to two hundred grams; in October it reached the fearful low of one hundred grams of food per man per day.

Kitamura made heroic efforts to keep up the morale of his starving, shaken command. He encouraged the composition of a defiant garrison anthem and daily made the round of each of the units, impressing upon each unit commander that he was personally responsible for the welfare of his men. Most important of all, he did his best to increase the food resources of the atoll, organizing the men into labor battalions for the nurturing of vegetables, but the limited area, the constant raids, and the poor soil made this an almost impossible task. By this time all the coconut palms had been stripped and all the fruit consumed; the men were scrambling after lizards and rats. So desperate had the plight of the garrison become that at the time of the battle for Pelelieu Kitamura radioed Thirty-first Army headquarters on Truk asking that his men be shipped to that front to die like soldiers rather than die of starvation where they were. But even had General Mugikura on Truk approved it, there were no ships left in the central Pacific to transport the men on Woleai.

In October a supply submarine arrived, the first of four that would get through to the garrison, delivering seventy tons of provisions and medical supplies. For a short time, the mortality rate slowed, but in the succeeding months it climbed sharply again. By March 1945 the garrison was down to twenty-five hundred men, one-third of its original size. By this time everyone was enfeebled: men collapsed while working in the pitiful vegetable patches or while engaged in burial duty. In May, the last of the supply submarines arrived. In August, when Kitamura received word by radio that Japan had surrendered, there were barely two thousand Japanese left on the atoll. On 19 September, when the *Takasago Maru* arrived to evacuate the garrison, there were just sixteen hundred men left to go aboard.

Surrender and Repatriation

For the Japanese, struggling, stranded, and abandoned on the southern rim of the empire, the end of the war came as a relief and an anticlimax. The stunning news of the nation's acceptance of defeat came to the isolated garrisons by various means. Most heard it on radio broadcasts from higher headquarters. The Wotje garrison first heard it on a broadcast from Australia; the men on Jaluit learned about it when a B-24 flew over the atoll and dropped a copy of the surrender document issued by the high command in Tokyo. No Japanese unit defied the order to surrender or resisted the American forces that came to occupy their islands, but here and there a Japanese commander, unable to confront the agony of defeat, took his own life.[97]

On 22 August 1945 the garrison on Mili Atoll had the mournful distinction of being the first Japanese Pacific command to capitulate, eleven days before the government itself formally surrendered. The arrangements for the overall capitulation of Japanese forces in Micronesia were concluded on 30 August in the wardroom of the destroyer *Stack* standing off the great fringing reef at Truk. Dazed from the shock of defeat, languid from long dietary privation, and shaking from various fevers, the Japanese military and naval staff on Truk laid bare the hollow shell of Japan's remaining defenses in Micronesia. Two days later, on board the cruiser *Portland*, General Mugikura and Admiral Hara formally turned over to the United States Navy the vast section of the Pacific Ocean and the scattered fragments of land that for all practical purposes Japan had already lost (Photo 43).[98] Over the next several weeks, in miniature reprise of the grand finale held on the deck of the battleship *Missouri* in Tokyo Bay, each of the senior officers of Japan's last shattered bastions in Micronesia went out by boat or launch to a waiting American warship, to be piped up the side and there confirm the capitulation of his command.

The end of Japan's rule in the Nan'yō not only required the liquidation of the Japanese administration and the disarming of the Japanese garrisons, but their repatriation to their homeland, along with all Japanese civilians who remained in Micronesia. All told, there were some 147,000 East Asians in the tropical Pacific when the war ended—Japanese, Koreans, Okinawans, and Taiwanese—of whom 95,000 were military personnel and 52,000 civilians. Just as the Japanese navy had

Photo 43. Japanese surrender on board USS *Portland*, Truk Atoll, 2 September 1945. Lt. Gen. Mugikura Shunzaburō, Thirty-first Army, Commanding (third from left); Vice Admiral Hara Chūichi, Fourth Fleet, Commanding (center); and Rear Admiral Aihara Aritaka, Governor, Eastern Branch District (just behind Admiral Hara).

ousted the handful of Germans from Micronesia when Japan entered the islands, so did the priorities of the new pax Americana in the Pacific (as well as simple justice to the Micronesians) demand the deportation of those on the losing side.[99]

The task of removing them was formidable. In the early autumn of 1945 there were few ships available: most Japanese shipping rested on the ocean floor and, as the United States was now burdened with the task of rushing food to Japan, as well as with the job of repatriating tens of thousands of American fighting men straining to return home, few American vessels could be spared until late in the year. In the meantime, the remnants of the Japanese navy and merchant marine—some hospital ships, a few surviving destroyers, and the *Hosho,* Japan's first and last surviving aircraft carrier—were assembled and pressed into service. Slowly, that early autumn of 1945, they made the rounds of islands and atolls, collecting an exhausted soldiery and the destitute survivors of a once vigorous colonial society for repatriation to Japan, Okinawa, and Korea.[100]

The smaller garrisons, particularly those whose troops were in the most desperate condition, were repatriated first. Among these was the ghostly remnant of the Woleai garrison that boarded the *Takasago Maru* on 19 September. Just before the transport left the lagoon and headed out to sea, officers and men lined the decks for a silent valediction to the dead, many weeping openly. Acting for them all, General Kitamura lighted an incense stick and, with palms pressed together and head bowed, stood facing the atoll as it receded from view. Ten days later, all that remained of the Fiftieth Independent Mixed Brigade disembarked at Beppu for two weeks of convalescence and demobilization. The incredible discipline of these soldiers and their loyalty toward their commander, both on shipboard and in demobilization camp, impressed even the American occupation authorities, it is said. Though he no longer had any command responsibility, General Kitamura never forsook the survivors of his unit during the demobilization process, staying with them until the last man was on his way home.[101]

During most of the autumn of 1945 the larger garrisons of Truk and Palau had been put to work cleaning away the debris of war, building roads and airfields for the victors, and storing supplies until sufficient transport could be arranged for their repatriation. All were thoroughly screened and questioned for information concerning Allied prisoners of war in the islands and for evidence of participation in wartime atrocities against Americans or Micronesians. In this way, damning evidence was uncovered concerning the conduct of a handful of Japanese officers and men, who were eventually tried and executed.[102]

As elsewhere in the Pacific, a few Japanese, mostly in the Marianas, held out long after their government had officially surrendered. Chief among these was Captain Ōba Sakae and his ragtag group of raiders on Saipan. Hiding in the bush and jungle around the slope of Mt. Tapot-chau, they had attempted to carry on the fight despite dwindling num-bers and the ever-increasing pressure of American mopping-up opera-tions. On 1 December 1945, finally convinced that the war was indeed over, Captain Ōba and forty-six survivors fired a last volley over the graves of their fallen comrades, donned fresh uniforms carefully pre-served during the months of their long travail, and marched down out of the hills singing an old Japanese infantry song, to surrender to the American command. They were the last Japanese fighting men in the Nan'yō to lay down their arms.[103]

In November, the Americans began to ship home the thirty-eight thousand soldiers and sailors and several thousand civilians from Truk, a task that took nearly two months, five demilitarized Japanese war-ships, and a number of American landing craft to complete. The Marianas were the last group to be evacuated, in part because of an ill-starred plan to let a large number of Okinawans settle on Tinian, and in part because some Japanese prisoners of war were held on Saipan to complete various tasks for the American occupation authorities.[104] By December 1947 these last unfortunates too, were on their way home to the hardships and uncertainties of war-ravaged Japan.

So ended the "southern destiny" of the Japanese empire.

Epilogue

THE VISITOR TO Micronesia can still see abundant evidence of Japan's wartime disasters. On all the main islands the battered, rusting, and crumbling remains of the Japanese bastions lie all around, largely covered by jungle growth but, because of their steel and concrete construction, destined to endure for decades. Along the island shorelines, few traces of the primary or secondary defense lines are still visible. The pillboxes constructed of coconut logs have long since rotted away, and many of the concrete coastal defenses are gone, blown up by American occupation forces after the war. But further inland, the massive concrete bunkers, the tunnels, the blockhouses, and other military buildings still stand, their blasted walls and roofs bearing witness to the awesome power of aerial bombs and naval shells.

On Eten Island in the Truk group, the roof of the naval air headquarters building sags like wet cardboard and the twisted steel reinforcement rods used in its construction hang out from the shattered concrete like spaghetti. Of the airfield itself one can see almost nothing. Decades ago, the island residents punched holes in it and planted coconut trees along its entire length. The layer of humus produced under the coconut plantation has become so thick that one must scrape vigorously with one's feet to find the concrete surface of the airstrip. The nearby hillside is pierced by great concrete tunnels, now used, the visitor is told, as typhoon shelters by the Trukese families on the island. Across the narrow strip of water, the stone causeway of Dublon's harbor shelters only an outboard motorboat or two. Of Dublon Town and its once closely packed military warehouses, barracks, and storage tanks, nothing remains visible to the visitor who steps out onto the crumbling dock. But during the walk along the jungle path that used to be the town's main street, where pigs now root in the bushes, the Trukese guide points out concrete slabs here and there and an occasional flight of steps that lead

311

to nowhere. On the slopes of Mt. Talomen, grave markers and tablets, themselves often in sad collapse, are evidence not only of the high wartime mortality rate upon these islands, but also of the general indifference of the present inhabitants to the disappearance of such memorials.

Over on Moen, perched atop one of the island's higher elevations, Xavier High School, perhaps the most prestigious educational institution in the islands, occupies the best-preserved of all the wartime relics in Micronesia. The main building of the school was once the former naval communications center, whose reinforced concrete walls and steel doors were so massive that only aircraft from a British carrier task force late in the war ever attempted to damage it and then with only slight success. For the most part, the meter-thick walls and roof held fast and now provide the kindly Jesuit fathers who run the school with what must be the world's most durable educational facilities. In the former radio room, where Japanese operators sought to coordinate the desperate reports and instructions from a battered command, youngsters from all over Micronesia bunk together. What was once the station commander's office is now used by the faculty as a lounge. Only the pockmarked walls and the large concrete slab pulled over a gaping hole in the ceiling of what is now the gymnasium, give evidence of war's furies. Standing on the sloping lawn in front of the building one has a superb view of Dublon and Fefan floating green and hazy in the distance.

The most dramatic war relics of the central Carolines lie invisible to any but those few passionate enthusiasts who, in small but increasing numbers, come each year to Truk to "dive the wrecks"—the blasted hulls of over two dozen ships that went down in the great air assault of February 1944. There in the liquid stillness, where the brilliant filigrees of coral blur the outlines of bridges, masts, deck guns, and gangways, and flashing schools of opal sweeper-fish zig-zag past the slanting decks and yawning hatches, the aqualunged intruder can slide through the holds of the *Shinkoku Maru*, the *Fujikawa Maru*, and their drowned sisters. More than four decades of marine life have given fantastic shape and coloration to the trucks, mines, tanks, gas masks, and bicycles that sank with them and now form part of this vast sub-surface graveyard.[1]

Few of the ruins of Japan's futile effort to ward off the enemy are regularly visited by sightseers. Most lie baking in the sun decade after decade, essentially forgotten because they are off the tourist track. It is obvious, for instance, that almost no one ever comes to kick through the weeds and rusting framework of what used to be Japan's main fighter base on Ponape. Driving along the paved road three kilometers west of Kolonia one can see at some distance from the road across the taro patches, the ribs of an aircraft hangar. A rough and prickly trek through the weeds is rewarded by a view of the foundations of barracks, sections of Japanese fighter aircraft strewn about, two small construction locomotives, trenches, bunkers, and other detritus of war. Such is the state of ruination, after decades of jungle growth and the postwar search for building materials, that it takes an effort to imagine the roar of airplane engines in this deserted place.

On Saipan, more directly in the path of the postwar tourist, the wreckage of war has been better preserved and is more easily accessible to the visitor. Near the present airport one can inspect the chipped and pockmarked bunkers from which the Japanese fought desperately to defend Aslito Airfield (identified as "Athlete's Airfield" on a brass plaque put up by some well-intentioned but misinformed Japanese war memorial mission). Driving north up the park-like expanse of Saipan's western coast to the island's northern tip, one comes to the most haunting of Japan's wartime travails in Micronesia. At Marpi Point—"Suicide Cliff"—the sea surges back and forth across the black face of the rock precipice, cradling its dreadful burdens—as the mind imagines it. Young Japanese honeymoon couples come to stand before the stone marker at the site bearing an appropriately admonitory message about peace and progress; they stare for a few moments at the pounding surf, then clamber back on their chartered bus chattering happily. The white terns and tropic birds skim endlessly along the cliffside, now dipping low over the water, now borne on the roiling air currents to soar high overhead. Across the road at the foot of the towering Banaderu escarpment—"Banzai Cliff"—one can see the shattered face of a concrete redoubt built into a deep recess in the cliff, the target of the main batteries of American battleships firing nearly point blank. Local legend has it that the coastal guns mounted in this fort were served by school-age Japanese boys. True or not, there is little doubt of the mercifully brief end of whoever fought and died here. Standing on the dirt floor inside the place and looking out from the picture-window-sized hole blasted in the concrete wall, the visitor has a panoramic view of the ocean horizon.

Far less evidence remains of the peacetime years of the Japanese in Micronesia. On Saipan it has been all but obliterated. Before 1944, the broad plains of the island were a rich patchwork of cultivated fields and plantations, but the firestorm of bombing and shelling so blackened and ravaged the island's surface that the topsoil threatened to slide away once Saipan was in American hands. To prevent this, the American occupation forces seeded the length of the island with tangan-tangan (*Leucaena leucocephala*), a tall, Philippine plant known for its soil-binding qualities. Where Matsue Haruji's sugarcane spread in lush profusion across much of Saipan, tangan-tangan now forms an impenetrable barrier to all but the most determined, machete-wielding visitors. A road cutting through this growth where the main street of Garapan used to run, a small park shaded by flame trees where a sugar-train locomotive and the statue of Matsue stand, the nearby shell of the Saipan hospital, and the ruins of the jail (where one can gawk at the roofless, weed-strewn cubicle which, a sign asserts, was Amelia Earhart's prison cell), are all that remain of the town. To the south, Chalankanoa, a twisted mass of rusting steel girders, boilers, and roof supports covered by brush, are the sole evidence that the Nan'yō Kōhatsu ever managed a thriving sugar industry here.

Of Kolonia, Ponape, somewhat more remains. Blackened foundations, various stone gateposts that announce the approaches to vacant lots, and a monument in the old park are practically the only artifacts of the Japanese civil period. But a school building and the tall Tropical Experiment Station, where Hoshino Shūtarō used to preside over his vegetable kingdom, still stand and are in use by the present Micronesian government. In Koror, on Palau, one can still see a number of the Japanese colonial buildings, now disguised by different uses. The present courthouse of the Republic of Palau was formerly the Palau Branch Government office, the Palau Legislature is housed in what used to be a telecommunications center, and the Palau museum was formerly a Japanese weather station. But, of the Nan'yō-chō headquarters building, with its sweeping verandas and graceful courtyard flanked by nipa palms, nothing remains except the concrete foundation, which bakes beneath the sun as a parking lot.

In the Marshalls, Jabor Town on Jaluit atoll was so utterly devastated by American bombardments that the district center was relocated to Majuro after the war. Only a Catholic mission occupies any portion of the old town, most of the rest of which lies under brush. But the huge trees that lined the lagoon shore at the northern end of Jabor in Japanese times still give shade to anyone who strolls beneath them.

For the first twenty years after the end of World War II, the United States military made only modest efforts to clear up the most dangerous or depressing remnants of war on the main islands of Micronesia. Then, in the mid-1960s, as the prospects for tourism in the islands began to increase, the United States Trust Territory administration spent considerable time, effort, and money to defuse or clear away the tons of unexploded bombs and shells that littered the islands. But the Americans had no idea how to make appropriate disposition of the most appalling reminders of the war: the tens of thousands of skeletons strewn through the jungles and fortifications, and heaped inside caves on islands where the fighting was most ferocious.[2]

Inevitably, the solution was Japanese, made imperative by the Buddhist tradition of setting at peace the souls of the dead by appropriate funerary ceremonies and cremation of human remains. Beginning in 1968, the Japanese Association of Bereaved Families, supported and encouraged by the Ministry of Health and Welfare, has sent annual bone collection missions to Micronesia to gather and dispose of the skeletons. Composed mostly of relatives of those who were killed, the missions combed the main Micronesian battle sites for over a decade. Bones were collected in burlap bags, which were then placed on funeral pyres, doused with kerosene, and set afire to the accompaniment of prayers for the dead intoned by Buddhist priests who were members of each mission. Year by year through the 1970s, the melancholy task went on, until all the known sites were sifted, the souls of the dead set at rest, and the lingering horrors of war at last exorcised from the islands.[3]

For the Japanese who survived, the intervening years have been devoted to recovery and renewal. Flung back upon a cold and shattered homeland at war's end, the Japanese repatriated from the Pacific inevitably gathered together for mutual aid and for the preservation of their collective memory of peacetime life or wartime agony in Micronesia. Thus were born the numerous groups that have kept alive the postwar Japanese interest in prewar Micronesia. Oldest and largest of these is the Nan'yō Guntō Kyōkai—South Sea Islands Association—formed in 1947 by former officials of the Nan'yō-chō as well as by private citizens who used to live in Micronesia. With links to Japanese business, an active office in Tokyo, and a monthly bulletin, the association continues today as the most important organization promoting understanding of the Japanese period in the islands. From the early years of the postwar period there have been dozens of smaller organizations, some regional or local in membership, like the Yamagata Prefectural Council of Repatriates from the South Sea Islands (founded in 1953 by a former Nankō employee who lost his daughter and seven grandchildren in the holocaust of war in Micronesia), others such as the Rota Remembrance and Friendship Association, composed of repatriates from a particular Micronesian territory. Some, like the Sakura-kai—Cherry Blossom Society—based in Palau, have brought Japanese and Micronesians together for a common philanthropic purpose.[4]

The veterans of the island garrisons that were bypassed or besieged have had their associations as well, such as the Zenkoku Mereon-kai whose members preserve the memory of the dreadful months on Woleai Atoll. Each year in dwindling numbers, the aging members of these groups congregate to sing the old songs, rekindle the comradeship, and relive the agonies of nearly half a century ago. Occasionally sharing in the prosperity of the new Japan, they are able to charter a flight to Palau or Truk or Kusaie to set up a marker, to lay a wreath, or just to look about and try to remember where and how it all happened.

If there are organizations in Japan devoted to preserving the memory of the colonial and wartime years in Micronesia, and a mass media interested in rediscovering that same period in books, magazines, and television documentaries, there are fewer and fewer Micronesians interested in doing so. As the Japanese period in the islands recedes farther into the past and the number of Islanders who remember it clearly dwindles each year, the colonial legacy of the Japanese becomes increasingly attenuated. For some decades after the war, Micronesians with prewar connections to the colonial administration or close links with the Japanese communities in the islands, still sprinkled their conversations with Japanese words, lived in Japanese-style houses, and, when they could, cooked Japanese meals. Putting the war years out of mind, they spoke with nostalgia of the old days and with a trace of pride in their youthful loyalty to Japan and its traditions.[5]

But this oldest generation of Micronesians, who remember the Japanese years in greatest detail, is passing from the island scene and with them whatever relevance the Japanese period may have had for Micronesians as a whole. Of all the formerly subject peoples of the Japanese colonial empire, the Micronesians, for better or for worse, received the least at Japanese hands. Their islands contain no great imperial structures, no broad avenues or public parks to remind them, as the Taiwanese are reminded, of the order and efficiency brought by their former rulers; nor are they endowed as are the Koreans with a bitter, energizing memory of the savage violation of their national soul. The visitor to Micronesia comes away with the impression that, for most Micronesians the "meaning" of the Japanese colonial presence has been written in foam: a dazzling incursion on their shores that has now all but evaporated.

Yet, looking here and there in Micronesia, one can appreciate that there is a legacy of sorts. One sees it, perhaps, in the habits and energies of present-day Palauans whose drive and sense of purpose may be in part due to the fact that Koror was the center of Japanese administration and the home of so many Japanese whose vigor and industry became a model for their Palauan neighbors.[6] One supposes it too, in the elevated status of a good number of islanders of mixed Japanese-Micronesian ancestry, many of whom had a *shōgakkō* education and have risen to positions of power and influence in the new autonomous states of Micronesia. Minoru Ueki has become a distinguished doctor and hospital administrator and served for awhile as minister of social services for the Republic of Palau. On Majuro, his counterpart, Trager Ishoda, serves as the most experienced medical professional in the Marshalls. The descendants and in-laws of Mori Koben flourish in the Carolines: Tosiwo Nakayama, Isabel's grand-nephew, is president of the Federated States of Micronesia; a grandson, Robert Mori, is lieutenant governor of Truk State; another grandson, Masataka Mori, runs the Truk Trading and Trucking companies; another descendant manages the Truk airport; still others hold influential positions in local government and business. A significant number of other Micronesians, who as youngsters were among the fortunate few able to obtain a Japanese secondary education, have also risen to prominence, exercising their Japanese-instilled habits of drive and initiative for the progress of their communities, as well as for their own personal advancement. These attitudes, fostered forty or fifty years ago by Japanese education in certain Micronesian and Japanese-Micronesian youngsters who are now community leaders and exemplars, may together constitute the most useful and enduring legacy that Japan has bequeathed to the island peoples.

If Micronesia's links to its prewar Japanese past are tenuous, the influence in the islands of the postwar Japanese industrial giant is now pervasive. Considering how completely Japan was separated from its tropical colony after World War II, the scale of the Japanese economic reentry into Micronesia has been remarkable. In 1945, the American occupation authorities in Japan scrapped all the institutions relating to overseas trade, banking, finance, and colonization, including the Nan'yō Kōhatsu.[7] Two years later the United States assumed responsibility for governing Micronesia under a strategic trusteeship agreement with the Security Council of the United Nations. Then in 1952, according to the terms of the San Francisco peace treaty, Japan not only accepted the 1947 United Nations agreement, but legally renounced all its claims and titles as a mandatory under the old League of Nations mandates system. Under a U.S. Trust Territory regulation that prohibited non-American investment in Micronesia, Japan was effectively blocked from significant economic relations with its former colony for the next two decades. Indeed, the only Japanese responsibility relating to Micronesia during these years concerned the settlement of claims arising from the destruction of Micronesian life and property during the Pacific War. The nettlesome reparations issue was formally settled by an agreement signed between the United States and Japan in 1969, though its terms remain far from satisfactory to the Micronesians themselves.

The reemergence of the Japanese industrial giant in the 1960s made it certain that it would play a major role in the economic development of Micronesia once the barriers to foreign investment in the islands were removed. When these were relaxed in the mid-1970s, Japanese enterprise, backed by significant amounts of capital, encouraged by the Japanese government, and guided by decades of accumulated Japanese experience in the islands, returned in force to Micronesia.[8] Today, Japan is the dominant economic presence there, in large part because the entrepreneurs who have made it so have pursued economic opportunity in the islands with the same energy and determination as those first few traders whose small boats pitched and rolled over the waters between Japan and Micronesia at the turn of the century. In the Marianas, Japanese now own eleven of the fifteen major hotels; in Belau (the new

name for the Republic of Palau) total Japanese investment is more than
the annual budget provided by the United States Trusteeship; in the
Marshalls, Japanese efficiency and reliability in commerce, construction, and industry have put them far ahead of the American competition. The lead in this economic drive has been undertaken by the Tōkyū
Corporation, an enormous conglomerate of hotels, real estate firms,
supermarkets, department stores, and trading companies in Japan, the
west coast of the United States, and around the Pacific. Tōkyū's head,
Gotoh Noboru, multimillionaire, confidant of prime ministers, and
chairman of scores of bank and company boards, exercises power and
influence in the Pacific on a scale that Matsue Haruji never dreamed.[9]

As in the mandate period, the Japanese government has worked
closely with Japanese business in pursuit of economic opportunity in
Micronesia. The Japan-Micronesia Association, chartered in 1974 as an
affiliate of the Foreign Ministry, is a prime example of this cooperative
effort. Founded by men of influence and position in Japanese politics
and business, some of whom held positions in the Nan'yō Kōhatsu
before the war, and supported by major shipping, construction, airline,
food, and real estate interests, the association has helped to ease the Japanese reentry into Micronesia through a carefully modulated program
of economic and cultural exchanges and a two-way dissemination of
information in Japan and Micronesia.[10]

In important respects, Japanese economic activity in Micronesia is
radically different from that of half a century ago. Most obviously, it is
no longer carried on within the sheltering protection of a colonial government, but depends upon the tolerance of newly or nearly independent Micronesian nations whose governments are sensitive to the merest
hint of exploitation. It has been accompanied, moreover, by a major
Japanese program of economic assistance to island peoples—nearly ten
million dollars in 1983—expended mostly in the form of grants, low-
interest loans, and technical assistance. For the Japanese, such largess is
as utilitarian as it is philanthropic. Not only does it help to insure access
to Micronesian resources, such as the preservation of fishing rights in the
Marshalls, but it also helps to strengthen the Japanese economic position
in Micronesia, since the Japanese government has been careful to insist
that Japanese companies be employed and Japanese materials used in its
various projects. Yet, Japanese self-interest in Micronesia is balanced by
a new sensitivity toward the interests of local Micronesian communities.
Where Nankō thought it natural to shut out Micronesians from participation in its activities—except as pick-and-shovel laborers at the
Angaur phosphate mines—a variety of Japanese ventures, ranging from
banking in Palau to a button factory in the Marshalls, include Micronesians as partners as well as laborers.[11]

In contrast to its place in the old colonial setting, the Japanese economic presence in Micronesia is directed from afar, in the boardrooms and offices of the giant companies in Tokyo and Osaka. Few Japanese live in the islands; the new states of Micronesia would never again permit a demographic onslaught of their islands by an alien people. But, in place of the tidal wave of Japanese immigrants who came to settle in the islands between the world wars has come a flood of Japanese products—cars, watches, refrigerators, radios, tractors, textiles, packaged foods, computers, heavy machinery, and other goods—in endless number and variety, all sold by affable, experienced, soft-spoken agents who pass through the islands with their briefcases and order forms—and depart.

The driving Japanese economic interest in the islands has changed dramatically in the postwar era. Of the four principal industries of the colonial period—sugar, phosphate, copra, and fishing—only the last retains an important place in the range of Japanese economic activities in Micronesia. Japanese tuna boats ply the waters of all the major island groups as they did years ago, though by and large, the rich loads that fill their holds are destined for the fish markets of Japan rather than for *katsuobushi* factories in Micronesia.

Neither sugar nor tuna is king in Micronesia. In the Marianas and the western Carolines, at least, tourism, specifically Japanese tourism, is the greatest money-maker for both Japanese investors and the island peoples. This new bonanza has been stimulated by the ease of air travel, by the burgeoning prosperity of a postwar middle class now able to afford foreign travel on a scale unprecedented for Japan, and by the common migratory impulse of tourists from competitive industrialized societies of the north to seek the warmth and languor of southern islands and seas, especially in winter. In the great cities of Japan, travel agencies churn out an endless flow of lavish brochures, posters, handbooks, and flyers beguiling young office workers and newlyweds with the natural splendors of the tropical Pacific.[12]

They come by the thousands, these affluent young Japanese, flying south on direct flights from Tokyo and Osaka, to bask on the beaches of Saipan, to explore the rock islands of Palau, or to go snorkeling in the limpid waters off Rota. To receive them at these places are growing numbers of luxury accommodations, mostly built and owned by Japanese firms, the largest of which is, not surprisingly, a Tōkyū subsidiary, Pan-Pacific Hotels. Where Japanese navy seaplanes used to come to rest on Arakebesang (Arakabesan) Island in the Palaus, Gotoh Noboru's vast resources have created the Palau Pacific Resort, a tropical Xanadu of sun-flecked terraces, sumptuous guest "cottages," open-air cocktail lounges, tennis courts, and conference facilities. Along the western shore of Saipan, where General Saitō's men fought and died in the rubble of their pillboxes and command posts, stretches a line of Japanese-owned luxury hotels where bikini-clad young office women sip cocktails at the poolside and honeymoon couples finger eighty-dollar Gucci scarves in the gift shops.

The carefree attitude of these young visitors to the islands contrasts sharply with the perception of the "South Seas" by Japanese of generations past. For the explorer-adventurers of young Mori Koben's day, the islands were a shimmering frontier that promised fulfillment of personal ambition and national destiny at the price of great risk; for the immigrant farmer and fisherman between the world wars they offered a new home and the chance for prosperity bought with struggle and sacrifice; for the Japanese administrator, businessman, or naval officer on the eve of the Pacific War, they were but stepping-stones in the southward advance of Japanese order, profit, and power. That Japanese today, no longer driven by the extremities of poverty or population or obsessed by a national quest for a tropical holy grail, can be content merely to linger for a few days amid the sunlit beauty of these islands before returning with but slight complaint to home and office, says much about the prosperity, the confidence, and the optimism of the new Japan.

Notes

Chapter 1: Distant Shores

1. See Preface for an explanation of the terms "South Seas" and "South Sea islands" in this study.

2. Two disasters drove these points home. In 1887 the protected cruiser *Unebi*, newly constructed at the Le Havre navy yard, left for Japan on its maiden voyage. Somewhere between Singapore and Japan the ship went down with all hands and without a trace. That same year the British steamship *Normanton*, sailing from Yokohama to Kobe with more than two hundred Japanese passengers aboard, struck a rock off the coast and sank. The captain, crew, and two hundred Western passengers all found places in the ship's lifeboats, while nearly two hundred fifty Japanese passengers were left to drown. A British consular court, which, under the unequal treaty arrangements between Britain and Japan, had jurisdiction in such a case, found the British captain and crew blameless. Both the initial act of callousness at the time of the disaster and the finding of the court created a storm of controversy and a public demand for the expansion of the Japanese merchant marine. See Kida 1970, 204–205.

3. Irie 1943, 35; and Itō Hirobumi Kankei Bunshō Kenkyūkai 1973, 258.

4. Kida 1970, 187, 196.

5. Takeshita 1942, 91–96.

6. Irie 1943, 115–116.

7. Miwa 1970, 14–16.

8. Quoted in Yano 1979, 24–26.

9. Pyle 1969, 158. Among the landfalls searched for by the officers and men of the *Hiei* was the "lost" island of Grampus, supposedly sighted by a Captain John Meares sailing from China to the coast of North America in 1786. Its existence was noted as doubtful on British navigational charts. That this island should have been the object of an avid search more than a century after its original "sighting" is an indication of the obsessive concern of some Japanese for Pacific discovery at this time.

10. Quoted in Pyle 1969, 159.

11. Nagasawa 1973, 240.

12. While Gotō Taketarō's family connection made him the nominal leader of the expedition I put Suzuki's name first because it is clear to researchers that nearly all the decisions and reports concerning it were made by Suzuki, eight

321

years his senior and a man with far greater experience. I have drawn my discussion of the puzzling circumstances surrounding the expedition principally from Suzuki's initial account of it, published in 1892, as the first half of his book, *Nan'yō tanken jikki*. I have also drawn on the expertise of Nakajima Hiroshi, executive director of the Pacific Society, who has undertaken considerable research on the subject. Nakajima's commentary is appended to the newest edition of that work (Suzuki 1983).

13. Nakajima 1984*a*.

14. During his sojourn in the Marshalls Suzuki made many sketches of what he saw there: indigenous houses, fishing spears, lures, tools, outrigger canoes, and all manner of fauna and flora. Some of the sketches appeared in rather crude form in his published works, but to accompany his report to the Foreign Ministry, Suzuki produced a series of delicately and precisely drawn ink and watercolor illustrations and maps. This collection, which he entitled *Nan'yō tanken zukai* (Sketches from an exploration in the South Seas), was filed away in the Foreign Ministry as a classified document and forgotten. It was long believed that all of Suzuki's original notes and sketches had been destroyed in the fire that devastated Yokohama after the Kantō earthquake of 1923, but in October 1983 the collection of illustrations and maps was discovered in the reference room of the Diplomatic Record Office in Tokyo, where they had lain for ninety-eight years in a forgotten file. They proved to be in mint condition, a superb anthropological and historical record of a largely bygone culture in Micronesia (Ōuchi 1984).

15. Suzuki 1892.

16. Nakajima 1983*a*. Suzuki Tsunenori's biographer, however, tells us that Suzuki and Gotō spent most of October 1884 based in a tent on Wotje atoll, from which they carried out thorough investigations of the topography, anchorages, and peoples of Wotje and Ailinglapalap. Takeshita 1943, 65.

17. Suzuki 1937, 9–10.

18. Nakajima Hiroshi believes that if Suzuki had the Japanese flag raised it was probably in front of the house of a chief on Ujae Atoll and was probably done more as a joke than as a serious step toward establishing Japanese sovereignty over the islands. I am more inclined to believe Suzuki's recollection of it. Nakajima Hiroshi, letter to author, 1 May 1984.

19. Nakajima 1983*b*. Nakajima Hiroshi believes that the truth about this affair was covered up by the government because in 1937, when Suzuki's memoirs appeared, the Marshalls were being subjected to an intensified program of "Japanization" and the government didn't wish to antagonize the Marshallese population.

20. Suzuki 1983, 95.

21. Suzuki 1893, 3–31.

22. Kida 1970, 192–194.

23. Yano 1979, 20–21; Kida 1970, 204. Synopses and analyses of these works can be found in Yanagida 1968: pt. 2, vol. 9, 279–287 and 487–501; and pt. 3, vol. 10, 95–103, 152–184, and 226–441.

24. Kida 1970, 204–205.

25. Yanagida 1968: pt.2, vol. 9, 153–184, and Yamada 1979, 97–110. The novel in its entirety can be found in Yano 1970, 77–178.

26. Purcell 1972, 56–57.

27. Yano 1979, 31–35. A biographic sketch of Taguchi can be found in Kaji 1973, 75–105.

28. Takeshita 1943, 19–20; Taguchi 1972, 138.

29. Purcell 1972, 57–58; Yano 1979, 31–35.

30. Kida 1968, 208–209; Yano 1979, 34–35.

31. Taguchi 1972, 138; Kida 1968, 208.

32. Nagasawa 1973, 251–254; Irie 1943, 107–109.

33. Cited in Kida 1968, 209.

34. Its lasting value was demonstrated years later, soon after Japan entered World War I and the navy was drawing up operational plans for the occupation of German territories in the Pacific north of the equator. Given the task of gathering information on Micronesia, particularly concerning possible landing sites, suitable construction materials, and available foodstuffs, the staff of the Naval Affairs Division of the Navy Ministry found no good guide books to Micronesia at hand. Then a staff officer remembered the Taguchi/Suzuki account, located a copy, and found it a mine of information—"the most detailed and dependable reference work which currently exists on the subject" (Admiral Hara Kanjirō in the 1942 edition, pp. 304–305 [Yamato Shōten]).

35. Joining the staff of the Nagoya *Fuso Shimbun,* Suzuki covered the Sino-Japanese War of 1894–1895 as a photographer-reporter for that paper. Never one to avoid adventure or the chance of a secret mission, he undertook several intelligence assignments for the Japanese Army General Staff prior to the Russo-Japanese War, including survey work in Manchuria and (incredibly) a stint as the interpreter for the prewar Russian ambassador to Japan. The rest of Suzuki's life was a long and dreary anti-climax—as an insurance agent. In the autumn of 1938 he died in Tokyo, unnoticed and almost penniless. Kida 1968, 193; Yano 1979, 38; Nagasawa 1973, 254; Nakajima 1983*a*, 30–32.

36. My understanding of the pioneering activities of Japanese traders in Micronesia between 1890 and 1914 is based largely on Yano 1979, 66–67; Purcell 1972, 58–62; and Gō 1942, 6–48.

37. Kida 1968, 196–198.

38. Takeshita 1943, 22–28; Kida 1968, 198; and Gō 1942, 14–17.

39. Purcell 1972, 59–60; Gō 1942, 44–46.

40. Gō 1942, 29–33.

41. Ibid., 14–23.

42. Ibid., 29–46.

43. Purcell 1972, 60–62; Yanaihara 1938, 26–27.

44. Unless otherwise noted the biographic sketch which follows has been drawn from a series of articles on Mori Koben and his times written by Morizawa Takamichi (1983).

45. Kashino Eiichi, 1944, "Mori Koben ō no kaikyūdan" [Recollections of the venerable Mori Koben], in Nan'yō Keizai Kenkyūjō 1944*b*, 10–11 (hereafter NKK).

46. Decades later, when Mori was an old man and a living legend, the story circulated in Japan that his adventurous life on Truk was a model for the highly popular Japanese comic strip of the 1930s, "Bōken Dankichi" [Dankichi the adventurous]. Drawn by Shimada Keizō, the strip portrayed the adventures of Dankichi, a young Japanese boy in the South Seas who wore only a childishly drawn crown and a grass skirt. In fact, Shimada seems never to have heard of Mori; rather, the strip was the culmination of boyhood daydreaming and its physical model was a composite of Shimada's children.

47. The Jaluit Gesellschaft moved into Truk in October 1889, less than a month after the German purchase of the Carolines, setting up operations on tiny Eten Island just south of Dublon. The relationship between Mori and the German company was of obvious mutual benefit. For his part, Mori now held a contract with a firm under the protection of Micronesia's new masters; to the

company's benefit, it now had as its Truk agent the son-in-law of the influential chief of one of the larger islands of the group (Nakajima 1984, 64–65).

48. Nakajima Hiroshi (1984, 65) believes that Mori was exempted from the expulsion order because he was too valuable as agent for the Jaluit Gesellschaft.

49. Morizawa, 3 June 1983.

Chapter 2: South into the Pacific

1. Morton 1959.
2. Bōeichō Bōei Kenshūjō Senshishitsu (hereafter BBKS) 1975, 132–134.
3. Pomeroy 1948, 44.
4. Quoted in Yano 1979, 48.
5. Ibid., 21–22; *Taiyō* (November 1913), 43–112.
6. Foreign Minister Katō Takaaki is known to have told the Japanese cabinet on the eve of the nation's declaration of war: "Japan, at this time, is not entering the war because it is obliged to do so by the Alliance. Rather, it considers a resolute decision to embark upon war as an opportune policy for two reasons: the request from Britain, which is based upon the friendship of this Alliance, and the opportunity to sweep up bases in Eastern waters and to advance the Empire's position in the world." Quoted in Ikeda 1967, 2:28–29.
7. Gaimushō 1966, 102–114.
8. Ibid., 114–117; Purcell 1967, 88; Spinks 1936.
9. Gaimushō 1966, 126–130.
10. Ibid., 665–666.
11. Purcell 1967, 152.
12. Nihon Gyōsei Gakkai 1934 (Section 6, Nan'yō), 68. Details of the movements of Yamaya's squadron at the time of the navy's seizure of Jaluit are provided in Kaigun Gunshireibu (n.d., 625–650). This unpublished and, at the time, classified history, which is on file in the War History Office of the Japanese Defense Agency's Defense Academy, is to my knowledge the only detailed account of Japanese naval operations in Micronesia during the First World War.
13. Gō 1942, 219.
14. Ibid., 220–223.
15. Kaigun Yūshūkai 1938, 672.
16. Details of the operations involved in the seizure of these places can be found in Kaigun Gunshireibu n.d., 659–669 (Kusaie), 675–702 (Ponape), 719–729 (Truk), 757–764 (Yap), 773–776 (Palau), and 741–749 (Saipan).
17. Gaimushō 1966, 675; Pomeroy 1948, 49; Kaigunshō n.d., vol. 16, "Tokubetsu rikusentai shikikan ni ataeru kunrei" [Instructions for commanding officers of special naval landing parties], 15 October 1914. This valuable collection of Navy Ministry materials on file at the War History Office of the Japanese Defense Academy was first given scholarly attention by Gabe Masaakira in his "Nihon no Mikuroneshia senryō to 'nanshin' " (1982), parts 1 and 2.
18. Jose 1943, 121–122.
19. Kajima 1980, 183–184.
20. Purcell 1967, 94.
21. See Matsumura 1918, 1–3.
22. Kajima 1980, 185.
23. Iklé 1965.
24. Nish 1972, 204–209.
25. Kajima 1980, 194–202.
26. Lansing 1935, 290–291.
27. Braisted 1971, 441–446; Levi 1948, 62.

28. Schilling 1954, 229–231.
29. Dingman 1976, 79–80.
30. An example of this *nanshin* fever was the attention given to the topic by the influential trade journal *Jitsugyō no Nihon*. In the spring of 1915, the journal devoted an entire issue to the Nan'yō, covering both Southeast Asia and Micronesia, stressing the natural riches of those regions, and providing information on travel, living conditions, and investment possibilities. Eight of the approximately thirty articles dealt specifically with Micronesia (*Jitsugyō no Nihon* 18 (3), 28 March 1915).
31. Kaigunshō n.d., vol. 16, "Nan'yō shinsenryōchi no shōrai" [Future of the newly occupied territories in the South Seas].
32. Yamamoto 1915, 115.
33. Kobayashi 1966, 785–789.
34. Yoshino 1919, 146a–147a.
35. Kawakami 1919, 63; Yano 1979, 209.
36. Kajima 1980, 388–389.
37. Whyte 1957, 382–383; *Literary Digest* 1919 (February 22), 22.
38. Kajima 1980, 389–391.
39. Dingman 1976, 81.
40. Cited in Yano 1979, 209–210.
41. Gabe 1982 (pt. 2), 70–74, 85–87.
42. Braisted 1971, 528–529.
43. Rattan 1972, 127.
44. Ibid., 127–128.
45. Ibid., 130–134.
46. United States Department of State 1938, 599–604.
47. Quoted in Freidel 1954, 135.

Chapter 3: The Iron Cherry Blossom

1. Kaigunshō n.d., vol. 16, "Tokubetsu rikusentai."
2. Hezel and Berg 1979, 442.
3. For an interesting biographic sketch of Matsuoka see Nakamura 1980–1981.
4. See Matsuoka's brief account of his experiences on Ponape at the head of the landing party in the introduction to his *Mikuroneshia minzoku shi* (1943, 6–9). For a discussion of his scholarly work, see NKK 1943*a*.
5. Palau Community Action Agency 1976–1978, 2:304–306.
6. It is obvious that these men gave a good deal of thought to the administration and development of Japan's new tropical territories. For example, Commander Matsuoka submitted an extensive report on the prospects for the development of Ponape, undertook the translation of a German work on the cultivation of coconut palms, and drafted a long essay on the importance of Micronesia as a stepping-stone to Japanese access to the riches of Southeast Asia. Commander Kurose Seiichi on Jaluit sent in a carefully considered series of recommendations to improve Japanese administration in the Marshalls, covering, among other things, improvement of relations between the Marshallese and Japanese officialdom, ways to promote copra production and land reform, and setting a standard time zone for Micronesia. Matsuoka 1943, 7; NKK 1943*a*, 3–4.
7. Crampton 1921; Hobbs 1923, 23–24; McMahon 1919.
8. Blakeslee 1922, 106. Similar in tone is Wood (1922).
9. NKK 1944*b*, 2–6.

10. Gō 1942, 231–239; Purcell 1976, 190–191.

11. Gabe 1982 (8), 77–83.

12. Nan'yō-chō 1932, 35–46. BBKS 1970, 15.

13. While Nan'yō-chō is usually translated as "South Seas Bureau," it actually meant the colonial government situated on Koror and was thus distinct from the actual South Seas Bureau in Tokyo, which served as a liaison office between the colonial government in Micronesia and the various ministries in Japan.

14. For a discussion of the legal structure of Japanese colonies, including the Nan'yō, see I-te Chen 1984.

15. The ranking system within the Japanese civil service added to its formalism and that of the Japanese bureaucracy, as well as identifying the relative degree of precedence and power possessed by those in any of its four levels. At its base were the thousands of *hannin* officials, "appointed by seal" of the various ministries in which they served, on the basis of a rather casual examination system. In military terms, they were the equivalent of noncommissioned officers. Next came the *sōnin* officials who were required to have passed the demanding civil service examinations and who were then "appointed by memorial," that is, by the highest minister within the ministry in which they would serve. They were the equivalent of field grade military officers. The *chokunin* officials, usually promoted from *sōnin* rank, were "appointed by decree," that is, by imperial order. They would be the equivalent of major and lieutenant generals. At the top were the *shinnin* officials, "personally appointed" by the emperor, enjoying the same privileges of protocol as cabinet ministers and sometimes drawn from the military services in which they were full generals and admirals. See Spaulding 1967, 327–329.

16. I-te Chen 1984, 270.

17. For a detailed description in English of the arrangement and functions of both the Nan'yō-chō and the branch governments, consult those veritable mines of information about Micronesia under Japanese rule, the wartime handbooks issued by the United States Navy, Office of the Chief of Naval Operations (OCNO) (1943; 1944*c;* 1944*d;* 1944*e;* 1944*f*).

18. I-te Chen 1984, 259, 266.

19. Among his other exploits Hayashi played a major role in spiriting Henry Pu-yi, the last heir to the Manchu throne, out of Peking in 1931, so that he could be installed as the puppet emperor of Japan's new client state of Manchukuo.

20. Nan'yō-chō 1932, 177; Nan'yō-chō 1937, 4–8. With this authority came considerable standing in the community. The American journalist Willard Price, visiting a village on Ponape in the mid-1930s witnessed the arrival of the new resident policeman and his wife, who were escorted to their new home by the entire village, including the chief. Some years later, the members of the 1941 Kyoto University research team on Ponape noted that the most prestigious family in each village they visited was usually that of the single Japanese police officer, in whose hands was the real authority for local government (Price 1936, 252); Umesao 1944, 455.

21. Nan'yō-chō 1937, 28; Palau Community Action Agency 1976–1978, 3:314; Umesao 1944, 455.

22. The American geologist William Hobbs, touring Ponape in 1922, wrote of one police official, assigned to him as a guide for travel in a remote part of the island, who had "features so hard and cruel that I was not surprised when I learned from the natives of his district that they no way belied his character, and that he had shortly before applied the cruel lash to a native woman in an

advanced state of pregnancy" (Hobbs 1923, 40). In contrast, Willard Price, touring the island over a decade later, had high praise for the Japanese police whom he encountered, particularly one new resident officer (see note 20) who seemed "a pleasant fellow, with none of the officiousness which sometimes characterizes the police in Japan." That Japanese police in Micronesia were not all thickheaded and brutal is exemplified by one policeman of long service in the Marshalls who retired to write an extensive anthropological study on Marshallese society based, one assumes, on a reasonably cordial relationship with his Micronesian informants (Price 1936, 252; Yanaihara 1938, 140).

23. Although there was considerable variation in leadership patterns throughout Micronesia, the following discussion is necessarily generalized. Space does not permit a more sophisticated discussion of the complexities and contrasts within traditional Micronesian societies or specific island communities.

24. For discussion of the local administration of Japanese communities in Micronesia, see Chapter 6, note 17.

25. Yanaihara 1938, 262–263; Yano Tōru 1978, 177.

26. Purcell 1967, 161–162.

27. Except for the somewhat exotic nature of a few of the offenses punishable under this code, it is similar in tone to the detailed and heavy-handed regulations posted in Japanese villages by shogunal authorities in Japan's feudal period. Crimes that could earn island offenders a month at hard labor on roads and docks included failure to carry out efforts to eradicate palm tree blight; conducting wedding banquets without permission of the authorities; holding dances without permission of the authorities; letting fires spread when clearing land for cultivation; making false translations; performing castration on others; tattooing oneself; practicing hypnotism; and being excessively noisy at religious devotions in public (cited in Yano 1978, 179).

28. Quoted in US Navy, OCNO 1948, 81.

29. Purcell 1967, 164; Yanaihara 1938, 263–266; Spoehr 1949, 95–96; Nason 1970, 208–210; Grahlfs 1955, 41.

30. For two different analyses of the *Modekngei* cult during the Japanese period, see Vidich 1980, 228–248; and Aoyagi 1985, 204–220.

31. My understanding of the organization and procedures of the Permanent Mandates Commission is based largely on Hall (1948) and to a lesser extent on Wright (1930).

Chapter 4: A Trust Betrayed

1. Purcell 1967, 249–252.

2. Likewise, this question can be asked of each and all the mandatory powers, not just Japan. Just as obviously, a detailed comparison with the conduct of European mandates in Africa and the Middle East is beyond the scope of this work. In the pages that follow I have, instead, made passing reference to the Australian and New Zealand mandates in the Pacific, since those comparisons seem more relevant.

3. My perspectives on these matters I owe to Hall 1948, 92–98.

4. American scholar Paul Clyde wrote of the "cheerful" Micronesian stevedores and laborers he observed during his tour of the islands in 1934, but after the Pacific War a number of Islanders in the Carolines recounted the traumatic effect of the departure of young men from their native communities for the mines at Angaur for periods of six months to four years. One Trukese recalled the wailing and crying of relatives at the dock at Dublon when the men were

taken by launch out to the waiting steamer (Clyde 1935, 147; Gladwin and Sarason 1953, 190–191).

5. For a discussion of Micronesian labor in the mandate in general, and on Angaur in particular, see Decker 1940, 130–150; Yanaihara 1938, 278–280; and Purcell, "Economics of Exploitation," pp. 191–194.

6. Yanaihara 1938, 288–289.

7. Ibid., 232–238.

8. Gaimushō Jōyakukyoku Hōkika 1962, 2:48.

9. Shuster 1982*b*, 20–22.

10. Ibid., 22–23; Spoehr 1954, 88.

11. Spoehr 1954, 50.

12. Gaimushō Jōyakukyoku Hōkika 1962, 2:111.

13. UK Naval Intelligence Division 1945, 345–346; Shuster 1978, 16–18.

14. Yanaihara 1938, 291.

15. Ibid., 273.

16. Shuster 1978, 22–26; Nufer 1978, 15.

17. The pattern of demographic change was uneven: between 1923 and 1933 Saipan, Ponape, and Palau showed noticeable increases; Truk and Jaluit remained static; and Yap showed a startling decrease. The Chamorros of the Marianas—by this time actually a mixed population—showed high birth and death rates, but the former was higher. The far larger population of Carolinians had far lower birth rates.

18. Taiheiyō Gakkai 1981, 73. In viewing the limited results of Japanese health care in Micronesia one must remember that Japanese medical staffs in the 1920s and 1930s possessed none of the wonder drugs developed during World War II and available to American authorities after 1945. Penicillin, for example, brought both yaws and gonorrhea under control in the early years of the American administration of Micronesia. I am grateful to Professor J. L. Fischer, Department of Anthropology, Tulane University, for pointing this out to me.

19. Nan'yō Guntō Kyōkai 1965, 39–40.

20. US Navy, OCNO 1948, 60.

21. Yanaihara 1938, 292–298.

22. Nan'yō Guntō Kyōiku-kai 1938, 632.

23. Gaimushō Jōyakukyoku Hōkika 1962, 2:3.

24. Until the mid-1930s there were still fourteen mission schools throughout Micronesia. These attracted some public school graduates who wished to have Bible classes or handicraft training. In a few of the remoter atolls where there were no public schools, the mission schools provided regular courses for a time at least (Yanaihara 1938, 241–242).

25. Ibid., 242–243.

26. These were the impressions, at least, of the young writer and bureaucrat Nakajima Atsushi who passed through the Mortlock Islands, southeast of Truk, in the autumn of 1941 (Ochner 1984, 160).

27. Nan'yō-chō 1932, 126.

28. The thrust of primary school education, according to the government's 1934 annual report to the League of Nations, was the "inculcation of moral education and the fundamentals of *national* education" [italics added], as well as providing Japanese students with "the *common* knowledge and capabilities essential to their livelihood . . ." [Italics added.] In other words, Japanese primary school students in Micronesia were to get the same education as their young compatriots in the homeland and for the same purpose: fully participating citizenship in a competitive society. In its discussion of public schools for Micronesians, the same report omitted any reference to "national education" or

"common knowledge," stating merely that they would be given "such knowledge and capabilities as are indispensable to the advancement and improvement of their lives" South Seas Government 1934, 46, 52.

29. Fischer 1961, 84.

30. Ramarui 1979, 5.

31. Shuster 1978, 35–36.

32. Ramarui 1976, 10; Fischer 1961, 85.

33. Konishi 1944, 34–35.

34. The official history of Japanese education in Micronesia explained the near total failure rate for Micronesians in Japanese schools as being due to "their lack of self-control [*jiseiryoku ni mazushiku*]; once having fallen into indolence they cannot overcome this fault and recover" (Nan'yō Guntō Kyōiku-kai 1938, 359).

35. Shuster 1978, 37; Ramarui 1976, 10; Nan'yō Guntō Kyōiku-kai 1938, 549.

36. It is instructive to compare the Japanese record in this regard with some other mandated territories and dependencies in the Pacific. On Nauru, for example, just four years after the beginning of the Australian mandate, all teachers on the island were Nauruan and some had been sent to Australia for further training. In the Cook Islands, New Zealand established a teacher training college at Rarotonga, and in Western Samoa it founded another (Shuster 1978, 38–39; Greenberger 1974, 160).

37. Fischer 1961, 86; Nufer 1978, 18.

38. Hall 1948, 95.

39. Interviews with such persons have been conducted by the field staff of the Micronesian Area Research Center at the University of Guam (see Dirk Ballendorf, Shuster, and Higuchi 1986).

40. Clyde 1935, 112; Price 1936, 295–296.

41. Moos 1974, 283–284.

42. US Navy, OCNO 1944*f*, 163.

43. Yanaihara 1938, 156.

44. Bascom 1950, 144–145; Nason 1970, 224.

45. Peoples 1977, 151–152; Emerick 1960, 51–52.

46. Ibid.

47. Spoehr 1954, 86; interview with Dr. Minoru Ueki, Koror, June 1983.

48. In the Marianas, the Japanese demand for land was heaviest, since it was into those islands that Japanese immigrants came in the greatest numbers. Not only the indigenous population of Saipan, but also the Chamorros on Rota, felt the pressure. After the Japanese economic development of that island began, indigenous farmers on the well-watered southeast coast of the island were pressured into exchanging their holdings for new land on the western shore. The exchange was made on the basis of equivalent area and the Rotanese were paid for their standing crops, but the new land was far less fertile; even so, none dared to resist the order. Following this removal of Rotanese farmers from their traditional lands, the residents of Songsong, the main village on the island, were obliged to move to Tatacho, three miles to the north (Bowers 1950, 79–80).

49. Bascom 1950, 145.

50. Peoples 1977, 152; Crocombe 1972, 232.

51. Shuster 1978, 44–45; Purcell 1976, 193–194.

52. Shuster 1978, 46–53.

53. Ibid., 48–49; Vidich 1980, 200; Gladwin and Sarason 1953, 42.

54. Shuster 1978, 50–51; Vidich 1980, 202; Nason 1970, 214–217.

55. Vidich 1980, 203–204; Shuster 1978, 47–48.

56. Bascom 1950, 144; Nason 1970, 220.
57. Nufer 1978, 18.
58. Peattie 1984, 96–98.
59. Betts 1971, 8–9.
60. Peattie 1984, 100.
61. Ibid., 119–124.
62. Shuster 1978, 31–33. A few Japanese educators did indeed urge a true assimilation of island children by providing a common education for Japanese and Micronesians in a single school system. Iwakuro Hideo, the Ministry of Education official who in 1915 drafted the guidelines for Japanese education in Micronesia, was one of these. But this degree of assimilation was seen as excessive by the colonial bureaucracy and suggestions like Iwakuro's were brushed aside (Nan'yō Guntō Kyōiku-kai 1938, 637–638).
63. Price 1936, 230–231; Ochner 1984, 161.
64. *Ishikawa Tatsuzō sakuhinshū* 1957, 234.
65. Shuster 1982b, 22–23.
66. Ibid., 36.
67. Nan'yō Guntō Kyōiku-kai 1938, 337–346.
68. Ibid., 348; Vidich 1980, 190–191; McMahon 1919, 32.
69. Nan'yō Guntō Kyōkai 1965, 57–60.
70. Moos 1974, 286.
71. South Seas Government 1934, 4. Not all Japanese bureaucrats were willing to relegate Micronesians to a permanent position of inferiority. Early in the Japanese occupation of Micronesia, Iwakuro Hideo (see n. 62) believed that true assimilation of Micronesians could lead to their "cultivation as genuine imperial subjects" [*junryō naru teikoku shimmin*]. Nan'yō Guntō Kyōiku-kai 1938, 630.
72. Spoehr 1954, 88; South Seas Government 1934, 4; League of Nations, Permanent Mandates Commission [hereafter, LN-PMC] 1933, 90. While the Japanese government flatly denied that it discriminated between the Chamorro and Carolinians (LN-PMC 1927, 2) the record of differences in conditions of employment would appear to be solid evidence that it did.
73. League of Nations, *Official Journal*, Third Year, no. 6 (June 1922), 592.
74. *Japan Chronicle*, 3 February 1921.
75. Shuster 1978, 3–6.
76. Shirase 1916, 63.
77. Quoted in Moos 1974, 286.
78. Shuster 1978, 7.
79. LN-PMC 1936, 178. Sensitive as always to cultural differences, without making racial judgments, Yanaihara Tadao offered a reasoned rebuttal of official Japanese prejudices. Rejecting claims that Micronesian children were inherently unintelligent and capable only of learning manual skills, Yanaihara pointed out that the textbooks used in public schools had little relation to daily Micronesian life and that Micronesian students were learning through a language that was not their own. Micronesian students, he insisted, "are not congenital mental cripples, but just uneducated children" (Yanaihara 1938, 246).
80. An example of one of the Micronesian practices with which the Japanese administration had to deal was encountered by Dr. Fujii Tamotsu, the noted medical investigator (mentioned earlier in this chapter), when he was director of the Yap Hospital. Invited to the funeral of a chief who had died of pulmonary tuberculosis, Fujii watched with uneasiness as the body was washed in coconut juice and then with horror as the liquid was collected in a bowl that was then passed around to the mourners in a last, symbolic communion with the

deceased. Offered a sip, Fujii avoided participation only by feigning (?) sudden illness (Nan'yō Guntō Kyōkai 1965, 42).

81. See, for example, Philip Curtin, 1964, *The Image of Africa: British Ideas in Action, 1780–1850* (Madison, WI: University of Wisconsin Press); Dominique Mannoni, 1956, *Prospero and Calaban: The Psychology of Colonization* (NY: Praeger); Alatas Syed Hussein, 1977, *The Myth of the Lazy Native* (London: Frank Cass).

82. South Seas Government 1922, 13; 1930, 135; 1937, 88.

83. Decker 1940, 45.

84. Hume-Ford's statement, cited in Shuster (1982, 178). See also Price 1936, 166.

85. Yanaihara 1938, 298.

86. Yanaihara's criticisms of Japanese colonial policies in general, brought about his professional eclipse in 1937, the year his book on the mandates was published in Japan. He was dismissed from his lectureship in colonial studies at Tokyo University, and in 1938 his works were banned and he was purged from public life. With considerable courage he continued to speak out against Japan's colonial abuses.

Chapter 5: Making Paradise Pay

1. Nan'yō Guntō Kyōkai 1965, 21–22; Imanishi 1944, 385.

2. Gō 1942, 85–89.

3. Ibid., 84–85.

4. Ibid., 85–86, 91–92.

5. Ibid., 98–100.

6. Rynkiewich 1981, 37–43.

7. Gō 1942, 116–118.

8. The failure of the initial agricultural/industrial ventures of these Japanese firms is discussed in detail by Irie Toraji (1942). The bungling of these firms on Saipan and the human chaos they wrought was paralleled by similar mismanagement on Tinian, first by the Kita Company which attempted in 1918, with little or no foresight, to start a coconut plantation with immigrant labor from Japan, and then in 1925, by the Diamond Company which attempted to set up a pork processing plant to make use of the countless wild pigs on the island. Both ventures folded, leaving the workers to get back to Japan as best they could. Even tiny Rota had its share of corporate failure: in 1918 the Nishimura Takushoku tried unsuccessfully to grow cotton with coolies from Japan and Korea and withdrew in 1921.

9. Matsue 1932, 55–56, 62–66, 79–80.

10. Ibid., 20–25, 53–58.

11. Ibid., 62–66.

12. While these were certainly rational and commendable reasons, Matsue neglects to list a fifth and obviously major consideration in his schemes: poor farmers from Okinawa would be satisfied with less than half the remuneration demanded by laborers from the more highly industrialized sections of Japan.

13. Matsue 1932, 84–90.

14. While on an inspection of the railway's branch line on the east coast, the open freight car in which he was riding up a steep gradient became detached from the locomotive and, slipping backward, began to pick up speed as it approached a dangerous curve. At the last moment Matsue jumped off, breaking his left arm in the process. Because of inadequate medical facilities on the

island, his arm never healed properly and for the rest of his life he could lift it only with difficulty (ibid., 112–114).

Little of the track and rolling stock of Matsue's railway still remain, most of it having been destroyed in the bombardment of Saipan in 1944 or ripped up for scrap during the American occupation. The sole remnant is a small steam locomotive which sits in a modest park in what used to be Garapan Town.

15. My summary of these reverses is based on Matsue 1932, 128–140, 151.

16. Ibid., 131–134, 140–142, 145–150.

17. In this way the sugar industry in the Marianas eventually produced alcohol for the distilling of various liquors, including a local "Scotch," flavored and colored to make it taste and appear so, and sold in the poorer sections of Tokyo, it has been said, as "Genuine Old Scotch Whisky Made in Saipan."

18. Matsue 1932, 152–156. The soil on Rota, however, proved too thin for first quality sugar and, by the eve of the Pacific War the refinery there had been turned over completely to alcohol, and many of the workers hired for the sugar industry had been sent to Tinian and Pagan to assist in the construction of airfields there.

19. After 1922 all trade taxes in the mandated territory were abolished, but a harbor clearance fee *(shukkōzei)* was imposed on such goods as sugar and alcohol, which were shipped to Japan or to other parts of the empire, and were subject to a consumption tax in the home islands (though the tax was not passed on to the Japanese consumer). In 1925, the fees accounted for less than five percent of the revenues of the mandate.

20. The statue, with a bullet in its left temple, still stands amid the flame trees in the same small park that displays the small rusting steam locomotive. The victim of wartime target-shooting by some unknown Marine sharpshooter, the statue is one of the few physical remains of Garapan Town, nearly obliterated in the fighting of June 1944.

21. In 1932–1933 Matsue acted upon this view by taking a number of trips to the Dutch East Indies to explore the possibility of Japanese commercial penetration of that region. Upon his return to Japan he spoke repeatedly in public and in private of the economic importance of Southeast Asia to Japan. Among his most attentive listeners were the navy brass.

22. South Seas Government 1937, 20–26.

23. Nantaku Kai 1982, 30–32.

24. Yano 1979, 118–119; Nantaku Kai 1982, 53–54.

25. The picture of economic cooperation between these three enterprises can be overdrawn, certainly. There was, for example, more than occasional friction between the Nan'yō Kōhatsu and the Nan'yō Takushoku, not just because more of their activities were mutually competitive, but also because the ranks of the Nan'yō Takushoku included many former government officials whose aloof and overbearing bureaucratic style was frequently resented by the branch directors of the Nan'yō Kōhatsu, which was noted for the close relations among its employees (Gondō 1939, 200–201).

26. Itō 1941, 411–435.

27. Clyde 1935, 144; US Navy, OCNO 1944a, 4–5. Nankō also established its own research station on Pagan in the Marianas, where it experimented with sugarcane, raw cotton, and vegetables.

28. One of Hoshino's pet projects was the development of a strain of rice that would meet Japanese tastes and yet be resistant to the humidity of Ponape. After considerable experimentation he succeeded, but perhaps for reasons of inadequate land and labor, rice cultivation was never really successful before the Pacific War (Price 1936, 248–250).

29. UK Naval Intelligence Division 1945, 342–343; US Navy, OCNO 1944, 23; Price 1936, 244–245; Nihon Keizai Kenyūkai 1941, 174–175.

30. But not entirely. Years after the war the American scholar John Coulter, wading through the tropical grass on Palau, came across "an acre of bright red oval fruit of the Malayan rambutan tree awaiting market in vain. In the vicinity were groves of East Indian mangosteens with ripe juicy fruit, tropical American cherimoyas, West Indian sour sap, cashew trees, mangoes and citrus—all introduced by the Japanese. The local American agriculturalist obtained his coffee from an abandoned plantation near his house, most of which was going to waste" (Coulter 1969, 40).

31. Bowers 1950, 137–138, 187–189, 202, 205–206; Farrell 1972, 54–55.

32. Fischer and Fischer 1957, 72–73, 79.

33. Bascom 1965; Matsue 1932, 74–76.

34. Bowers 1950, 154; Bascom 1965, 89; Farrell 1972, 54; Nan'yō Keizai Kenkyūjō 1943c.

35. US Navy, OCNO 1944b, vi, 1–4.

36. Yanaihara 1938, 60; Price 1936, 253; Bascom 1965, 120; US Navy, OCNO 1944b, 6–7; Hall and Pelzer 1946, 89–92.

37. US Navy, OCNO 1944b, 10; Nihon Gyōsei Gakkai 1934 (Nan'yō section), 67; Ōgimi 1939, 202.

38. Bascom 1965, 125–126; Price 1936, 259; US Navy, OCNO 1944b, 14; Cockrum 1970, 94–97.

39. Price 1936, 257–258; US Navy, OCNO 1944b, 14; Bartlett 1954, 280–291. Considering that the Japanese came late to Australian waters and that they operated at great distance from their home ports, their rapid domination of the Australian pearl grounds is remarkable. Their success appears to have been due to a number of factors: the diving experience and skills they had gained fishing in Japan's Inland Sea, as well as in the service of Australian pearlers; the fact that Japanese pearling enterprises employed only Japanese, which made for tighter, more effective operations; and the use of superior technology, especially larger, faster ships. See Konishi 1944, 32–36.

40. Gondō 1939, 196–200.

41. Nihon Gyōsei Gakkai 1934, 51; UK Naval Intelligence Division 1945, 435–437.

42. UK Naval Intelligence Division 1945, 369–373; Ehrlich 1984, 43–44.

43. US Navy, OCNO 1944f, 130–134; Bascom, 1965, 50; Price 1936, 23; Ochner 1984, 147–150; *Nihon Yūsen Kaisha* 1956, 226–227.

44. One of the ships, the *Shizuoka Maru*, came to grief in April 1933, when it ran aground on a reef off the northern tip of Yap. R. V. C. Bodley, a British journalist who was aboard the vessel at the time, later wrote an interesting but stiff-upper-lip account of the coolness and discipline of the captain, crew, and Japanese passengers. Although all aboard were safely evacuated, the vessel, pounded by enormous waves, became a total loss. The American journalist Willard Price passed the wreck several years later aboard the *Yokohama Maru* and noted that it was surrounded by canoes as the Yapese stripped it of stateroom doors, portholes, bunks, wash cabinets, railings, and planking (1936, 25); Nan'yō Guntō Kyōkai 1965, 151; Bodley 1933, 193–206.

45. Nippon Yūsen Kaisha 1935, 123; Umesao 1944, 402; Ochner 1984, 147–150.

46. There was also a Truk interisland line that circuited all the principal islands within the enormous lagoon once or twice a week.

47. Information on the NYK routes noted in this paragraph derived from Nihon Gyōsei Gakkai 1934, 52–54; US Navy, OCNO 1944f, 130–131; US Navy,

OCNO 1944*d*, 116–117; US Navy, OCNO 1943, 88; Nason 1970, 213–214. By the 1930s the Nantaku also ran a number of interisland lines and there were several smaller lines like the Palau Transportation Company, which serviced specific groups of islands.

48. The trailblazing of Micronesian skies was not without its sacrifices, most notably the mysterious disappearance in 1938 of a Douglas flying boat purchased by the Nan'yō-chō from the Japanese navy. Piloted by the same navy captain who pioneered the Yokohama-Palau flight in 1935 and carrying a crew of seven, the plane was heading south on the same route when, after having passed the Bonins, it ceased radio communication. As the skies were clear at the time, engine failure was the most likely cause of the crash, but why the pilot and crew did not send out a distress call has never been explained. Japanese warships searched along the route of the aircraft, but no trace was ever found. Some years later a monument was erected to the memory of the lost aviators in the park near Koror, but it is now gone, destroyed in the aerial bombardment of the city in 1944. Nan'yō Guntō Kyōkai, 1965, 102–104; "Nan'yō-chō Dagurasu hikōtei junnan shichi yūshi tsuitō go" 1939, 104–109.

49. Nozawa 1960.

50. Yanaihara 1938, 267–268; Lockwood 1954, 312n; Nan'yō-chō Chōkan Kanbō 1937, 150–151.

51. Gaimushō Jōyakukyoku Hōkika 1962, 2:297; US Navy, OCNO 1944*d*, 117–118.

52. Mizoguchi 1980, 133.

53. Mitsubishi Keizai Kenkyūjō 1937, 161.

Chapter 6: From Ripple to Riptide

1. In 1981 the estimated population of the US Trust Territory of the Pacific was 135,600 (*Britannica Book of the Year, 1984* [Chicago: Encyclopedia Britannica, 1984], 295).

2. Russell 1984, 60; Shuster 1978, 11–12.

3. Decker 1940, 37–39; Yamagata ken 1971, 871.

4. Decker 1940, 40–41.

5. Yamagata ken 1971, 872.

6. Nankō seems to have worked with the Japanese government in identifying those prefectures where population and economic pressures seemed greatest: Okinawa, Kagoshima, Miyazaki, Kumamoto, Tottori, Tokyo (particularly Hachijojima), Fukushima, and Yamagata. Selection and counseling of prospective immigrants at the recruiting centers in those areas appears to have been careful and fair, the company weeding out all who seemed unsuitable as settlers and admonishing all applicants that Micronesia was no place for the mere opportunist, the drifter, or the incompetent. But the paperwork for applicants was minimal: a copy of the family register, a letter of reference, a doctor's certificate of good health, and a photograph (Ōgimi 1937, 321–322).

Nankō's recruiting efforts paid off. Throughout the Japanese period the company was the largest single employer in Micronesia. In 1929, out of a total immigrant population of approximately 16,500, approximately 10,000 were directly employed by the company or its subsidiary firms, or were dependents of such employees. In 1935, the number had risen to approximately 28,000 (out of nearly 50,000 immigrants); in 1940, to 30,000 (out of more than 85,000); and in 1943, approximately 48,000 (out of more than 96,000) (Takemura Jirō, ed., 1984, *Nankō shi* [A history of the South Seas Development Company], Nankō Kai, 111).

7. Kerr 1958, 393–399, 436–439.

8. Matsue Haruji himself soon became convinced that it was unwise for his enterprise, as well as for the colonization of the Marianas, to depend entirely on immigrants from one region. Determined to recruit farmers and laborers from other parts of Japan, he selected Fukushima, Yamagata, and Iwate prefectures in Tohoku (northern Honshu) as special areas of recruitment, along with Kagoshima Prefecture in Kyushu. Sending immigrants from the snow country to Micronesia was thought to be somewhat risky, but an emigrant group from Fukushima had gone to the Philippines and proved successful. Matsue counted on the hardihood of farmers from Tohoku in dealing with extreme weather conditions to stand them in good stead in the South Seas. As it turned out, Matsue was correct, since Tohoku emigrants came to make up a significant portion of the immigrant population in Micronesia (Matsue 1932, 181).

Nevertheless, the Okinawan majority in the islands continued to soar. By 1939, Okinawans numbered over 45,000, constituting nearly 60 percent of the immigrant population. Next, but far below the Ryūkyū Islands, came Tokyo with approximately 4500, Fukushima with 3700, Kagoshima with 2500, and Yamagata, Hokkaido, Shizuoka, and Fukuoka with approximately 1000 each. There were also some 2000 Koreans in Micronesia on the eve of the Pacific War. The remainder of the immigrant population—approximately 15,000 souls—represented all the other prefectures in Japan, plus the tiniest handful from the other colonies (Okinawa Ken 1974, 390–392).

9. Asai 1944, 320.

10. In 1935, out of a total immigrant population of nearly 40,000 in the Marianas—setting aside dependents—just over 11,000 were directly engaged in agriculture. Following, but fewer in number, were shopkeepers and tradespeople (1255), construction workers (940), commercial fishers (609), hotel and restaurant workers (829, of whom 552 were women) and transportation workers (533) (Nan'yō-chō Chōkan Kambō 1937, 14–17).

11. Akamine 1978, 215.

12. Taeuber 1958, 181.

13. Nan'yō-chō Chōkan Kambō 1937, 4, 14; Price 1936, 161–173.

14. Spoehr 1954, 85–86.

15. Matsue 1932, 179–182, 184–185.

16. Nan'yō-chō Chōkan Kambō 1937, 6. As usual the great majority of these came from Okinawa, though Matsue made efforts to bring in immigrants from other regions. In 1929, a particularly large group arrived from Kagoshima aboard the *Shizuoka Maru* (Matsue 1932, 182).

17. By the 1930s, the largest Japanese communities in the Marianas had sufficiently developed in population and function that they needed some sort of municipal administration. Therefore in 1932, by executive order, the South Seas Government established in Micronesia the town-village *(buraku)* system that existed in rural Japan. For each substantial Japanese community in the Islands a town council *(kyōgikai)* was created, consisting of 12 to 24 members, serving four years without pay, and elected by their male compatriots over twenty. The council determined the town budget, taxes, loans, disposal of real property, basic finances, and other contractual obligations, as well as publicizing directives from the branch governor. Acting as a sort of mayor, representing the council to the branch governor, was a representative *(sōdai)*, appointed in theory by the branch governor, but in practice taking office only after election by the town council, which also voted him a small salary. This type of municipal government came to operate at Garapan and Chalankanoa on Saipan; Tinian Town; Koror; Dublon Town, Truk; and Kolonia on Ponape. Nan'yō-chō 1932, 64; US Navy, OCNO 1948, 81–84; and Nan'yō Guntō Kyōkai n.d.

18. Bowers 1950, 96; Matsue 1932, 219–220.

19. Bowers 1950, 79–80, 82–83.

20. Ehrlich 1984, 40–43.

21. NKK 1943d, 1–12; Yamagata ken 1971, 886–887.

22. NKK 1943b, 17.

23. Ibid., 16; NKK 1943d, 19; Yamagata ken 1971, 888.

24. NKK 1943b, 1–2.

25. Ibid., 5–9.

26. Ibid., 9–12, 17. In the same name-change Ailai became Mizuho Mura, Gardok became Kiyomizu Mura, and Gabadon became Yamato Mura.

27. Ibid., 12–15; Price 1936, 171.

28. Yanaihara 1938, 59–60.

29. In the late 1930s, for example, the South Seas Pineapple Company substantially dropped the price it was willing to pay for pineapples, causing the agricultural settlements to cut back drastically on production. Since the revenue of the colonial government did not depend upon pineapples, as it did on sugar, there was no incentive to rescue the crop through price supports or subsidies. In 1940, Nantaku and Tōyō Bōseki, as a joint venture, established the Asahimura Tropical Fiber Association to produce commercial fibers from pineapple skins and leaves, but two years later, after failing to show a profit, the project was abandoned by both firms (NKK 1943b, 12–15).

30. Asai 1944, 328; NKK 1943d, 12.

31. Ehrlich 1984, 44–46, 52.

32. Price 1936, 161–162.

33. Ehrlich 1984, 52; Gondō 1939, 196–200.

34. Bascom 1965, 120; US Navy, OCNO 1944d, 54; Hanlon 1981, 100–101.

35. Bascom 1965, 5, 36; Price 1936, 172; Umesao 1944, 459.

36. Umesao 1944, 430.

37. Ibid.

38. Ibid., 429.

39. In all of this, of course, little thought was given to the place or future of the island's indigenes. Indeed, there was even talk among the Japanese community of completely taking over Ponape and moving the local population to some smaller island (Bascom 1950, 145).

40. Nan'yō-chō Chōkan Kambō 1937, 6; BBKS 1966, 60.

41. Oddly, despite the relatively small Japanese presence on Truk between the wars, compared to the near total Japanese occupation of the Marianas, the Truk group was among the very few Micronesian islands to which Japanese names were applied (as opposed to Japanese pronunciation of Micronesian names). The Japanese gave the names of seasons or days of the week to the larger or more important islands, and names of plants, flowers, or birds to the others. For example, Moen was known as Harujima (Spring Island), Dublon as Natsujima (Summer Island), Udot as Getsuyōtō (Monday Island), and Tol as Suiyōtō (Wednesday Island).

42. Nan'yō-chō Chōkan Kambō 1937, 7–8.

43. UK Naval Intelligence Division 1945, 408–409.

44. US Navy, OCNO 1943, 37; UK Naval intelligence Division 1945, 421; Tobin 1970, 20.

45. Yamagata ken 1971, 860–862.

46. Kikuchi 1937, 50–58.

47. Nan'yō Guntō Kyōkai 1965, 119.

48. Kikuchi 1937, 272–273; Ballendorf, Shuster, and Higuchi 1986.

49. Kikuchi 1937, 275–276.

50. Yamagata ken 1971, 862–864.

51. Kikuchi 1937, 267–268.

52. Toyama Misao, ed., 1981, *Kaigun hen* [Navy volume], vol. 2 of *Riku-kaigun shōkan jinji sōran* [A conspectus on general officers of the Japanese navy] (Fuyō Shobō), p. 179; Nan'yō Guntō Kyōkai 1965, 108; Konishi 1943, 4, 5.

53. Years later, in 1942, Hijikata's valuable study, based on his notebooks of that time, *Folk Legends of Palau* [*Parao no shinwa*] was published in Tokyo (Hijikata Hisakatsu Ten Kaisai Iinkai 1971, 9–14).

54. Ibid.

55. Ibid., 146–147.

56. NKK 1944*b*, 2–6.

57. Ibid.; Morizawa, 9 June 1983.

58. Morizawa, 10 June 1983. His family kept Mori's photographs after his death, but sadly, when the Mori home was blown down in a hurricane after the war, they were all destroyed.

59. Ibid.

60. Ibid., 9 and 10 June 1983.

61. One can still find the marker, slightly tilted and moss covered, at the edge of the field, though only the first few lines are clearly legible: "Many years ago, Mori Koben, venerable pioneer on Truk, set sail with great ambition for the South Seas, crossing the ocean in 1892. It has been more than fifty years since he began to teach and guide the island peoples . . ."

Chapter 7: Japan in the Tropics

1. Ishikawa 1957, 215–249.

2. My understanding of Nakajima's Micronesian sojourn is almost entirely based on Ochner 1984, 135–194.

3. Nan'yō Guntō Kyōkai 1965, 139.

4. Nan'yō-chō 1937, 32–33.

5. On Majuro atoll in the Marshalls there still stands a monument set up by the Japanese navy to commemorate a vast typhoon that struck there on 8 November 1918, during which time an enormous wave swept over Majuro drowning more than two hundred people. The coconut palms were so devastated that no copra was produced for ten years (Spoehr 1949, 21; Rynkiewich 1981, 31).

6. Metropolitan newspapers had a circulation of no more than five hundred in Micronesia, being bought mostly by government offices, companies, and larger stores. Most Japanese in Micronesia bought locally published papers which ranged from the *Nan'yō Asahi Shimbun* on Saipan, with a circulation of three thousand and branch offices on Tinian and Rota, to the *Torakku Jihō* [Truk Times], a somewhat irregular paper of two to four mimeographed sheets with a circulation of only two hundred (Kikuchi 1937, 249–251).

7. Umesao 1944, 450.

8. Asai 1944, 370–371; Bowers 1950, 107, 112–113.

9. Asai 1944, 370–371.

10. Umesao 1944, 445–446; Bodley 1934, 101; Asai 1944, 371.

11. Umesao Tadao noted, however, that despite these concessions to the temperature, other efforts brought forth derision from old Micronesia hands. Use of a folding fan, for example, marked one as the rawest tenderfoot, as yet unable to bear the heat (Umesao 1944, 368).

12. Andō 1936; Asai 1944, 368; NKK 1943*d*, 30.

13. Asai 1944, 368; Gaimushō Jōyakukyoku Hōkika 1962, 1:243–266. In the 1930s, however, this official obsession with correct attire still seemed incapable of lapse. R. V. C. Bodley remembered one young Japanese functionary who showed him about in the heat and humidity of Ponape, dressed in a white duck suit, stiff butterfly collar, black tie, straw boater, and silver-topped walking stick (Bodley 1934, 166).

14. Andō 1936, 35–36, 86; Umesao 1944, 450.

15. Asai 1944, 352–358; Ochner 1984, 140, 177.

16. Bodley 1934, 110, 120, 143–144.

17. Kikuchi 1937, 254–255; US Navy, OCNO 1944*f*, 58.

18. Nan'yō Guntō Kyōkai 1965, 113.

19. Ibid., 115.

20. Ibid., 92–93.

21. Tobin 1970, 27; Ballendorf, Shuster, and Wakako 1986.

22. Kikuchi 1937, 254; Fischer 1957, 79.

23. Gondō 1939, 64; Umesao 1944, 450.

24. Nan'yō-chō 1937, 54.

25. Kikuchi Masao, who seems to have informed himself in some detail on these matters, estimated that there were some eighty brothels throughout Micronesia, employing some six hundred women, and bringing in some two hundred thousand yen annually (Kikuchi 1937, 254). There is little doubt that amidst the boomtown atmosphere of some of the Japanese settlements in the Marianas, prostitution was a very lucrative profession. Andō Sakan asserted in his travel account that, in the row of brothels amid the palm groves at the southern end of Rota Town, each woman had five or six customers a night, so that within a year they earned an average of one thousand yen (approximately $2850), after which they usually returned to Japan (Andō 1936, 18–20).

26. Nan'yō Guntō Kyōkai n.d.; comments by Antolin Sotan, my guide on Truk in June 1983.

27. Bodley 1934, 142; Andō 1936, 37.

28. Ishikawa 1957, 223.

29. Price 1944, 50.

30. Umesao 1944, 418.

31. Ibid., 425.

32. Hanlon (1981, 94–98) provides a detailed discussion of the layout of streets and buildings of Kolonia.

33. Umesao 1944, 308–309. I have slightly rearranged the sentences of Umesao's original Japanese to make it more intelligible in English.

34. Price 1944, 143.

35. Ibid., 268.

36. Nan'yō Guntō Kyōkai 1965, 120–121.

37. The song, "The Daughter of the Village Chief" (*Sonchō no musume*), written in 1925 by Ishida Hitomatsu, was recorded on Polydor records in Osaka in May 1930 and quickly became popular in the Kansai region. Later, after Ishida revised it to make it easier to sing, it was again recorded by Polydor and soon became a national hit. During the Pacific War, it was much in demand in entertainment programs for Japanese soldiers and was often accompanied by a slightly obscene dance in which someone painted black played the role of the chief's daughter (Osada Gyōji, ed., 1968, *Nihon gunka dai zenshū* [Complete collection of Japanese military songs], Zen Ongakufu Shuppan, p. 188).

38. Umesao 1944, 451.

39. Ibid.; Barnett 1960, 16.

40. Shuster 1982*a*, 156.

41. Matsue 1932, 41.

42. Gondō 1939, 80–81; Andō 1936, 87.

43. Ochner 1984, 186.

44. Bascom 1965, 13; Ochner 1984, 155; Vidich 1980, 207; Tobin 1970, 27; Umesao 1944, 452.

45. Interview with Minoru Ueki, June 1983; Ballendorf, Shuster, and Higuchi 1986.

46. Ueki interview; NKK 1942, 2–3.

47. Price 1936, 88–89; Umesao 1944, 487.

48. Bascom 1965, 13; Hanlon 1981, 89.

49. Umesao 1944, 487.

50. Gondō 1939, 25–26; Ishikawa 1957, 223; Nonaka 1936, 126.

51. Umesao 1944, 407.

52. NKK 1943*d*, 44–45; NKK 1944*a*, 10. Oddly, no references to the 1941 ban on further Okinawan emigration to Micronesia appear in any of the Japanese sources I have used other than those cited here. Even the postwar history of Okinawan emigration (Okinawa Ken 1974) is silent on the subject.

53. Akamine 1978, 215.

54. The flood of Japanese commentary on Japan's role in the tropics may also have been influenced by the fact that during the 1930s the future of Caucasians in the tropics had been the subject of investigations in a number of Western works, most notably A. Grenfell Price's *White Settlers in the Tropics* (New York: American Geographic Society, 1939).

55. Komeda Masatake, writing in a contemporary journal of colonial studies, asserted the supposedly unique collective experience of the Japanese people in adjusting to the notoriously humid conditions of their summer rainy season and stressed that Westerners lacked an equivalent acclimatizing tradition. It is obvious from his argument that he had never spent a summer on the eastern seaboard of the United States (Komeda 1939, 79–81).

56. Umesao 1944, 409–410.

57. Ibid., 449.

58. Ishikawa 1957, 444.

59. Shuster 1982*b*, 23.

60. My discussion of the establishment of the Kampei Taisha Nan'yō Jinja at Koror is almost entirely based on Shuster's interesting and detailed account (1982*b*, 27–33).

61. The shrine itself had a brief and inauspicious life. Umesao Tadao visited it a half year after the enshrinement ceremonies and thought its buildings and precincts still too raw and gaudy, but considering the fertile nature of the tropics, looked to the day some years forward when, suitably sheltered by trees and growth, they would be majestic in appearance. Nature has more than done its part in the four and a half decades since, but in the vicissitudes of war the shrine has disappeared. Though it was untouched in the American bombing runs over Koror in 1944, its sacred symbols were returned to Japan by submarine late that year. After the war, it was dismantled for building material in the reconstruction of Koror. Today, only a few minutes walk from the Nikko Hotel, the site is almost unrecognizable. Only the steps, the great stone lanterns, and a marker remain, and all are covered by dense overgrowth and trees whose gnarled branches stretch across what was once the courtyard. As of 1983 plans were afoot by a Japanese Shintō sect to reconstruct the shrine at a cost of two million dollars (Umesao 1944, 406; Koror State Government, *Newsletter* 1:5, 1983).

Chapter 8: A Question of Bases

1. My own perspectives on this historical problem as outlined in this chapter have largely been shaped by the following three sources, even where they have not been specifically cited: Burns (1968), the most judicious study of the problem; Wilds (1955), an apparently authoritative review of the Japanese documentary evidence of the period; and BBKS (1970, 18–48), the most complete published record on the problem from the Japanese side.

2. For a more detailed overview of the strategic features of the principal Micronesian islands see Hobbs (1945, 3–135).

3. The Japanese navy's interceptive strategies of the 1920s and 1930s are discussed in Ikeda (1960, 2:137–138) and in Pelz 1974, 34–39.

4. Gabe 1982, 55 (8): 83, and BBKS 1970, 55.

5. Cited in Gabe (1982, 55 [8]: 82–83), these documents are to be found in Kaigunshō n.d., vols. 52 and 53.

6. Reber 1977, 54–55; Ballendorf 1983, 53–54.

7. During the 1922 Washington Naval Conference, for example, the Hearst newspapers were claiming, without factual evidence, that Japan was well on the way to building a "great fortified submarine base" on Saipan (*San Francisco Examiner*, 12 January 1922). In the immediate post–World War II years, American writers, including some who should have known better, were still at it, dropping in eyebrow-raising references to long-standing Oriental treachery. "The 'Little Prussians of the East' " wrote the author of a popular book on American submarine warfare published a few years after the war, "immediately violated their diplomatic promises not to fortify these island groups, and set out to turn Truk into a west-central Pacific Gibraltar. How the Japanese could build this oceanic fortress behind a veil of secrecy remains one of those secrets of the armament world . . ." (Roscoe 1949, 154).

8. Ballendorf 1984*a*, 84–86. The Japanese government tolerated the presence of Burns Philp in the Marshalls only to lend support to its request to the Australian government that reciprocity be granted to Japanese vessels seeking to trade along the coast of the Australian mandated territory in New Guinea. When nothing came of the extended negotiations on this issue, Japan applied sufficient pressure on Burns Philp to force it out of the Micronesian trade. I am indebted to Professor R. D. Walton of Griffith University, Brisbane, for information on this point. See also note 10.

9. Blakeslee 1922, 105; Wood 1921, 752; Pomeroy 1948, 59; Gaimushō Jōyakukyoku Hōkika 1962, 2:297. Though couched in terms of the naval administration during World War I, these regulations remained in force throughout the mandate period and were regularly reprinted in Japan's annual reports to the League of Nations Permanent Mandates Commission.

10. As British Commonwealth representatives to the Paris Peace Conference in 1919 had doggedly rejected Japanese proposals that all the mandated territories be open to trade, rejections which had not been opposed by the United States delegates, Western governments were in no position to make an issue of the situation.

11. Ballendorf 1984*a*, 88. In evaluating such reports one must keep in mind that the Japanese navy, which occupied the islands for nearly eight years, would naturally have maintained some facilities ashore.

12. Ibid., 86.

13. Burns 1968, 449–450.

14. Ballendorf 1984*a*, 86–89.

15. Ibid., 90–93.

16. Ibid., 94–95.

17. While the last word on the Ellis mission remains to be written, the two best summaries are the articles by Ballendorf (1984a) and Reber (1977).

18. It is ironic that several years after Earl Ellis had stumbled around Micronesia, his movements and intentions well known to the Japanese and his accomplishments nearly worthless, the Japanese army general staff quietly infiltrated an expert topography specialist, Lt. Maeda Masami, into the Philippines. Maeda spent three years in those islands, particularly in Luzon, gathering topographical, meteorological, and tide data. On the basis of his reports, by 1929 the general staff had worked out meticulous contingency plans for operations against all important areas in the Philippines (BBKS 1967b, 300–301).

19. Ballendorf 1984a, 96–97.

20. United States Department of State (hereafter, USDS) 1944, 256–259.

21. Ibid., 260.

22. USDS 1954, 984–992.

23. BBKS 1970, 14–15; Nan'yō Guntō Kyōkai 1965, 107–109.

24. The speaker was Lord Moyne, who was traveling around the world with his wife collecting ethnographical material for the British Museum. The arrival of his yacht off Koror in 1935 was met with a good deal of suspicion by Japanese harbor and police officials (Moyne 1936, 192–197).

25. USDS 1944, 260.

26. Ibid.

27. LN-PMC 22nd Session, 11 November 1932, 114–115, and Annex 7, 319–320.

28. The best summary of the conflict of scholarly opinion at the time can be found in Clyde (1935, 178–201).

29. Shakai Mondai Kenkyūkai, eds., 1976: *Kampō gōgai* [Official Gazette, extra edition], *Sokkiroku* [Minutes], 1 February 1934, p. 407, and 2 February 1934, p. 21, in *Teikoku gikaishi* [Records of the Imperial Diet], 1st ser., vols. 17–18, 65th Diet Session (1976 re-edition, Tōyō Bunka Sha).

30. There is reason to believe, however, that even after their withdrawal from the League of Nations the Japanese were still vexed by world opinion concerning the legitimacy of Japan's position in Micronesia. One recent researcher has claimed that, as Japan's relations with Germany became closer in the 1930s, the Japanese government (taking a different stance from that of Hirota) seriously considered the idea of returning the islands to Germany, then buying them back again, in order to settle Japan's claim once and for all. The idea was discussed, supposedly, among the war, navy, and foreign ministries and authority was received from the throne early in 1938 to enter into such an arrangement, but nothing ever came of it (Hatano 1984, 282).

31. USDS 1950, 339; NKK 1943c, 6–7.

32. See, for example, Kaigunshō 1933.

33. Yano 1979, 171–191; Hatano 1984, 277–284.

34. LN-PMC 26th Session, 6 November 1934, 90–94; USDS 1950, 338.

35. One of the obstacles facing prospective foreign travelers to Micronesia after 1933 was the difficulty in obtaining passage on any NYK steamer to the islands, due largely to a confidential NYK policy, made apparently under pressure of the Nan'yō-chō and the navy, of refusing passage to foreigners wishing to enter the mandate. The company's agents overseas were told to discourage prospective foreign passengers by advising them that the line was not suited to accommodation of foreigners, that hotel facilities in the islands would not be to foreign taste, that sailing schedules between the islands were inconvenient, and so on. If a foreign traveler persisted in trying to obtain passage, the application

was to be accepted only after it had been secretly approved by the Nan'yō-chō. However, no restrictions were placed on travel to the islands by ordinary Japanese. This evasive policy, encountered and eventually overcome by Willard Price in traveling to Micronesia in 1935, was revealed in evidence presented at the Tokyo war crimes trials (Price 1936, 176–180, 183–184; International Military Tribunal for the Far East (hereafter IMTFE), *Transcript Record*, vol. 21: pp. 9140–9143, and 9147–9150.

36. *Palo Alto Times*, 8 November 1934; Bodley 1934, 104–107.

37. Clyde 1935, vi, 222.

38. Price 1936, 15–18, 176–180, 183–184, 188–189. On the question of Japanese perfidy or innocence in Micronesia, Price trimmed his sails to the winds of national sentiment. During World War II, using essentially the same material presented in his 1936 book, he wrote *Japan's Islands of Mystery* (1944), which made it appear as if Japan had been using the islands for military purposes all along.

39. As of this writing, the most recent entry in the ever-growing list of works on Earhart and her disappearance is *Amelia Earhart: The Final Story* (Loomis with Ethell 1985). Using some interesting new testimony from Marshallese, some plausible guesswork, and alleged evidence from the logs of several Japanese warships, Loomis has given slightly more substance to the theory that Earhart and her navigator, Fred Noonan, beached their aircraft on the reef of Mili Atoll in the Marshalls, were captured by the Japanese, and eventually were transported to Saipan, where Noonan was executed and Earhart died of dysentery. While the argument is superficially plausible, careful reading shows that it raises more questions than it answers. Moreover, Loomis provides no specific citations from the evidence he claims to have used, except for reproduction, at the end of the volume, of the originals and translations of what he calls "secret Japanese record traffic" during the period immediately after Earhart's disappearance. These, in fact, utterly fail to support Loomis' contention that the government lied to cover up Earhart's capture.

In recent years, some Japanese writers have picked up and embellished some of the more sensational theories surrounding Earhart's disappearance (see for example, Aoki 1983). For a point-by-point refutation of such views, see Nakajima (1984*b*).

40. See Burke (1970, 233–240) for a good summary of the reasons why it is illogical to believe that Earhart was on an espionage mission or was captured by the Japanese.

41. BBKS 1970, 55. Testifying for the defense at the Tokyo war crimes trials, Hayashi Hisao, governor of the Nan'yō from 1933 to 1936, claimed that these facilities were constructed specifically for civil air transportation, which was to be a key part of the government's ten-year plan, begun in 1935, for the development of Micronesia. Kondō Shunsuke, governor from 1940 to 1943, also testifying at the trials, claimed that the navy was asked to provide technical, material, and logistical assistance to the project, which was, however, essentially civilian. IMTFE, *Transcript Record*, vol. 60, pp. 26,491–26,497.

42. In the 1930s similar improvements to certain American island territories offer an interesting and often overlooked parallel. In 1935, Guam and Midway became stops on Pan American Airways' pioneering trans-Pacific mail and passenger route. With the cooperation of the United States Navy, the channel at Apra Harbor at Guam was improved and landing ramps and hangars erected for the big Pan American clippers; at Guam and Midway radio beacons were installed. The next year the United States announced that it would spend $2 million to improve seaplane bases at Midway and Wake. The American navy

insisted that these facilities had nothing to do with militarizing the islands, but acknowledged that they would be available for "emergencies." Strategy-minded Japanese were not so sure and continued, mistakenly, to refer to Guam as a major American military base (Burns 1968, 452–453).

43. BBKS 1970, 56–57, 70–72.

44. Ibid., 60 (chart). The plannine for these and later naval air facilities in Micronesia was initiated by Captain (later Vice Admiral) Kusaka Ryūnosuke, chief of the First Section, Naval Air Headquarters (Hatano 1986, 220).

45. In April 1937, a Norwegian ship captain, whose freighter had foundered in the Marshalls, was rescued and then detained by the Japanese on Jaluit. Upon his release, he claimed to have observed an aircraft carrier and three destroyers anchored in the Jaluit lagoon (USDS 1954*b*, 812–813).

46. Testifying at the Tokyo war crimes trials, former navy captain Yoshida Hidemi, section chief in the naval affairs division of the Navy Ministry, 1941–1945, with duties relating to the defense of Micronesia, declared that the Japanese navy made a distinction between "naval bases" *(konkyochi)* and sites that could be used for operations *(kichi)*. The former possessed important facilities necessary for use by the fleet (accommodations for major fleet units, repair facilities, dry docks, stores for naval ammunition, supplies, etc.); the latter simply designated places where ships could anchor, planes could land, or supplies could be delivered (though the definition left unclear the question of whether it included sites that had been improved by construction). According to Yoshida, fortifications were defined, in the navy's view, by two characteristics: first, armaments and fixed defenses enabling such places to repel enemy attack by land, sea, or air; and second, the presence of land forces to defend them (IMTFE, *Transcript Record*, vol. 60, pp. 26,471 and 26,485–26,486).

47. Wilds 1955, 402. After 1937, the navy's liaison officer at Koror, a position that had been a sinecure in the 1920s and early 1930s, became the most influential official in Micronesia. It was his job to supervise a whole range of activities—harbor improvements, communications, entry and departure of warships, procurement of supplies, and so on—in which the navy did not wish to show its hand. According to one former Nan'yō-chō official, the navy's liaison office at Koror worked closely with the Nan'yō-chō governor on these matters, and the costs were buried in the Nan'yō-chō budget (BBKS 1970, 14–15; Nan'yō Guntō Kyōkai 1965, 107–109).

48. United States Department of the Army [hereafter USD Army] 1943, 1–2; USD Army 1944, 4–6.

49. BBKS 1970, 60–61. As of May 1940, the Fourth Fleet essentially consisted of an older light cruiser (the fleet flagship), two seaplane tenders, a destroyer flotilla, a submarine flotilla, and twenty-four Kawanishi Type 97 flying boats of the Yokohama Naval Air Corps (ibid., 72–73, 78–79).

50. Wilds 1955, 404–406; BBKS 1970, 72–79.

51. An example of this reliance on human labor was the construction of the airstrip on Eten Island, Truk. Leveling one half of the island for the airstrip took nearly seven years, from 1934 to 1941, largely because nearly all the work was undertaken by dynamite, pickax, and shovel (conversation with Antolin Sotan, my guide on Truk and Eten, June 1983).

52. *Kochi Shimbun,* 15 June 1983; Spoehr 1949, 33; IMTFE, *Transcript Record*, vol. 21, p. 135.

53. BBKS 1970, 62–64.

54. Of all the monuments erected to the futile Japanese military effort in Micronesia, surely the saddest must be those on Wotje and Moen in memory of convict prisoners who died there even before a shot was fired. One of those who

survived, but remained in the islands through the Pacific War, was Kubota Kiyoshi, who was sentenced to Yokohama Central Prison for his political views,
released at age twenty-one for conscript labor in Micronesia, and sent to Moen
with the "Green Battalion" (so called, because its members wore green
fatigues). Kubota stayed on at Moen with over one hundred others of his group,
of whom only ten survived the bombing, starvation, and disease of the war. His
Harujima monogatari (1968) became a classic tale of war's privations and horrors.

55. Wilds 1955, 406–407; BBKS 1970, 58–59.

56. As of 8 December 1941 the major units of the Fourth Fleet were deployed
as follows: Headquarters at Truk; Fleet Surface Force (four light cruisers, eight
destroyers, three mine layers, and various auxiliary vessels), variously disposed;
Fleet Submarine Force (nine submarines and tender), variously disposed;
Twenty-fourth Air Flotilla, Kwajalein, Wotje, and Palau; Fifth Base Force,
Saipan; Third Base Force, Palau; Fourth Base Force, Truk and Ponape; and
Sixth Base Force, Kwajalein, Wotje, Jaluit, and Maloelap. The militarization of
Japanese Micronesia in the last years before the war was entirely a navy under-
taking; indeed, no army troops were dispatched to the islands until 1943.

57. Wilds 1955, 406; Denfeld 1984, 8–9.

58. Wilds 1955, 404. It is a mark of how little the United States knew, even
after World War II, of Japanese prewar naval preparations in Micronesia, that
at the Tokyo trials the prosecution not only failed to prove its charge that Japan
had fortified the islands in violation of international agreement, but chose not
to challenge any of the defense testimony (some of it patently false) that argued
otherwise. In the decades since the trials, efforts have been made by Japanese to
disprove the sweeping indictment of Japan on the fortification by marshaling
additional testimony, but these rebuttals, while worthy of serious consideration, are themselves flawed by a rather selective presentation of evidence. See,
for example, Okumiya 1968, 66–73.

59. Sadao Asada, 1973, the Japanese Navy and the United States, in *Pearl
Harbor as History: Japanese-American Relations, 1931–1941,* edited by Doro-
thy Borg and Shumpei Okamoto (New York: Columbia University Press), p.
255; Sadao Seno, 1974, A Chess Game with no Checkmate: Admiral Inoue and
the Pacific War, in *Naval War College Review* (January–February): 26–39.

60. Denfeld 1981*a*, 1–3.

61. Okumiya 1968, 71.

Chapter 9: "Crushed Jewels" and Destitute Garrisons

1. USD Army 1943, 5–6; USD Army 1944, 9–10; BBKS 1970, 288–300. Morison 1950, 160–163, 184–186, 230–254.

2. Morison 1950, 74–75; BBKS 1970, 379–388.

3. Japan maintained a number of fleets, mostly according to capital ship categories. However, the Combined Fleet [Rengō Kantai] was a composite armada
of battleships, cruisers, destroyers, submarines, auxiliaries, and aircraft, making it the largest force in the Japanese navy, though it rarely operated in its
entirety.

4. Morison 1951, 316.

5. My description of the atmosphere surrounding the Combined Fleet at
Truk is based on Agawa (1979, 206, 326–328, 338–339) and Niina 1978, 206–
207.

6. BBKS 1974, 5–6; Hayashi and Coox 1959, 72–73.

7. In 1943, the navy reassumed an old responsibility: direction of civil affairs

in Micronesia. In November of that year, the last civilian governor of the Nan'yō-chō, Kondō Shunsuke, was replaced by a naval officer who had fallen from grace, Vice Admiral Hosogaya Boshirō, former commander of the Fifth Fleet. He had been placed on reserve after what the navy high command had considered his lackluster performance at the Battle of the Komandorski Islands in the North Pacific, in March 1943. In 1944, after the American invasion of Palau, the administrative center of the Nan'yō-chō was moved back to Truk.

8. BBKS 1973, 519–521; Crowl and Love 1955, 210–211. It is mark of the deep and continuing fissures between the army and the navy that, on a number of islands—Saipan and the Palaus in particular—the introduction of army units was to create arguments and jealousies. Unlike the rarely serious jeering between enlisted men in the various branches of the American armed forces, these interservice antagonisms between the Japanese services had their origins in the hubris of their high commands and proved to be a preposterous and crippling obstacle to a truly coordinated strategy in the Pacific.

9. Denfeld 1981a, 16–21; Momm 1945.

10. Denfeld 1981b, 6–7.

11. Ibid., 1–2; Morison 1951, 302–303.

12. Crowl and Love 1955, 193–195.

13. Ibid., 195–199; Morison 1951; Craven and Cate 1950, 305–310.

14. Morison 1951, 225–227; Shaw, Nalty, and Turnbladh 1966, 142–143.

15. BBKS 1973, 596–597, 600–601; Morison 1951, 223.

16. BBKS 1973, 597–598; Shaw, Nalty, and Turnbladh 1966, 143–152, 155–175.

17. BBKS 1967, 228–236; Shaw, Nalty, and Turnbladh 1966, 175–179; Crowl and Love 1955, 230–301.

18. BBKS 1967, 258–259.

19. Ibid., 259–262; Shaw, Nalty, and Turnbladh 1966, 191–193.

20. BBKS 1967, 263; Shaw, Nalty, and Turnbladh 1966, 192.

21. BBKS 1967, 263–266; Shaw, Nalty, and Turnbladh 1966, 193–205.

22. BBKS 1967, 266–268; Shaw, Nalty, and Turnbladh 1966, 205–209; Morison 1951, 299.

23. BBKS 1967, 268–271.

24. BBKS 1973, 637.

25. The mop-up campaign, conducted almost entirely by marines from the invasion force on Kwajalein, lasted from early March to late April. Arno Atoll, only a few miles from the holdout Japanese base on Mili, had already been occupied without incident on 12 February. On Wotho, occupied on 8 March, all twelve Japanese on the atoll, survivors of a plane crash, committed suicide rather than surrender, as did all but one of the six weather observers on Ujae two days later. Lae Atoll, which had been the initial focus of Japanese interest in Micronesia some sixty years before, was lost by Japan on 10 March, as was Lib the next day. But on Ailinglapalap, where Suzuki Tsunenori had landed in 1884, a thirty-nine man garrison, well entrenched, offered furious resistance before being annihilated, on 21 March. Two days later, the marine landing party on Ebon met with similar do-or-die defense in which all of the seventeen-man garrison were killed, about the same time as Namorik and Kili, without any Japanese soldiers, were occupied peacefully. On Namu, the sole Japanese policeman, a schoolteacher, his wife, and three children came down to the beach with a white flag to surrender. No Japanese were found on Ailuk or Likiep, which were occupied on 30 March, but every member of the six-man weather station on Mejit fought to the death that same day. Without any Japanese garrisons, Ailingnae, Rongerik, and Bikar atolls were taken without inci-

dent, but the five Japanese soldiers on Bikini committed suicide on 30 March. On 5 April the marines taking Utirik had to kill the fourteen-man garrison before they could occupy the atoll, but those landing the same day on Rongelap found it to be unoccupied. On 17 April, Erikub (five miles from Wotje) and Aur (ten miles from Maloelap) were occupied without incident. The last of the Marshall atolls, Ujelang, was taken by American army troops on 21 April, after desperate resistance by the eighteen-man garrison (Shaw, Nalty, and Turnbladh 1966, 216–219).

26. Introduction to Yoshida 1985, xxi–xxii.

27. Derived from an ancient Chinese reference, the term was apparently revived in the nineteenth century by the great Satsuma figure and revered military hero of the early Meiji period, Saigo Takamori.

28. BBKS 1966, 523–525.

29. Morison 1951, 317.

30. BBKS 1974, 245–246.

31. Ibid., 254; BBKS 1973, 627–628; Hayashi 1959, 77, 84.

32. Craven and Cate 1950, 684–687; Morison 1953, 38–40.

33. Blair 1975, 310, 453, 535; Takeuchi 1982.

34. BBKS 1973, 611–612; Craven and Cate 1950, 307; Morison 1953, 40–41.

35. Morison 1953, 32.

36. Craven and Cate 1953, 299.

37. Craven and Cate 1950, 685–687, 692.

38. Morison 1951, 307.

39. Never really having been a fighting force, the Fourth Fleet at Truk was now relegated to a theoretical and melancholy function, command over all the bypassed atolls and islands of the Marshalls and Carolines.

40. Shaw, Nalty, and Turnbladh 1966, 256–257.

41. BBKS 1967, 615, 618.

42. Ibid., 399–401, 406.

43. Ibid., 395–396, 417–418, 421; Shaw, Nalty, and Turnbladh 1966, 258.

44. BBKS 1967a, 407.

45. Ibid.

46. Ibid., 407–408; Shaw, Nalty, and Turnbladh 1966, 258–262.

47. BBKS 1967a, 463–466.

48. Dull 1978, 303–309.

49. Shaw, Nalty, and Turnbladh 1966, 292.

50. See the harrowing account of a Japanese nurse at the hospital in Toland (1970, 507–510).

51. All accounts in English state that Saitō composed this final order to the Saipan garrison. The wording of the message in its entirety suggests that was so, but the official Japanese history of the campaign specifically appends Nagumo's name to the message since he was technically overall commander on Saipan (BBKS 1967a, 500–503).

52. Ibid., 503–506; Shaw, Nalty, and Turnbladh 1966, 340; Toland 1970, 512–513.

53. BBKS 1967a, 506–508; Sherrod 1945, 145–148.

54. For discussions of the Japanese internment at Susupe from both sides of the wire, see Russell (1983) and Hamaguchi (1985).

55. BBKS 1967a, 512–513. Ōba's saga has been recounted in a popular work by Don Jones, *Oba, The Last Samurai: Saipan, 1944–45* (Novato, CA: Presidio Press, 1986).

56. Shaw, Nalty, and Turnbladh 1966, 364.

57. BBKS 1967a, 610–612.

58. Ibid., 638–641.

59. According to the official Japanese history of the campaign nearly 9500 Japanese and nearly 2700 Korean noncombatants survived the battle. Tragically some 3500 civilians were killed or committed suicide (ibid., 642).

60. As in the Marshalls, there were now a number of bypassed and beleaguered garrisons in the Marianas: a battalion and a company each of engineers and artillery on Rota; a regiment and some service units on Pagan; and on Aguiguan forty men of the Fiftieth Regiment.

61. BBKS 1966, 65.

62. Smith 1953, 461–462.

63. Ibid., 462–463.

64. Ibid., 461; BBKS 1966, 151–153; Garand and Strobridge 1971, 70–73.

65. Garand and Strobridge 1971, 222.

66. Ibid., 68–69.

67. Ibid., 221–222.

68. BBKS 1966, 221–222.

69. Morison 1958, 35.

70. BBKS 1966, 199.

71. Ibid., 204.

72. Morison 1958, 47–52.

73. Ochner 1984, 180–184; Nan'yō Guntō Kyōkai 1965, 94.

74. Bowers 1950, 47; Fischer and Fischer 1957, 61–62, 79. Such enforced separation appears to have contributed to a further drop in the Micronesian birth rate.

75. Bascom 1950, 145; Brower 1975, 45, 101.

76. *Kochi Shimbun*, 16 June 1983.

77. Bowers 1950, 56; Nan'yō Guntō Kyōkai 1966, 114–116.

78. Bascom 1965, 120–121.

79. Nan'yō Guntō Kyōkai 1966, 116–117; Nan'yō Guntō Kyōkai 1965, 94.

80. *Kochi Shimbun*, 18 June 1983.

81. These elements and the growing anti-Japanese mood they inspired among Micronesians existed only on islands where there were substantial numbers of Japanese troops. On the remoter atolls of the Marshalls and the Carolines, where Japanese garrisons were either minuscule or nonexistent, and which in consequence were untouched by American bomb or shell, the impact of the war was slight. Principally, with an end to the copra trade, the Micronesians were without a cash crop and were thrown back on their own resources, but this was scarcely a genuine hardship.

82. Shuster 1982a, 173–177; Kitaoka 1974, 16 (4): 39.

83. Kitaoka 1974, 16 (4): 39; Watakabe (1965, 120–152) provides a moving account of the innocent bravado and forlorn aftermath of the volunteer unit from Ponape. The saga of the 104th Construction Detachment from Palau was dramatized after the war in a film, *Minami no shima ame ga furu* [It rains in the southern islands].

84. At least on some of the larger islands, however, there is evidence that amicable relations continued to exist between Micronesians and Japanese civilians, particularly the remaining officials of the Nan'yō-chō. One former official recalled years later that when the Japanese were evacuated from Koror at the end of the war, Palauan friends came down to the docks weeping bitterly, to bid them farewell.

85. Joseph and Murray 1951, 47; Spoehr 1949, 33. There is at least some evidence that the brutality and desperation of some Japanese garrisons in the war's last months may have reached the point where local Japanese commanders

seriously considered the slaughter of all nearby Micronesians, though for what purpose is not clear. I encountered an account of such plans in the Marshalls and I understand that a similar story circulates on Ponape and Truk. Its most dramatic and detailed version is recounted on Rota, where it is claimed that just before the end of the war Japanese officers supervised the digging of a secret pit into which the bodies of the Chamorros were to have been thrown after being cut down with machine guns (conversation of author with Dr. William Peck, longtime resident on Rota, July 1983). Elsewhere in the Pacific, Japanese garrisons most certainly carried on massacres on Ocean and Nauru islands at the very end of the war. See Nakajima (1986).

86. Hall and Pelzer 1946, 100; Bascom 1950, 130.

87. Heine 1979, 19–20.

88. BBKS 1966, 450.

89. Ibid., 448–449.

90. Because of its location, Rota was perhaps the only island that continued to serve even a minimally useful purpose. Since the garrison could observe American flights from Saipan, Tinian, or Guam, its lookouts would telephone the high command in Tokyo every time B-29s were observed taking off for bombing runs against the Japanese islands (ibid., 599).

91. Ibid., 496–497.

92. Ibid., 541.

93. Ibid., 599–601, 606–607.

94. Craven and Cate 1950, 692.

95. BBKS 1966, 440–441, 460, 465, 538, 548, 550, 556–557.

96. My summary of the torment of the Woleai garrison is based on BBKS (1966, 559–590), and Asahi Shimbun Sha (1966, 332–350).

97. BBKS 1966, 451–453, 460, 465.

98. The surrender is described by Charles Blackton (1946), an eyewitness. See also Frank and Shaw (1968, 452–455).

99. Requiring, as they did, the expulsion of all Japanese citizens from Micronesia, American deportation and repatriation policies resulted in some bitter and anomalous situations. For example, young Minoru Ueki, son of a Japanese father (by that time deceased) and a Palauan mother, was forced to go to Japan, a country he had never seen, all because he technically held Japanese citizenship. Some Japanese who had married Micronesian women left their wives and children behind rather than subject them to the uncertainties of a strange and ravaged land (conversation of author with Minoru Ueki, July 1983). Eventually, twenty-two Japanese and eleven Koreans were allowed to stay in Micronesia because of special circumstances in their cases (US Navy, OCNO 1948, 65).

100. BBKS 1966, 451–453, 460, 465, 497, 550, 557, 513.

101. It is said that when word of the privations of the Woleai garrison and the utmost devotion and loyalty of its commander reached the emperor he was so moved that he asked that Kitamura be brought to him, so that he might thank the general in person. But such was the confusion in Japan that autumn of 1945 that word never reached Kitamura. For the next two years he spent his time looking up as many as he could find of the bereaved families of his old command, in order to express his condolences. His task completed, General Kitamura Katsuzō committed seppuku at his home in Nagano City on the second anniversary of Japan's surrender (ibid., 589–590).

102. The most spectacular war crimes trial of Japanese officers who had served in Micronesia involved charges against navy Captain Iwanami Hiroshi, former fleet surgeon and commander of the naval hospital on Truk. Along with

eighteen codefendants, he stood accused of torturing to death eight American prisoners of war at Truk in 1944. Other trials involved four navy officers accused of murdering three American airmen on Jaluit in 1944, and various army and navy officers charged with beheading Marshallese and Rotanese as spies (Piccigallo 1979, 75–83).

103. BBKS 1967*a*, 513.

104. Because the American forces had taken over so much of their home islands for use as military facilities, many of the Okinawans imprisoned on Saipan were offered the opportunity to settle on Tinian, now empty except for the American base at its northern end. At first, many indicated interest in taking up the offer, but most who tried to make a new life on the war-devastated island eventually gave up, and by the end of 1946 all Okinawans had been repatriated.

Epilogue

1. For those who will never don aqualung and flippers, Sylvia A. Earle (1976) provides a fascinating pictorial tour of the wrecks and their accumulations of marine life.

2. Minoru Ueki, Palau's most distinguished physician, recalled that, years ago when he needed skeletal structures to teach human anatomy in his medical classes, he used to go to the caves of Pelelieu where the skeletons were heaped together in great piles (conversation with author, June 1983).

3. Robert Kiener (1978, "A Bulwark of the Pacific," *Glimpses of Micronesia and the Western Pacific* 18 [1], 33–38). The bone collection missions still continue, though on a reduced scale and generally only in response to specific sightings of remains that have been confirmed by the nearest Japanese consulate.

4. The Sakura-kai was originally founded by Minoru Ueki in the mid-1950s for the purpose of reuniting Japanese and Japanese-Palauan children with their Japanese parents who had left them in Palau, either because one parent had been forced to return to Japan or because the parents were fearful of conditions in the war-ravaged homeland. By the 1980s, with most of its cases closed either through successful reunions or conscious decisions to leave certain family separations as they were, the organization became largely ceremonial and commemorative (conversation of author with Dr. Ueki, June 1983).

5. Kitaoka 1974, 39–41; Mainichi Shimbun Sha 1978, 173.

6. Conversations of author with Minoru Ueki and with the late David Ramarui, June 1983.

7. In 1954 this closure order was lifted and Nankō was technically permitted to operate once more. But with no assets and all its prewar personnel dispersed, it never started up again. Takemura 1983, 94–96.

8. Fluker et al. 1978, 289–293. "Special Report on Japanese Investment in the Pacific Islands," *Pacific Magazine* (May–June 1985), 34–47.

9. "Mr. Pacific Surveys His Favorite Ocean," *Pacific Islands Monthly* (July 1985), 35–38.

10. Fluker et al. 1978, 295–297.

11. "Special Report," 34.

12. "Japanese Sigh for the 'Last Paradise' " *Pacific Islands Monthly* (July 1985), 33–35.

Bibliography

NOTE: All Japanese language titles were published in Tokyo, unless otherwise stated.

Agawa Hiroyuki
   1979   *The Reluctant Admiral: The Life of Yamamoto Isoroku*, translated by John Bester. Kodansha.

Akamine Hideo
   1978   "Nan'yō" fuchin shita Okinawa jin [Vicissitudes of Okinawans in the South Seas]. In Mainichi Shimbun Sha 1978, 215.

Andō Sakan (Sei)
   1936   *Nan'yō ki* [An account of the South Seas]. Shoshin Sha.

Aoki Fukiko
   1983   A. Iyahaato wa shokei sareta ka? [Was Amelia Earhart executed?]. *Bungei Shunjū* 61 (April), 392–418.

Aoyagi Machiko
   1985   *Modekngei: Mikuroneshia-Parao no shin, shūkyō* [A new religion in Palau, Micronesia]. Shinsensha.

Asahi Shimbunsha [Asahi Newspapers], eds.
   1966   *Mereon-to: sei to shi no kiroku* [Woleai Atoll: A record of life and death]. Asahi Shimbunsha.

Asai Tatsurō
   1944   Nihonjin [The Japanese]. In Imanishi 1944, *Ponape-tō: seitaigaku-teki kenkyū*, pt. 3, 315–398.

Ballendorf, Dirk A.
   1983   Earl Hancock Ellis: The Man and His Mission. United States Naval Institute *Proceedings*, November, 53–60.

   1984a   Secrets without Substance: U.S. Intelligence in the Japanese Mandates, 1915–1935. *Journal of Pacific History* 19 (2): 83–99.

   1984b   Micronesian Views of the Japanese: The Palauan Case. Paper presented at Micronesian Area Research Center, 3 October 1984.

Ballendorf, Dirk A., D. R. Shuster, and Higuchi Wakako
   1986   An Oral Historiography of the Japanese Administration in Palau. Micronesian Area Research Center monograph, University of Guam.

351

Ballendorf, Dirk A., et al.
1986   An Oral History of Japanese Schooling Experience of Chamorros in the Northern Mariana Islands. American Association of State and Local History monograph. Micronesian Area Research Center, University of Guam.

Barnett, H. G.
1960   *Being a Palauan.* New York: Holt, Rinehart, and Winston.

Bartlett, Norman
1954   *The Pearl Seekers.* London: Andrew Melrose.

Bascom, William R.
1950   Ponape, the Cycle of Empire. *Scientific Monthly* 70 (March): 141–150.

1965   *Ponape: A Pacific Economy in Transition. Anthropological Records* 22. Berkeley: University of California Press.

Betts, Raymond
1971   *Assimilation and Association in French-Colonial Theory.* New York: Columbia University Press.

Blackton, Charles
1946   The Surrender of the Fortress on Truk. *Pacific Historical Review* 14:400–408.

Blair, Clay, Jr.
1975   *Silent Victory: The U.S. Submarine War against Japan.* Philadelphia: Lippincott.

Blakeslee, George H.
1922   The Mandates of the Pacific. *Foreign Affairs* 1 (1): 98–115.

Bodley, Ronald Victor Courtenay
1933   *A Japanese Omelette: A British Writer's Impressions of the Japanese Empire.* Tokyo: Hokuseido Press.

1934   *The Drama of the Pacific.* Tokyo: Hokuseido Press.

Bōeichō Bōei Kenshūjō Senshishitsu [Self-Defense Agency, Self-Defense Research Institute, War History Office, BBKS]
1966   *Senshi Sōsho* [War history series]. Vol. 13, *Chūbu Taiheiyō rikugun sakusen, 2: Periryū, Angaru, Iōtō* [Army operations in the Central Pacific, part 2: Pelelieu, Anguar, & Iwo Jima]. Asagumo Shimbun Sha.

1967a   *Senshi Sōsho.* Vol. 6, *Chūbu Taiheiyō rikugun sakusen, 1: Mariana gyokusai made* [Army operations in the Central Pacific, part 1: Up to the loss of the Marianas].

1967b   *Senshi Sōsho.* Vol. 8, *Dai Hon'ei Rikugunbu, 1: Shōwa jūgonen gogatsu made* [Imperial General Headquarters: Army Division, part 1: Up to May 1940].

1970   *Senshi Sōsho.* Vol. 38, *Chūbu Taiheiyō hōmen kaigun sakusen, 1: Shōwa jūshichinen gogatsu made* [Naval operations in the Central Pacific area, part 1: Up to May 1942].

1973   *Senshi Sōsho.* Vol. 62, *Chūbu Taiheiyō hōmen kaigun sakusen, 2: Shōwa jūshichinen rokugatsu ikō* [Naval operations in the Central Pacific area, part 2: After June 1942].

1974   *Senshi Sōsho.* Vol. 71, *Dai Hon'ei Kaigun-bu; Rengō Kantai, 5: Dai sandan sakusen chuki* [Conduct of operations by Imperial General

Headquarters, Navy Division and Combined Fleet Headquarters, part 5: Middle phase of the third stage operation].

1975   *Senshi Sōsho*. Vol. 91, *Dai Hon'ei, Kaigun-bu; Rengō Kantai*, 1: *Kaisen made* [Imperial General Headquarters, Navy Division and Combined Fleet Headquarters, part 1: Up to the opening of hostilities].

Bowers, Neal M.
1950   *Problems of Resettlement on Saipan, Tinian, and Rota, Mariana Islands*. Coordinated Investigation of Micronesian Anthropology Report no. 31. Ann Arbor: Pacific Science Research Board and National Research Council.

1951   The Mariana, Volcano, and Bonin Islands. In *Geography of the Pacific*, edited by Otis W. Freeman, 205–235. New York: J. Wiley.

Braisted, William Reynolds
1971   *The United States Navy in the Pacific, 1909–1922*. Austin: University of Texas Press.

Brower, Kenneth
n.d.   *Micronesia: The Land, the People, and the Sea*. Singapore: Mobil Oil Micronesia. (1981, Baton Rouge: Louisiana State University Press.)

Burke, John
1970   *Winged Legend: The Story of Amelia Earhart*. New York: Putnam's Sons.

Burns, Richard Dean
1968   Inspection of the Mandates, 1919–1941. *Pacific Historical Review* 37 (4): 445–462.

Chen Ching-chik
1984   Police and Community Control Systems in the Empire. In *The Japanese Colonial Empire, 1895–1945*, edited by Ramon H. Myers and Mark R. Peattie, 213–239. Princeton: Princeton University Press.

Chen, I-te
1984   The Attempt to Integrate the Empire: Legal Perspectives. In *The Japanese Colonial Empire, 1895–1945*, edited by Ramon H. Myers and Mark R. Peattie, 240–275. Princeton: Princeton University Press.

Clyde, Paul H.
1935   *Japan's Pacific Mandate*. New York: Macmillan.

Cockrum, Emmett E.
1970   The Emergence of Modern Micronesia. PhD dissertation, University of Colorado.

Coulter, John Wesley
1969   *Trade Winds: Stories of the South Seas*. Milford, NH: Cabinet Press.

Crampton, Henry E.
1921   A Journey to the Mariana Islands—Guam and Saipan. *Natural History* 21 (2): 126–145.

Craven, Wesley Frank, and James Lea Cate, eds.
1950   *The Army Air Forces in World War II*. Vol. 4, *The Pacific: Guadalcanal to Saipan, August 1942 to July, 1944*. Chicago: University of Chicago Press.

1953   *The Army . . .* Vol. 5, *The Pacific: Matterhorn to Nagasaki, June,
        1944 to August, 1945.*

Crocombe, R. G.
1972   Land Tenure in the South Pacific. In *Man in the Pacific Islands:
        Essays on Geographical Change in the Pacific Islands,* edited by
        R. Gerard Ward, 219–251. Oxford: Clarendon Press.

Crowl, Philip A., and Edmund G. Love
1955   *Seizure of the Gilberts and Marshalls.* Washington, DC: Office of the
        Chief of Military History, Department of the Army.

Decker, John Alvin
1940   *Labor Problems in the Pacific Mandates.* London: Oxford University
        Press.

Denfeld, D. Colt
1979   *Field Survey of Ponape: World War II Features.* Micronesian Ar-
        chaeological Survey Report no. 2. Saipan: Historic Preservation
        Office, Trust Territory of the Pacific Islands.

1981a   *Field Survey of Truk: World War II Features.* Micronesian Archaeo-
        logical Survey Report no. 6. Saipan: Historic Preservation Office,
        Trust Territory of the Pacific Islands.

1981b   *Japanese Fortifications and Other Military Structures in the Central
        Pacific.* Micronesian Archaeological Survey Report no. 9. Saipan:
        Historic Preservation Office, Trust Territory of the Pacific Islands.

1984   Korean Laborers in Micronesia during World War II. *Korea Observ-
        er* 15 (1): 3–14.

Dingman, Roger
1976   *Power in the Pacific: The Origins of Naval Arms Limitation, 1914–
        1922.* Chicago: University of Chicago Press.

Dull, Paul S.
1978   *A Battle History of the Imperial Japanese Navy (1941–1945).* Annap-
        olis: U.S. Naval Institute Press.

Earle, Sylvia A.
1976   Life Springs from Death in Truk Lagoon. *National Geographic* 44
        (4): 578–603.

Ehrlich, Paul M.
1984   *Koror: A Center of Power, Commerce and Colonial Administration.*
        Micronesian Archaeological Survey Report no. 11. Saipan: Historic
        Preservation Office, Trust Territory of the Pacific Islands.

Emerick, Richard G.
1960   Homesteading on Ponape: A Study and Analysis of a Resettlement
        Program of the United States Trust Territory Government in Micro-
        nesia. PhD dissertation, University of Pennsylvania.

Farrell, Bryan H.
1972   The Alien and the Land of Oceania. In *Man in the Pacific Islands:
        Essays on Geographical Change in the Pacific Islands,* edited by
        R. Gerard Ward, 34–73. Oxford: Clarendon Press.

Fischer, John Lyle
1961   The Japanese Schools for the Natives of Truk, Caroline Islands.
        Human Organization 20:83–88.

Fischer, John L., and Ann M. Fischer
1957   *The Eastern Carolines*. New Haven: Pacific Science Board, National Academy of Sciences, National Research Council in association with Human Relations Area Files.

Fluker, Robert, Grant Goodman, Carl Lande, Nobleza Lande, Chae-jin Lee, and Felix Moos
1978   *The United States and Japan in the Western Pacific: Micronesia and Papua New Guinea*. Manhattan, KS: University of Kansas.

Frank, Benis M., and Henry I. Shaw, Jr.
1968   *History of U.S. Marine Corps Operations in World War II*. Vol. 5, *Victory and Occupation*. Historical Branch, G-3 Division Headquarters. Washington, DC: U.S. Marine Corps.

Frei, Henry
1984   Japan Discovers Australia: The Emergence of Australia in the Japanese World View, 1540's–1900. *Monumenta Nipponica* 39 (1): 55–81.

Freidel, Frank
1954   *Franklin D. Roosevelt: The Ordeal*. Boston: Little Brown.

Gabe Masaakira
1982   Nihon no Mikuroneshia senryō to "nanshin" [Japan's occupation of Micronesia and the "southward advance"]. Keiō Daigaku *Hōgaku Kenkyū* 55 (6): 71–89; 55 (8): 67–87.

Gaimushō [Japanese Foreign Ministry], eds.
1966   *Nihon gaikō bunshō* [Documents on Japanese foreign policy]. Vol. 3, *Taishō sannen* [1914].

Gaimushō Jōyakukyoku Hōkika [Foreign Ministry, Treaties Division, Laws and Regulations Section]
1962   *Gaichi hōsei shi* [Record of legislation for external territories]: *Inin tōchiryō Nan'yō guntō* [South Sea islands mandated territory], 2 vols.

Garand, George W., and Truman R. Strobridge
1971   *History of U.S. Marine Corps Operations in World War II*. Vol. 4, *Western Pacific Operations*. Historical Branch, G-3 Division Headquarters. Washington, DC: U.S. Marine Corps.

Gladwin, Thomas, and Seymour Sarason
1953   *Truk: Man in Paradise*. New York: Wenner-Gren Foundation.

Gō Takashi
1942   *Nan'yō bōeki go-jūnenshi* [Fifty years of commerce in the South Seas]. Nanyo Boeki KK.

Gondō Shigeyoshi
1939   *Nan'yō wa maneku* [The South Seas call]. Nihon Kōronsha.

Grahlfs, Francis
1955   The Effects of Japanese Administration of Micronesia: An Example of Culture Contact. MA thesis, Columbia University.

Greenberger, Allen J.
1974   Japan as a Colonial Power: The Micronesian Example. *Asian Profile* 2 (2): 151–164.

Hall, Edward T., and Karl J. Pelzer
  1946   *The Economy of the Truk Islands: An Anthropological and Eco-
         nomic Survey.* Honolulu: U.S. Commercial Company.

Hall, H. Duncan
  1948   *Mandates, Dependencies, and Trusteeship.* Washington, DC: Carne-
         gie Endowment for International Peace.

Hamaguchi Sadae
  1985   Saipan-tō minkan jinshūyōjō-nai no sangeki [The tragedy at the Sai-
         pan civil internment camp]. *Rekishi to Jimbutsu,* no. 171 (Decem-
         ber): 187–199.

Hanlon, David
  1981   *From Mesenieng to Kolonia: An Archaeological Survey of Historic
         Kolonia, Ponape, Eastern Caroline Islands.* Micronesian Archaeo-
         logical Survey Report no. 5. Saipan: Historic Preservation Office,
         Trust Territory of the Pacific Islands.

Hatano Sumio
  1984   Shōwa kaigun no nanshin ron [The Shōwa navy's southward ad-
         vance concept]. *Hishi: Taiheiyō senso* [Secret history: The Pacific
         War]. Special issue of *Rekishi to jimbutsu* (December): 277–285.

  1986   Nihon kaigun to "nanshin": sono seisaku to riron no shiteki tenkai
         [The Japanese navy and the "southward advance": Historical shifts
         in policy and theory]. In *Ryōtaisen kanki Nihon-Tōnan Ajia kankei
         no shōsō* [Various aspects of Japan–Southeast Asia relations between
         the world wars], edited by Shimizu Hajime, 207–236. Ajia Keizai
         Kenkyūjō.

Hayashi Saburo, in collaboration with Alvin D. Coox
  1959   *Kōgun: The Japanese Army in the Pacific War.* Quantico, VA: The
         Marine Corps Association.

Heine, Dwight
  1979   Reminiscence. *Micronesian Reporter* 27 (1): 18–21.

Hezel, Francis X., and M. L. Berg
  1979   *Winds of Change: A Book of Readings on Micronesian History.*
         Saipan: Trust Territory of the Pacific Islands, Education Depart-
         ment.

Hijikata Hisakatsu
  1973   *Ryūboku* [Driftwood]. Miraisha.

Hijikata Hisakatsu Ten Kaisai Iinkai [Committee for the exhibition of the works
of Hijikata Hisakatsu], eds.
  1971   *Hijikata Hisakatsu ten: Minami Taiheiyō ni romansu o motometa*
         [The Hijikata Hisakatsu exhibit: Pursuing the romance of the South
         Pacific].

Hobbs, William H.
  1923   *Cruises along the By-ways of the Pacific.* Boston: The Stratford Co.

  1945   *The Fortress Islands of the Pacific.* Ann Arbor, MI: University of
         Michigan Press

Ikeda Kiyoshi
  1967   *Nihon no kaigun* [The Japanese Navy]. 2 vols. Isseido.

Imanishi Kinji, ed.
1944   *Ponape-tō seitaigakuteki kenkyū* [Ponape island: Ecological research]. Shoko Shōin.

Inklé, Frank
1965   Japanese-German Peace Negotiations during World War I. *American Historical Review* 71:62–76.

Irie Toraji
1942   Haizan no yume no ato: Nan'yo gunto kaitakusha [Remnants of a defeated dream: Pioneers of South Seas development]. In *Hōjin kaigai hatten shi* [History of the progress of overseas Japanese], vol. 2: 234–256. Ida Shoten.

1943   *Meiji nanshin shikō* [A short history of Japan's southward movement]. Ida Shoten.

Ishikawa Tatsuzō Sakuhinshū [Collected works of Ishikawa Tatsuzo], vol. 6.
1957   Shinchōsha.

Itō Hirobumi Kankei Bunshō Kenkyūkai [Research association for documents relating to Itō Hirobumi], vol. 1.
1973   Hanawa Shobō.

Itō Toshio
1941   Nan'yō guntō nōgyō no tokushitsu [Special characteristics of South Sea islands agriculture]. *Nihon Tokushoku Kyōkai Kihō* 2:411–435.

Jose, Arthur W.
1943   *The Royal Australian Navy, 1914–1918*. Sydney: Angus & Robertson.

Joseph, Alice, and Veronica Murray
1951   *Chamorros and Carolinians of Saipan*. Cambridge: Harvard University Press.

Kaigun Gunshireibu [Naval General Staff]
n.d.   *Taishō san-yonnen kaigun senshi* [History of naval operations, 1914–15], vol. 5, pt 5. War History Room, Self-Defense Agency, Setagaya, Tokyo.

Kaigun Yūshūkai, eds.
1938   *Kinsei teikoku kaigun shiyō* [An outline history of the modern Imperial Japanese Navy]. Maruzen.

Kaigunshō [Navy Ministry]
n.d.   *Taishō sen'eki senji shorui* [Documents on wartime campaigns of the Taisho period]. War History Room, Self-Defense Agency, Setagaya, Tokyo.

Kaigunshō, Kaigun Gunji Fukyūbu [Navy Ministry, Naval Affairs Information Section]
1933   *Umi no seimeisen* [Our ocean lifeline].

Kaji Ryūichi
1973   *Meiji igo no godai kisha* [Five reporters since the Meiji period]. Asahi Shimbunsha.

Kajima Morinosuke, ed.
1980   *The Diplomacy of Japan, 1894–1922*. Vol. 3, *First World War, Paris Peace Conference, Washington Conference*. Kajima Institute of International Peace.

Kawakami, K. K.
1919   *Japan and World Peace*. New York: Macmillan.

Kerr, George
1958   *Okinawa: The History of an Island People*. Rutland, VT: Charles Tuttle.

Kikuchi Masao
1937   *Yakushin no Nan'yō* [The South Seas advance]. Toa Kyōkai.

Kida Jun'ichirō
1970   Nangokki [Records of southern lands]. In *Ajia e no yume* [Dreams of Asia], edited by Hanzawa Hiroshi, 186–232. Vol. 6 of *Meiji no gunzo* [Meiji images]. San'ichi Shobō.

Kitaoka Kazuyoshi
1974   Mikuroneja to Nihon o Kangaeru [Thinking about Micronesia and Japan]. *Asahi Jaanaru* 16 (3, 25 January): 70–74, and 16 (4, 1 February): 38–42.

Kobayashi Tatsuo
1966   *Suiso nikki: Itō-ke monjo* [The green rain dairy: Itō family documents]. Hara Shobō.

Komeda Masatake
1939   Nettai kankyō no ijūsha ni oyobasu eikyō: shū toshite Mariana guntō ni tsuite [The influence of tropical environment on Japanese emigrants, with special reference to the Mariana Islands]. *Takushoku Shōreikan Kihō* [Japanese Colonial Institute Quarterly] 1 (2): 75–92.

Konishi Tatehiko
1943   Nan'yō no kishō [Meteorology of the South Seas]. *Nan'yō Shiryō*, no. 331 (October). Nan'yō Keizai Kenkyūjō.

1944   Nan'yō guntō gaikan [Overall view of the South Seas islands]. *Nan'yō Shiryō*, no. 294 (August). Nan'yō Keizai Kenkyūjō.

Kubota Kiyoshi
1968   *Harujima monogatari* [A tale of Moen island]. Tōhō Shuppansha.

Lansing, Robert
1935   *War Memoirs*. Indianapolis: Bobbs-Merrill.

League of Nations, Permanent Mandates Commission (LN-PMC)
var.   *Minutes*.

Levi, Werner
1948   American Attitudes toward Pacific Islands, 1914–1919. *Pacific Historical Review* 17 (1): 55–64.

Lockwood, William
1954   *The Economic Development of Japan: Growth and Structural Change, 1868–1938*. Princeton: Princeton University Press.

Loomis, Vincent V., with Jeffrey Ethell
1985   *Amelia Earhart: The Final Story*. New York: Random House.

McMahon, J.
1919   Japanning the Marshall Islands. *Sunset*, July, 31–33.

Mainichi Shimbun Sha [Mainichi Newspapers], eds.
1978   *Taiwan, Nan'yō guntō, Karafuto* [Taiwan, South Sea islands, and Karafuto]. Vol. 3 of *Nihon shokuminchi shi* [A history of Japanese

colonies], in *Ichiokunin no Shōwa shi* [A history of one hundred million Japanese in the Shōwa period].

Matsue Haruji (Harutsugu)
1932   *Nan'yō kaitaku jūnen shi* [A record of ten years of development in the South Seas]. Nan'yō Kōhatsu, K.K.

Matsumura, Akira
1918   Contributions to the Ethnography of Micronesia. *Journal of the College of Science* 40: Article 7. (Tokyo Imperial University, 15 December.)

Matsuoka Shizuo
1943   *Mikuroneshia minzoku shi* [Ethnological record of Micronesia]. Iwanami Shoten.

Mitsubishi Keizai Kenkyūjō [Mitsubishi Economic Research Institute], eds.
1937   *Taiheiyō ni okeru kokusai keizai* [International economic relations in the Pacific]. Mitsubishi Keizai Kenkyūjō.

Miwa Kimitada
1970   Shiga Shigetaka (1863-1927): A Meiji Japanist's View of and Actions in International Relations. *Research Papers*, Series A-3. (Institute of International Relations, Sophia University.)

Mizoguchi Toshiyuki
1980   *Nihon tōjika ni okeru Nan'yō guntō no keizai hatten, 1922-1938* [Economic development of the South Pacific islands under Japanese administration, 1922-1938]. Discussion Paper Series, no. 31, April. (Economic Research Institute, Hitotsubashi University.)

Momm, Albert O.
1945   *Ponape: Japan's Island in the Eastern Carolines.* (n.p.)

Moos, Felix
1974   The Old and the New: Japan and the United States in the Pacific. In *Political Development in Micronesia,* edited by Daniel T. Hughes and Sherwood Lingenfelter, 278-298. Columbus, OH: Ohio State University Press.

Morison, Samuel Eliot
1950   *A History of United States Naval Operations in World War II.* Vol. 3, *The Rising Sun in the Pacific: December 1931 to April 1942.* Boston: Atlantic, Little, Brown.

1951   *A History* . . . Vol. 7, *Aleutians, Gilberts, and Marshalls: June 1942-April 1944.*

1953   *A History* . . . Vol. 8, *New Guinea and the Marianas: March 1944-August 1944.*

1958   *A History* . . . Vol. 12, *Leyte, June 1944-January 1945.*

Morizawa Takamichi
1983   Sekidō ni ikiru: Mori fuamirii no hyakunen [Living at the equator: A hundred years of the Mori family]. *Kochi Shimbun* (May 30-June 23).

Morton, Louis
1959   War Plan Orange: Evolution of a Strategy. *World Politics* 11:221-250.

Moyne, Walter Edward Guinness
1936   *Walkabout: A Journey in Lands between the Pacific and Indian Oceans.* London: William Heinemann.

Myers, Ramon H., and Mark R. Peattie, eds.
1984   *The Japanese Colonial Empire, 1895–1945.* Princeton: Princeton University Press.

Nagasawa Kazutoshi
1973   *Nihonjin no bōken to tanken* [Adventures and explorations of Japanese]. Hakusui sha.

Nakajima Hiroshi
1983a   Commentary. Appended to Suzuki 1983, pp. 1–34.

1983b   "Maasharu guntō tanken shimatsu" no nazo [The puzzle of particulars of an exploration in the South Seas]. *Taiheiyō Gakkai shi,* no. 20 (October): 9–12.

1984a   The First Japanese Officials Sent to Micronesia, 1884–85. *Asian Profile* 12:485–488.

1984b   Iyahaato no saigo no hikō ni tsuite [Concerning Earhart's last flight]. *Taiheiyō Gakkai shi,* no. 22 (April): 28–32.

1984c   Meiji sanjū yonen no Torakku zaichū Nihonjin zen'in tsuihō jiken [The expulsion of the entire Japanese community on Truk, 1899]. *Taiheiyō Gakkai shi,* no. 23 (July): 62–65.

1986   Nauru, Ōshiyan no Nihon no kaigun [The Japanese navy on Nauru and Ocean islands]. *Taiheiyō Gakkai shi,* no. 30 (April): 8–9.

Nakamura Yoshihiko
1980–   Kaigun taisa Matsuoka Shizuo to sono kyōdai [Navy captain Matsu-
1981   oka Shizuo and his brother]. *Kaigun Geppō,* no. 3 (October 1980): 41–50; no. 4 (December 1980): 52–62; no. 5 (February 1981): 38–47.

Nantaku kai
1982   *Nantaku shi* [Annals of the South Seas Colonization Corporation]. Nantaku kai.

Nan'yō-chō, eds.
1932   *Nan'yō-chō jūnen shisei shi* [A ten-year history of the South Seas Government]. Nan'yō-chō Chōkan Kambō.

1937   *Nan'yō-chō guntō keisatsu gaiyō* [A summary of the police in the South Sea islands]. Nan'yō-chō.

Nan'yō-chō Chōkan Kambō
1933,   *Nanyōchō tōkei nenkan* [Statistical yearbook of the South Seas
1937   Bureau]. Nan'yō-chō.

Nan'yō-chō Dagurasu hikōtei junnan shichi yūshi tsuitō go [Memorial issue on the seven brave martyrs aboard the South Sea Government's Douglas flying boat].
1939   *Nan'yō Guntō* 5 (2, February).

Nan'yō Guntō Kyōiku-kai
1938   *Nan'yō Guntō Kyōiku shi* [History of education in the South Sea islands]. Palau.

Nan'yō Guntō Kyōkai [South Sea Islands Association], eds.
1965   *Omoide no Nan'yō guntō* [Recollections of the South Sea islands]. Nan'yō Guntō Kyōkai.

1966   *Yashi no ki wa karezu: Nan'yō guntō no genjitsu to omoide* [The unwithered palms: Realities and recollections of the South Sea islands]. Sōdo Bunka.

n.d.   *Nan'yō Guntō Kyōkai Kaihō* [Bulletin of the . . . Association]. Special issue on Tinian.

Nan'yō Keizai Kenkyūjo [South Economic Research Institute, NKK], eds.

1942   *Garumisukan shokumin kaihatsu kaiko* [Recollections of the development of Garumisukan colony]. *Nan'yō Shiryō*, no. 163.

1943*a*   Taiheiyō minzokugaku no kaiso: kaigun taisa Matsuoka Shizuo [The founder of the ethnology of the Pacific: Navy captain Matsuoka Shizuo]. *Nan'yō Shiryō*, no. 152.

1943*b*   *Parao Asahimura kensetsu nenpyō* [A chronological record of the founding of Asahi Village on Palau]. *Nan'yō Shiryō*, no. 242.

1943*c*   Parao Asahi Mura ni okeru dai-kagyū hanshoku gaiyō [A summary of the propagation of African snails near Asahi Village, Palau]. *Nan'yō Shiryō*, no. 260.

1943*d*   *Uchi Nan'yō hōmen senkakusha monogatari* [Tales of pioneers of Japanese Micronesia]. *Nan'yō Shiryō*, no. 277.

1943*e*   *Parao Asahimura kensetsu zadankai kiroku* [A record of a roundtable discussion on the founding of Asahi Village on Palau]. *Nan'yō Shiryō*, no. 295.

1944*a*   *Garumisukangawa o sakanoborite* [Going upstream on the "Garumiskan" River]. *Nan'yō Shiryō*, no. 327.

1944*b*   *Uchi Nan'yō kizuki shi hitobito* [Persons who built Japanese Micronesia]. *Nan'yō Shiryō*, no. 474.

Nason, James D.

1970   Clan and Copra: Modernization on Etal Island, Eastern Caroline Islands. PhD dissertation, University of Washington.

Nihon Gyōsei Gakkai [Japan Administration Study Association], eds.

1934   *Bankin dai Nihon takushoku shi* [The recent colonial history of Japan]. Nihon Gyōsei Gakkai.

Nihon Keizai Kenyūkai [Japan Economic Research Association], eds.

1941   *Nanshin Nihon shōnin* [Japanese traders in the southward advance]. Ito Shoten.

Nihon Yūsen Kaisha [Japan Mail Steamship Company]

1935   *Golden Jubilee History of the Nippon Yūsen Kaisha, 1885–1935.*

1956   *Shichijūnen shi* [A seventy year history].

Niina Masuo

1978   Rengō Kantai no konkyochi, Torakku [Truk, the base of the Japanese Combined Fleet]. In Mainichi Shimbun Sha, eds., 1978, 206–207.

Nish, Ian

1972   *Alliance in Decline: A Study in Anglo-Japanese Relations, 1908–23.* London: Athlone Press.

Nonaka Fumio

1936   *Sekidō o sen ni shite* [With the equator at my back]. Chūō Kōron Sha.

Nozawa Takashi, ed.
1960   *Nihon kōkū gojūnen shi* [Fifty years of Japanese aviation]. Shuppan Kyodo Sha.

Nufer, Harold F.
1978   *Micronesia under American Rule: An Evaluation of the Strategic Trusteeship, 1947–1977.* Hicksville, NY: Exposition Press.

Ochner, Nobuko Miyama
1984   Nakajima Atsushi: His Life and Work. PhD dissertation, University of Hawaii.

Ōgimi Tomomori
1939   *Nan'yō guntō annai* [Guide book to the South Sea islands]. Kaigai Kenkyūjō.

Okinawa Ken [Okinawa prefecture], eds.
1974   *Okinawa Ken shi* [A history of Okinawa prefecture]. Vol. 7, *Imin* [Emigration]. Iwanamido Shoten.

Okumiya Masatake
1968   For Sugar Boats or Submarines? United States Naval Institute *Proceedings* 94 (8): 66–73.

Ōuchi Seiko
1984   "Nan'yō tanken zukai" zakken [Miscellaneous impressions of "Sketches from an exploration in the South Seas"]. *Taiheiyō Gakkai shi*, no. 22. (April): 55–65.

Pacific Islands Monthly
1985a   Japanese Sigh for the "Last Paradise." July, 33–35.
1985b   "Mr. Pacific" Surveys His Favorite Ocean. July, 35–38.

Pacific Magazine
1985   Special Report: Japanese Investment in the islands. May–June, 34–47.

Palau Community Action Agency
1976–   *A History of Palau.* 3 vols. Koror: Palau Community Action Agency.
1978

Peattie, Mark R.
1984   Japanese Attitudes toward Colonialism. In Myers and Peattie 1984, 80–127.

Pelz, Stephen
1974   *Race to Pearl Harbor: The Failure of the Second London Naval Conference and the Onset of World War II.* Cambridge, MA: Harvard University Press.

Peoples, James G.
1977   Deculturation and Dependence in a Micronesian Community. PhD dissertation, University of California, Davis.

Piccigallo, Philip
1979   *The Japanese on Trial: Allied War Crimes Operations in the East, 1945–1951.* Austin, TX: University of Texas Press.

Pomeroy, Earl
1948   American Policy Respecting the Marshalls, Carolines, and Marianas, 1898–1941. *Pacific Historical Review* 17 (2): 43–53.

Price, Willard
1936   *Pacific Adventure.* New York: John Day.
1944   *Japan's Islands of Mystery.* New York: John Day.

Purcell, David C., Jr.
1967   Japanese Expansion in the South Pacific, 1890–1935. PhD dissertation, University of Pennsylvania.

1972   Japanese Entrepreneurs in the Mariana, Marshall, and Caroline Islands. In *East Across the Pacific: Historical and Sociological Studies of Japanese Immigration and Assimilation*, edited by Hilary Conroy and T. Scott Miyakawa, 56–70. Santa Barbara, CA: ABC Clio Press.

1976   The Economics of Exploitation: The Japanese in the Mariana, Caroline, and Marshall Islands, 1915–1940. *Journal of Pacific History* 11 (3): 189–211.

Pyle, Kenneth
1969   *The New Generation in Meiji Japan: Problems of Cultural Identity, 1885–1895.* Stanford, CA: Stanford University Press.

Ramarui, David
1976   Education in Micronesia: Its Past, Present and Future. *Micronesian Reporter* 24 (1): 9–20.

1979   Putting Educational Critiques into Perspective. *Micronesian Reporter* 27 (1): 2–7.

Rattan Sumitra
1972   The Yap Controversy and Its Significance. *Journal of Pacific History* 7:124–136.

Reber, John J.
1977   Pete Ellis: Amphibious Warfare Prophet. United States Naval Institute *Proceedings*, November, 53–63.

Roscoe, Theodore
1949   *United States Submarine Operations in World War II.* Annapolis: U.S. Naval Institute Press.

Russell, Scott
1983   Camp Susupe: Postwar Internment on Saipan. *Pacific Magazine* May–June, 21–23.

1984   *From Arabwal to Ashes: A Brief History of Garapan Village: 1818 to 1945.* Micronesian Archaeological Survey Report no. 19. Saipan: Historic Preservation Office, Trust Territory of the Pacific Islands.

Rynkiewich, Michael
1981   *Traders, Teachers, and Soldiers: An Anthropological Survey of Colonial Era Sites on Majuro, Marshall Islands.* Micronesian Archaeological Survey Report no. 8. Saipan: Historic Preservation Office, Trust Territory of the Pacific Islands.

Schilling, Warner R.
1954   Admirals and Foreign Policy, 1913–1919. PhD dissertation, Yale University.

Shaw, Henry, Bernard C. Nalty, and Edwin Turnbladh
1966   *History of U.S. Marine Corps Operations in World War II.* Vol. 3,

Central Pacific Drive. Washington, DC: Historical Branch, G-3 Division Headquarters, U.S. Marine Corps.

Sherrod, Robert
1945   *On to Westward: War in the Central Pacific.* New York: Duell, Sloan, & Pearce.

Shinozuka Masaharu and Yamamoto Tomio
1985   Senzen, sen-chū no Maasharu guntō ni tsuite [Concerning the Marshall Islands before and during the war]. *Taiheiyō Gakkai shi,* no. 25 (January): 14–29.

Shirase Satoru
1916   Wareware ga mitaru Nan'yō no shinsō [True facts about our view of the South Seas]. *Chūō Kōron* 31 (13): 55–63.

Shuster, Donald R.
1978   Major Patterns of Social Change Instituted in Micronesia during Japanese Colonial Rule, 1914–1940. MA thesis, University of Hawaii.

1982*a*   Islands of Change in Palau: Church, School, and Elected Government, 1891–1981. PhD dissertation, University of Hawaii.

1982*b*   State Shinto in Micronesia during Japanese Rule, 1914–1945. *Pacific Studies* 5 (2): 20–43.

Smith, Robert Ross
1953   *The Approach to the Philippines.* Washington, DC: U.S. Department of the Army, Office of the Chief of Military History.

South Seas Government
var.   *Annual Reports to the League of Nations on the Administration of the South Sea Islands under Japanese Mandate.* Tokyo.

Spaulding, Robert
1967   *Imperial Japan's Higher Civil Service Examinations.* Princeton, NJ: Princeton University Press.

Spinks, Charles N.
1936   Japan's Entrance into the World War. *Pacific Historical Review* 5 (4): 297–311.

Spoehr, Alexander
1949   *Majuro: A Village in the Marshall Islands. Fieldiana: Anthropology,* vol. 39. Chicago: Chicago Natural History Museum.

1954   *Saipan: The Ethnology of a War-Devastated Island. Fieldiana: Anthropology,* vol. 41. Chicago: Chicago Natural History Museum.

Suzuki Tsunenori (Keikun)
1892   *Nan'yō tanken jikki* [A true account of explorations in the South Seas]. (Included both *Maasharu guntō tanken shimatsu* [Particulars of an exploration to the Marshall Islands] and *Nan'yō junkō nisshi* [A diary of a voyage through the South Seas].) Hakubunkan.

1893   *Nan'yō fūbutsushi* [An account of the customs and landscapes of the South Seas]. Yatsuo Shinsuke Shoshi.

1937   Nan'yō ō kaikodan [Recollections of a venerable of the South Seas]. *Meiji-Taishō shi dan* [Historical tables of the Meiji-Taisho periods], nos. 5–12.

1983   *Nan'yō tanken jikki* [Record of an expedition to the South Seas]. Sozo Shobō for Taiheiyō Gakkai [the Pacific Society].

Täeuber, Irene
1958   *The Population of Japan.* Princeton, NJ: Princeton University Press.

Taguchi Chikashi
1972   "Tenyū Maru" no bōken [The adventure of the *Tenyū Maru*]. In *Fukoku kyōhei* [Rich country, strong military], vol. 6 of *Nihonjin no hyakunen* [A hundred years of the Japanese]. Sekai Bunka Sha.

Taiheiyō Gakkai, eds.
1981   Shōwa kunendō Yappu shichō "kannai jōkyō" [1933 report of the Yap branch government]. Reprinted with commentary in *Taiheiyō Gakkai shi* [Journal of the Pacific Society], April, 62–73.

Takemura Jirō
1983   Senzen no Nan'yō guntō ni okeru Nihon kigyō no kōbō [The rise and fall of pre-war Japanese enterprises in Micronesia]. *Taiheiyō Gakkai shi,* no. 20 (October): 87–105.

Takeshita Gennosuke
1942   *Suzuki Tsunenori.* Nihon Kōen Kyōkai.

1943   Yokō Tōsaku to Nampō senkaku shishi [Yokō Tōsaku and the pioneers of the south]. *Nan'yō shiryō,* no. 258 (June).

Takeuchi Atsushi
1982   *Parao Maru* minami no umi bosshita. [The *Palau Maru* sank in southern seas]. *Nan'yō Kyōkai Kaihō* (1 July).

Tobin, Jack A.
1970   Jabwor: Former Capitol of the Marshall Islands. *Micronesian Reporter* 18 (4): 20–30.

Toland, John
1970   *The Rising Sun: The Decline and Fall of the Japanese Empire, 1936–1945.* New York: Random House.

Umesao Tadao
1944   Kikō [Travel account]. In Imanishi 1944, pt. 4, 399–489.

United Kingdom Naval Intelligence Division
1945   *Pacific Islands.* Vol. 4, *Western Pacific (New Guinea and Islands Northward).* London: HMSO.

U.S. Department of the Army, Office of the Chief of Military History
1945–   Inner South Seas Islands Area Naval Operations, Part 1, Gilbert
1960a   Islands. (November 1941–November 1943) *Japan Monographs,* no. 161.

1945–   Inner South Seas Islands Area Naval Operations, Part 2, Marshall
1960b   Islands. (December 1941–February 1944) *Japan Monographs,* no. 173.

U.S. Department of State (USDS)
1938   *Foreign Relations of the United States 1922,* vol. 2. Washington, DC: U.S. Government Printing Office.

1944   *Foreign Relations . . . 1929,* vol. 3.

1950   *Foreign Relations . . . 1934,* vol. 3.

1954a   *Foreign Relations . . . 1936,* vol. 4.

1954b   *Foreign Relations . . . 1937,* vol. 4.

1954c   *Foreign Relations . . . 1938,* vol. 3.

U.S. Department of State
1943   *Papers Relating to the Foreign Relations of the United States and Japan, 1931–1941.* Washington, DC: Government Printing Office.

U.S. Navy, Office of the Chief of Naval Operations (OCNC)
1943   *Military Government Handbook: Marshall Islands.* OPNAV P22-1 (Formerly OPNAV 50E-1). Washington, DC: Government Printing Office (GPO).

1944a   *Civil Affairs Guide: Agriculture in the Japanese Mandated Islands.* OPNAV 13–17. Washington, DC: GPO.

1944b   *Civil Affairs Guide: The Fishing Industry of the Japanese Mandated Islands.* OPNAV 50 E-20. Washington, DC: GPO.

1944c   *Civil Affairs Handbook: Administrative Organization and Personnel of the Japanese Mandated Islands.* OPNAV 50-E. Washington, DC: GPO.

1944d   *Civil Affairs Handbook: East Caroline Islands.* OPNAV P22-5 (Formerly OPNAV 50E-5). Washington, DC: GPO.

1944e   *Civil Affairs Handbook: West Caroline Islands.* OPNAV P22-7. Washington, DC: GPO.

1944f   *Civil Affairs Handbook: Mandated Marianas Islands.* OPNAV P22-8 (Formerly OPNAV 50E-8). Washington, DC: GPO.

1948   *Handbook on the Trust Territory of the Pacific Islands.* Washington, DC: GPO.

Vidich, Arthur J.
1980   *The Political Impact of Colonial Administration.* New York: Arno Press.

Watakabe Mitsuo
1965   *Ponape-tō to misuterareta Ponape-tōmin kesshitai* [Ponape island and the abandoned Ponapean "do or die" unit]. Privately printed.

Whyte, W. Farmer
1957   *William Morris Hughes: His Life and Times.* Sydney: Angus and Robertson.

Wilds, Thomas
1955   How Japan Fortified the Mandated Islands. U.S. Naval Institute *Proceedings* 81 (4): 401–407.

Wood, Junius
1921   Japan's Mandate in the Pacific. *Asia* 21:747–753.

Wright, Quincy
1930   *Mandates under the League of Nations.* Chicago: University of Chicago Press.

Yamada Munechika
1979   Yano Ryūkei to Natsume Sōseki. In *Jimbutsuumi no Nihon shi* [Maritime personalities in Japanese history]. Vol. 10, *Nanatsu no umi e* [Toward the seven seas], 79–110. Mainichi Shimbun Sha.

Yamagata ken [Yamagata prefecture]
1971   *Yamagata ken shi* [A history of Yamagata prefecture]. Vol. 4, *Takushoku* [Colonization]. Iwanamido Shoten.

Yamamoto Miono
1915   Nan'yō shinsenryōchi jijō [Conditions in the newly occupied territo-

ries in the South Seas]. *Taiyō* 21 (September, October): 74–80, 107–115.

Yanagida Izumi
1968   *Seiji shōsetsu kenkyū* [Studies concerning political novels], parts 2 and 3; vols. 9 and 10 of *Meiji bungaku kenkyū* [Studies in Meiji literature]. 2 vols. Shinjusha.

Yanaihara Tadao
1938   *Pacific Islands under Japanese Mandate*. London: Oxford University Press.

Yano Ryūkei
1970   *Meiji bungaku zenshū* [Collected works of Meiji literature]. Vol. 15, *Yano Ryūkei shū* [Works of Yano Ryūkei]. Chikuma Shobō.

Yano Tōru
1978   Nan'yō-chō no inin tōchi [The South Seas Government's mandated territory]. In Mainichi Shimbun Sha 1978, 176–179.

1979   *Nihon no Nan'yō shikan* [Japan's historical view of the South Seas]. Chūō Kōron Sha.

Yoshida Mitsuru
1985   *Requiem for Battleship Yamato*, translated and introduced by Richard Minear. Kodansha.

Yoshino Sakuzō
1919   Kōwa kaigi ni teigen subeki waga kuni no Nan'yō shōtō shobun an [A proposal concerning our country's South Seas islands which should be presented to the peace conference]. *Chūō Kōron*, 34:146a–147a.

Index

About the Author

Mark R. Peattie is currently professor of history and director of the program in East Asian Studies at the University of Massachusetts in Boston. Previously, he served with the U.S. Information Agency for thirteen years, nearly ten of which were spent in Japan. There he held the position of director of the American Cultural Center in Sendai, northern Honshu, and later in Kyoto. He received his Ph.D. in modern Japanese history at Princeton University in 1972 and has taught at Pennsylvania State University and the University of California, Los Angeles. He is also an associate in research at the Edwin O. Reischauer Institute of Japanese Studies at Harvard University.

Other works include *Ishiwara Kanji and Japan's Confrontation with the West* and *The Japanese Colonial Empire, 1885–1945* (coeditor), and articles on Japanese imperial, naval, and military history.

Printed in the USA
CPSIA information can be obtained
at www.ICGtesting.com
LVHW051103020124
767951LV00007B/63